E

Economics

L W ROSS and J R SHACKLETON

The Chartered Association of Certified Accountants

Longman

PUBLISHED BY LONGMAN GROUP UK LTD IN CO-OPERATION
WITH THE CHARTERED ASSOCIATION OF
CERTIFIED ACCOUNTANTS

© Longman Group UK Ltd 1988

ISBN 0 85121 4568

Published by

Longman Professional and Business Communications Division
Longman Group UK Limited
21–27 Lamb's Conduit Street, London WC1N 3NJ

Associated Offices

Australia   Longman Professional Publishing (Pty) Limited
130 Phillip Street, Sydney, NSW 2000

Hong Kong   Longman Group (Far East) Limited
Cornwall House, 18th Floor, Taikoo Trading Estate,
Tong Chong Street, Quarry Bay

Malaysia   Longman Malaysia Sdn Bhd
No 3 Jalan Kilang A, Off Jalan Penchala,
Petaling Jaya, Selangor, Malaysia

Singapore   Longman Singapore Publishers (Pte) Ltd
25 First Lok Yang Road, Singapore 2262

USA   Longman Group (USA) Inc
500 North Dearborn Street, Chicago, Illinois 60610

A CIP catalogue record for this book is available from the British Library.

Printed in Great Britain by Bell & Baine Ltd, Glasgow.

For further information and enquiries please contact your local Longman office.

Europe, Latin America, Iran
Please contact our International
Sales Department
Longman House
Burnt Mill
Harlow
Essex CM20 2JE

Arab World
Longman Arab World Centre
Butros Bustani Street
Zokak el Blat
PO Box 11-945
Beirut
Lebanon

New Sphinx Publishing Co. Ltd.
3 Shawarby Street
Kasr el Nil
Cairo
Egypt

Librairie Sayegh
Salhie Street
PO Box 704
Damascus
Syria

Longman Arab World Centre
Al-Hajairi Building
Amir Mohammed Street
PO Box 6587
Amman
Jordan

Longman Arab World Centre
15th Street
PO Box 1391
Khartoum
Sudan

Cameroon
M A W Ngoumbah
BP 537
Limbe
Cameroon

Australia
Longman Cheshire Pty Ltd.
Longman Cheshire House
Kings Gardens
91-97 Coventry Street
South Melbourne
Victoria 3205

Botswana
Longman Botswana (Pty) Ltd.
PO Box 1083
Gaborone

Canada
James D Lang
Marketing Manager
Carswell Legal Publications
2330 Midland Avenue
Agincourt
Ontario
M1S 1P7

Ghana
Sedco Publishing Co. Ltd.
Sedco House
PO Box 2051
Tabon Street
North Ridge
Accra

Hong Kong
Longman Group (Far East) Ltd.
18th Floor Cornwall House
Taikoo Trading Estate
Tong Chong Street
Quarry Bay

India
Orient Longman Limited
5-9-41/1 Bashir Bagh
Hyderabad 500 029

UBS Publishers Distributors
5, Ansari Road
PO Box 7051
New Delhi 110 002

Japan
Longman Penguin Japan Co. Ltd.
Yamaguchi Building
2-12-9 Kanda Jimbocho
Chiyoda-ku
Tokyo 101

Kenya
Longman Kenya Ltd.
PO Box 18033
Funzi Road, Industrial Area
Nairobi

Lesotho
Longman Lesotho (Pty) Ltd.
PO Box 1174
Maseru, 100

Malawi
Dzuka Publishing Co. Ltd.
Blantyre Printing & Publishing
Co. Ltd. PMB 39
Blantyre

Malaysia
Longman Malaysia Sdn, Berhad
No. 3 Jalan Kilang A
Off Jalan Penchala
Petaling Jaya
Selangor

New Zealand
Longman Paul Ltd.
Private Bag
Takapuna
Auckland 9

Nigeria
Longman Nigeria Ltd.
52 Oba Akran Avenue
Private Mail Bag 21036
Ikeja
Lagos

Pakistan
Tahir M Lodhi
Regional Manager
Butterworths
7 Jahangir Street
Islamia Park
Poonch Road
Lahore

Singapore
Longman Singapore
Publishers Pte Ltd.
25 First Lok Yang Road
Off International Road
Jurong Town
Singapore 22

South Africa
Maskew Miller Longman (Pty) Ltd.
PO Box 396
Howard Drive
Pinelands 7405
Cape Town 8000

Swaziland
Longman Swaziland Ltd.
PO Box 2207
Manzini

Tanzania
Ben & Co. Ltd.
PO Box 3164
Dar-es-Salaam

USA
Longman Trade USA.
Caroline House Inc.
520 North Dearborn Street
Chicago
Illinois 60610

Transnational Publishers, Inc.
PO Box 7282
Ardsley-on-Hudson
NY 10503

West Indies
Longman Caribbean (Trinidad) Ltd.
Boundary Road
San Juan
Trinidad

Longman Jamaica Ltd.
PO Box 489
95 Newport Boulevard
Newport West
Kingston 10
Jamaica

Mr Louis A Forde
'Suncrest'
Sunrise Drive
Pine Gardens
St Michael
Barbados

Zimbabwe
Longman Zimbabwe (PVT) Ltd.
PO Box ST 125
Southerton
Harare

Preface

We have written this introductory text for all students of economics but specifically to meet the needs of students preparing for examinations of the accountancy and other professional institutes. The structure and content of the book are, of course, geared closely to the particular requirements of the revised Level 1 Economics syllabus of the Chartered Association of Certified Accountants (ACCA). However, we are confident that the coverage and treatment will cater for the similar economics papers set by other professional examining bodies.

We know from our own experience in teaching and examining that professional students tend to have special problems with economics. The subject itself often seems to have only peripheral relevance both to the student's prospective career and to the other papers in the overall curriculum. This has certainly been true in the past when many of the professional institutes failed to think through the rationale for studying economics and drew up syllabi largely devoid of empirical content or practical relevance. Sadly, this is still the case with the papers of one or two of the institutes. Several others, however, including the ACCA, have responded to the criticisms of irrelevance with a thoroughgoing review of the economics syllabus designed to stress the applications of the subject and its links with other papers.

One of our principal aims has, therefore, been to reflect this fresh approach. For example, we have excised some of the more arid pieces of economic theory (such as indifference curves) with which generations of students have been forced to grapple for no ostensible good reason. We still think theory of prime importance but we have tried to bring out its relevance to a full understanding of 'real world' problems and issues. We have deliberately introduced discussion of live topics such as privatisation, deregulation, unemployment and Third World debt. In doing so, we want to show that economics *is* relevant and that the subject itself is continually changing to reflect the radical shifts in thinking about and in policy towards the economy over the last decade.

Our other main concern is with the more general problems of students preparing for professional exams. The majority have full-time jobs and very limited time for study. Even those who are able to follow day-release and evening classes typically receive tuition in large groups and seldom have the personal tutorial guidance which most full-time students get. Although we strongly advise all students to attend classes if they can we have aimed to make this book as self-contained as possible to facilitate independent study. Students, obviously, should read widely and, in particular, keep themselves up-to-date on economic issues and developments with regular reading of newspapers and periodicals such as the *Financial Times*, *Wall Street Journal* and *The Economist*. But students who master this book should, we think, have little difficulty in passing the exam.

We advise students to work systematically through the chapters reading each one first fairly quickly and then again more slowly taking notes. Note-taking reinforces learning and is extremely valuable at the revision stage. The **self-test questions** at the end of each chapter should not be attempted till you feel you have thoroughly mastered it. Whether you get the right answer or not, spend some time thinking about why only one answer is correct and the others are wrong—it is not always obvious!

We also provide our own model answers to the end of chapter exercises, the questions being largely drawn from recent papers of the professional institutes. Additional questions are provided towards the back of the book and students are encouraged to attempt these. Solutions to these can be found in the manual available to lecturers only which complements this book. We suggest that after studying each chapter you attempt the question yourself and then compare your answer with ours. Remember that in the exam you will usually have only about half an hour for each question. Therefore, it is essential to be concise and to answer the question directly and without waffle and padding. Again, we give our own answers to the questions on the ACCA paper set in June 1988. You might use this to give yourself a mock exam a few weeks before the proper one.

Finally, we have ordered the chapters in a traditional fashion with what is called microeconomics in the first half followed by macroeconomics. Most students fresh to economics find macroeconomics intrinsically more interesting (because it deals with topics like unemployment and inflation with which they are already familiar). Lecturers using this as a course book therefore might prefer to deal with macroeconomics early on in the course. If so, we suggest that Chapters 1 to 3 are covered before going on to Chapter 11. However, this is not something that we advise to students studying independently since much of the macroeconomics, in fact, leans heavily on the micro concepts developed in the first half of the book.

L W Ross
J R Shackleton

Polytechnic of Central London
June 1988

Contents

Introduction to Economics

This chapter introduces the nature and scope of the discipline of economics. It deals with the central problem of resource scarcity faced by all economies and how this forces societies to make choices about the allocation of those resources. In turn, societies can organise their economic systems in alternative ways making use of markets or planning or both. After studying this chapter you will have an appreciation of the merits and demerits of different systems of organisation and a better understanding of how economists approach their analysis of the economy and the policy problems and issues which arise in the operation of the economic system.

1.1 INTRODUCTION

Everyone is familiar with the kind of economic issues discussed daily in the media—issues such as inflation, unemployment, interest rates, the budget deficit, government spending, privatisation, and so on. Most people will have views on these matters and about the policies which should be pursued in order to improve the economic situation both for themselves and for society at large. This is so even when people have a much less than perfect comprehension of the nature of and relationship between these problems which arise in the operation of the economic system. A central purpose of this book is to remedy that lack of understanding.

1.2 THE SCOPE OF ECONOMICS

Economics is primarily concerned with the economic system through which societies attempt to use their available resources to meet people's material needs and wants through the production of goods and services. Goods are tangible things like motor cars, carrots and houses; services, such as hairdressing, health care and education, are consumed simultaneously with their production. Production itself is the process of transforming inputs of resources like labour power and raw materials into goods and services. The final goal of production is consumption—individuals satisfy their material needs and wants by using up or 'consuming' goods and services. Their capacity to do so is constrained by their income so that the size of a household's income is usually taken as an indicator of its material living standards or economic welfare.

FACTORS OF PRODUCTION

All societies have available to them quantities of productive resources or what economists call **factors of production**. Traditionally, these factors are classified into three main groups:

1 **Labour**—Labour resources include all types of physical and mental power of human beings. Labour as a factor of production is clearly very diverse or heterogeneous, ranging from the raw labour power of an unskilled worker to the highly specific services provided by a musician, a trained accountant or a surgeon. People may inherit some part of their particular talents and their physical and mental abilities, but these must be developed and enhanced through education and training. Modern economists in fact prefer to separate the raw labour power available to an economy (measured by the numbers in the working population) from **human capital** which is the value of the increase in the quality and productivity of labour as the result of investment in education and training.

2 **Land and natural resources**—This is largely self-explanatory. Countries are differently endowed with land of various quality for farming and other uses and also with natural resources such as oil, coal and other mineral deposits, water, fish from the sea, the climate and terrain.

3   **Capital**—Here we mean the economy's stock of physical assets such as machinery and plant installed in manufacturing firms, the premises and offices of all types of business and also the social infrastructure of roads, railways, sewers and so on commonly provided by the government. Capital stock in this sense should not be confused with financial capital consisting of financial assets like bank deposits, bonds and equity shares. The distinguishing feature of a capital good like a machine is that it is not produced for its own sake to satisfy the requirements of consumers, but to assist in further production. Thus, the application of capital increases the efficiency and productivity of labour and land and is a potent source of economic growth. In turn, physical capital like human capital is accumulated over time by **investment**—the diversion of part of the economy's resources into the production of capital goods rather than final consumer goods.

In order to produce goods and services, factors of production must be combined with the essential element, **entrepreneurship**. Here the owners of an enterprise put up the financial risk capital and undertake the overall coordination of factors of production. The efficiency with which these factors are used depends very much on the **technology** deployed. The application of knowledge or science to production is what is meant by technology.

Experience in production will usually lead to a firm's organisation and management becoming more efficient and it will introduce more advanced technology and production methods. The result will be a greater output of goods and services from given inputs of resources. Modern economies typically grow over time with increasing output and corresponding increases in real income per head of population. This occurs because of a combination of investment in human and physical capital and by the application to production of advances in organisation, management skills and technology.

1.2.1 Scarcity and choice

Even though economies, particularly those of the Western industrialised countries, have grown very rapidly in modern times to achieve historically high average living standards it still remains the case that the central economic problem for all societies is a **scarcity** of resources. Productive resources are finite while the demands which can be placed on them in the shape of consumer needs and wants are infinite. In poor countries—euphemistically called developing or less developed countries (LDCs) by economists—there may be a problem of absolute scarcity. Especially during times of natural disaster like drought or flood the country may be unable to produce enough to satisfy even the basic needs of food and shelter. At best this may result in malnutrition; at worst it can be starvation. In normal times, living standards in many LDCs are still abysmal for a great part of the population with low levels of literacy, a short life expectancy and near-zero ownership of goods such as cars and washing machines which are often taken for granted in the rich countries.

In developed countries (DCs) by contrast, the problem is largely one of relative scarcity. While there remain significant pockets of poverty, they are the outcome of an uneven distribution of the national income. Average income per head is generally well above subsistence level enabling people to enjoy unprecedented levels of consumption of 'luxury' goods and services. But economists usually assume that human wants are virtually insatiable; even the wealthiest individual will get positive satisfaction (or so it is argued) from another villa on the Mediterranean, a private chef or gardener or a chauffeur for the Rolls! At the more mundane level it is clear that the average household in countries like Britain, West Germany and the United States would not reject an increase in income, while the acute scarcity of resources to meet collective as well as private consumption and investment demand is highlighted by the continuing political debate over the size of government spending and how it should be allocated among competing programmes such as defence, welfare, health and education.

1.2.2 The problem of resource allocation

Scarcity of resources imposes choice on societies. Decisions, often very difficult ones, have to be taken about the **allocation of resources** among competing claims. This core problem of resource allocation is usually said to have three dimensions:

1 Decisions must be made about **what** to produce with the available resources. At the broadest level a choice has to be made between production of, say, capital goods and consumer goods. More investment in machines and education may increase productivity and income in the future but only at the sacrifice of present consumption. Even when the divison of current output between investment and consumption has been determined there still remains the question which, of the thousands of possible capital and consumer goods which can be produced, should resources be devoted to. Do we train more accountants or build more roads? Do people want more rice or more cat food or more television sets?

2 Having decided what to produce, it is necessary to determine **how**. The methods of production and the appropriate technology have to be chosen. Presumably, people will want to use the most efficient methods and technologies within the constraints of the quantities and quality of resources available to their own economies.

3 Finally, there must be mechanisms for deciding **who** is to get what is produced. This is the problem of the **distribution of income** among households and among various social classes and groups such as workers, landowners and capitalists; the employed and unemployed; the sick; large families and pensioners.

1.2.3 The production frontier

We can get an insight into the central question of resource allocation by drawing up a simple model of an economy. The use of 'models' is the dominant method by which economists analyse and try to make sense of economic behaviour. Because the real world is so complex, it is necessary to make simplifying assumptions regarding the structure of the economy and about the way people behave, for example, in what determines their decisions to buy, produce and sell goods and services. Thus, in order to analyse the resource allocation problem more deeply, suppose we simplify by dividing all the many goods and services into just two categories—capital goods, which we label 'machines', and consumer goods labelled 'bread'. The question of what is produced therefore narrows down to a simple choice between bread and machines.

At any time, the economy has available only limited quantities of resources which determine its productive capacity. It follows that there must be an absolute maximum output of either bread or machines. If all resources were used with maximum efficiency to produce bread suppose the output each week was 300 units (each unit equal, say, to one million loaves). Similarly, if only machines were produced the greatest possible output might be 600 per week. These values fix the extreme points, J and K, on what is termed the economy's production frontier or production possibilities (PP) curve drawn in Figure 1.1.

FIGURE 1.1 **The production possibilities curve or production frontier**

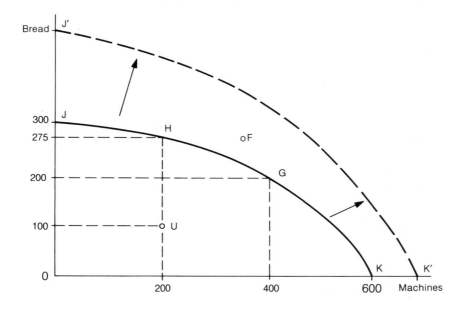

OPPORTUNITY COST

The graph measures output of the two goods on the axes. But, of course, no economy would wish to produce at the extremes of J or K. Consumption goods, bread, must obviously be produced but not to the exclusion of capital goods, machines. If the country is merely to maintain its existing stock of capital it must devote part of its resources to replacement investment. That is, it must produce enough machines to replace those wearing out or depreciating over time. To do so, however, it will have to shift labour and other factors out of bread production and into the production of machines. Producing more machines, therefore, has a real cost in terms of the sacrifice of bread which could have been produced by the diverted resources. That cost is called **opportunity cost**. Economists argue that practically every good or service has a positive opportunity cost—production of one commodity, bread, involves forgoing output of something else, in our example, machines.

The opportunity cost of bread and machines is illustrated by the production frontier or PP curve, JK. The curve shows the maximum output of one good given the output of the other. At the extreme point, J, where we are producing no machines at all, the maximum output of bread is 300 units (300B). If we want to produce, say, 200 machines (200M) we have to move down the production frontier to point H where the maximum output of bread is 275B. In going from J to H, therefore, we have had to sacrifice 25B to produce 200M—each machine on average has an opportunity cost of one eighth a unit of bread. If we then want to double machine output to 400M we must shift further down the production frontier from H to G. Maximum bread output falls to 200B so that the extra 200M has cost 75B or an average per machine of three-eighths of a unit of bread. That is three times as much as the average cost of the first 200 machines.

This illustrates the important principle of **increasing** opportunity costs—as the output of any good is expanded so we expect the cost of further output of it ultimately to rise. There are various reasons for this which we examine in a later chapter, but we can note that different productive factors will be better suited to production of one good rather than another. When the economy specialises in bread at point J it will be using factors, say, mechanical engineers, which are not really very productive in the bread industry. As a result, it is initially possible to raise machine output at a very low opportunity cost by diverting engineers into the machine industry where they are hugely more productive. The more machine output is expanded, however, the more we have to use up resources like bakers and wheat-growing land which are highly productive in bread but clearly not in making machines.

The real cost of additional machines goes higher and higher as we approach point K. Increasing costs are shown by the bulging shape of the PP curve, more formally described as concave to the origin. The principle applies in reverse; starting at K with complete specialisation in machines, then expansion of bread production incurs a heavier and heavier cost in terms of the loss of machines.

The production frontier shows all the maximum feasible combinations of goods which can be produced. There are insufficient resources to produce above the frontier, for example, at point F. Attempts to do so will place such pressure of demand on resources that, as we shall see, inflation is likely to result. However, it is possible to produce inside the production frontier at a point like U. This will be for one of two reasons: either the country is not using its resources efficiently or factors of production like labour are not fully employed. Inefficiency can have a variety of sources such as the operation of restrictive practices resulting in overstaffing, or bad management and organisation of firms. Inefficiency means a failure to achieve the maximum output from given inputs of labour and other factors.

In turn, we shall see that economies always have some degree of unemployment, most visible in the form of workers unable to find jobs or unwilling to take the jobs available. Capital and land may also be underemployed. Both inefficiency and unemployment will push output below the PP curve so that the economy can, in principle, have more of either good without any loss of the other. Thus, at point U production is 100B and 200M. By improving efficiency or increasing employment, output of bread can be raised all the way to 275B at point H on the PP curve with no loss of machines. Alternatively, machine output can be raised without sacrificing bread. In other words, the opportunity cost of extra output is zero. If countries want to maximise their material income, they must therefore try to eliminate both inefficiency and unemployment in order to push production as close as possible to the production frontier.

ECONOMIC GROWTH

The diagram also demonstrates the effects of economic growth. Suppose the economy is initially operating at points JK at H and on the output of 200 machines is just enough to replace existing capital as it wears out. With no source of growth other than a rise in the capital stock, the production frontier will remain where it is. But then imagine that the country expands machine output to 400 by moving to G on the PP curve. Its **gross** investment (output of capital goods) is 400M but it now has positive **net** investment (gross investment minus depreciation) of 200M; the capital stock is growing by that amount each week. This is likely to raise the productivity of other factors and allow an increase in the output of either bread or machines with no reduction in production of the other. In short, the whole production frontier is pushed outwards from the origin to, say, the broken curve J'K' in the diagram.

The same would result from technological progress or application of improved management techniques or more investment in human capital. Growth, unless it comes from a population increase, means a higher output per head and, potentially at least, improved living standards. However, the analysis shows that growth has an opportunity cost—higher future income nearly always requires a sacrifice of current consumption as resources are shifted into physical or human investment or into research and development. For poor countries where the sacrifice is bread, the cost may be unacceptable without extra capital resources from outside by way of aid and investment from developed countries.

1.3 ECONOMIC ORGANISATION

If all economies have the same central problem of allocating scarce resources, then they must, also, have some decision-making system to enable choices to be made about what is produced, how it is produced and who gets what is produced. Historically, societies at an early stage of economic development have tended to rely on systems in which power, wealth, status and occupation derive primarily from birth and inheritance. Such a system may work tolerably well in predominantly agricultural societies with a limited range of occupations and products. But, even ignoring the glaring inequities likely to arise, systems based on inheritance are clearly inappropriate to modern industrial economies.

1.3.1 Division of labour

Economic development invariably goes hand in hand with increasing complexity and specialisation. Today's economies produce a bewildering diversity of goods and services while a primary source of development itself is an increase in the division of labour. Workers are not just specialised in producing particular goods and services, but typically in quite minor stages and operations in the production process. This is because specialisation raises productivity: there may be hundreds of separate operations in making products like motor cars and television sets. If it was left to individuals to acquire and apply all the necessary skills then it is dubious whether even one car would ever be produced. However, with people specialising in particular aspects of production: design; engineering; administration; assembly of parts and components, modern economies can produce millions of cars each year.

1.3.2 Central planning

Societies today make use of two main modes of economic organisation—central planning and the market system. The first is perhaps the easier to understand. In a **centrally planned** or what some call a 'command' economy, all questions about the allocation of resources are determined by the government. For example, in the Soviet Union and other East European countries where planning is the dominant form of economic organisation, the government takes policy decisions about the broad division of output among classes of goods and services such as consumption, investment, defence and education. These decisions are translated into plans, both medium-term (like the famous 'five-year plans' in the Soviet Union) and short-term for the year ahead. The plans attempt to lay down feasible targets for the production of almost every conceivable good and service. The task of the planners is enormous as witnessed by the millions of bureaucrats employed in the Soviet Ministry of Planning

(Gosplan). Targets must be set for thousands of different products and, if they are to be realistic, those targets should relate to the resources and technology available. The planners therefore have to decide not only what is produced, but also how it is all to be produced.

Targets have then to be communicated to the producing enterprises whose actual performance must be continually monitored. Failure of any one enterprise, say, a plant producing tractor engines, to meet its targets may have damaging effects on large parts of the economic plan. Inadequate supplies of engines will jeopardise the target for tractors themselves which may result in under-production of grain and other farm products. 'Planning failures' can and do arise, sometimes on a massive scale. Under-performance may mean shortages of goods even when the original targets themselves are adequate to meet consumer demand. Shortages lead to the queues often associated with planned economies. Moreover, though targets may be achieved in quantitative terms, the managers of plants and factories may cut corners and skimp on materials and quality control in order to do so. The result may be the production of poor quality goods.

In a complete command economy, it is possible to guarantee everyone a job. The elimination of unemployment is a major potential advantage of planning. But the corollary of this is that the government will also have to determine the allocation of labour to different occupations. The planners will therefore need to calculate the requirements for the many types of skills to fulfil their overall production targets. People will have to be educated and trained appropriately and directed or induced into particular jobs. Restrictions may have to be imposed on individual freedom of choice of jobs and places of work. Finally, the government will have to decide the distribution of income. This is often claimed as another major advantage of planning since, in principle, the national income can be shared out on an equitable basis of what people need rather than on their luck in inheriting wealth or intelligence. The reality, however, will be different as those in power, including the planners, use their influence to secure privileges for themselves.

1.3.3 The market economy

Using markets to allocate resources is diametrically opposed to planning. In a pure market system decisions about what is produced, how and who gets what is produced, would be **decentralised**. All these things would be the outcome of millions of separate individual decisions made by consumers, producers and owners of productive services. As such, of course, decisions reflect private preferences and interests. The next chapter looks in detail at the operation of individual markets, but to see how a market system would work, let's return to the production frontier model. Suppose both bread and machines were bought and sold in free and competitive markets. That means that there is no attempt by the government to influence or regulate the decisions of buyers and sellers and that there are large numbers of them with no one sufficiently powerful to 'corner' the market. Essentially, the two markets will be self-regulating through the medium of prices.

Imagine that we start at point H in Figure 1.1 (page 3) with production of 275B and 200M. Producers of both goods are making adequate profits at the current prices and buyers too are getting all they want at those prices. In other words, there is a matching-up of supply and demand. Then, suppose the firms which buy machines decide for some reason that they want to increase their investment, perhaps in order to enable them to increase their capacity to meet an expected growth in demand. At the current price they now want to buy, say, 500 machines. We know that, so long as bread output stays at 275B, the economy cannot meet this extra demand for machines; resources will have to be diverted out of bread and into machine production along the PP curve. In a market economy, the increased demand for machines will drive up their price and make machine production more profitable than bread. Firms making machines will therefore expand their output and will attract factors of production out of the bread industry by offering higher wages for labour and bigger rents for land, while some bread producers might be induced to move into machine production.

The upshot is that the rise in machine prices will divert resources into machines and out of bread: in the diagram production will move away from H towards G. Also, the rise in machine prices will choke off some of the original increase in investment demand to, say, 400M. Point G, in fact, could be a new point of 'equilibrium' at which producers in both industries are again satisfied with their profitability and buyers can obtain precisely the quantity they want of both goods at the new prices. This adjustment of supply to demand has taken place purely as a result of the independent decisions of producers, consumers and resource owners in response to an automatic change in the relative prices of bread and machines and with no need for intervention by some external planning agency. It was analysis of this kind which, over 200 years ago, prompted Adam Smith, the founder of modern economics, to describe the market system operating to allocate resources as if regulated by an 'invisible hand'. Smith was a great admirer of the market, but he was also aware of its potential weaknesses or 'market failures' which are discussed in the next section.

1.3.4 Markets versus planning

Debate over the relative merits of planning and the price mechanism is at the very core of politics since what is at issue is (1) the role of the government; and (2) who wields power in the economy. In practice, no country uses one system to the exclusion of the other; every economy is a **mixed economy** making use of both planning and markets in different degrees. Planning is the dominant system in 'socialist' countries such as the Soviet Union. The main feature of socialism in this context is the ownership of capital and land by the government or the 'state'. Since the private profit motive, which is essential to the operation of markets, is largely removed, socialist countries almost inevitably tend to rely on centralised planning. That is not to say that there is no scope for markets in a socialist economy; managers, workers and planners themselves can all be offered a variety of incentives such as higher pay, bonuses and rewards in kind like holidays and better housing as inducements to work harder and more efficiently to meet their targets. These incentives perform the same function as private profit and allow the emergence of markets, particularly when state-owned enterprises are given freedom in turn to compete against each other and to set prices for their output related to the demand for it. It is precisely this shift towards the use of market mechanisms and away from planning which forms the basis of economic reforms which have been initiated in the Soviet Union and other East European countries in the 1980s.

THE PRIVATE SECTOR AND THE PUBLIC SECTOR

'Capitalism' on the other hand, with its private ownership and control of resources is strongly linked to the use of markets. What are often referred to as capitalist countries—the United States, Britain, West Germany, Japan and so on—are, however, all mixed economies. They all have a large **private sector** in which markets are the chief mode of organisation. Producers, ranging from the self-employed and small businesses to giant corporations, buy their inputs of productive services and sell their output in markets. For the most part, producers take their own independent decisions about what and how to produce; people are free to sell their labour services in the market and consumers choose for themselves on what they spend their incomes. At the same time, these countries have a large government or **public sector** in which resources are controlled by the government. In Britain, for example, public sector spending amounts to around 40 per cent of the national income. Much of that is in the form of **transfer payments** such as pensions and welfare benefits to the sick and unemployed, but the government is massively involved in the provision of services such as education, health, the police and defence. These, for the most part, are not sold in markets; they are either free of charge at the point of consumption or provided at prices usually below the cost of production.

Governments of 'market' economies are also involved in varying degrees in the ownership and management of producing enterprises. There are first the **nationalised** or state-owned firms. Sometimes, as with the nationalised banks in France, these firms may compete with others in the private sector. In other cases, the nationalised industry may have a monopoly and its prices may be closely regulated by the government. This is so, for example, with the publicly owned railways and coal industry in Britain. Then there are privately owned firms like British Telecom and British Gas (formerly nationalised industries) whose prices and services are monitored by special government regulatory agencies. Moreover, governments intervene throughout the private sector in a great variety of ways like price controls, taxes, subsidies, planning of land use, licensing, regulation and even prohibition of certain activities like selling drugs. The upshot is that a large proportion of economic activity is either planned directly in the public sector or is subject to close regulation by the government.

The argument regarding the merits of markets and planning proceeds at different levels. For example, opponents of the market system are often found to be really attacking capitalism. Private ownership of the means of production, involves, it is claimed, an inequitable distribution of income and wealth and to the exploitation of labour by the capitalist class. That was the basic thinking of Karl Marx in his monumental work, *Capital*, published in 1867. At the other end of the political spectrum there are those (like the contemporary American economist, Milton Friedman) who are fundamentally opposed to socialism and planning on the grounds that it restricts the freedom of individuals to choose where they work and invest, what they produce and what they consume.

PLANNING FAILURES

Economists tend to concentrate on the efficiency with which the two systems operate in the allocation of resources. In the real world neither system works with maximum efficiency in the sense of achieving the greatest possible satisfaction of people's wants from the resources available. We have already mentioned 'planning failures'; by the same token there are also 'market failures'. The failures of planning include the lack of realism in setting targets and inevitable mismatches in supply and demand resulting in shortages and queuing for some goods and unwanted surpluses for others. Target-setting may tend to make production the goal of economic activity rather than consumption and to overemphasise quantity at the expense of quality. The sheer size of the planning task absorbs an immense proportion of resources into unproductive administration, while the overriding objection to planning is that decisions about what and how to produce are made not by consumers, but by bureaucrats who are likely to allocate resources in their own interests.

CONSUMER SOVEREIGNTY

On the face of it, the decentralised decision-making in a market system gives it what many think is a decisive advantage over planning. The whole pattern of production of goods and services is determined by what people want as expressed by the countless separate spending decisions by consumers. Consumers, it is said, are sovereign. In a planned economy people get what the planners decide they should have. In a market system consumers themselves can ensure that production matches their demands for different goods and services. However, this consumer sovereignty can be impaired or even eliminated by the existence of market failures.

MARKET FAILURES

We shall examine market failures in detail in Chapter 9. For the moment, we can just note some of the more important reasons why markets may work inefficiently.

(a)   Markets may not be competitive; supply may be in the hands of a single firm—a monopoly—or dominated by just a few—an oligopoly. We shall see that this can result in high prices and restricted output to the cost of the consumer while a monopolist can foist shoddy products on to the market. At the same time, large firms can manipulate and shape consumer wants by advertising and other sales promotions. In short, in monopolistic markets the consumer may be no more sovereign than in a planned economy.

(b)   In many markets prices are often unstable or volatile. This is so, for example, in the foreign exchange market with continual see-sawing of currencies like the US dollar. Prices of many primary commodities like copper and coffee are also very unstable. The volatility may arise from speculative buying and selling and for other reasons unrelated to production costs or to the final demand of consumers. Such instability may prevent prices serving their function of acting as a signal to producers and buyers to alter their output and consumption. The signals may be false; a rise in price from speculative buying may bring an unwarranted expansion of output which will later have to be reversed.

(c)   In other markets prices may be inflexible and fail to respond to supply and demand changes. This may have serious results. In the labour market, for example, a failure of wages to adjust after a change in demand may lead to inefficiency and possible unemployment.

(d)   Markets may result in under-production of certain kinds of goods known as 'public goods'. Similarly, the existence of 'externalities' can also cause under-production of some goods in relation to consumer wants and over-production of others, such as pollution. These ideas are explained in Chapter 9.

(e)   As noted already, a market system may result in an arbitrary and inequitable distribution of income and wealth unrelated to the pattern of people's needs or their contribution to the national income.

The existence of market failures does not mean we should reject markets as a system of organisation in favour of planning any more than planning failures imply the reverse. There is no presumption that either system works better than the other and it is ultimately a matter of politics rather than economics and of making judgments about such things as 'equity' and 'freedom' as to which system is preferred and implemented. The economist's role is to analyse the relative efficiency of the alternative systems. The commonsense view is that societies should make use of either system where it has clear advantages over the other. Where there are market failures there may be good reason for the government to intervene and even to produce goods and services itself. But the same reasoning applies when goods can be more efficiently produced through markets. The discovery that this is so for a very wide range of goods and services no doubt explains Mr Gorbachev's drive to introduce market mechanisms in the Soviet Union as well as the widespread movement by governments in the West to curb the role of the government in the economy through 'privatisation' of nationalised enterprises and dismantling of government control and regulation of private sector industries.

1.4 THE SCIENCE OF ECONOMICS

1.4.1 Positive and normative economics

It is common to speak of economics as a social science. If we use the word, 'science', in its broad sense to mean simply a body of knowledge then there is unlikely to be any problem in describing economics in that way. However, many modern economists would like to go further and place economics in the same category as the physical sciences such as physics and biology. Arguably, the distinguishing feature of these sciences is that they attempt to formulate theories about the real world from which we can derive testable propositions or hypotheses. But, in doing so, physical scientists often have the great advantage of being able to conduct their tests under controlled laboratory conditions. In economics, because we are studying social behaviour, we are rarely able to approach that ideal and any hypotheses we make, for example, about the causes of unemployment can only be imperfectly tested against experience.

Nevertheless, this does not mean that economists should not adopt a scientific approach. That is what they do in so-called **positive economics** which attempts to make an objective analysis of economic behaviour. Positive economic theory is concerned with explanation of the workings of the economy as a whole or with particular aspects such as the operation of markets. We have noted already that, because the real world is extremely complex, economic theories are presented in models in which we make simplifying assumptions about the structure of the economy and about people's economic behaviour. Models in turn enable us to make 'predictions' about the economy, for example, that unemployment will fall if the government spends more. Those predictions can in principle be tested against what happens when the government does boost its spending. Our problem is that the prediction is made on the assumption of 'other things equal' or, to use the Latin phrase, *ceteris paribus*—unemployment will drop if all other things like wages which can affect unemployment remain unchanged. In practice, of course, other things do not stay the same. Our tests of economic theories are rarely conclusive and that is a major reason for the frequent complaint that economists can never agree about the way the economy works.

If there are often many competing theories in positive economics, the scope for disagreement expands immeasurably in **normative economics** which is less concerned with the way people actually behave than with how they ought to behave in order to achieve certain objectives. While *positive economics* might analyse and explain the causes of inflation, normative economics is concerned with what should be done to bring inflation down. Normative economics is ultimately concerned therefore with economic policy. Even when economists can agree on the positive theory of inflation there is still room for conflict about what, if anything, should be done to reduce it.

1.4.2 Microeconomics and macroeconomics

Economics is often split into two broad areas of study known as micro- and macroeconomics. The terms come respectively from the Greek words for 'small' and 'large'. Thus, microeconomics is concerned with the behaviour of small parts of the economy—with individual firms and consumers and with particular markets. The implicit assumption in microeconomics is that the individual behaviour being studied is such a small part of the total that we can ignore its impact on the workings of the economy as a whole. A change in the price of, say, matches or pepper will have a negligible effect on the inflation rate.

Macroeconomics deals with the economy in the large—with big aggregates like the national income, employment and unemployment, the rate of inflation and a country's exports and imports. There are certain markets, like those for labour and foreign exchange, where we cannot ignore their impact on the economy as a whole. If wages generally rise there could be significant effects on employment, inflation and the balance of payments.

In this book we follow what has become a convention of separating these two broad areas of economics, dealing in the first half with microeconomics and then with macroeconomics. But note that the two areas in fact share common concepts and methods. Many economists believe that the split is largely artificial and this is reflected in many of the recent developments in thinking about macroeconomic concerns.

1.5 ECONOMICS AND THE ACCOUNTANT

This book is specifically written for accountancy and other professional students whose main aim is to pass an examination in economics. It is all too easy, therefore, for the student to take a purely instrumental approach to the subject, learning material by rote, trying to spot exam questions and so on. That sometimes works and the exam is passed. But more often it doesn't work, partly because economics, unlike one or two other subjects, does not lend itself to that kind of learning. Economic concepts and models will often seem meaningless and useless when they are first encountered and their relevance only becomes clear when they are applied to analysis of practical problems and issues. For instance, the notion of opportunity cost which we have already encountered is highly relevant to decision-taking of all kinds. It stresses the real cost, rather than, say, the money or nominal cost of doing one thing rather than another. Management accountants are, in large degree, concerned with the measurement of opportunity costs to assist management to reach better decisions or choices about where to invest or disinvest, where to raise capital etc. Proper understanding of opportunity cost does not come from learning a definition by heart but by seeing how the concept can usefully be deployed.

An understanding of economics is relevant to accountants in two ways:

1   Economics is centrally concerned with the efficient allocation of scarce resources, with maximisation subject to constraints. In whatever organisation the accountant works that too should be his or her primary concern. Economics tries to lay down certain principles for the efficient achievement of the organisation's goals, whether it is to make the biggest possible profits or to provide a given level of service for the least cost. Those principles are just as relevant to commercial business as to a government department or agency concerned with assessing the social costs and benefits of pursuing different policies and ways of implementing them.

2   The organisations in which accountants work do not themselves operate in a vacuum. They have internal constraints in the form of limited resources but they also face external constraints on what they can and cannot do. The economic environment has many different aspects. In decision-taking, organisations must be aware of the effects of changes in the markets in which they buy and sell, of the competitive structure of markets, and of the industrial, economic and fiscal policies of the government. Economics provides the framework for a deeper understanding of the economic environment to enable accountants to make a fuller assessment of the costs and benefits of management decisions.

SUMMARY

This chapter has reviewed the general nature and scope of economics which studies the economic system in which societies deploy their resources to satisfy material wants. The central problem is the allocation of scarce resources. Scarcity imposes choice about what and how to produce and who gets what is produced. The problem is illustrated by the production possibilities frontier; societies must choose where to be on the frontier, but expansion of output in one direction invariably involves an increasing opportunity cost. Countries can use two main systems of economic organisation to allocate resources—central planning by the government and decentralised decision-making through the market. All economies in practice are mixed economies using both systems in different degrees. Economists focus on the relative efficiency of the two systems in resource allocation and identify sources of both planning failure and market failure. However, the choice between the two systems may ultimately be more a matter of politics than economics.

SELF-TEST QUESTIONS

1   Refer to the production possibilities diagram in Figure 1.1. Which one of the following statements is wrong?

(a)   The PP curve is concave towards the origin because expansion of bread output is achieved only with increasing cost in terms of lost machine output.

(b)   At point F the opportunity cost of either good is zero.

(c)   A country may operate at a point like U because it is not using its resources fully.

(d)   The production frontier may shift out to J'K' as a result of positive net investment.

(e)   At point J the opportunity cost of machines is close to zero.

2   Which one of the following is correct?

(a)   Socialist countries prefer planning because it eliminates the problem of scarce resources.

(b)   Capitalist countries prefer markets because they eliminate the problem of scarce resources.

(c)   Markets can provide a decentralised system of decision-making.

(d)   Planning is preferable to markets because it can more easily guarantee consumer sovereignty.

(e)   A mixed economy combines capitalism with markets.

3   Which one of the following is not a potential source of market failure?

(a)   A shift of resources into production of a good whose price has risen.

(b)   Dominance of markets by oligopolies.

(c)   The existence of public goods.

(d)   Wages remaining unchanged after a fall in the demand for labour.

(e)   Speculative buying and selling of commodities.

4   Which of the following is *not* a potential source of planning failure?

(a)   Concentration by producers on meeting quantitative targets.

(b)   Fixing prices for food and other essential goods below the cost of production.

(c)   Fixing prices for luxury goods above the cost of production.

(d)   Payment of bonuses to managers who exceed their production targets.

(e)   Setting prices in order to match output with demand as closely as possible.

5   Which one of the following statements is wrong?

(a)   Human capital is the value of investment in education and training.

(b)   Positive economics is concerned with objective explanation of economic behaviour.

(c)   Macroeconomics assumes that changes in prices in all individual markets will have insignificant effects on the economy as a whole.

(d)   Normative economics is ultimately concerned with questions of economic policy.

(e)   Economists find it difficult to test hypotheses because the *ceteris paribus* assumption never holds in the real world.

EXERCISE

Explain the concept of consumer sovereignty. How does the existence of large corporations affect the sovereignty of consumers?

Answers on page 237.

Prices and Markets

This chapter shows how prices are determined in free and competitive markets. The concepts of demand and supply are explained and used to show the effects on price and quantity of changes in demand and supply. Finally, we look at the impact of government controls on prices with the setting of either minimum or maximum prices.

2.1   INTRODUCTION

In the last chapter we saw that one of the principal methods for organising the economic system was to rely on decentralised market forces. Given the pervasiveness of markets it is essential to have a thorough understanding of how markets operate to allocate resources. By 'markets' we don't just mean particular geographical locations where buyers and sellers meet to trade commodities. We certainly include markets like the Stock Exchange in London, the various commodity and financial futures exchanges in the commercial centres of most countries and the commonplace wholesale and retail markets in commodities like meat and fruit and vegetables. The term 'market' is however used in a wider sense in economics. Modern communications mean that buyers and sellers no longer have to meet face-to-face to make transactions. They can trade over the phone, sometimes with the aid of prices displayed on screens as in most of today's financial markets, or consumers can respond to suppliers' advertisements in newspapers or on television and radio.

The central point is that, so long as buyers and sellers can communicate, we can conceive of a market in goods and services. Transactions are made at differing prices and a key concern of this chapter is to look at the forces at work which determine prices in free and competitive markets. A free market is one where prices and quantities are settled by buyers and sellers without outside intervention or controls. In particular, there is no intervention in the market by the government or government agencies. A competitive market is one with a sufficiently large number of buyers and sellers so that none of them individually is able to control prices or 'corner' the market. No market in practice ever completely satisfies either condition and we shall look more closely at intervention and the degree of competition in markets in later chapters. For the moment, it helps to focus on the basic forces in price determination by assuming a perfectly free and competitive market.

2.2   SUPPLY AND DEMAND

Suppose then that we have some commodity traded freely and competitively. Let us call it 'fish' and assume that, after landing, it is traded every working day in the quayside fish market. For convenience, we also assume that all the fish is of the same kind and quality and that it is sold in 'boxes' of a given weight. Our immediate concern is to see how the price of fish is determined on any market day. The short answer is that it comes about through the interaction of **supply and demand**; we first need therefore to understand these concepts.

Obviously, the market is composed of two kinds of traders—the sellers and the buyers. The sellers represent the owners of fishing boats whose catch has been landed; the buyers are largely wholesalers and retailers of fish as well as people like restaurant owners and individuals who may want to stock up their freezers. Imagine that before trading starts we were to conduct a survey among all the operators in the market about their buying or selling intentions. What we are particularly interested in is how much fish they plan to buy or sell at different market prices. Concentrate first on the fish suppliers. We ask each one how many boxes he or she will be willing to sell at the prices shown in the first column of Table 2.1. When, at each price, we add up all the answers we get the quantity supplied shown in the second column of the table. The two columns together are the **supply schedule** showing the total amount which suppliers are willing to offer at each price.

TABLE 2.1 **Supply and Demand Schedules for Fish**

Price (£ per box)	Quantity Supplied (boxes)	Quantity Demanded (boxes)
10	20	120
20	40	100
30	60	80
40	80	60
50	100	40
60	120	20

It is important to interpret the quantity supplied as the number of boxes the suppliers would like to sell and not what they will actually sell at each price—when trading starts they may be unable to sell all they want. Note that the quantity supplied increases as the price rises—the two are said to be **positively related**. Normally, that is the relationship we assume between price and quantity supplied. For example, at low prices the suppliers might prefer to hold fish off the market and bring it back the next day in the hope of better prices; or some suppliers may know that they can get higher prices elsewhere. Similarly, when the price is high they will want to sell off most or all of their stocks immediately. The relationship is actually more complicated than that and we shall look at supply in more depth in Chapters 5 and 6.

We can follow the same procedure with the buyers. When we add up the amounts they would like to buy at each price we end up with the 'quantity demanded' in the third column. Again, these are not necessarily the amounts they actually buy because they may not be available. The 'price' and 'quantity demanded' columns together are the demand schedule. This time the two are **negatively related**—when price goes up the quantity demanded falls since buyers will know from experience that their own customers will buy less fish as it becomes dearer. We investigate this in Chapter 4.

It is convenient to translate the supply and demand schedules to a graph. This is done in Figure 2.1 where we measure price on the vertical axis and quantity on the horizontal axis. Since quantities supplied and demanded both change by regular amounts as price alters we end up with straight lines when they are plotted on the graph. Note that this is assumed for simplicity's sake; there is no reason to expect either quantity supplied or demanded to behave quite like this in real world markets.

FIGURE 2.1 **Supply and demand for fish**

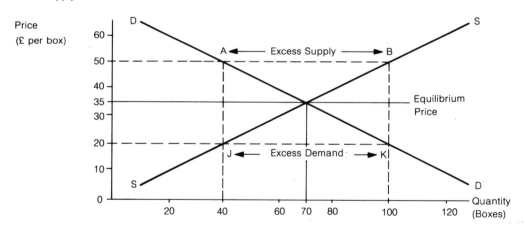

EQUILIBRIUM PRICE

When the supply and demand schedules are plotted they are referred to as the supply and demand curves respectively and are labelled with S and D. The supply curve has a positive gradient (slopes upwards from left to right) reflecting our assumption that quantity supplied increases as price rises. The demand curve has a negative slope—quantity demanded falls as price goes up. The two curves therefore intersect at a unique price and quantity—in our example at a price of £35 per box and a quantity of 70 boxes. The price at which quantity supplied equals quantity demanded is known as the **equilibrium** or **market-clearing** price. Our basic proposition is that, in a free and competitive market, the actual price at which the good is traded will tend to move towards the equilibrium price. Note that this is not to say that fish will not change hands at prices other than £35. It almost certainly will, but market forces, we argue, will tend to drive the price back to £35.

To understand this proposition, suppose trading takes place at prices different from the market-clearing price. Take a first price of £50, above the equilibrium. At this price we can read from the curves that the quantity supplied at 100 boxes is much greater than the quantity demanded at only 40 boxes. We call this a situation of **excess supply** and it is measured in the diagram by the horizontal distance between the two curves at the price of £50. At this price buyers are simply unwilling to take as much as the suppliers are offering. Sellers are therefore likely to try to avoid having unwanted stocks on their hands by lowering their offer prices. Buyers, conversely, seeing that suppliers cannot sell their fish at £50 are likely to bid down the price. Thus, whenever there is excess supply, we expect market forces to bring down the price. As it comes down, the quantity supplied falls and the amount demanded increases to reduce the excess supply.

Now, take a price below the equilibrium, of say, £20. The situation is reversed with buyers wanting 100 boxes of fish and suppliers willing to offer only 40 boxes. There is **excess demand** and we can expect buyers to bid up the price and sellers to raise their offer prices. We move up and along both curves to reduce the excess demand. In short, price will tend to rise when there is excess demand and to fall when there is excess supply. There is only one price at which there is neither excess demand nor excess supply—the equilibrium price of £35. Once that price is reached both buyers and sellers are satisfied—buyers can obtain all the fish they want and suppliers can sell all they want. There is no further pressure for the price to change.

2.3 SUPPLY AND DEMAND FUNCTIONS

We argue then that, given the supply and demand schedules or curves, the price will tend to move towards the equilibrium or market-clearing level. Yet, we know that in many real-world markets the prices of goods and services are continually changing. This is especially so in relatively free and competitive markets like that for fish. Other markets with fluctuating prices are those for perishable fruit and vegetables, for primary commodities like coffee, cocoa, tin and copper, and for financial assets such as equity shares and foreign exchange. The explanation for price fluctuations in these markets is simply that supply and demand are both changing to bring rises or falls in the market-clearing price. In graphical terms the supply and demand curves are forever shifting to bring new equilibrium prices at the point of intersection of the curves. To understand this we need to introduce the idea of supply and demand 'functions'. We look first at the demand function.

2.3.1 The demand function

When we drew up the demand schedule and curve for fish we showed the relationship between the price and the quantity demanded on the implicit assumption that all other things which affect the purchases of fish remain unchanged. We thus made the *ceteris paribus* or 'other things equal' assumption introduced in the last chapter. *Ceteris paribus*, when the price of fish goes up the quantity demanded comes down. But there are many determinants other than price of what people want to buy of a good and we incorporate these into what is termed the demand function for the good. The word 'function' is used here in a slightly technical sense and comes from mathematics. When the value of one variable, x, is determined by or is dependent on another, y, then we say x is a function of y. In mathematical shorthand we write that as:

$$x = f(y)$$

In the same way, the quantity demanded of a good is said to be a function of a range of variables, some more important than others. If we have a commodity, X, then the generally more significant determinants of the quantity demanded of X (Dx) are likely to be as follows:

1   **The price of X itself** (Px)—We have already seen that the relationship between Px and Dx is shown in the demand curve itself. Other things equal, we observe how Dx is affected by changes in Px by moving along the demand curve.

2 **The prices of other goods** (Pa, Pb, Pc....)—Changes in the prices of other goods may have an effect on Dx depending on whether they are substitutes or complements for X:

(a) **Substitutes**—Goods which are substitutes for each other satisfy similar consumer wants. Many people might regard fish and meat as substitutes, in which case, if there is a rise in the price of meat, they will buy less meat and consume more fish. Generally, a rise in the price of one substitute leads to an increase in demand for the other.

(b) **Complements**—These are goods which are consumed together or we can say they are in joint demand. Examples are bread and butter, shirts and ties or, in Britain, fish and chips! A steep rise in the price of fish will lead to a drop not only in consumption of fish but of chips as well even though the price of chips is unchanged. In short, a rise in the price of a complement leads to a fall in demand for X.

3 **Consumers' incomes** (Y)—A rise in the incomes of consumers will allow them to buy more of good X without any less of other goods. But whether consumers buy more or less of X after a rise in income depends on whether it is a 'normal' good or an 'inferior' good:

(a) **Normal goods**—These are defined simply as goods for which demand rises after a rise in consumers' incomes.

(b) **Inferior goods**—With two substitute goods one will be 'inferior' to the other. For example, margarine commands a lower price than butter, showing that the majority of consumers prefer butter to margarine. Similarly, expensive foods like meat and fish may well be preferred to cheap staple foods such as rice, bread and potatoes. But, at low incomes, households can only afford the staple foods. As their income rises they therefore tend to have a more diverse diet, increasing their consumption of meat, but reducing that of 'inferior' foods. An inferior good, then, is one for which demand falls after an increase in income (or rises after a reduction in income).

4 **Tastes** (T)—People's tastes or preferences for goods and services can be affected by a great variety of non-economic factors such as fashions (clothes, hair styles), the weather (cold drinks, fuel, ice cream), dissemination of medical knowledge about smoking, drinking and diet. Advertising and other sales promotion will also influence tastes.

5 **Expectations** (E)—Expectations about the future prices of goods can have a potent effect on demand. If buyers of, say, coffee expect the price to rise they are likely to buy more than their current needs in order to increase their stocks. Similarly, they will run down stocks and cut current purchases if the price is expected to fall.

All these determinants of demand for X enter into the demand function. This is written as:

$$Dx = f(Px; \ Pa, \ Pb.....Pn; \ Y; \ T; \ E)$$

Remember, we read this as the quantity demanded of X is a function of the price of X, the prices of other goods, etc.

2.3.2 Shifts of demand

When we drew the demand curve for fish we varied only Px; all other things were held constant. Now, suppose we change one of the other determinants of Dx. Imagine consumers' incomes rise and that fish is a normal good. This means that at each price people will demand more fish. Instead of 60 boxes at £40 they might now want 80 boxes; at £30 they want 100 boxes instead of 80. In graphical terms the demand curve shifts to the right, from DD to D_1D_1 in Figure 2.2—more is demanded at each price. Alternatively, if the price of meat—a substitute—dropped there would be a fall in demand for fish. Less would be demanded at each price and the demand curve for fish would shift to the left.

We can also see the effects of the shifts in demand on the price and quantity traded of fish. The original equilibrium price and quantity are at P_1, but there is a greater quantity demanded, that is, there is now excess demand at the original price. We already know that in a free and competitive market excess demand will push up the price. That is what happens here; the price rises until a new equilibrium is reached where the new demand curve cuts the supply curve. At that point we have a higher price, P_2, and a new higher quantity, Q_2. Thus we expect an increase in demand to raise both price and quantity.

FIGURE 2.2 **Effects of shifts in the demand curve**

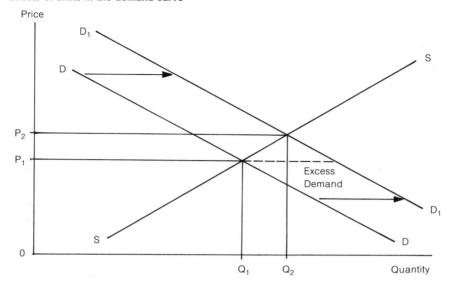

A fall in demand, as might be expected, will have the opposite effects. It will create excess supply at the original price and that will push the price down to a new market-clearing level. Students should draw their own diagrams to show this.

2.3.3 The supply function

It is easy now to make a parallel analysis of supply. First, any supply curve is drawn under the same ceteris paribus assumption that all the determinants of quantity supplied (Sx) remain unchanged except for Px, the price of the good itself. Again, there is a supply function incorporating the variables which may affect Sx. The more important ones other than Px are:

1   **The prices of other goods**—Some goods are in joint supply. Farmers raising cattle primarily for beef will also produce hides for leather. A rise in the price of beef will increase not only the quantity supplied of beef (a movement up its supply curve) but also, as more cattle are raised, an increase in the supply of hides (a shift to the right of the supply curve as more hides are produced at each price). Other goods may compete in production for similar resources, eg, a rise in the price of wheat may lead to land being taken out of production of other crops, say, potatoes. The supply of potatoes therefore falls; the supply curve shifts to the left.

2   **Costs** (C)—Costs of production are examined in depth in Chapter 4, but it should be clear that a rise in costs through an increase in factor prices (such as wages) is likely to mean that producers will want a higher market price to produce any given quantity. This is shown by an upward shift of the supply curve. In turn, if the supply curve is positively sloped, as we have assumed so far, then the upward shift is equivalent to a shift to the left or a fall in supply. Similarly, a reduction in costs because of, say, higher productivity of factors, will shift a positively sloped supply curve down and to the right—more will be supplied at each price.

3   **Indirect taxes** (T) and **subsidies** (S)—Indirect taxes are those imposed on goods and services (rather than directly on factor owners). For instance, governments commonly levy special taxes on cigarettes. For the producers the tax is equivalent to a rise in costs and the effect is to shift the supply curve up and to the left. A subsidy can be treated as a negative tax. A subsidy payment to wheat farmers will increase supply—the supply curve shifts down and to the right.

4   **Expectations** (E)—Producers as well as consumers will be influenced by their expectations of *future* prices. This is important when there is a lag between planning and realisation of production. If farmers, for example, expect the price of carrots to rise next season they will sow more seed and the supply curve will shift to the right.

5   **Other factors** (F)—As well as these general supply determinants production of particular goods will be influenced by specific factors like favourable or adverse weather for farm products and in construction, natural disasters or strikes and other industrial disruption. These factors are analogous in their effects to tastes in the demand function.

Using the shorthand once again we can write the supply function for X as:

$$Sx = f(Px; Pa, Pb....Pn; C; T; S; E; F)$$

2.3.4 Shifts of supply

Shifts of supply can be handled in the same way as shifts of demand. Suppose, for example, the government imposes a tax of £20 on every box of fish sold. Using the figures in Table 2.1 the suppliers will now want a market price of £20 more to induce them to offer any given quantity—they require £50 instead of £30 to supply 60 boxes and so on. The whole supply curve shifts upwards vertically by the £20 tax per box. This is shown in Figure 2.3.

FIGURE 2.3 **Effects of a tax on fish**

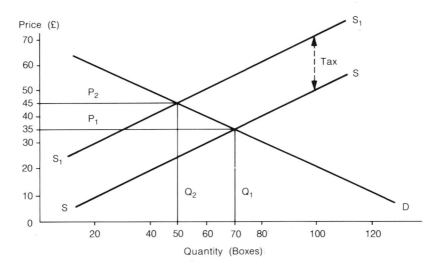

Note that the upward shift of the supply curve is equivalent to a shift to the left (a fall in supply) only when the curve is positively sloped. This may be important since supply curves, as we shall see, may not always slope upwards. For instance, if the supply curve was vertical (perfectly inelastic as explained in the next chapter) then a tax or subsidy would leave it unchanged. However, in this case the tax does bring a fall in supply with a shift of the curve to S_1. That creates excess demand at the original equilibrium price of P_1 or £35. The result is a rise in price to a new equilibrium of P_2 (£45) and a fall in the equilibrium quantity to Q_2 or 50 boxes of fish. The general conclusion is that a fall in supply will tend to raise price and reduce the quantity traded. The student should be able to see that the opposite will happen after an increase in supply, for example, work out the effects of a £10 per box subsidy to fish producers.

Notice also in this particular example that the tax of £20 leads to a rise in market price of only £10. After paying the tax to the government producers are left with a net supply price of £25, £10 less than before. In other words, suppliers have only been able to pass on half the tax to consumers in higher prices and have had to absorb the other half themselves. The **tax burden** is shared equally between producers and consumers. Sharing the burden is the most likely outcome of a tax, but it is not necessarily a 50/50 split and, in special cases, the whole of the burden could fall on consumers or on producers. The actual division depends on the elasticities of supply and demand which are dealt with in Chapter 3.

2.4 PRICE CONTROLS

So far, we have assumed that the market is both free and competitive. We shall keep the second assumption until later chapters, but suppose we have a market which is not free, that is, traders in the market are subject to control or regulation. Such regulation is common and usually comes from the government either directly or through agencies established by government. In organised markets, like the commodity exchanges and Stock Exchange in London, there is self-regulation of trading practices. Market regulations can take many forms (dealt with in later chapters) but here we concentrate on price controls. In principle, these are of two kinds—the setting of maximum prices or minimum prices. Also, government agencies may intervene to stabilise or influence prices indirectly by buying or selling of the commodity.

2.4.1 Maximum prices

Fixing a maximum or ceiling price for a good or service is aimed at holding the price below its free-market level to the benefit of the consumers. There would certainly be no point in setting a maximum price above the eqilibrium; in our fish market a ceiling of £50 a box is redundant when the market-clearing price is only £35. But suppose the government lays down a maximum price, backed up by law, of only £20. The immediate effects are clear. Using our original supply and demand figures in Table 2.1, consumers at that price would like to buy 100 boxes, but producers are willing to offer only 40 boxes. There is an excess demand of 60 boxes which cannot now be choked off by a rise in price. This is our central prediction of the effects of fixing and enforcing maximum prices; they invariably lead to excess demand or a market shortage.

Excess demand created by a maximum price will in turn have other effects partly dependent on how strictly the legal price is enforced. At one extreme, if the penalties for selling above the maximum are very light, say, a small fine, or the probability of detection and conviction are small, then the effects will be correspondingly slight. The legal price might be largely ignored and traders are likely to treat the fines like a tax, as an addition to their costs. If so, the supply curve will be shifted up and to the left resulting perversely in a higher equilibrium price. Fixing a maximum price would have precisely the opposite effect to that intended! Consumers would all end up paying higher prices.

At the other extreme the legal price might be backed up with severe penalties—heavy fines and imprisonment—together with a high level of policing. In this case no supplier might be willing to risk conviction and the excess demand cannot be eliminated by a rise in price. There has to be some means therefore of allocating or 'rationing' the reduced supplies among the consumers—there are only 40 boxes of fish available at £20 each to buyers who want 100 boxes at that price. There are two possibilities—informal or formal rationing:

1 **Informal rationing**—This would be undertaken by the suppliers themselves either individually or collectively. The possible principles for rationing by suppliers are many. They include combinations of queuing and 'first-come-first-served', restricting customers to maximum quantities, and discriminating in favour of certain consumers like regular customers or the supplier's family and friends or others who can offer other favours in return. Whatever rationing method is used there is bound to be arbitrariness and inequity among consumers.

2 **Formal rationing**—The government might introduce a formal rationing system. For example, during and for some years after World War II (1939–1945) the British government had rationing for most food and other basic goods like clothing and coal. The main method was to issue coupons to households which each week entitled them to specific amounts of butter, sugar, meat, and so on. Certain people like manual workers got bigger rations. Formal rationing of this sort is certainly fairer than informal rationing and can ensure that even the poorest households have minimum amounts of essential goods which are in short supply in wartime or other emergency periods. But all rationing schemes are arbitrary and have some degree of unfairness; with formal rationing it is administrators who decide who gets what irrespective of individual household needs.

Enforcement of price controls tends to lie in practice between the two extremes. Penalties are severe enough to deter some traders from breaking the law but not for others. Even if only a minority is willing to take the risk of conviction and fines the result will be the emergence of illegal trading in **black markets**. Thus, consumers who are going short at the legal price will be willing to pay the premium price necessary to compensate suppliers for their extra costs in black market trading.

There are countless practical examples to support our analysis of price controls. Wartime controls and the need for rationing are just one. Another is the legislation in Britain, first enacted in 1915, to hold down rents for privately let housing. The result has been a dramatic shrinkage in the availability of rented housing in the private sector together with an effective black market as private landlords collude with tenants to evade the controls. The only gainers have been households fortunate enough to have secured or inherited protected tenancies at some time in the past. Others have been forced into buying houses even when renting may have been more appropriate to their needs, or have had to pay inflated rents in the black market. In the extreme, those who can afford neither option may actually become homeless.

2.4.2 Minimum prices

It is easy to see the superficial attractions to politicians of holding down prices below market levels. Legislation to stop rents or bread prices from rising has a short-term popular appeal and might even win votes in the next elections. Laws which do the opposite, to hold up prices to minimum levels, are more difficult to understand. Yet in many countries price fixing of this kind is far more prevalent than the setting of maximum prices. The reasons are often political. Keeping prices up to minimum levels is almost always designed to protect producers who are often well organised and able to exert pressure on politicians and civil servants for the introduction of protective measures including laws for the maintenance of minimum prices and the effective removal of price competition. For example, in Britain, the rest of the European Community (EC) and other industrial countries like Japan and the USA, farmers have successfully deployed arguments for special treatment to win a massive degree of protection for agriculture. In the EC this has culminated in the Common Agricultural Policy (CAP) a major feature of which is the setting of most food prices in the EC way above world market levels.

Another example is the international airlines cartel which fixes fares on scheduled flights, again above the free-market prices. The International Air Transport Association (IATA) is backed by most national governments which wish to support their largely publicly-owned airlines. Although cartels—agreements between producers to fix prices and carve up markets between them—are illegal in most countries governments typically make exceptions for a wide range of industries and professions.

To see the effects of fixing minimum prices we can again return to our model of the market for fish. Suppose the fishing industry succeeds in persuading the government to protect it by fixing a legal minimum price at which fish can be sold. To have any effect, it must be above the free-market price of £35, say, £50 a box. At that price the quantity demanded is only 40 boxes but the suppliers are willing to sell 100 boxes. There is excess supply of 60 boxes. If the minimum price is to be sustained, one of three things must happen. First, the fish producers could agree among themselves to limit their total supplies to only 40 boxes to match demand at the high price. But that would mean allocating the restricted quantity among individual suppliers each of whom wants as big a share or 'quota' as possible. Even if they can agree on quotas they will then have to introduce a policing system to stop cheating—suppliers selling above their quota, possibly at prices below the legal minimum. We know from the experience of the oil producers' cartel (OPEC) that eventually this kind of restrictive agreement breaks down. Once one producer breaks ranks the rest will see little point in keeping within their own quotas. Competition resumes and the price slumps back to its free-market level (as the oil price did in 1986).

Cartels are unlikely then to survive on their own. The second possibility is that the government steps in to impose and enforce the quota restrictions on output. It might try to ensure compliance with quotas by imposing fines on producers who exceed them. Alternatively it could reward producers who keep within their quotas. They would be paid therefore for not producing! Government-enforced quota restrictions are more likely to succeed in keeping down output but have the same disadvantage of policing costs (borne this time by the taxpayer) while many producers, particularly the efficient ones, may feel unfairly penalised.

THE EUROPEAN COMMON AGRICULTURAL POLICY (CAP)

Producers will much prefer the third means of holding up the price. This is to allow them to produce as much as they want at the minimum price but for the government itself to buy up the excess supply or surplus output. This is precisely what happens in the EC's agricultural policy. The EC ensures that prices do not drop below minimum target levels by setting up intervention agencies to which farmers can sell at guaranteed prices all the surplus output which they cannot sell on the market. Prices have been set so high that the EC has had to accumulate vast stocks of most food products—the notorious beef, butter and grain mountains and the milk, wine and olive oil lakes. If the government did that in our fish market it would buy up 60 boxes a day which it would have to keep in cold store. It would not be long before it had a fish mountain.

The costs of the CAP are huge. EC taxpayers have to pay the bill for buying up surpluses and storing them. Eventually the food mountains have to be disposed of. This is done sometimes by physically destroying food or dumping it—in the sea, down old mine shafts or literally down the drain. Another way is to 'dump' it on overseas markets at subsidised prices. That depresses world prices to the detriment of more efficient foreign farmers, often in less developed countries which rely on exports of products like sugar for their vital foreign exchange earnings. In turn, EC consumers bear a heavy cost in being forced to pay wildly excessive food prices while the burden is especially hard for poorer households who spend a higher proportion of their incomes on food.

All these costs are incurred to secure the protection of a minority of the population—farmers and landowners. Because of the immense expense of the surpluses, proposals have been made to introduce quota restrictions on output of the kind just discussed. In fact a quota system is already in force for milk with fines for farmers who over-produce. More recent suggestions involve farmers to take land out of use! The point here is that there may well be good arguments for protecting agriculture such as the need for domestic sources of food supply in wartime or for preservation of the countryside. However, the CAP's method of achieving this—pushing up market prices—is extremely inefficient. Farmers could be given protection by other less costly means. For example, in Britain, before she joined the EC (in 1973), farmers received subsidies on their output and consumers were able to buy food at low prices established in world markets. This avoided the need to buy up surplus production and simultaneously avoided the burden on consumers from high prices.

We should note that the effects of minimum prices may differ in some respects when they are applied to services rather than goods. This is because surplus output of services obviously cannot be stored. In the case of the IATA cartel, the excess supply from fixing high fares on scheduled services shows itself in excess capacity—aeroplanes on scheduled routes typically fly with a high proportion of empty seats. In turn, the banning of price competition leads to extensive non-price competition with heavy advertising and claims by airlines that they offer more in-flight comforts and delights than their competitors. The cartel is also threatened by airlines selling discounted tickets and setting up charter flight subsidiaries to which the fixed prices do not apply.

To sum up on both maximum and minimum prices, our analysis indicates that interference with the allocation of resources through free market mechanisms can impose heavy costs on society. While we can sometimes find good reasons (like wartime shortages) for price controls and other kinds of market intervention, it is important that governments weigh up the potential benefits against the costs. More likely than not it will be found either that there is a net cost for society or that some more efficient method can be used to achieve the desired results which interferes less harmfully with the operation of the market. For example, cash grants to poor households are likely to be a better way of helping them than rent controls and subsidies to farmers much less costly than high food prices. The general question of the alternative means governments can use to intervene in markets is taken up in Chapter 9.

SUMMARY

In a free and competitive market the price of a commodity will tend to move towards an equilibrium or market-clearing level at which quantity demanded equals quantity supplied. This can be shown graphically using supply and demand curves drawn on the ceteris paribus assumption that all factors in the supply and demand functions, other than the price of the good itself, remain unchanged. Changes in these other factors bring shifts in the supply or demand curves and movements in equilibrium price and quantity. Analysis of intervention in markets to fix maximum or minimum prices reveals potentially heavy costs from interfering with the price mechanism as a means of allocating resources.

SELF-TEST QUESTIONS

In most of these questions it will help to sketch diagrams.

1   Ceteris paribus, which one of the following statements is wrong?

(a)   A positive relation between quantity supplied and price means that suppliers are willing to offer less when the price falls.

(b)   Consumers will normally be willing to buy more of a good when its price falls.

(c)   At all prices the quantity bought equals the quantity sold.

(d)   Demand curves are negatively sloped because people want less when the price rises.

(e)   The equilibrium price is the only price at which the quantity bought equals the quantity sold.

2   Which one of the following statements is correct?

(a)   An excess of quantity demanded over quantity supplied will lead to a fall in price.

(b)   When there is excess supply buyers will bid up the price.

(c)   When price is above the market-clearing level suppliers can sell all they want.

(d)   Excess demand of 10 units combined with excess supply of 10 units will leave the price unchanged.

(e)   When price is below the equilibrium buyers will be unable to buy all they want.

3   Which one of the following statements is correct?

(a)   An increase in the price of gas will shift the demand curve for gas to the left.

(b)   A rise in the price of electricity will shift the demand curve for gas to the left.

(c)   A steep fall in the price of video recorders will shift the demand curve for video cassettes to the right.

(d)   A subsidy to bread producers will raise the price at which they are willing to sell any given quantity.

(e)   A tax will shift a vertical supply curve to the left.

4   Which one of the following statements is correct?

(a)   At the original equilibrium price, a 10% increase in quantity demanded combined with a 10% fall in quantity supplied leaves the price unchanged.

(b)   The price of a good will rise if the price of a substitute rises at the same time as the price of a complement falls.

(c)   A subsidy of 10p per kilo of oranges will normally lead to a 10p fall in price.

(d)   A tax on beer will have no effect because any rise in price will reduce demand and bring the price down again.

(e)   An increase in productivity in tea plantations at the same time as a rise in the price of coffee will clearly push up the price of tea.

5   Which one of the following statements is wrong?

(a)   Imposition of a maximum price above the market-clearing level will leave the price unchanged.

(b)   Fixing a minimum price below the free-market level will leave price unchanged.

(c)   Rent controls will ensure an adequate supply of rented housing at low prices only if the controls are strictly enforced.

(d)   Cartels aimed at raising price above the free-market level will fail if producers exceed their quotas.

(e)   Fixing fares on scheduled flights at less than their free-market level will lead to insufficient capacity to satisfy demand.

EXERCISE

Many governments impose controls on the rents of private property with the object of assisting lower-paid workers. What are the likely consequences of such policies?

Answers on page 239.

Elasticities

This chapter completes basic supply-and-demand analysis of markets with an examination of the concept of **elasticity** with which we measure the responsiveness of quantity demanded or supplied to changes in price and other variables in the demand and supply functions. After studying this chapter you should know how to calculate elasticities and understand their determinants. You should also be able to appreciate the importance of elasticities to the pricing decisions of firms, to the government in imposing indirect taxes and as an explanation of price instability in many markets.

3.1   INTRODUCTION

When we analysed the effects of shifts in the supply and demand functions in the last chapter we came to the general conclusions, for example, that an increase in demand will lead to a rise in both price and quantity and that a fall in supply will result in a higher price and a lower quantity. We said nothing about how much price and quantity will change, but that can be important in many business decisions. For example, if firms in the steel industry formed a cartel to raise price by a restriction of output they would actually be worse off in terms of their revenue if, to push up the price by 10 per cent, they had to cut back steel output by 20 per cent. Their revenue would drop by roughly 10 per cent and the cartel is likely to be abandoned. On the other hand, if they could achieve 10 per cent better prices by cutting output by only 5 per cent, then the cartel would clearly be worthwhile; they would make about 5 per cent extra revenue for less output.

The difference between the two cases is that, in the first, the quantity demanded falls away four times as much as in the second. Quantity demanded is much more sensitive to the rise in price. To measure the response we use the concept of elasticity; we say that demand is more **elastic** in the first case than in the second. Before examining the particular notion of **price elasticity of demand** which is involved here, we should note that elasticity is a general measure of the response of a **dependent** variable, x, to a change in an independent variable, y. Thus, in our demand function in Chapter 2 we included a whole range of factors which can influence the demand for commodity X. If Px changes we can calculate the change in quantity with the 'price' elasticity of demand; if incomes change we can use the 'income' elasticity of demand, and so on. We shall look first at the price elasticity of demand and then at other elasticities in respect of both demand and supply.

3.2   PRICE ELASTICITY OF DEMAND

Price elasticity of demand (PED) measures the response of quantity demanded of a good to a change in its price. PED has a numerical value calculated as the percentage change in quantity demanded resulting from a one per cent change in price. Suppose we refer to the demand schedule for fish in the previous chapter. At £20 the quantity demanded was 100 boxes and at £30 it was 80 boxes. Thus, when the price went up by 50 per cent the quantity fell by 20 per cent—for every one per cent rise in price the quantity demanded declined by 0.4 per cent. Writing quantity demanded as QD and price as P the value of PED can be calculated approximately by using the following formula:

$$PED = \frac{\text{Percentage change in QD}}{\text{Percentage change in P}}$$

The formula can be set out more succinctly by using the mathematical shorthand for 'a change in', the Greek capital letter 'delta' (Δ). We shall encounter Δ quite frequently in later chapters. The formula then becomes:

$$PED = \frac{\%\Delta QD}{\%\Delta P}$$

Suppose we set out the calculation of PED for fish along with two more examples:

TABLE 3.1 **Calculating the price elasticity of demand**

(a) *Fish*

Price (£)	Quantity Demanded
20	100
30	80
%ΔP = 50	%ΔQD = −20

PED = −20/50 = −0.4

(b) *BMW cars*

Price (£)	Quantity Demanded
16,000	10,000
20,000	5,000
%ΔP = 25	%ΔQD = −50

PED = −50/25 = −2

(c) *Vacuum cleaners*

Price (£)	Quantity Demanded
80	160,000
70	180,000
%ΔP = −12.5	%ΔQD = 12.5

PED = 12.5/−12.5 = −1

Note two points about PED. First, we are interested in the percentage or proportionate changes and quantity and not in the absolute changes. This is because we want to make comparisons of demand responsiveness for different goods and services. If we just took the absolute changes in the prices and sales of BMWs and vacuum cleaners there is no immediate basis for saying that the demand for either is more or less sensitive to price than the other. The PED values, however, tell us at once that the demand for BMWs is twice as responsive to price changes as that for vacuum cleaners. The second point is that, so long as demand curves have a negative slope, then the PED must have a negative value; P and QD change in opposite directions so that, if ΔQD is positive, ΔP must be negative and vice versa. However, unless we are doing mathematical work, it is conventional to ignore the minus sign.

Taking the absolute size of PED, ie, ignoring its sign, its value can range between the extremes of zero and infinity (∞). If PED=0, we say that demand is **perfectly inelastic**—the quantity

FIGURE 3.1 **Perfectly inelastic and perfectly elastic demand curves**

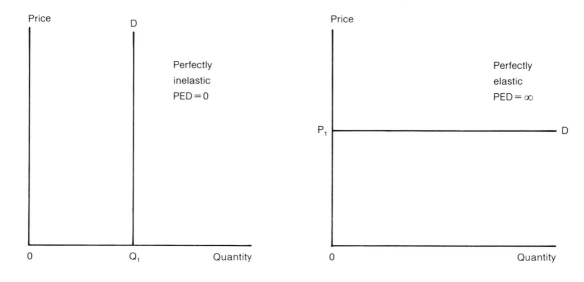

demanded of the good remains the same at all prices. If PED = ∞ then even the smallest change in price brings an 'infinite' change in quantity. Demand is then said to be infinitely or **perfectly elastic**. The practical interpretation of perfectly elastic demand is that there is only one relevant price. Figure 3.1 shows what the demand curves look like in these two limiting cases of PED. For nearly all goods, we expect the PED to lie between these two extremes and it is usual to distinguish three cases:

1   PED < 1; Relatively inelastic demand

An example here is the value of PED for fish which we calculated as 0.4 when the price rose from £20 to £30. Quantity demanded is relatively insensitive to price; proportionately the change in quantity is only 0.4 times the change in price. (Commonly, we drop the word 'relatively' and just say 'demand is inelastic' to mean PED is less than one.)

At this point we can note that the size of PED determines what happens to consumers' expenditure on a good when the price changes. Expenditure (E) equals price times quantity (P.Q). In our example, E increased from (£20 × 100) = £2,000 to (£30 × 80) = £2,400. This is because the 50 per cent rise in price, which on its own increases expenditure, more than offsets the 20 per cent fall in quantity, and reduces expenditure. This will always be the case when demand is inelastic—the price change will dominate the quantity change in its effect on spending. This means that, when demand is inelastic, price and expenditure will change in the same direction as we move along a given demand curve. A relatively inelastic demand curve is shown in Figure 3.2. Expenditure on the good at each price is measured by the area of the rectangle beneath the demand curve. You can see the area increases as the price goes up from P_1 to P_2.

2   PED > 1; Relatively elastic demand

In our example BMW cars have a relatively elastic demand; when the price is increased by 25 per cent sales volume drops by 50 per cent. In turn, there is a fall in expenditure (the producer's revenue) from £160 m to £100 m because the effect on revenue of the drop in volume dominates over that of the rise in price. This will always be the case when demand is elastic—as we move along the demand curve price and revenue change in opposite directions. It can be seen in Figure 3.2 that, as the price rises, the rectangle beneath the elastic demand curve decreases in area.

3   PED = 1; Unit elastic demand

When PED = 1, as with vacuum cleaners, price and quantity change by the same percentage but in opposite directions. That will keep expenditure on the good approximately the same; we say approximately because it will only stay precisely the same for very small, (strictly speaking, infinitesimal) changes in P and QD. Thus, when the vacuum cleaner price is reduced by 12.5 per cent, expenditure falls slightly from £12.8 m to £12.6 m. For practical purposes, expenditure or producers' revenue can therefore be treated as staying constant for small price changes. That gives us a simple method of drawing a demand curve on which PED = 1 at all points; it is a curve along which all the expenditure rectangles have a constant area. This is shown in Figure 3.2. By drawing rectangles of equal area (P.Q) and joining up the corner points we trace out a smooth curve called a 'rectangular hyperbola'. This is alternatively termed a 'constant-expenditure' curve.

PED ON A STRAIGHT LINE DEMAND CURVE

Because for convenience we commonly show an inelastic demand curve as a steep straight line and an elastic one with a flat straight line it is a frequent error to say that a unit elastic demand curve is like the one in Figure 3.3, a straight line at 45 degrees to both axes. That is quite wrong; a unit elastic demand curve is, as we have just seen, a rectangular hyperbola. Any straight line curve (not just one at 45 degrees) will pass through all values of PED, from infinity at point A, where it cuts the price axis to zero where it meets the quantity axis at C. Exactly halfway along the line at B, PED = 1.

Along a straight-line demand curve the slope remains constant equal to $\Delta Q/\Delta P$. But that is the ratio of the *absolute* changes in price and quantity. In measuring the PED we are interested in the percentage or *relative* changes, $\Delta Q/Q$ and $\Delta P/P$. The PED in fact can be rewritten simply as $\Delta Q/Q$ divided by $\Delta P/P$. Rearranged that gives us:

$$PED = \frac{\Delta Q}{\Delta P} \cdot \frac{P}{Q}$$

FIGURE 3.2 **Cases of price elasticity of demand**

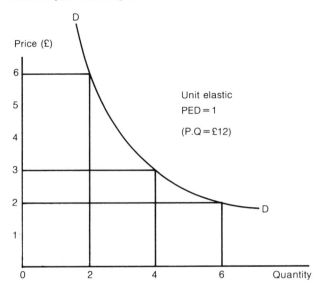

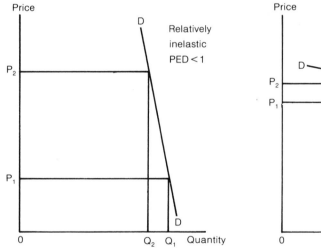

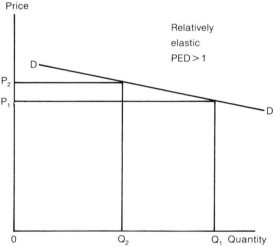

At any point on a straight-line demand curve therefore we have two determinants of PED. $\Delta Q/\Delta P$ is constant but P/Q changes as we move down the line. At the extreme point A, Q is zero so that both P/Q and the PED itself must equal infinity. At C, P is zero so that PED is also equal to zero. Halfway along the curve, PED must equal one. The PED continuously declines as we slide down the curve. This means that between A and B, PED is greater than one—demand is relatively elastic. Similarly, in the lower half of the curve between B and C, PED is less than one, so that demand is relatively inelastic. This can also be seen by noting what happens to the expenditure rectangles. At A the area is plainly zero but as we move from A the area increases till it reaches a maximum at the mid-point, B. In other words, expenditure rises as price falls, showing that demand is elastic between A and B. In moving down from B, however, the rectangles shrink in area until expenditure once again becomes zero at C. In the lower half of the demand curve, expenditure falls as price falls so that demand is inelastic.

It should be stressed that we have measured the PED at **points** along the line. PED, for example, equals one at point B only for an infinitesimal change in price. If we have finite changes in price, as in our examples in Table 3.1, our estimates of PED are only approximations. This is a general problem in calculating PED along any demand curve, not just along a straight-line curve. Some writers try to resolve it by distinguishing between **point elasticity**, which measures PED for infinitesimal changes in price, and **arc elasticity** which calculates it over a finite distance along the curve. The notion of arc elasticity will not be found to be helpful at this stage and we will not pursue it

FIGURE 3.3 **Price elasticity along a straight-line demand curve**

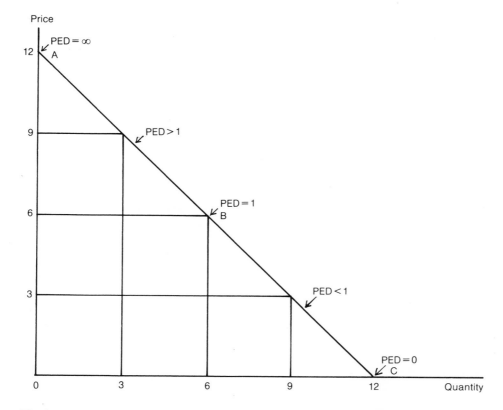

further. The important point is to be aware that measures of PED for significant changes in price **are** approximate and should therefore be treated with caution.

DETERMINANTS OF PED

In Chapter 4 we shall show that when the price of a good rises, the effect on quantity demanded can be broken down between two components. First, there is a **substitution effect**—consumers will tend to switch to what are now relatively cheaper substitutes. This gives us one of the main determinants of the value of the PED for any good. If there are close substitutes available then we might expect a relatively large reduction in consumption of the good after a rise in its price. For example, motor cars imported into Britain are a close substitute for cars produced at home. If the pound drops against other currencies imported cars will become more expensive and consumers may switch to home-produced models. The result may be a relatively big fall in imports; in short, the demand for imported cars may be relatively elastic. Conversely, demand for goods with no close substitute (cigarettes, alcohol, salt) will tend to be inelastic and a rise in their price will have relatively little effect on consumption.

However, the demand even for goods with no close substitutes is unlikely to be perfectly inelastic. This is because of the **income effect** of a price change. When the price of a good rises, consumers effectively suffer a reduction in their **real** income, ie, their capacity to buy goods and services generally out of their money income. With a normal good the fall in real income after a rise in its price will reduce consumption so that the income effect reinforces the substitution effect. The importance of the income effect depends on the proportion of the consumer's income spent on the good. With a product such as pepper or salt even a large rise in price will normally have a negligible income effect. But, if there is a general rise in clothing prices, the reduction in real incomes will be significant, especially for poor households. If clothing is a normal good the fall in demand may be correspondingly large.

Note though that with inferior goods, for which consumption falls after a rise in income, the income effect opposes the substitution effect of a price change. Suppose poor households, for example, spend a high proportion of their income on an 'inferior' staple food such as potatoes. A rise in the price of potatoes may so far reduce their ability to buy 'superior' foods like cheese and meat that they are forced to buy more potatoes after the price increase. The perverse income effect could be strong enough not just to make demand inelastic but to swamp the substitution effect completely. In that case, we could have a positively sloped demand curve where quantity demanded increases after a rise in price. Such goods are known as **Giffen goods** after a nineteenth century statistician, Sir Robert Giffen, who is supposed to have first identified goods with positively sloped demand curves. Modern economists, however, believe that, though Giffen goods may exist for individual households, they are very rare at the level of market demand.

Finally, consumers will often need **time** to adjust their consumption patterns after a change in price. For example, when the OPEC cartel pushed up oil prices by more than four times in the early 1970s, households and firms with oil-fired central heating boilers did not immediately switch to alternative fuels such as gas. They wanted to be sure the price increase was permanent before incurring the capital expenditure in changing their boilers. Similarly, motorists did not replace their 'gas guzzling' cars straightaway with more economical ones and it was months and years before car manufacturers fully responded with the development of more fuel-efficient models. This meant that, in the short run, demand for oil was inelastic and that oil producing countries were able to reap a rise in their revenues almost in proportion to the increase in price. As time passed, however, consumption did respond to higher prices and long-run demand for OPEC oil became price-elastic. This is shown in Figure 3.4; the long-run demand curve, D_L, is more elastic than the short-run curve, D_S. Falling consumption to Q_3 in the longer run helps to explain the declining power of the OPEC cartel to control the price of oil.

FIGURE 3.4   **Increasing long-run PED for oil**

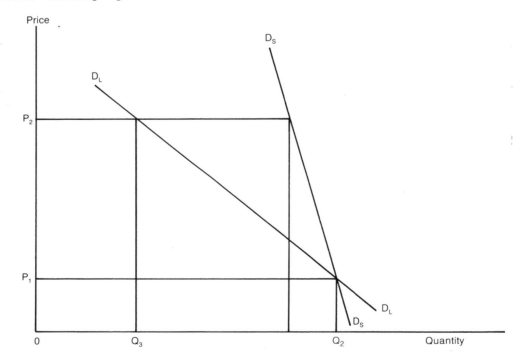

IMPORTANCE OF PED

Price elasticity of demand has a wide range of practical applications. As we have just seen, it is important for producers in cartels or with a degree of monopoly power in their markets to be aware of how their sales volume is likely to respond to a change in price. OPEC producers were able to gain a huge increase in export revenues in the short run because demand for oil was inelastic, but those revenues have fallen away quite drastically as demand has become more elastic. In the same way, if an enterprise calculates that demand is price-elastic then it will get increased revenue by **lowering** its price. An example of this was a large cut in fares on London buses and underground trains in the early 1980s. This appeared to lead to a disproportionate increase in passengers and higher revenues. It is quite possible also that airlines could be better off if they abandoned their cartel on scheduled flights—if demand proves to be elastic, revenue will increase while the extra cost of filling otherwise empty seats will be small.

Governments also find knowledge of the PED useful in imposing taxes on goods and services. A tax on a good, remember, shifts the supply curve upwards. The less elastic is demand, the greater the increase in the equilibrium price and the smaller the fall in consumption. For a given tax, therefore, the lower the PED the more the government raises in revenue. This no doubt explains why in most countries we find the heaviest taxes on goods like tobacco and alcohol, for which demand is likely to be inelastic. However, the country's finance minister (ie the Chancellor of the Exchequer in Britain) is not solely concerned with maximising revenue. The less elastic the demand the greater the share of the tax burden borne by consumers (the easier it is for producers to pass on the tax in a higher price). The minister might want to avoid unpopular price increases and burdens on households. If so, indirect taxes might be directed towards goods with elastic demand where the taxes would largely be absorbed by producers having to take a cut in their own supply prices. The effect of a tax on price and the way the tax burden is shared between consumers and producers depend very much on the PED for the good. Students should confirm this by redrawing Figure 2.3 in Chapter 2 with both inelastic and elastic demand curves.

3.3   OTHER DEMAND ELASTICITIES

We pointed out earlier that elasticity is a general concept and that we can use it to measure the response of demand to changes in other variables in the demand function. We shall focus on two other demand elasticities—the income elasticity and the cross elasticity.

3.3.1   Income elasticity of demand

With this elasticity we measure the responsiveness of quantity demanded of a good to changes in consumers' incomes. Using our previous notation and letting Y stand for income, the income elasticity of demand can be written as:

$$YED = \frac{\%\Delta QD}{\%\Delta Y}$$

Thus, if income rises by 20 per cent and consumption increases by 30 per cent the YED equals 1.5. That means that, other things being equal, quantity demanded goes up by 1.5 per cent for every one per cent increase in income. Remember that the rise in demand is shown by a shift to the right of the demand curve—more is demanded at each price. The YED therefore determines how far the curve shifts after a given rise (or fall) in income. The value of the YED gives us a more precise way of classifying goods:

1   **Normal goods** It has been seen that these are goods for which the demand rises (falls) after an increase (reduction) in income. QD and Y are therefore positively related and the YED must have a positive value. We can define normal goods simply as those with a YED greater than zero. In turn, we can subdivide normal goods, depending on whether the YED is greater or less than one. In the first case, demand for the good is **income-elastic**, so that expenditure on the good will increase as a proportion of income as income rises. In the second, demand is **income-inelastic** and spending on the good becomes a smaller proportion of rising income.

    Some writers refer to goods with income-elastic demand as luxuries and those with income-inelastic demand as necessities. However, in our view these labels are confusing and misleading since demand for a good such as meat may be income-elastic for a poor household but income-inelastic for a richer one. The same point can be made about almost all goods and we think it better therefore to avoid use of these terms in this context. This is not to say, of course, that the size of the YED is unimportant. For instance, in a growing economy with rising real incomes, firms producing goods for which demand is income-elastic will have more rapidly-growing sales than those concentrating on products for which demand is income-inelastic. Firms are likely therefore to bias their investment towards goods and services with a high YED, which are not necessarily luxuries in the every-day sense.

2   **Inferior goods** With these quantity demanded falls (rises) after an increase (decrease) in income. The YED must therefore have a negative value.

Calculation of the YED can again be useful to businesses and the government. Firms, for example, will often want to make forecasts of sales revenue. If in turn they can make estimates of the YED for their various products and prepare projections of the growth of consumer incomes in the future, it is simple to turn these into sales forecasts. Estimating the YED for the firm's existing and new products will also help it to take decisions about the best way of allocating its investment and research and development resources to secure its own growth prospects. For example, a company with a static or even falling market in food products may wish to diversify by taking over firms in more dynamic industries such as financial services and personal computers, products which may have a high YED. Finally, knowledge of the YED for different goods and services will assist finance ministers to predict revenue from indirect taxes.

3.3.2 Cross elasticity of demand

This measures the response of quantity demanded of one good to changes in the price of another. If we have two goods A and B, then the cross elasticity of demand (CED) is calculated as:

$$CED = \frac{\%\Delta QDa}{\%\Delta Pb}$$

We know that there are two classes of goods related to each other in demand—substitutes and complements. If A and B are substitutes, then a rise in the price of B will increase the demand for A and the CED will therefore be positive. Substitutes are defined as goods with a positive CED and the greater is the value of CED the greater is the degree of substitution between them.

Similarly, if the goods are complements, a rise in the price of one leads to a fall in the demand for the other. Complementary goods thus have a negative CED. If they are highly complementary the CED will have a correspondingly high value, eg, right and left shoes should have a negative CED of close to infinity. The CED is largely useful in economic analysis. For example, when we want to identify an 'industry' we might include in it only those firms producing products which are close substitutes, ie, those with a high CED.

3.4 PRICE ELASTICITY OF SUPPLY

The concept of elasticity applies to supply as well as demand. Thus, we can use elasticity to measure the response of quantity supplied to any of the variables in the supply function. However, we tend to make most use of the **price elasticity of supply** (PES) which measures the sensitivity of the quantity supplied of a good to changes in its own price. We are therefore measuring elasticity along a given supply curve. The formula for calculating PES is analogous to that for the PED. If we write quantity supplied as QS it is:

$$PES = \frac{\%\Delta QS}{\%\Delta P}$$

The cases of PES which we distinguish are the same as those for PED. We thus have the two extreme cases of perfectly elastic and perfectly inelastic supply with respective values of infinity and zero. The supply curves also look the same as the corresponding demand curves—perfectly elastic supply is represented as a horizontal straight line and perfectly inelastic supply by a vertical straight line. The interpretation too is the same. When supply is infinitely elastic, the industry will supply any quantity at one price; when it is perfectly inelastic the same quantity will be supplied at all prices. In turn, we have three corresponding intermediate cases shown in Figure 3.5.

1   **PES < 1; Relatively inelastic supply** After a rise in price of one per cent, quantity supplied increases by less than one per cent. Supply is clearly relatively insensitive to price. An inelastic supply curve is usually depicted with a steep positively sloped line but in fact any straight-line supply curve cutting the quantity axis will be inelastic, irrespective of its slope. This is because we are interested, not in the absolute slope of the line ($\Delta Q/\Delta P$) which stays constant, but in the relative changes in quantity and price. If a straight line cuts the horizontal axis at some positive

FIGURE 3.5 **Cases of price elasticity of supply**

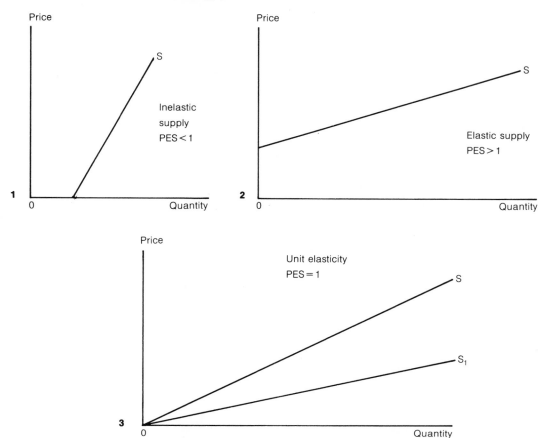

quantity then the relative or percentage change in quantity will always be less than the relative change in price. As we move up the line, the PES will increase and will get closer to but never exceed one. In other words, supply along such a line will be relatively inelastic.

2 **PES > 1; Relatively elastic supply** A one per cent price rise will bring a more than one per cent increase of quantity supplied—supply is relatively responsive to price changes. Elastic supply can be easily represented by any straight line cutting the price axis. Again, the absolute slope of the line is immaterial. As we move up the line from the quantity axis, the relative increase in quantity will exceed the relative rise in price. The PES is greater than one and although its value rises the limit is infinity. Supply is therefore relatively price-elastic.

3 **PES = 1; Unit elastic supply** A one per cent price increase will induce a one per cent rise in quantity supplied. Unit elasticity is again simple to show graphically by drawing any straight line passing through the origin. Note again that the *absolute* slope of the line is irrelevant and that it is not necessary to draw it at 45 degrees—both S and S_1 in Figure 3.5 have unit elasticity. The *relative* changes in price and quantity are equal along any straight line passing through the origin. The student can confirm this, as well as the similar points just made about inelastic and elastic supply curves, by drawing straight-line curves on a graph and calculating the elasticities along them.

The PES measures the ease with which an industry responds to a change in price as a result usually of a shift in the demand curve. Firms in all industries will require time to adapt their output to price changes and it is common as a result to distinguish between short run and long run supply curves. Suppose there is an increase in demand for fish as shown in Figure 3.6 by the rightward shift in the demand curve. In the short run we might expect the supply of fish to be relatively inelastic like the curve S_s. This is because at any one time the industry will have a limited productive capacity, in this case, determined by the number of fishing boats in commission. Up to a point, these can be used more intensively so that supply is not perfectly inelastic. Nevertheless, there will be a constraint on expansion of output to meet the increase in demand. As a result, there is a steep short run increase in price from P_1 to P_2.

FIGURE 3.6 **Short-run and long-run effects of an increase in demand**

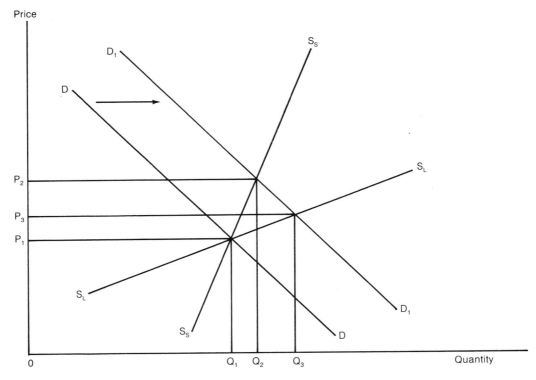

However, the short run rise in price will increase the profits of the fishing firms and will induce them to increase their capacity by bringing old boats back into commission and having new ones built. The high price might also attract new firms to enter the industry. In the long run therefore, supply becomes elastic as shown by the curve S_L. The price then recedes to a new long run equilibrium level of P_3 with an expansion of output to Q_3. (The distinction between the short run and the long run is explained in Chapter 5.)

3.5 PRICE INSTABILITY

Inelastic short run supply is an important explanation of the observed wide fluctuations in prices of many goods. We find that price instability is particularly pronounced in the markets for many primary commodities—agricultural and mineral products such as tea, coffee, potatoes, copper, tin and sulphur. With agricultural products farmers clearly cannot respond to a rise in price without a time lag determined by the 'gestation period' of the product. If demand for potatoes increases farmers may increase their plantings to produce more next year but, in the meantime, supply is highly inelastic and the price may soar. The same goes for mineral products. A boom in the industrial countries may boost demand for raw materials but producers will require time to expand capacity with exploration for and development of new sources of supply. Until then prices may increase sharply. The reverse is true when there is a slump in demand.

If fluctuations in demand combined with inelastic short run supply can lead to price volatility so too can shifts in the supply curve interacting with inelastic demand. Supply of agricultural products can be particularly vulnerable to changing weather conditions, pests and crop diseases. A fall in supply with a shift to the left of the supply curve will bring a disproportionate price rise if demand is inelastic. Favourable growing conditions may bring an unplanned increase in supply. If demand is inelastic the fall in price will outweigh the extra quantity sold, leading to the paradox that a good harvest will reduce farmers' incomes. Supply of other products can similarly be unstable. World oil production, for instance, was severely disrupted by the Iran-Iraq conflict in the early 1980s leading to a sharp rise in prices.

Inelasticity of demand and supply can sometimes explain wide price fluctuations but note that other factors will frequently be more important. Changes in expectations are especially significant, for example, in markets for financial assets such as foreign exchange, shares and bonds. The slump in equity prices in the world's stock markets in October 1987 can only be explained by a sudden downward revision of investors' expectations of future returns on equities relative to other assets such as bonds. Also, price instability is largely confined to competitive markets where individual producers have no control over prices. The relative price stability of prices of manufactured goods is only partly explained by more elastic supply in the short run (manufacturing firms can more rapidly adjust output to demand). The major factor is that manufacturing industries are typically less competitive than primary producing industries. Individual firms in manufacturing therefore have much greater control over their prices.

SUMMARY

Elasticity is a general measure of the response of one variable to changes in another. The price elasticity of demand (PED) shows the sensitivity of quantity demanded to a change in price. The value of PED for a good will be influenced by the availability of substitutes, by the proportion of income spent on the good and by the time needed for consumers to adjust to a price change. The PED is useful to firms in predicting the effects of price changes on their revenue. The income elasticity and the cross elasticity of demand measure the sensitivity of demand to changes in income and in the prices of other goods. Price elasticity of supply (PES) indicates the ease with which industries can respond to price changes. Supply is likely to be less elastic in the short run than in the long run. Inelastic supply and demand may be important explanations of large fluctuations in many prices, particularly in the prices of primary commodities.

SELF-TEST QUESTIONS

1 Which one of the following statements is wrong?

(a) Restriction of output by a cartel when demand is price elastic will increase its revenue.

(b) Elasticity measures the sensitivity of a dependent variable to changes in an independent variable.

(c) If quantity demanded rises by 20 per cent after a 15 per cent fall in price demand is relatively elastic.

(d) When demand is relatively price inelastic consumers' expenditure will increase when price goes up.

(e) Along a unit elastic demand curve, expenditure is the same at all prices.

2 Draw a supply/demand diagram for fish assuming a relatively elastic demand curve. Which one of the following best describes the effects of a fall in supply?

(a) Price rises and fish suppliers obtain more revenue.

(b) Price stays the same and consumers spend less on fish.

(c) Price falls so that producers obtain less revenue.

(d) Price falls but elastic demand means consumers spend more on fish.

(e) Price rises but suppliers' revenue falls.

3 Which one of the following statements is wrong?

(a) Goods with no close substitutes are more likely to have a low PED.

(b) A strong income effect from a price change will tend to increase the PED of inferior goods.

(c) Other things equal, the government will raise more revenue from taxes on goods with inelastic demand than on goods with elastic demand.

(d) Giffen goods must have a negative income elasticity of demand.

(e) The less price elastic is demand the bigger the burden of an indirect tax on consumers.

4 Draw a supply/demand diagram for tin on the assumption that supply is inelastic in the short run and elastic in the long run. Which of the following best describes the effects of a fall in demand?

(a) In the short run price drops steeply but producers' revenue goes up.

(b) Price falls more in the long run than in the short run so that there is a bigger fall in the long-run output.

(c) In the long run, elastic supply means that producers get more revenue despite the fall in price.

(d) Price falls steeply in the short run but moves back towards its original level as producers reduce their productive capacity in the long run.

(e) Production of tin will be cut sharply in the short run but by only small amounts in the long run.

5   Which one of the following statements is correct?

(a) Gin and tonic are likely to have a high positive cross elasticity of demand.

(b) Spending on luxury goods will tend to take an increasing share of incomes when consumers' incomes fall.

(c) When demand for coffee is price-inelastic producers will achieve higher incomes from higher production.

(d) Fluctuations in demand for primary products will cause unstable prices when supply is inelastic.

(e) A high degree of competition in manufacturing industries compared with primary producing industries is an important cause of relatively stable prices for manufactured goods.

EXERCISE

Why are the prices of many primary commodities unstable relative to the prices of manufactured goods? Examine the role of elasticities of demand and supply in price instability.

Answers on page 241.

Consumer Behaviour

This chapter deals with the way in which consumers allocate their incomes between purchases of different goods and services. In order to maximise satisfaction, consumers must have the same 'marginal utility' of expenditure on all goods. If this principle is combined with diminishing marginal utility we have an explanation of negatively sloped demand curves. The concept of consumer surplus and its practical use in measuring changes in consumers' welfare are explained.

4.1   INTRODUCTION

In the supply-and-demand analysis of the previous two chapters we have so far assumed that demand curves are negatively sloped; *ceteris paribus*, when the price of a good rises the quantity demanded of it falls. In this chapter we shall examine that proposition more closely. Since the market demand curve for a good is found by adding up the quantities demanded at different prices by all the separate buyers, we focus on the behaviour of individual households or consumers and how they allocate their income between spending on different goods and services. To help us in this, we make a simplifying assumption that **rational** consumers will want to achieve the greatest possible satisfaction from their spending.

Economists are often criticised for this assumption of rational behaviour. People, it is said, frequently behave irrationally so that any theory based on rationality will inevitably yield poor predictions. The criticism, though, is misplaced for at least two reasons. First, the term 'rational' is used in a narrow sense to mean that consumers behave consistently, **as if** they are attempting to maximise satisfaction from spending. We assume that consumers themselves are the best judge of what is in their own interests. The fact that they may behave in a way that seems irrational to other people is irrelevant. Thus, a person who smokes despite the medical evidence of serious health risks or who behaves altruistically in giving large sums to what others think is a worthless charity is in neither case 'irrational' in our use of the word. The consumer is assumed to have weighed up the potential costs against the satisfaction derived from smoking while donation of money to a cats' home is presumed to give the animal-lover satisfaction, irrespective of the actual good it may do.

Secondly, the aim of consumer theory is not to explain the behaviour of particular individuals—we leave that to psychologists. Rather, our interest is in questions about aggregate behaviour—if the price of a good falls will there be an increase or a reduction in the amount purchased by consumers as a group? The test of our theory is not whether some people behave inconsistently but whether it yields good predictions about real-world behaviour.

4.2   UTILITY THEORY

A number of theories have been put forward by economists to explain the spending behaviour of consumers. However, we shall concentrate on one known as the **marginal utility** theory which originated in the late nineteenth century. The term 'utility' is particularly associated with the English philosopher, Jeremy Bentham (1748–1832), who developed Utilitarianism, a theory of the means of ensuring 'the greatest happiness of the greatest number'. In economics, utility has come to mean the capacity of a good or service to satisfy consumers' wants. Any good has utility so long as consumption of it satisfies people's needs or wants: the word has no moral significance in this context. Cigarettes have utility in satisfying the wants of some consumers and so do the services of doctors in curing the ailments which result from smoking! Similarly, economists make no moral judgments about the way people satisfy their wants—they can read romantic novels or economics textbooks, or listen to rock music or Beethoven. Utility therefore is subjective—it exists in the mind of the consumer and cannot be objectively measured.

DIMINISHING MARGINAL UTILITY

The central hypothesis of utility theory is that of **diminishing marginal utility**. This says that, as consumption of a good is increased, we normally expect the individual's satisfaction or utility also to increase but that it will do so at a diminishing rate. Particular wants are **satiable** so that consumption of goods which satisfy those wants must logically reach some point at which further consumption will yield no further utility and might even give negative utility or **disutility**. We should first see what is meant by marginal utility. It can be defined as the change in the total utility of a good which results from a change of one unit in its consumption. It can formally be written as:

$$MUx = \frac{\Delta TUx}{\Delta Qx}$$

where MU and TU stand for marginal and total utility and Qx is the quantity consumed of good x. For example, suppose we can measure utility in some units, say 'utils'. If a coffee drinker consumes two more cups of coffee a day and calculates that his or her total utility has increased as a result by 10 utils, then the marginal utility of coffee is 5 utils, the rate of increase in total utility for each extra cup.

To understand the relation between TU and MU more clearly let us extend this example. Imagine on a particular morning we measure a consumer's total utility from drinking coffee with breakfast in a café. The first cup might yield a high utility, say, 20 utils. The second cup also gives satisfaction but not as much as the first—TU, suppose, goes up to 35 units so that the second cup has a marginal utility of 15 utils. Each additional cup yields less and less extra utility—there is diminishing marginal utility, MU, in fact, may shrink to zero by, say, the fifth cup and conceivably may then become negative. The sixth cup might make the consumer ill and he or she would be prepared to pay not to have to drink it. The relationship between TU and MU is shown in Figure 4.1.

FIGURE 4.1   **Total utility and marginal utility**

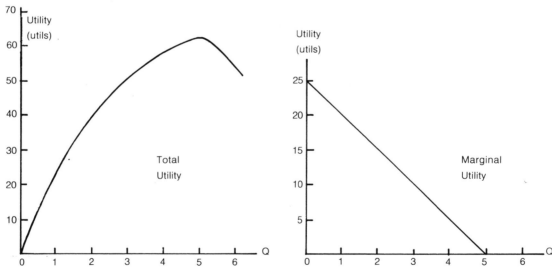

In the left-hand diagram we can see that total utility increases but at a diminishing rate—the slope of the TU curve gets flatter and flatter. That is also shown in the right-hand graph where we plot marginal utility (but on a bigger vertical scale). MU (the rate of change of TU) diminishes; once it reaches zero at 5 cups the consumer is satiated—TU ceases to increase and the TU curve becomes horizontal. If MU becomes negative the TU curve dips downwards—its slope, measured by MU, becomes negative. Note that, since total utility for any quantity can be found by adding up the marginal utility for all the preceding units consumed, total utility can be measured by the area beneath the marginal utility curve up to that quantity.

We should stress that this principle of diminishing marginal utility follows from our assumption that human wants of a particular kind are ultimately satiable. That may seem to be plain commonsense, but it is not a proposition that can be proved by logical deduction. It is an empirical proposition that can only be tested against our real-world experience. Because we never find a consumer want which is not ultimately satiable the proposition is often given the status of a 'law'—the law of diminishing marginal utility.

WILLINGNESS TO PAY

We have already noted that utility is not objectively measurable. However, we have an indirect way of calculating the utility of a good to an individual consumer with the concept of willingness to pay. Thus, imagine we asked our coffee-drinker how much he or she would be willing to pay for the first cup. Since it gives a high utility, the consumer, irrespective of the actual cost per cup, would be willing to pay quite a high price to obtain it—at, say 80p. The second cup has a lower utility so that the consumer is willing to pay, say, only 60p. As marginal utility decreases so we have a corresponding diminishing **marginal** willingness to pay—the maximum amount the consumer is prepared to pay for one more unit of the good. Once the MU of coffee is zero at five cups the marginal willingness to pay becomes zero as well. If MU is negative you would have to pay the consumer to drink more coffee. We can easily translate the MU curve therefore into a curve of the consumer's marginal willingness to pay (MWP). This is shown in Figure 4.2.

FIGURE 4.2   **the Marginal willingness to pay**

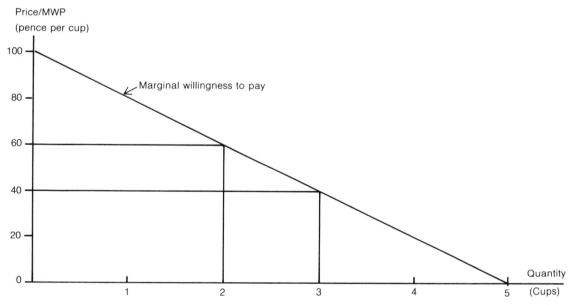

The MWP curve can also be interpreted as the consumer's demand curve for coffee. Goods normally are sold by suppliers at a uniform price. Thus, suppose the café owner charges 40p a cup. We know that the consumer, perhaps an accountant on the way to see a client, is willing to pay up to 80p for the first cup and up to 60p for the second, so he will definitely drink at least two cups of coffee. However, the accountant's willingness to pay for the third cup is 40p, the same as the price being charged. He or she will therefore buy up to three cups. Certainly, the customer will not buy a fourth cup since the MWP or valuation of it is only 20p, less than the cost. The same goes for the fifth and all subsequent cups.

We argue then that the consumer goes on buying extra cups of coffee so long as the MWP exceeds the price which measures the **marginal** cost or the cost of acquiring one more cup. The ambiguity about the third cup can be removed by assuming that the consumer can buy coffee in small fractions of a cup rather than one cup at a time. This allows us to draw a smooth MWP curve as in the diagram and it can then be seen that the consumer's MWP exceeds the price for quantities up to three cups. Consumption is therefore increased up to that level but not beyond. If the price falls to 20p consumption increases up to four cups. At 60p it drops to two cups. The MWP curve is equivalent to the consumer's demand curve for coffee since it describes the relationship between quantity demanded and price. Diminishing marginal utility thus gives us an explanation of downward-sloping demand curves—as the price falls quantity demanded increases.

This example also illustrates an important principle of decision-making. In order to maximise total utility it is necessary to take decisions at the margin—the consumer should go on buying coffee or any other good until the value of the marginal utility (revealed by marginal willingness to pay) equals the marginal cost of the good which is usually (but not always) the same as the price. A price of 40p measures the sacrifice that has to be made of other goods and services if the consumer buys one more cup—it is the marginal opportunity cost of coffee. By buying coffee and other goods up to the point where the marginal utility of each equals its marginal cost, the consumer will maximise total utility from his or her income. This principle of equating marginal benefit with marginal cost in order to maximise net benefits is of general application. In the next chapter, for example, we shall see that it applies just the same to a firm which wishes to maximise profits from its production.

THE PARADOX OF VALUE

The concept of marginal utility helps to resolve the famous 'paradox of value' which vexed, amongst others, Adam Smith. Smith pointed out that a commodity like water has an extremely high total utility but is usually provided at a very low price. Diamonds on the other hand have little total utility but are very expensive. Smith's answer to the diamond-water paradox was unsatisfactory—he had to content himself with the observation that goods have a 'value in use' which may differ from their 'value in exchange'. Marginal utility theory provides a much better solution. If the curve in Figure 4.2 represents the demand curve for coffee then, in a competitive market, the price of coffee will be determined by both demand and supply. If we draw in a supply curve to cut the demand curve at 40p, that will be the equilibrium price. Consumers' total utility (Smith's 'value in use') is measured by the area beneath the demand curve; the price or 'value in exchange' is determined by marginal utility at the equilibrium point—by what consumers are prepared to pay for the last unit. Thus, water is normally in relatively abundant supply and has a low marginal utility even though the total utility is very large. Diamonds are scarce and command a high price—marginal utility is large but total utility may be small.

4.3 CONSUMER EQUILIBRIUM

We have focused so far on how a consumer decides how much to buy of a particular commodity on the implicit assumption that spending on that commodity takes up only a small part of the individual's total income. Buying another cup of coffee had a negligible effect on the consumer's real income or capacity to buy other goods and services. In other words, we ignored the income effect (introduced in the last chapter) of changes in the price of coffee. In reality, we often need to take the income effect into account—buying one more cup on one day may have an insignificant effect on income, but drinking one more every day will not. In a more general theory of consumer behaviour we need to examine how the consumer allocates income between all the available goods and services with a given set of prices. If one price changes we can then see how the consumer will reallocate spending between all goods, not just the one whose price has changed. In doing so, we should consider both the income and the substitution effects of the price change.

To simplify, suppose the consumer has to allocate income between just two goods which we label 'bread' (b) and 'wine' (w). Assume that all income is spent and that the consumer wants to maximise utility from total spending. When that is achieved the consumer is in equilibrium. Given diminishing marginal utility for both goods the condition for **consumer equilibrium** is that income should be allocated in such a way that the marginal utility of expenditure on each good is the same. The marginal utility of expenditure on a good is the extra utility derived from one more unit of spending (a penny or a pound). Thus, the marginal utility of a pound spent on bread is MUb/Pb, where MUb is the marginal utility of bread and Pb is the price in pounds. If MUb is 4 utils and Pb is £2 then the MU of another pound spent on bread is 2 utils. The condition for consumer equilibrium can therefore be written as:

$$\frac{MUb}{Pb} = \frac{MUw}{Pw}$$

Spending should be distributed in such a way as to equate the MU of expenditure on each good. If the two are unequal, say $MUb/Pb > MUw/Pw$, then utility can be increased by reallocating income away from wine on to bread. Thus, assume the consumer is initially in equilibrium and there is then a fall in the price of wine. The MU of spending on wine is increased and we have:

$$\frac{MUb}{Pb} < \frac{MUw}{Pw}$$

The consumer can now gain by spending a pound less on bread and spending it instead on wine since the reduction in utility from consuming less bread is outweighed by the increase in utility from another pound's worth of wine. But, because of diminishing marginal utility, as each pound is redistributed in this way the lower consumption of bread results in a higher MUb and the increased wine consumed leads to a fall in MUw. Eventually, the equality between the two ratios is restored and the consumer is again in equilibrium buying less bread and more wine than before.

We once more have an explanation of downward-sloping demand curves. The fall in the price of a good leads to a switching of spending from other goods and to an increase in the quantity demanded of it. However, this is strictly just the substitution effect of the price change. On its own, the substitution effect invariably leads to a rise in quantity demanded after a fall in price. But, when the price of wine falls, there is an increase in the consumer's real income since he or she can now buy the same amount of wine as before and have more left over for bread. The change in real income may itself alter the relative marginal utilities of the two goods. If wine is a normal good the rise in income leads to an increase in consumption and the income effect reinforces the substitution effect—the demand curve for wine will definitely be negatively sloped. But if wine is an inferior good it is conceivable that the negative income effect outweighs the positive substitution effect to produce a **fall** in consumption after the fall in price—the consumer's demand curve would have a positive slope. However, as we pointed out in Chapter 3, instances of Giffen goods with positively sloped market demand curves are thought to be rare.

Our conclusion then is that the demand curves for nearly all, if not all, goods and services can be presumed to be downward-sloping. This often seems to fly in the face of experience. For example, when the prices of shares rise on the Stock Exchange it will sometimes be followed by an increase in trading volume, suggesting that investors are buying more shares after a rise in price. However, this does not mean the demand curve for shares is positively sloped. Remember that any demand curve is drawn under the *ceteris paribus* assumption—it shows the relation between price and quantity demanded on the assumption that all other variables in the demand function are constant. When share prices rise, investors' expectations of future prices may be revised upwards, shifting the demand curve to the right and leading to increased purchases of shares. With *constant* expectations the demand curve is negatively sloped.

There are other instances of price increases apparently leading to a greater quantity demanded. When people buy goods like carpets, they will often tend, other things being equal, to go for the more expensive one. But this again does not mean the demand curve for carpets is positively sloped. Consumers don't have the technical knowledge to compare the quality of different carpets and tend therefore to use price as a guide to quality. The demand curve for carpets generally is almost certainly downward-sloping. Again, a washing powder producer may market two physically identical brands at different prices and support sales of the higher priced one with an advertising campaign. The consumer who buys the more expensive powder has been convinced by the advertising that it is superior to the cheaper one and is worth paying a higher price. He or she will still have a downward-sloping demand curve for washing powder.

4.4 CONSUMER SURPLUS

We've seen that the price of a good reflects not its total utility to consumers but its marginal utility. Since consumers are normally charged a uniform price for goods and services, however much they buy, the total utility derived from buying a given quantity is usually in excess of the loss of utility measured by the amount spent. This can be seen in Figure 4.3, which repeats our illustration of marginal willingness to pay. At a price of £0.40 the coffee drinker buys three cups at a total cost of £1.20, measured by the rectangle OABC. Yet we know the consumer would have been willing to pay £0.80 for the first cup, £0.60 for the second and then £0.40 for the third. That adds up to a total willingness to pay of £1.80. In fact, with our assumption that the consumer can vary the quantity bought by small fractions of a cup we constructed a continuous MWP or demand curve. As we move down the MWP curve from point E we can add up the consumer's extra willingness to pay for increasing amounts of coffee; we can thus measure the total willingness to pay (TWP) for a given quantity as the area beneath the MWP curve. In the diagram the TWP for three cups is the area

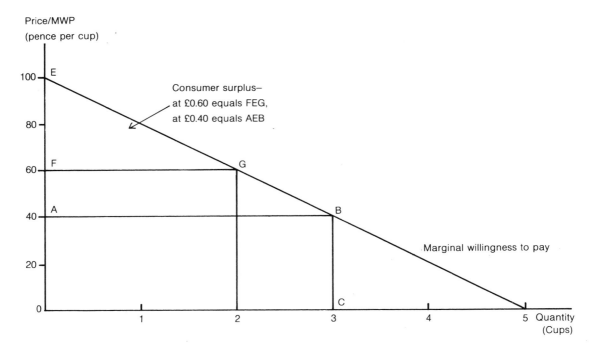

FIGURE 4.3 **Consumer surplus**

OEBC; since we have a straight-line MWP curve this is easily calculated as £2.10. In other words, the consumer is able to buy three cups of coffee, which he or she values at £2.10, for only £1.20. There is therefore what we call a **consumer surplus** of 90p measured by the triangle AEB. It can be seen that if the price goes up to 60p, consumption drops to two cups and consumer surplus contracts to FEG or 40p, a loss of AFGB or 50p. There are some conceptual problems with consumer surplus, but despite these, the notion of consumer surplus is often very useful. Why?

Firstly, changes in the surplus can be used to estimate the effect of price charges on consumers' utility or **welfare**. The reduction of 50p in the surplus measures the loss of welfare to the coffee drinker when the price goes up from 40p to 60p. Similarly, if the government imposes a tax on a good, the burden on consumers is calculated as the loss of surplus from the rise in market price. The European Common Agricultural Policy (CAP) which we looked at in Chapter 2 raises food prices sharply; estimates of the loss of consumer surplus which results indicate that this is a major cost of the CAP, greater even than the direct cost to taxpayers from having to finance the buying-up of surplus output.

Secondly, suppliers of goods and services who are able to control their prices can in principle extract all or part of the consumer surplus by practising **price discrimination**. This means varying the price to different consumers or according to the amounts purchased. For instance, if the café owner in our example were able to estimate our consumer's MWP curve, he or she could increase revenue by charging, instead of a uniform 40p a cup, 80p for the first one, 60p for the second and 40p for the third. Since the consumer takes decisions at the margin he or she would still be willing to buy three cups. But now the café owner takes £1.80 in revenue instead of £1.20 by exploiting the consumer's willingness to pay more for the first and second cups. (Note here that we have ignored any income effect from the consumer paying 60p more for three cups). Similarly, if the proprietor could charge different prices to different customers, he or she could benefit by asking more from those with a higher willingness to pay (say, business executives with expense accounts) and less from poorer customers.

Extraction of consumer surplus by price discrimination is quite a common practice. Gas and electricity companies, for instance, typically have a fixed or standing charge irrespective of the amount consumed and then a tariff of so much per unit. The fixed charge can be viewed as the price of the first unit and takes advantage of the consumer's high marginal valuation of the initial quantities consumed. The actual level of consumption depends principally on the variable tariff per unit—consumers will increase their consumption to the point where the marginal value to them of the last unit used equals the tariff. Similarly, suppliers of goods will often offer quantity discounts—a record shop, for example, might sell one compact disc for £10, two for £18 or £9 each, and three for £24 or £8 each. In this case, note that the consumer will decide how many discs to buy not by the average price but by the marginal cost for an extra disc. The marginal cost of the second is £8 and of the third £6. The consumer will buy three therefore so long as his or her marginal valuation of the third disc exceeds £6, not £8. If so, the shop takes £24. But if it had charged a uniform price of £8 a disc it would have sold fewer and made less money.

SUMMARY

The marginal utility theory of consumer behaviour postulates that people's wants are satiable and that this leads to diminishing marginal utility as consumption of a good is increased. On the assumption that a consumer wishes to maximise utility from income spent, he or she will achieve equilibrium by distributing spending between goods so that the marginal utility of expenditure on each of them is the same. This principle allows us to predict negatively sloped demand curves for all normal goods though, when both income and substitution effects of price changes are taken into account, it is theoretically possible to have positively sloped demand curves for some types of inferior goods. Consumers will usually derive satisfaction from consumption in excess of a good's cost—the excess is known as consumer surplus. The concept of consumer surplus can be used to measure changes in welfare resulting from price changes while suppliers of goods and services can extract consumer surplus by price discrimination.

SELF-TEST QUESTIONS

1   Which one of the following best describes diminishing marginal utility?

(a)   People have a smaller range of wants to satisfy as their incomes increase.

(b)   As consumption of a good is increased the total satisfaction derived from it usually increases but at a diminishing rate.

(c)   A consumer will always expand consumption of a good to the point where the extra utility from one more unit is zero.

(d)   For any good X, $\Delta Qx/\Delta TUx$ declines as consumption of X rises.

(e)   Consumers get diminishing total satisfaction from increasing their consumption of most goods.

2   Which one of the following statements is wrong?

(a)   In economics, a 'rational' consumer attempts to maximise his or her utility from spending income on different goods and services.

(b)   A consumer's total willingness to pay for a given quantity of a good can be calculated by the area beneath the marginal willingness to pay curve up to that quantity.

(c)   If the price of baked beans is 30p a tin the consumer can maximise satisfaction

by buying them up to the point where his or her total willingness to pay is just equal to 30p.

(d)   A consumer's MWP curve for a good can validly be interpreted as his or her demand curve for it only if expenditure on the good is an insignificant proportion of the consumer's income.

(e)   Goods which have a very high total utility do not necessarily have a high exchange value when prices are determined by supply and demand.

3   There are two goods, a and b; Pa = £8 and Pb = £4. A consumer will achieve equilibrium when:

(a)   He or she spends twice as much on a as on b.

(b)   Total utility from a is twice as great as that from b.

(c)   The marginal utility of expenditure on a is twice as great as that for b.

(d)   MUa/Pa is double MUb/Pb.

(e)   The marginal utility from another pound spent on a equals the marginal utility of a pound spent on b.

4   If there are the same two goods as in 3 and the price of b rises to £8, which of the following best describes how the consumer restores equilibrium?

(a)   He   or   she   redistributes   spending

between the two goods until the ratio of the marginal utilities of the two goods equals one.

(b)   The consumer switches spending away from a on to b until $MUa/Pa = MUb/Pb$.

(c)   So long as b is a normal good the consumer responds to the rise in its price by reducing quantity demanded of it until total utility is the same as that from a.

(d)   If b is an inferior good the negative income effect will always change MUa and MUb in such a way that the consumer ends up buying more of b in the new equilibrium.

(e)   If b is a normal good the consumer switches spending from b to a, raising MUa and reducing MUb until $MUa/Pa = MUb/Pb$.

5   Which one of the following statements is correct?

(a)   Consumer surplus is an alternative way of measuring a consumer's total utility from a given level of consumption of a good.

(b)   Consumer surplus is measured by the difference between total willingness to pay and marginal willingness to pay for a given quantity of a good.

(c)   When the price of gas is £0.10 a unit, a consumer is in equilibrium when using 10 units a day. She would have been willing to pay a total of £3 for 10 units so her consumer surplus is £2.

(d)   The increase in consumer surplus when the price of a good rises is a good way of measuring the loss of consumers' welfare.

(e)   Suppliers who offer quantity discounts are taking advantage of consumers' increased marginal willingness to pay for greater quantities.

EXERCISE

What do you understand by 'consumer surplus'? How can producers use price discrimination to take advantage of consumer surplus?

Answers on page 243.

Production and Costs

This chapter develops the study of supply with a general analysis of how a profit-maximising firm determines its optimum level of output. We make a simplifying assumption about the firm's revenue and concentrate on the behaviour of the firm's costs. In the short run the firm operates under an output constraint which results in diminishing returns and increasing marginal costs. In the long run the constraint is removed; the firm is free to increase the scale of its output and to take advantage of economies of scale which lower its unit costs.

5.1   INTRODUCTION

Our study of consumer behaviour in the last chapter gave substantial theoretical backing to the economist's usual assumption that demand curves slope downwards—as price rises quantity demanded falls. We now turn to supply. So far, we have made what looks to be the intuitively reasonable assumption that supply curves have positive slopes, that suppliers are willing to offer greater quantities of goods and services as their prices rise. Since, in a competitive industry, the total amount supplied is found by adding up the output of all the firms in the industry, our central focus in the theory of supply is on the individual firm and how its output responds to changes in price.

To simplify our initial analysis we shall make two general assumptions about the firm. The first is that the firm produces just a single product and is operating in a **perfectly competitive** industry. We shall look more closely at perfect competition in Chapter 6. For the present, it is enough to note that in such an industry the individual firm is just one of a large number of firms producing an identical or **homogeneous** product. As a result, the firm has no control over the price at which it sells its product—it has to accept the prevailing market price and is what we call a **price taker**.

The second assumption is that the firm, in common with others in the industry, aims to **maximise its profits**. This, of course, is analogous to our assumption that consumers attempt to maximise utility and it is subject to the same kind of criticisms. We know, for example, that firms in the real world often have goals other than profit maximisation. But in economic analysis we argue that making profits is the most pervasive goal among firms, certainly in the private sector of the economy. Theories based on the assumption that firms behave **as if** they were maximising profits yield more powerful predictions than those making more complex assumptions about firms' goals. The 'realism' of the assumptions we make is subsidiary to how well the theory predicts the behaviour of firms in the real world.

Our central aim in this chapter is to show how a firm determines its output in order to maximise profits. The concept of profits is itself not straightforward and we shall have to look at it in more detail later on. But let's provisionally define a firm's profits (Π) simply as the difference between its total revenue (TR) from sales and its total costs (TC):

$$\Pi = TR - TC$$

It should be stressed that the firm is aiming neither at maximising revenue nor at minimising its costs; its aim is to maximise the difference between revenue and costs. To find the firm's optimum level of production, therefore, we need to study the behaviour of both revenue and costs as the firm varies its output.

5.2   THE REVENUE FUNCTION

Given our assumption that the firm is a price taker in a competitive industry the **revenue function**, the relationship between revenue and output, is a very simple one:

$$TR = P.Q$$

where P is the price per unit and Q is the firm's output (assumed to be equal to sales). P is the firm's revenue per unit of output or its **average revenue** (AR = TR/Q). More important, because the firm is only one of many firms selling the same product, it can effectively produce and sell as much as it likes without having any significant effect on the market price. Taking the prevailing market price as given, revenue varies directly with output. If we define **marginal revenue** (MR) as the increase in revenue from selling one more unit of output, then MR must also be equal to price. Marginal revenue can formally be defined as:

$$MR = \frac{\Delta TR}{\Delta Q}$$

It is therefore the rate of change in total revenue from increases in output. Under perfect competition:

$$P = AR = MR$$

Another way of putting this is to say that the individual firm faces a perfectly elastic demand curve for its output at the prevailing market price. This is shown in Figure 5.1.

FIGURE 5.1   **The firm's marginal and average revenue curves under perfect competition**

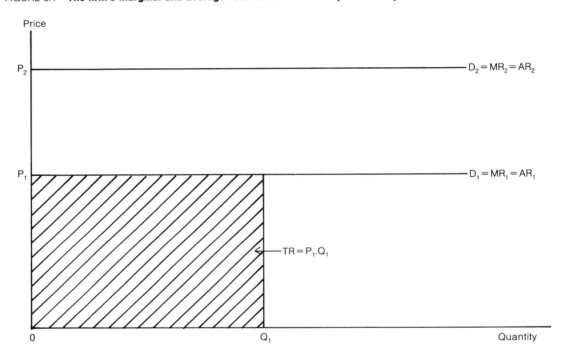

At the price of P_1 the *firm's* demand curve is D_1 and its average revenue and marginal revenue are both equal to P_1. If the price rises to P_2, say, because of an increase in *market* demand, the firm's demand curve shifts upwards to D_2 and both AR and MR rise to the same level. In both cases we measure total revenue as price or average revenue multiplied by output. Since P stays constant along any demand curve, we can see again that TR increases directly with output. We have, therefore, a very simple revenue function. To find out what happens to profits as output changes we must next study the firm's **cost function**, the relationship between costs and output.

5.3   COSTS IN THE SHORT RUN

The firm's costs arise because it has to purchase **inputs** of productive resources—labour, land and capital—and to combine them to produce output. The cost of producing any output therefore is determined by the quantities and prices of the inputs used. To study the behaviour of costs we shall again make simplifying assumptions. First, we assume that all input prices—wages, rent, interest and materials prices—are determined in competitive markets. The firm therefore is a price taker for its inputs as well as its output. Given the prices the firm must pay, costs are determined purely by the quantities of inputs employed by the firm. Secondly, the firm is assumed always to use the most efficient productive techniques available and to combine inputs to produce any level of output at the lowest possible cost.

Students should note that in economics we are concerned with *opportunity costs*. When a firm buys inputs such as labour and materials in the open market the prices paid reflect their opportunity cost to the firm, that is, the alternatives foregone by using these inputs and not others. However, with factors *owned* by the firm, such as premises and machinery, the opportunity cost has to be *inputed*. For example, the opportunity cost of using an owned machine is what could have been earned by hiring it out to another firm.

5.3.1 The short run and the long run

Consider a firm which is already established in producing, say, table tennis bats. The firm, remember, is in competition with many other firms and we are assuming for simplicity that bats are homogeneous—all firms produce an identical product. At any one time, the owner of the firm has two types of decision to make about production—a short run and a long run decision. The **short run** is defined as a period of time in which the firm's productive capacity is constrained by the fixed supply of at least one factor of production. Most commonly, this will be the firm's fixed assets in the form of plant, machinery, premises and so on.

Our bat manufacturer has, let us suppose, a factory equipped with machines and other equipment. To make bats the firm has to buy in materials and employ labour to work the machines— labour and materials are the **variable factors** or **inputs**. The level of output per day can be altered but only within certain limits. At one extreme, of course, output is zero if no variable factors are employed and the fixed assets are left standing idle. But there is also an upper limit to output determined by the absolute capacity of the fixed assets. The firm can increase production by buying more materials, hiring more workers and using the fixed assets more intensively but it can logically do so only up to the maximum productive capacity of the machines. There must come a point when output can no longer be expanded.

In the short run the central decision to be made by the firm is what output to produce within the ceiling of its productive capacity. The situation is different in the **long run**. This is the period in which all factors of production, including the firm's physical capital, are variable. The firm can increase its productive capacity by investment. If our bat producer takes over another similar-sized factory and installs the same amount of machinery as in the existing one it will have doubled its capacity—we say it has doubled the **scale of production**. It then, of course, faces a new short run situation in which it has to choose some level of output within the higher capacity constraint. In the long run, then, the firm has to make investment decisions—whether to add to its stock of capital in order to expand its scale of production, or whether to maintain the existing scale with zero new investment, or to reduce scale by **disinvestment**. It might even decide to go out of the business of making bats altogether.

Note that we don't specify the length of the short run period. It will vary enormously from industry to industry and even from firm to firm. Expanding the scale of output might be achieved very quickly in industries where production is labour intensive and requires the application of only small amounts of capital. A window cleaner could double the scale of production by buying another ladder and a bucket and employing an assistant. At the other extreme, a significant increase in scale by an oil producer or a motor car manufacturer might take months or years. Similarly, in farming a time constraint is placed on increasing productive capacity by the 'gestation period' for crops and livestock. It takes many months for farmers to expand their scale of production for products like coffee and beef. However, the general point is that all firms face a constraint on their production decisions in the short run. Only the severity of that constraint will differ.

5.3.2 Fixed and variable costs

Take first the firm's production decision in the short run. Our table tennis bat producer makes bats by buying materials and employing capital and labour to **add value** to them. Let's focus on how the firm combines capital (K) and labour (L) to produce **value added** (a concept we will return to in Chapter 11). Capital consists of machines and premises and is the firm's fixed factor in the short run. In turn, the costs associated with capital, such as rent on premises and depreciation of machines, are assumed to be completely **fixed** costs in the short run. The firm has to meet these expenses irrespective of its level of output. Labour on the other hand is the **variable factor**. We assume the firm has complete freedom to employ any number of workers it likes. Labour costs or wages are therefore the firm's **variable** costs which will change with the level of employment and output.

We have assumed that the firm can hire as much labour as it wants at the going market wage, say, £20 a day. The variable cost per bat produced—the **average variable cost** (AVC)—is equal to the wage (W) divided by the output per worker each day. This last is called the **average physical product of labour** (APP_L), found simply by dividing the total output (Q) by the amount of labour employed (L) − $APP_L = Q/L$. We thus have:

$$AVC = \frac{W}{APP_L}$$

With a wage of £20 and APP_L of 10 bats a day, the AVC is £2 per bat. So long as the wage is given, AVC is determined purely by APP_L, the productivity of labour. The higher is APP_L, the lower is AVC and vice versa. To see what happens to variable costs as output is varied we need to examine the behaviour of labour productivity as more people are employed to work the fixed number of machines.

5.3.3 Diminishing returns

We argue that in the short run all firms, as they expand output by employing more variable inputs, will inevitably come up against the phenomenon of **diminishing returns**. The 'law' of diminishing returns states that as we increase the quantity employed of a variable factor in combination with a fixed factor, then eventually the marginal physical product of the variable factor will decline. To see what this means we can first define **marginal physical product** (MPP). The MPP of a factor is simply the increase in output from employing one more unit of it. In our example, the MPP of labour is the extra bats produced each day by taking on another worker:

$$MPP_L = \frac{\Delta Q}{\Delta L}$$

MPP_L thus expresses the rate of change of output as more labour is employed. With diminishing returns, increased employment may lead to increased output but at a declining rate. The existence of diminishing returns in production (like the analogous diminishing marginal utility in consumption) cannot be proved by logical deduction. However, as we have already seen, there must be an upper limit to output when a firm has factors in fixed supply. Once that limit is reached the marginal product of the variable factors must be zero—increased employment of them will add nothing to output. Also, the principle is a general one. A farmer, for example, who applies fertiliser to a piece of land to increase crop yields will find diminishing returns—the extra output from each additional unit of fertiliser will decrease. The marginal product of fertiliser may even become negative if too much of it poisons the crops!

TABLE 5.1 **Product schedules for table tennis bats**

	Output of bats per day		
No of Workers	Total Product (per worker) (Q)	Marginal Product (per worker) $MPP_L = \frac{\Delta Q}{\Delta L}$	Average Product (per worker) $APP_L = \frac{Q}{L}$
1	30	30	30
2	80	50	40
3	150	70	50
4	220	70	55
5	275	55	55
6	300	25	50
7	315	15	45
8	320	5	40
9	320	0	35.5

Diminishing returns may not set in the moment that employment of the variable factors is increased. The bat manufacturer, for instance, may find that employing just one worker in the factory is rather unproductive. He or she would have to carry out all the separate operations involved in making bats (shaping the blade, applying the handle, and so on). Two workers could more efficiently divide up the work between them and so again might three workers. Output may therefore rise initially at an increasing rate; the MPP_L may increase. But at some level of employment diminishing returns set in and the MPP_L declines. This is shown in Table 5.1 in which we draw up hypothetical **product schedules** for the firm. At each level of employment we show the total product (Q), the marginal product (MPP_L) and the average product (APP_L).

There are a number of points we can make about the schedules. First, the total product goes on rising until the ninth worker is employed. The marginal product of the ninth worker is therefore zero and the firm has reached the limit of its productive capacity. Secondly, the marginal product rises at first (as explained above) to reach a peak of 70 bats for the third and fourth workers. We can imagine that the maximum MPP_L is a little more than 70 bats and is reached for, say, 3.5 workers (which makes sense if the firm can employ workers part-time). After that point, diminishing returns set in and MPP_L falls away quickly.

AVERAGE AND MARGINAL PRODUCT

The third point concerns the average product or APP_L. This too rises initially but more slowly than MPP_L. Also, APP_L reaches its highest value of 55 bats for the fourth and fifth workers. Suppose the precise peak occurs with 4.5 workers. APP_L therefore reaches its maximum value at a higher employment level than MPP_L. From there, APP_L declines but at a slower rate than MPP_L. The relationship between the MPP_L and APP_L schedules can be understood more clearly if we show them as curves as in Figure 5.2. Note that we have drawn up smooth curves for MPP_L and APP_L and have therefore assumed that the firm can vary the employment of labour by fractional amounts rather than by one worker at a time as shown in the table.

FIGURE 5.2 **Marginal and average product of labour**

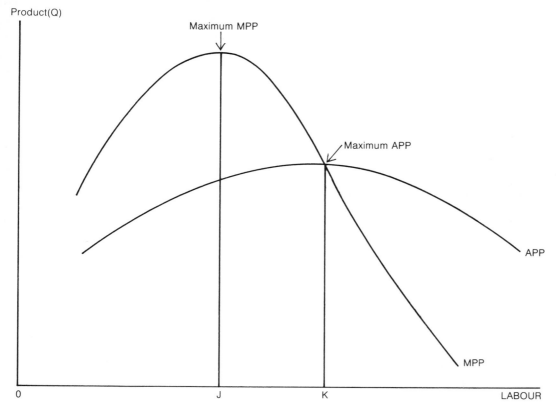

The behaviour of the MPP_L and APP_L curves can be explained by considering the general relationship between marginal and average values of any variable. Imagine a golfer, for instance, marking a card as he or she completes each hole. The score on the last hole completed is the marginal score which is added to the cumulative total. Suppose at the same time we work out the average score per hole, the total to that point divided by the holes completed. After four holes the total is 16 strokes and the average is four. If, on the fifth hole, he or she takes more than four strokes the average must clearly rise—if he or she lands in a bunker and ends up taking 9, the total goes up to 25 and the average to five. On the other hand, if less than four strokes are taken the average must fall—with a birdie two, the total for five holes is 18 and the average drops to 3.6. Then, if he or she takes four strokes at the fifth the average clearly stays the same at four.

To generalise, when the marginal value is greater than the average, the average must rise. When the marginal value is less than the average, the average must fall. When the two are equal the average stays constant. In the case of the product curves, MPP_L lies above APP_L initially so that the APP_L is pulled up. This is so even after MPP_L reaches its peak at the employment level OJ. Although MPP_L is itself falling it is still greater than APP_L so that APP_L continues to rise up to OK. From then on, MPP_L is less than APP_L causing APP_L to decline. APP_L is therefore at its maximum at employment of OK where the MPP_L curve cuts the APP_L curve. Here, MPP_L equals APP_L so that APP_L is momentarily constant at its turning point.

AVERAGE AND MARGINAL COSTS

Construction of the firm's short run cost curves is now relatively straightforward. Total costs for any output are of two kinds—fixed costs and variable costs. **Total fixed costs** (TFC) by definition remain constant at all levels of output. As output expands, fixed costs (roughly what accountants call 'overheads') are spread more and more thinly over a greater number of units of output. **Average fixed cost** (AFC), the fixed cost per unit, is defined as:

$$AFC = \frac{TFC}{Q}$$

AFC therefore gets smaller and smaller as output rises. This is shown in Figure 5.3. Note that TFC is equal to AFC times Q, the number of units of output. TFC is measured therefore by the area of the rectangle beneath any point on the AFC curve. Since TFC is constant we construct the AFC curve by drawing rectangles of equal area and joining up the corner points. The AFC curve is therefore a rectangular hyperbola like the unit elastic demand curve in Chapter 3.

FIGURE 5.3 **Average fixed costs**

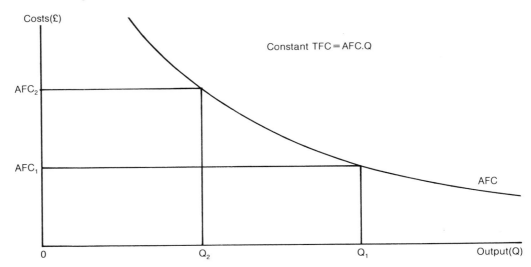

Let's now turn to variable costs. We have already noted that, when labour is the only variable input, the **average variable cost** (AVC), the variable cost per unit of output, can be found by dividing the wage by the average product of labour:

$$AVC = \frac{W}{APP_L}$$

Assume the wage is given at £20 a day. If we return to the product schedules in Table 5.1 we see that when two workers are employed their APP_L is 40 bats. The average variable cost for their total output of 80 bats is therefore £20/40 or 50p. We can similarly calculate the AVC for other output levels—for 150 bats AVC is £20/50 or 40p, and so on. We can thus easily draw up a curve for AVC plotted against output as in Figure 5.4. Notice that, since the wage is assumed to be given, AVC initially falls as APP rises. At the output B when APP_L reaches its peak the AVC is at its minimum. Further increases in output are associated with declining APP_L so that AVC rises. The AVC curve is therefore U-shaped, a crude mirror image of the inverted U-shape of the APP_L curve in Figure 5.2.

Marginal cost (MC) is the addition to total cost (TC) of producing one more unit of output:

$$MC = \frac{\Delta TC}{\Delta Q}$$

It expresses the rate of change of total cost as output rises. Since fixed cost remains constant when output goes up, the marginal cost must be the increase in variable cost for an extra unit of output. If we again look at the product schedules in Table 5.2 we see that increasing employment from three to four workers raises output by 70 bats, the MPP of labour. If wages are £20 a day, then the marginal cost per bat when output is increased from 150 to 220 is £20/70 or nearly £0.29. When employment is raised from five to six workers, output goes up by 25 bats to 300 and the marginal cost per bat is £20/25 or £0.80. In other words, we find the marginal cost by dividing the wage by the marginal product of labour:

$$MC = \frac{W}{MPP_L}$$

At any given wage therefore we can easily find the marginal cost of any output. Plotting the values on to a graph gives us a marginal cost curve like the one in Figure 5.4. The MC curve falls initially because the MPP_L rises. At the output where MPP_L is at its highest, MC is at its minimum. After that, diminishing returns set in; MPP_L falls and MC rises.

To find the **average total cost** (ATC) of any output we add together the AFC and AVC for that output. Graphically, we add the AFC (in Figure 5.3) vertically to AVC at each output to give

FIGURE 5.4 **The firm's average and marginal cost curves**

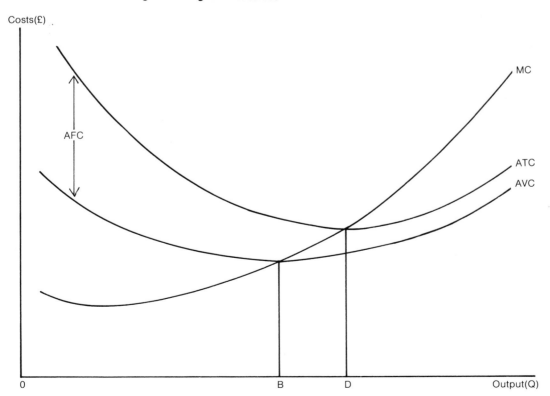

c

the ATC curve in Figure 5.4. Since the AFC is continuously falling the ATC and the AVC curves get closer and closer together as output increases. Note also that the general relationship between marginal and average values holds good for marginal cost and **both** the average cost curves. At first, MC is falling and is less than AVC and ATC so that both average values decline. MC then starts to rise but the average curves continue to fall so long as MC lies below them. At output OB, the MC curve cuts the AVC curve at the minimum point of AVC. From there, MC is greater than AVC, so AVC rises. Similarly, the MC curve eventually intersects the ATC curve at the lowest point of ATC at the output OD. ATC too rises after that. Minimum ATC therefore occurs at a higher output than minimum AVC. This is because falling AFC continues to pull down ATC for some further increases in output until rising AVC takes over.

5.3.4 Profit maximisation

We are now in a position to see how the firm determines its optimum or profit-maximising level of output in the short run. We have already concluded that a firm in perfect competition faces a perfectly elastic demand curve for its output at the prevailing market price which will also equal the firm's marginal and average revenue. In Figure 5.5 we show demand curves at the prices P_1 and P_2 and superimpose them on the firm's cost curves. Focus first on the firm's output decision when the price is P_1. There is a simple general rule for the maximisation of profits—this is that the firm should produce that output at which **marginal cost equals marginal revenue**:

$$MC = MR$$

FIGURE 5.5 **Determination of maximum profit output**

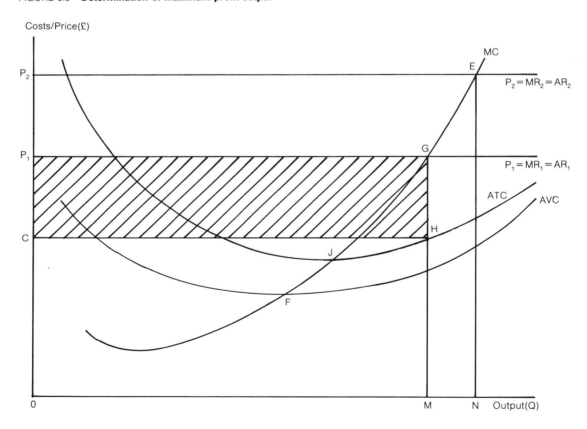

Remember that the price P_1 is the same as the firm's marginal revenue. We find that MC equals MR at the output OM—this is the firm's maximum profit output. Up to that output, MR is greater than MC so that each extra unit of output adds more to revenue than to costs and profits must increase. Beyond OM, on the other hand, MC rises above MR—expansion of output therefore adds more to costs than to revenue and profits necessarily fall. It follows that profits are maximised at output OM.

Profits can be measured by noting that P_1 is also the firm's average revenue. OC is the firm's average total cost of producing OM. If we subtract OC from OP_1, we have CP_1 which is the profit per unit of output. Multiply that by OM and total profits are measured by the shaded rectangle CP_1GH.

Consider what happens if the market price rises to P_2, perhaps because of an increase in market demand. The firm's marginal revenue also rises and maximum profits are achieved by equating the new MR with MC at the output ON. As the price changes therefore the firm responds by moving along the marginal cost curve to equate MC with MR. But since MR equals P for a firm in perfect competition **the MC curve is equivalent to its short run supply curve**. However, this only applies to the rising portion of the MC curve above F, the minimum point of AVC. If the price drops to F the best the firm can do is just to cover its variable costs and it will make losses equal to its fixed costs. If the price falls even further there is no output at which the firm can cover even its variable costs—the costs of labour and materials—and the firm might as well go out of business immediately to restrict its losses to the fixed costs which it cannot avoid in the short run. The firm's short run supply curve is thus the MC curve where it lies above the AVC curve.

CLOSE-DOWN DECISIONS

This implies that the firm will stay in business if the price is less than J, the minimum point on the ATC curve, but above F—that is, when it is able to cover its variable costs but not its total costs. Why should it continue producing when it is making overall losses? The answer is that it will only do so in the short run, the period in which it has to go on paying its fixed costs. Take a simple example to illustrate the point. Suppose an oil company has an oil well with variable costs of £10 a barrel. The fixed costs derive from the past investment in developing the well—exploration and drilling, installation of the rig, pumping equipment, pipework and so on. The company estimates these fixed costs—interest on loans to finance the investment and depreciation—at £5 a barrel. So long as the price of oil is above £15 a barrel the company is making overall profits. If the price slumps to, say £8, the company cannot cover the variable costs of £10 and it will close down the well. But if the price falls to, say, £12 it will keep the well going. It can meet the variable costs and have £2 left over to contribute towards the fixed costs which have to be met anyway.

The important principle here is that the fixed costs have no part to play in short run 'close-down' decisions and should be ignored. All that matters in the short run is whether the firm can cover its variable or operating costs. If it can do so but cannot cover total costs then it should continue in business in the short run—for the oil company that might mean until the well runs dry. For our table tennis bat producer the short run may be the period it takes to terminate rental agreements on premises and machinery or to sell any assets owned by the firm.

The principle that fixed or unavoidable costs are irrelevant in the short run can be applied to a wide range of situations. Firms facing what they believe to be a temporary fall in demand and prices for their products may decide to stay in production till demand recovers because they can still cover their variable costs. In a general economic recession we often find firms in capital-intensive industries such as steel and chemicals continuing to produce despite making heavy overall losses. For them, the major part of costs is fixed costs; variable costs are relatively small. Similarly, firms in industries with big seasonal fluctuations in demand—airlines, holiday hotels and restaurants, travel agents—must decide whether or not to close down in the off-season. In resorts on the Mediterranean, for example, some hotels stay open through the winter charging very low prices to people like pensioners. Although they are almost certainly making overall losses the hotels are more than meeting variable costs such as staff wages and heating and lighting which they could avoid by closing down.

5.4 COSTS IN THE LONG RUN

In the long run all inputs including capital become variable and the firm has to decide its scale of output. In principle, the nature of the firm's long run decision is the same as in the short run—it will want to choose that scale of output which will maximise its profits. If our firm producing bats is considering investing in an expansion of its capacity it will need to make forecasts, first, of its likely future revenue and, second, of the effect on its costs of the increased scale of production. Revenue will be dependent on the future price of bats. Obviously, in any industry there will be some degree of uncertainty about future prices and most firms will make revenue forecasts on different assumptions about price levels. However, suppose the bat producer bases its decision on a single expected price of, say, £1 a bat. It then needs to calculate its costs of operating on a bigger scale, say, at twice its existing capacity.

5.4.1 Economies of scale

Now, if a firm doubles its capacity by doubling the size of its premises, installing twice as much machinery and other equipment and using the same technology, we might expect its average or unit costs to be exactly the same so long as wages and other variable costs remain unchanged. However, we often find in practice that when firms expand their scale of production their unit costs change; most commonly, they decline as firms take advantage of **economies of scale**. Thus, as a firm grows in size it is often able to reorganise production and to introduce more efficient plant and machinery which would not have been fully employed at a lower scale. The result may be increased productivity of factors giving rise to **increasing returns to scale** and falling long run average costs.

There are various potential sources of economies of scale. One of the more important ones was identified by Adam Smith in his revolutionary work *The Wealth Of Nations* (1776). This is the principle of the **division of labour** which we referred to in Chapter 1. Production of all goods and services can be broken down between different stages and operations. We have already pointed out that there will be numerous operations involved in making even relatively simple products like table tennis bats. For complex goods like motor cars, dishwashers and computers the number of separate operations will run into hundreds. Smith noted that at a low scale of output the productivity of labour is constrained by the need for individual workers to carry out a number of tasks. At a bigger scale, workers can become more specialised in particular operations. Their productivity increases as they acquire specific skills and are able to concentrate on what they do best. Production meanwhile can be organised more efficiently in the **flow or assembly lines** now commonplace in modern manufacturing industries. These mean that materials and components are continually being worked on as they pass down the line and are hardly ever at rest.

Exploitation of the principle of division of labour has undoubtedly been a major cause of the huge gains in productivity and real incomes in industrial economies, but specialisation does not stop with labour. Greater scale also allows the economical use of specialised capital—machines and equipment—with similar gains in productivity. Increased scale in farming permits land to become more specialised for particular crops. Note that a major underlying cause of economies of scale from specialisation is the **indivisibility** of factors. A small business, for example, might have enough work only for a quarter of a management accountant but may have to employ one full-time or not at all. If the latter, either the firm's general managers carry out the specialist work inefficiently or it has to buy in accountancy services at a high cost. When the firm expands it is able to keep a specialist fully employed.

Specialisation overlaps with another general source of scale economies from the **substitution** of one factor for another. Again, in the small business there would be little point in installing a computer which might only be used a few minutes a day, say, to do basic book-keeping or to calculate wages and tax deductions. The owner of the firm may do this more cheaply by hand. Once the firm grows beyond a certain size it may pay to replace manual labour with computerised accounting systems. There is substitution in this case of capital for labour but the gains derive once again from indivisibility.

There are also other more specific sources of increasing returns which are important in certain kinds of production:

1   **Geometrical or dimensional economies** are particularly significant in processing and transporting of liquids and bulk products. For example, the cost of building a cylindrical storage tank may be largely related to its surface area which determines the amount of steel and other materials used. Given the height of the tank the surface area of the walls is related to the circumference, given (students might recall from their school days) by the formula $2\Pi r$, where r is the radius. The storage capacity, however, is determined by the area of the circular cross-section for which the formula is Πr^2. In other words, it is theoretically possible to build a tank with four times the capacity of another at only twice the cost. In practice, the relationship is not quite as simple as that and engineers often use the **rule of two-thirds** meaning that costs of building storage vessels, ocean-going and road and rail tankers, chemical plants, oil refineries, factories and so on, rise roughly by two-thirds of the increase in capacity. These dimensional

economies are clearly an important explanation of the massive scale of plant and installations in the steel, oil, chemicals and other industries and also the trend towards bigger and bigger goods vehicles, cargo ships and tankers.

2   **Set-up costs** In many industries goods are produced in batches or 'runs' and machines and plants have to be specially 'set-up' before the run can commence. A good example is the writing, publishing and printing of books. There are more or less fixed costs in preparing the manuscript and proofs and in setting the printing and book-binding plant and machinery. The longer the production run (the more books are printed and sold) the lower are these set-up costs per book.

3   **Stocks or inventories** All producers need to hold stocks or, to use the American term, inventories of materials, components, spare parts and of finished goods. As the level of output rises theory shows that the optimum level of inventories increases in smaller proportion. For instance, the spare parts that have to be kept in stock to deal with possible breakdown of one machine might have to be almost the same as for two or three machines since it is unlikely that more than one machine will fail at a time. Similarly, a book publisher will have to keep relatively large numbers of copies of books with low sales to meet booksellers' orders compared with books sold in high volume.

An important cost saving which is not strictly related to the scale of production comes from **dynamic economies of learning**. Here, the cost reductions emerge over time as workers and managers learn from experience the best production methods and techniques and become more skilled in particular tasks and operations. Dynamic economies are clearly significant in firms producing new products or existing products incorporating new technology. Engineers in the aircraft industry, for instance, have constructed 'learning curves' which show reductions in the cost of building new aeroplanes. The cost of the second plane built may be dramatically lower because of the experience gained in building the first.

Most of the economies mentioned above relate to increases in the scale of particular factories or plants. A firm may grow by building or taking over more plants, each operating at the optimum size with no further scope for exploiting economies of scale. However, the increase in the size of the firm itself may still allow further economies. If two firms merge they may save by **pooling their overheads**: thus, they can have common central services in administration, sales and marketing, finance and accounting. Since many of the costs here are fixed they can be spread more thinly over the joint production volume. Bigger firms also have more **market power**. They can more easily negotiate better terms and quantity discounts with their suppliers and offer better career prospects to their employees and attract higher quality staff. The large firm may also have a better credit-rating and be able to borrow more cheaply from banks and the capital market.

5.4.2 Integration

All these economies of scale give powerful incentives to firms to grow in size either through internal expansion or by **integration** with other firms by takeovers and mergers. Integration can be of various kinds. First, there is **vertical integration** where a firm moves either into earlier stages of production (backward integration) or into later stages (forward integration). A motor car manufacturer might, for example, integrate backwards by buying up its suppliers of components or setting up its own foundry. Oil companies are often highly integrated forwards with the control of the distribution and marketing of their products. Vertical integration may lead to the various economies of large firms and allows the firm to plan, coordinate and control the production process as a whole.

Horizontal integration occurs with the merger of firms producing similar products. In this case, there may be potential economies at the plant and factory level as well as with the growth of the firm. Finally, there is **conglomerate integration**, when two firms producing different goods and services merge. This frequently occurs for purely financial reasons—'asset-stripping' and tax avoidance. But we also find firms taking over others in order to diversify out of their own possibly static or declining business. The slow growth of cigarette sales, for example, has led tobacco firms in Britain to diversify into often quite unrelated fields like financial services.

5.4.3   Diseconomies of scale

Once economies of scale become exhausted we have two possibilities. Either the growing firm will have constant returns to scale, or else **diseconomies of scale** set in to give decreasing returns through falling productivity of one or more factors. The possibility of diseconomies of size has long been debated by economists but many agree that once firms grow beyond a certain point **managerial diseconomies** may arise. Thus, the management of the firm, particularly at the top level, is in relatively fixed supply even in the long run. The decision-making capacity of the board of directors and chief executive may therefore become over-stretched as the decisions, such as those on investment, become more numerous and the information required more voluminous and complex. Much of the work involved has to be delegated to less senior managers and to working parties and committees representing different departments and interest groups in the firm. The result is that the organisation becomes administratively top-heavy and bureaucratic and its costs increase.

Another possible source of diseconomies is a deterioration in industrial relations. Both managers and workers, as they become more narrowly specialised, tend to lose any identity with the firm's goals and products. As sociologists say, workers may become 'alienated', leading to increased frequency of strikes and other industrial action. Also, specialisation means greater interdependence among workers which may give them more market power in bidding up wages or insisting on restrictive working practices. A strike by a small group of, say, maintenance workers may bring a whole production line or factory to a standstill.

5.4.4   The long run cost curve

If firms enjoy increasing returns up to a certain scale but then suffer from diseconomies it is possible to draw up a U-shaped **long run average cost** (LAC) curve of the kind shown in Figure 5.6. This shows the lowest possible unit cost producing any output. The falling part of the curve up to output OB indicates increasing returns to scale. At B there are constant returns at the minimum point of the curve and then decreasing returns as diseconomies take over to cause a rise in LAC. Note that as a firm increases its scale it continually moves into new short run situations in which the short run cost curves become relevant. The LAC curve can therefore be interpreted as being tangent to all the infinite number of short-run average cost (SAC) curves, each one related to a different scale of production. Two of these are shown in the diagram. SAC_1 is tangent to the LAC curve at F where

FIGURE 5.6   **The long run average cost curve**

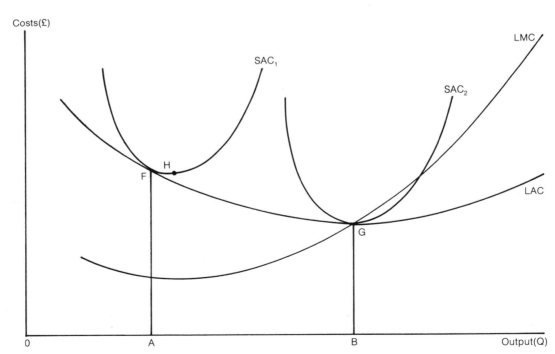

both SAC and LAC are falling. This doesn't mean that, having expanded to a scale which generates SAC_1, the firm should produce at point F, to the left of the minimum SAC at H. Rather, the firm will have to determine its short run output by the principles we set out above in the light of the current level of prices. SAC_2 is tangent to the LAC curve at G, the minimum point on both curves. Using our same relationships between margins and averages we can construct a **long run marginal cost** (LMC) curve cutting both average curves at their minimum points. In turn, we can argue that the firm should determine its maximum-profit long run output in exactly the same way as for the short-run—by equating marginal revenue (the same as price for a firm in perfect competition) with long-run marginal cost. However, we shall see in Chapter 6 that in the long run under perfect competition, the price will be driven down to the minimum of LAC and the firm will therefore produce output OB.

SUMMARY

To maximise profits any firm must consider the behaviour of revenue and costs as it varies output. Assuming perfect competition, a firm is a price-taker; its revenue varies directly with output and marginal revenue is equal to price. In the short run the firm has a finite productive capacity and its costs are centrally determined by diminishing returns. These result in falling marginal product of the firm's variable factors and in increasing marginal cost. The maximum profit output is where marginal revenue equals marginal cost. In the short run the firm's fixed costs are irrelevant in determining its output and it should stay in business so long as it can cover its variable costs. In the long run unit costs may fall because of economies of scale but, once these are exhausted, diseconomies may give rise to decreasing returns to scale and rising average costs.

SELF-TEST QUESTIONS

1   Which of the following best describes the revenue function of a firm operating in a perfectly competitive industry?

(a)   Total revenue equals price times quantity.

(b)   Marginal revenue is greater than average revenue but is equal to price.

(c)   The firm can influence its revenue by altering its price.

(d)   As the firm increases its output total revenue increases but by relatively less than price.

(e)   At the prevailing market price marginal revenue equals average revenue.

2   Which one of the following statements is correct?

(a)   In the long run there is only one fixed input and in the short run only one variable input.

(b)   In the long run all costs are variable so that the cost of capital can be ignored.

(c)   If labour is the only variable factor in the short run the variable cost per unit of output is found by dividing the hourly wage rate by the average product of labour per hour.

(d)   Diminishing returns in production

mean that increased inputs of variable factors will ultimately give rise to a fall in marginal utility.

(e)   When the firm reaches the ceiling of its productive capacity the average product of the variable factor is zero.

3   Which one of the following statements is correct?

(a)   The average product of labour reaches its minimum point when it is equal to the marginal product.

(b)   The average product of labour rises as output is first increased but at a faster rate than the marginal product.

(c)   The average product of labour continues to increase after the marginal product reaches its maximum so long as average product is less than marginal product.

(d)   The firm's fixed costs per unit of output remain constant at all outputs.

(e)   Because AFC falls continuously AVC reaches its minimum point after ATC.

4   Which of the following best describes the profit-maximising position of a firm in perfect competition?

(a)   Total costs are rising at the same rate as output.

(b) Total costs are increasing at the same rate as total revenue.

(c) Marginal revenue is equal to the rate of change in average total cost.

(d) Average revenue exceeds marginal cost by the greatest amount.

(e) Price equals marginal revenue which is greater than marginal cost.

5   Which one of the following statements is wrong?

(a) A tin mine with operating costs of £500 a ton and fixed costs of £1,000 a ton should be kept working in the short run when the price of tin is £900 a ton.

(b) Some Spanish seaside hotels stay open in the winter because, although they make overall losses, they can cover their variable costs.

(c) If a firm doubles all its inputs and achieves more than double the output its LAC curve is rising.

(d) Backward vertical integration occurs when a firm sets up a plant to produce its own components.

(e) When LMC equals LAC there are constant returns to scale.

EXERCISE

Distinguish between fixed and variable costs. Consider the significance of fixed and variable costs to a firm's decision whether to close down.

Answers on page 245.

Competition

In this chapter we first extend the theory of supply with a study of how a perfectly competitive industry responds to changes in demand and price. We find that under perfect competition any excess short run profits are competed away in the long run by the entry of new firms into the industry and that in equilibrium firms will produce with minimum unit costs. This suggests that perfect competition leads to an optimal allocation of resources. We then consider monopolistic competition where firms can engage through product differentiation in non-price, as well as price, competition. Although simple comparison with perfect competition indicates that non-price competition leads to inefficient resource allocation we find that the analysis ignores benefits to consumers from greater product choice.

6.1 INTRODUCTION

Goods and services are supplied in a wide variety of **market structures**. For most goods, certainly for consumer products, there are very large numbers of potential buyers who compete against each other in the market. Individual buyers normally don't have the market power to control the prices they pay and it is usually (but not always) safe to assume that competitive conditions prevail on the demand side of the market. This is clearly not the case with the supply of goods. A basic condition for effective competition is a large number of suppliers of a good. There are industries such as agriculture, accountancy practices and some areas of retailing, where this condition is met but there are many more where supply is dominated by just a few firms and, in extreme cases, by a single firm.

Because deviations from competition occur most frequently on the supply side economists conventionally make an initial classification of market structures according to the number of significant suppliers in the market.

On the supply side we thus have a spectrum of market forms:

1   **Perfect competition** Large numbers of suppliers each selling a homogeneous product.
2   **Imperfect or monopolistic competition** Again, large numbers of suppliers but with each selling a **differentiated product** (explained below).
3   **Oligopoly** Only a few suppliers each with a significant share of the market. (The word comes from the Greek for 'a few sellers'.)
4   **Monopoly** Just one supplier. (From the Greek for 'one seller'.)

In this chapter we shall concentrate on the first two market forms in which there is competition among many firms. We start with perfect competition.

6.2 PERFECT COMPETITION

We have already done much of the spade work for our analysis of perfect competition in Chapter 5 where we examined the output decision of an individual producer in a perfectly competitive industry. The model of perfect competition is drawn up on a number of assumptions:

1   **A large number of firms** Each firm, remember, has such a small share of the total market that it can be considered to be a **price taker**—the demand curve for its output is perfectly elastic at the prevailing market price.
2   **A homogeneous product** The product of each firm is identical in the minds of buyers to the products of the others. Firms' products are therefore perfect substitutes for each other, eliminating price differences between firms.

3 **Free entry and exit** This means that there are no barriers to the entry of new firms into the industry while existing firms can leave the industry without incurring significant costs.

4 **Perfect information** Buyers are assumed to have enough information to **know** that different firms are selling identical products. Similarly, suppliers all have access to the lowest-cost technology and production methods.

We also assume that firms aim to maximise their profits and that they buy inputs in perfectly competitive markets so that they are price takers for their inputs. All these assumptions are of course so restrictive that we could never hope to find a real-world industry that conformed precisely to any one of them let alone to all of them. But the model has a dual purpose. First, it yields predictions about the behaviour of prices and output which help us to understand the workings of industries whose structures approximate to perfect competition. Secondly, as an idealised model it gives us a basis for drawing comparisons between other models of imperfect markets—what are price and output likely to be under monopoly or oligopoly compared with perfect competition? Are resources allocated more or less efficiently under other market structures? Should government intervention be directed towards making markets more competitive?

6.2.1 The industry supply curve

In the last chapter we concluded that the individual firm's short-run supply curve is its marginal cost curve where it rises above the close-down price equal to minimum average variable cost. As the price rises the firm increases output along the MC curve, keeping MC equal to price in order to maximise profits. Now, if we imagine the industry is composed of a large number of firms with identical cost curves it is a simple matter to construct the industry's short-run supply curve as in Figure 6.1. In the left-hand diagram we show the average and marginal cost curves for a representative firm like those drawn up in Chapter 5. In the right-hand diagram we show the market situation for the industry as a whole. The demand curve for the industry's product is drawn together with two short-run supply curves, SS_1 and SS_2. Focus first on SS_1.

FIGURE 6.1 **Equilibrium under perfect competition**

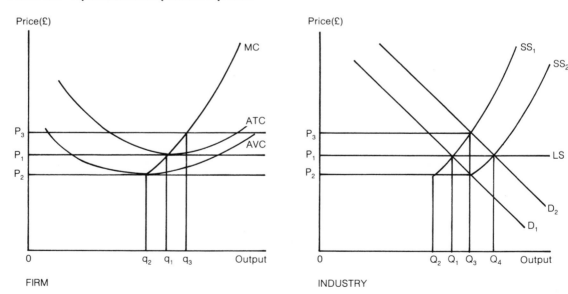

If there are 100 firms in the industry then, at each price, the output of the industry must be 100 times the output of each firm. To generalise, denote the firm's output with q and the industry's with Q; if there are n firms in the industry, then:

$$Q = n.q$$

The output axis for the firm in Figure 6.1 is on a scale n times bigger than that for the industry. The curve SS_1 is constructed by summing the outputs of the n firms at each price as they move up and down their MC curves. Using the Greek capital letter Σ to stand for 'the sum of':

$$SS_1 = \Sigma MC$$

Given the difference in the output scales, therefore, the MC curve for the firm is identical to the industry's short-run supply curve SS_1. Suppose we start with an equilibrium market price of P_1 where the demand curve D_1 cuts SS_1. Each firm's output is q_1 and the industry's output is Q_1. Notice that this price is just equal to each firm's minimum ATC. Since price equals average revenue firms are just breaking even with zero profits. In the economist's terminology they are making **normal profits**.

NORMAL PROFITS

There is an apparent paradox here. The graph tells us that firms are making zero profits; economists tell us they are making normal profits. The problem is resolved by considering what is meant by normal profits. In economics we argue that the capital invested in a business has an opportunity cost—the business must offer the investor a prospective return on capital at least equal to the return available on equivalent alternative investments. Suppose an individual has £100,000 which can be safely invested in, say, government bonds to yield 10 per cent or £10,000 a year. He or she then considers buying a hotel for £100,000. Clearly, the investor, before going ahead with the purchase, is going to require a return in profits from the business of at least 10 per cent. The required expected return is likely to be higher at, say, 15 per cent because of the additional uncertainty and risk involved compared with leaving the money in bonds.

This minimum return required to attract capital into the business is what economists call **normal profit**. Since it represents the opportunity cost of risk capital to the business it is treated as part of the firm's fixed costs which have to be paid if the firm is first to come into existence and then to survive in the long run. Returning to the diagram, at the price P_1 equal to minimum ATC the firm is just making normal profits. This is enough to keep it in business in the long run but not enough to attract new firms into the industry. If the price drops below P_1 the firm will be making less than normal profits and will leave the industry in the long run (although, as we saw in Chapter 5, it may stay in business in the short run if the price is above the close-down level P_2). Correspondingly, if price rises above P_1 the firm makes **super-normal** profits: it is earning a **surplus** over and above what is necessary to keep it in business (the surplus is often referred to in economics as **economic rent**—see Chapter 8). However, super-normal profits will attract new firms into the industry to drive profit levels back to normal.

LONG RUN EQUILIBRIUM

If we also assume that all the firms in the industry are operating at an optimum scale so that the short run ATC curve is tangent to the LAC curve at its minimum point, then our initial position is one of **long run equilibrium**. At the market-clearing price of P_1, all firms are making normal profits and there is therefore no incentive for new firms to move in or incumbent firms to move out. But suppose there is an increase in market demand with a shift of the demand curve to D_2. Excess demand at the old price will drive up the market price inducing firms to move up their MC or short run supply curves. This continues until a new **short run equilibrium** is established at price P_3. Each firm has expanded its output to q_3 and the industry's output has risen by the same proportion to Q_3.

This is only a temporary or **short run** equilibrium. At the higher price each firm is now making super-normal profits which will attract new firms into the industry because the prospective returns are higher than can be obtained outside the industry. As each new firm comes in we have to add its MC curve to the industry short run supply curve, SS_1. SS therefore is pushed to the right and as it does so there is a fall in the market-clearing price. The process continues until super-normal profit and, hence, the incentive for new firms to enter, is eliminated. In other words, the price has to drop back to its original level at P_1 through a shift of the short run supply curve to SS_2 which cuts D_2 at that price. We then have a new **long run equilibrium** in which all firms are again making normal profits, each producing the old output q_1, while the industry has fully responded to the rise in demand by expanding output to Q_4 through the entry of new firms.

THE LONG RUN SUPPLY CURVE

In this analysis we end up with a perfectly elastic long run supply curve at a price equal to minimum long run average cost. Thus, whatever happens to demand, the industry always returns to the long run equilibrium position. If we analysed a fall instead of a rise in demand the short run effect would be a reduction in price. That would leave firms with sub-normal profits and, as they quit the industry, the SS curve would shift to the left to push the price back again to P_1. But the perfectly elastic long run supply curve is the result of two of our simplifying assumptions which are unlikely to hold in the real world. The first is that all firms have identical costs. This is clearly unrealistic. The costs of inputs will vary for a variety of reasons. Some firms will have locational advantages, such as proximity to the market or to sources of raw materials, and these may reduce their transport and distribution costs. In agriculture, some farmers will have better land and higher crop yields; in mining, costs of extracting minerals will depend on the depth and quality of deposits—both investment and operating costs of oil wells in the North Sea are far higher than land-based wells in, say, Saudi Arabia.

These cost differences between firms mean that the minimum LAC, which determines the price necessary for normal profits, varies among firms. Thus, the cost diagram in Figure 6.1 is representative only of the **marginal firm**, the one which can just make normal profits at its **entry price** of P_1. The **intra-marginal firms** have lower cost curves and lower entry prices. At P_1 they are therefore earning super-normal profits or rent, more than enough to keep them in the business. When demand rises, firms with still higher costs are induced to enter by the higher price but in the new long run equilibrium the price is above P_1 and there is a new marginal firm. The long-run supply curve is more elastic than the short run curve but is now upward sloping. The analysis here is the same as in our discussion of supply elasticities in Chapter 3 (see Figure 3.6).

The second assumption we made, which led to a perfectly elastic long-run supply curve, was that input prices remain constant at all levels of output, but if a whole industry is expanding its output after a rise in demand for its product it will correspondingly be increasing its own demand for inputs of labour, capital, land and materials. The most likely outcome is a rise in input prices to all firms in the industry and therefore a general upward shift of their cost curves. The normal-profit price therefore rises and we again end up in a new long run equilibrium with a higher price—the long run supply curve is upward-sloping. We should stress that the rise in costs here applies to all firms as the industry expands. It is not the same therefore as the increase in costs in the individual firm when it independently expands its scale because of **internal diseconomies** of scale discussed in Chapter 5. The cost increase now is, we say, internal to the industry but external to the firm—the firm suffers from **external diseconomies** from the expansion of the industry.

We can also conceive of **external economies** if input prices drop after an increase in the industry's output. This could occur if firms supplying an input, say, components or materials, are themselves able to reduce their costs because of unexploited economies of scale in their own production. This is certainly not improbable in practice. For example, the huge expansion of the computer industry in recent years has massively boosted the demand for memory chips. Chip producers have substantially cut their prices partly, if not largely, because of cost reductions as they have expanded their own scale. External economies can lead therefore to a **downward-sloping** long run supply curve. After a rise in demand the price may still rise in the short run but ultimately falls in the new long run equilibrium.

EFFICIENCY UNDER PERFECT COMPETITION

The adjustment of output to a long run equilibrium in which price equals minimum average cost leads to the conclusion that perfect competition results in optimum efficiency in the allocation of resources. If we were to imagine an economy in which all markets were perfectly competitive then, in a situation of general equilibrium (equilibrium in all markets) all goods and services would be being produced at lowest unit cost. Moreover, all consumers would be in equilibrium maximising their utility with equal marginal utility of expenditure on every good (see Chapter 4). For any one good the marginal valuation of it as expressed by marginal willingness to pay (MWP) is equal to price which is equal to marginal cost:

$$P = MWP = MC$$

This equality of the two marginal values is often described as a **Pareto condition for optimality** in the allocation of resources after the Italian economist, Vilfredo Pareto (1843–1923). Any deviation from the equilibrium position will lead to an inequality and a reduction in allocative efficiency. For instance, an increase in output by the industry leads to a rise in MC and a fall in MWP; more is added to costs by the extra output than is added to utility as measured by willingness to pay and there is a reduction therefore in **social welfare**.

Formal proof of the Pareto conditions for maximising allocative efficiency is outside the scope of this book while they have to be applied to the real world with great caution. For example, their validity strictly depends on perfect competition in all markets. Even so, the notion of perfect competition leading to maximum efficiency has been very influential in public policy with a presumption that competition between a larger number of firms leads to greater efficiency and welfare. Before we reach conclusions of that kind, however, we should first look at other market structures. We move next to imperfect competition.

6.3 IMPERFECT OR MONOPOLISTIC COMPETITION

PRODUCT DIFFERENTIATION

This model goes under alternative names because of its virtually simultaneous but separate development by two economists who both published books in 1933, *The Economics of Imperfect Competition* was published by Joan Robinson in England and *The Theory of Monopolistic Competition* by Edward Chamberlin in America. Their particular models had differences but both stressed the importance of **product differentiation** in real-world markets. Thus in what has become the standard version of monopolistic competition we make the same assumptions as in perfect competition except that we now have differentiated products instead of a single homogeneous product. We therefore have an industry with large numbers of competing firms and with free entry and exit. But the product of each firm is now only a close, not a perfect, substitute for those of other firms.

Firms are all producing the same class of good or service which satisfies similar consumer wants. But each firm attempts to differentiate its product from its rivals' products either by producing it with different physical characteristics or through the use of brand names, advertising, packaging and other marketing techniques. Product differentiation is clearly much more widespread than the selling of homogeneous products. Nearly every manufactured product is available in a wide variety of shapes, sizes and qualities. Motor cars range from small, basically-equipped hatchbacks to plush executive limousines and high performance coupés. All these are available in different colours, trim and so on. The same differentiation applies to washing machines, refrigerators, TVs, video recorders and even to simple products like instant coffee, tea, breakfast cereals, biscuits, washing-up liquid and petrol. Differentiation is found also in the marketing of services such as banking and insurance, airlines and holidays. Note though, that many of these products are produced under oligopoly, dealt with in the next chapter.

Product differentiation is essentially **non-price competition**. If the product is homogeneous, like most primary products, producers have little option but to compete on price. The possibility of improving the quality of a product or selling more of it by advertising gives producers an alternative to price reductions as a method of increasing sales. To examine the effects of product differentiation let's first see how it may change the conclusions we reached from the perfect competition model.

The primary effect of product differentiation is on the revenue functions of firms. With a homogeneous product the demand for the output of each firm is perfectly elastic at the prevailing price so that marginal revenue equals price and total revenue varies directly with output. However, under monopolistic competition the more successfully a firm differentiates its product the less elastic will be the demand for it and the more control it will have over the price it can charge. A firm which has built up brand loyalty for, say, its own washing powder among its customers will be able to retain some sales even when the price is higher than the products of its competitors. The demand curve for its product is therefore downward-sloping. But, given our assumption of a large number of firms and many competing products, we can assume that demand will be relatively elastic—a rise in price leads to a bigger proportionate fall in sales.

AVERAGE AND MARGINAL REVENUE

If the demand curve is downward sloping, marginal revenue (MR) is now less than price or average revenue (AR). The relation between the two can be seen by looking at a straight-line demand or AR curve as in Figure 6.2. In Chapter 3 we saw that the price elasticity of demand (PED) changes continuously along such a curve from infinity at A to unity at its mid-point B and zero at C. Total revenue (TR = P.Q) is measured by rectangles beneath the demand curve and is plotted in the right-hand diagram (with a smaller vertical scale).

FIGURE 6.2 **Revenue with a downward-sloping demand curve**

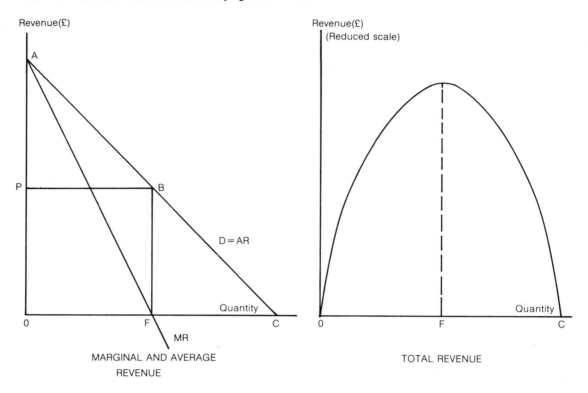

We can note that, as output is increased from zero, TR increases so long as demand is elastic between A and B on the demand curve and between a zero output and output of OF. Marginal revenue (MR), remember, measures the rate of change of TR:

$$MR = \frac{\Delta TR}{\Delta Q}$$

MR therefore is given by the slope of the TR curve. This is positive but diminishing as TR increases at a declining rate till it reaches its peak at output OF. Since MR equals AR for the first unit of output, the MR curve starts at point A and then declines to zero at F. At F the TR curve has a zero slope (is flat) so MR is also zero. As output is increased further from F, demand becomes inelastic and TR declines all the way to zero at output OC where the price is zero. MR therefore must be negative once output exceeds OF. With a straight-line demand curve we thus have a simple relationship between the MR and AR curves. They both begin at the same point on the price axis when output is zero but the MR curve then lies below the AR curve and falls twice as steeply. MR is zero at F, halfway between the origin and C. From F, MR is negative.

6.3.1 Equilibrium under monopolistic competition

Figure 6.3 shows the revenue and cost curves for a representative firm in monopolistic competition. The average cost curve is for the long run and is assumed to be U-shaped. Take first the demand or average revenue curve, D_1. As we have just explained, this is downward-sloping but is assumed to be relatively elastic—if it was extended to cut the output axis then the firm's demand curve lies wholly in the top half (between A and B in Figure 6.2). The marginal revenue curve can then be constructed as we have shown—MR is therefore less than AR or price at all outputs except zero where they are the same. D_1 lies above minimum average cost implying that the firm can make super-normal profits. The actual maximum profit output is found as before where the MR curve cuts the MC curve at H, at output Q_1. This must be the maximum profit output for the same reasons as under perfect competition—MR is greater than MC up to Q_1 and is less beyond Q_1. But there is now a gap between MR and price. The firm can sell Q_1 at the price, P_1, equal to the distance Q_1J. This is also the firm's average revenue while the average cost is measured by Q_1K. The profit per unit of output is therefore equal to the distance JK. Multiply that by Q_1 and we have the firm's total profits (strictly speaking, super-normal profits).

FIGURE 6.3 **Equilibrium under monopolistic competition**

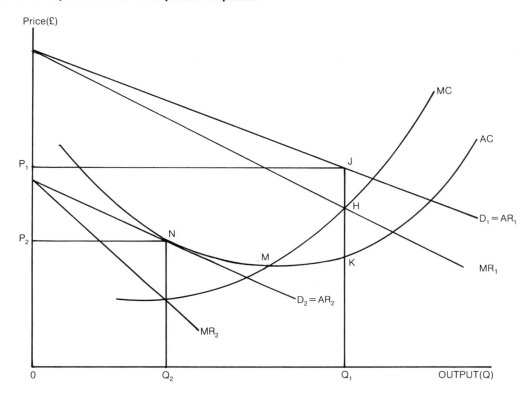

However, this can only be a position of short run equilibrium. With free entry into the industry, new firms will be attracted by super-normal returns and, as they come in, they will erode the sales of the incumbent firms and force down the average market price. The typical firm will therefore sell less at each price and will find its demand curve moving down and to the left. This continues until the firm is earning only normal profits where AR equals AC. This can only occur at a point like N where the AR or demand curve has shifted to a point of tangency with the AC curve. At N, the best the firm can do is sell the output Q_2 at the price or average revenue of P_2. Its average cost is the same so that it is just making normal profits. If this applies to all firms (or at least to the marginal firm) there will be no further entry into the industry. We have a position of long run equilibrium.

EXCESS CAPACITY

The process of adjustment to long run equilibrium is the same as for perfect competition but there is a difference in the price and output at the equilibrium point. Under perfect competition the firm would be operating at minimum AC at point M, with a lower price and a greater output. The firm under imperfect competition is at rest in the long run at N, which must be on the downward-sloping part of the AC curve at an output lower than the minimum AC output. Comparing the two positions we can say that firms under monopolistic competition will end up producing less and charging a higher price than under perfect competition. This is often summarised by saying that monopolistic competition results in **excess capacity**, meaning that there is scope for an expansion of output with further cost and price reductions.

Since the single difference between the two models is product differentiation, we apparently conclude from the comparison that non-price competition lowers allocative efficiency and social welfare. In equilibrium at N we can see that price is greater than marginal cost and we have a sub-optimal allocation of resources. The value of marginal utility at N exceeds marginal cost so that an expansion of output will add more to utility than to costs and increase welfare until excess capacity is removed at M. There is nothing faulty with the logic of this conclusion that in the allocation of resources monopolistic competition is inferior to perfect competition. But it would be quite wrong to argue that governments should take measures to prohibit product differentiation. This is because the analysis fails to distinguish different kinds of product differentiation some of which may benefit consumers in ways not captured in the model.

There are two broad types of non-price competition. The first is based on artificial product differentiation produced by brand names, advertising, packaging and sales promotion generally. In the extreme case, it is conceivable that a firm may succeed in persuading some consumers that its product is superior to those of its competitors even though the product is actually identical to the others. There is a presumption that this type of non-price competition is wasteful and that the costs of advertising and sales promotion reduce consumer welfare through higher prices. But even then we need to be careful in condemning product differentiation of this kind. A producer of, say, table salt might apparently convince a sizeable number of consumers that its brand X has superior qualities, like greater purity and added vitamins, even though chemically the brand is identical to all the others. But the consumers who are willing to pay a premium price for brand X have not necessarily been hoodwinked. They may know well enough that the salt is the same but they are prepared to pay the higher price because the salt is more conveniently or attractively packaged or is easier to pour. In other words, there is an element of the second type of non-price competition based on real physical differences in the product.

Thus, for any product type consumers differ in their preferences for such things as size, colour and style. If they didn't, producers would gain no competitive advantage from producing anything other than the standard product which all consumers want. In practice, preferences do differ for the great majority of goods and services, even for salt. Preferences for many product characteristics will lie along a continuum of the kind shown in Figure 6.4. Here, we take a product, microwave ovens, and plot a frequency distribution of people's preferences for ovens of a different size. Single people with small kitchens want small ovens; families with big kitchens want large ovens. The preferences are assumed to be 'normally distributed', meaning that most people want medium-sized ovens and that the numbers wanting smaller or bigger ovens tail off the further away we move from the most popular size in the middle—the distribution is therefore bell-shaped. (It is not necessarily like that in practice.)

FIGURE 6.4   **Size preferences for microwave ovens**

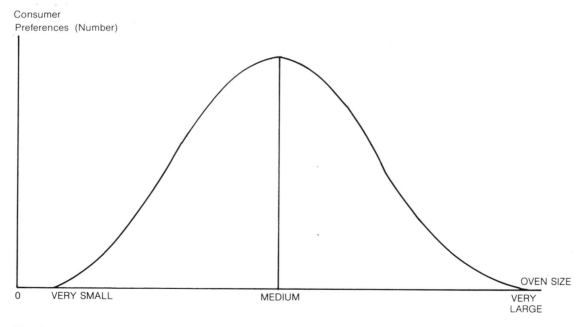

The first firm to enter the microwave oven market is very likely to offer a product which most nearly meets the preferences of the majority of consumers, in other words, a medium-sized oven. People right in the middle of the distribution are completely satisfied while others near the middle will probably still buy. Those at the extremes who want very small or very big ovens are the least likely to buy. As new producers enter the market they too are likely to locate at or close to the middle. But, eventually, the centre becomes congested and new firms will start to move further and further from the middle ground, offering smaller or bigger ovens. We can imagine that once the market is saturated we might have just one or two firms producing very large and very small ovens to satisfy the few consumers in the tails of the distribution.

The point, of course, is that non-price competition in this example increases consumer satisfaction through greater product variety and wider consumer choice. Also, consumers may benefit over time as producers attempt to increase their market share by product innovation and improvement. There are countless practical examples of this type of competition—in motor cars, all kinds of consumer durables, houses, food products, and so on. Moreover, it is not limited to goods; it is found in services as well. In retailing, for example, supermarkets tend to cater for the middle ground of consumers, usually with cars. But small shops survive, commonly charging higher prices, because they are more conveniently located and stay open at different times or because they offer higher standards of service like deliveries to the home.

Clearly, government regulation of non-price competition with restrictions on product differentiation runs the risk of lowering consumer welfare by restriction of consumer choice. This is arguably the case, for instance, in the regulation of radio and TV broadcasting in many countries which restricts the number of channels. When the choice of TV channels is limited, as in Britain, to four, then there is a natural tendency to compete for the mass audience with a similar range of what many think are mediocre programmes. Another example is the restriction on shop opening hours in many countries. There may be good arguments in favour of such regulation but often these are not weighed against the cost in terms of the loss of consumer choice.

SUMMARY

Output in a perfectly competitive industry adjusts to a long run equilibrium in which the marginal producer makes only normal profits and price is equal to minimum average cost. Since, in equilibrium, the long run marginal cost is equal to the value of marginal utility, perfect competition leads to the optimal allocation of resources. If all producers have identical costs and there are no external economies or diseconomies of scale, the industry long run supply curve is perfectly elastic. Upward-sloping long run supply curves can be explained by cost differences among producers or by external diseconomies which drive up input prices. External economies may lead to a downward-sloping long-run supply curve. Under monopolistic competition, product differentiation apparently leads to sub-optimal resource allocation with excess capacity in the industry. However, the analysis ignores the important benefits which flow from non-price competition in the form of wider consumer choice and product innovation and improvement.

SELF-TEST QUESTIONS

1 Which one of the following statements is wrong?

(a) Under perfect competition, firms' products are close but not perfect substitutes for each other so that there can be small price variations between them.

(b) The short run supply curve under perfect competition is given by summing the marginal cost curves of the individual incumbent firms.

(c) When AR equals ATC a firm's profits are just enough to keep the firm in business in the long run.

(d) When price exceeds minimum ATC a firm can earn a super-normal return on capital.

(e) If input prices are constant and there are only internal economies or diseconomies of scale, the long run supply curve is perfectly elastic.

2 Under perfect competition, an industry's long run supply curve may slope upwards because:

(a) of external economies of scale;

(b) industries which supply inputs enjoy economies of scale;

(c) only the marginal firm makes profits

while the intra-marginal firms make losses though covering their variable costs;

(d) cost differences between firms mean that a rise in price is necessary to induce higher-cost firms to enter the industry;

(e) firms leave the industry when the price falls.

3 Which one of the following statements is correct?

(a) Perfect competition allocates resources efficiently because, in equilibrium, firms produce with minimum average variable cost.

(b) The Pareto conditions for optimality are satisfied when price is equal to both marginal cost and consumers' marginal willingness to pay for all goods and services.

(c) Product differentiation occurs in industries where each firm diversifies its output between different types of goods and services.

(d) Monopolistic competition is the same as perfect competition except that there is no longer free entry and exit to and from the industry.

(e) Firms operating under imperfect competition face inelastic demand curves for their output.

4 Which of the following best describes long run equilibrium in monopolistic competition?

Answers on page 247

(a) Firms earn super-normal profits because price is greater than marginal cost.

(b) There is excess capacity because firms could expand their output with falling average costs.

(c) The marginal revenue curve is tangent to the average cost curve.

(d) Price equals marginal cost but not average cost.

(e) Resources are allocated efficiently because firms make only normal profits.

5 Which one of the following statements is correct?

(a) Excess capacity in equilibrium under monopolistic competition proves that product differentiation produces a sub-optimal allocation of resources.

(b) Non-price competition is more likely to occur for homogeneous products.

(c) Non-price competition is wasteful because it invariably means that a firm persuades consumers to buy its products which are the same as those of its competitors.

(d) Consumers' utility is increased when non-price competition leads to a wider range of products to meet differences in consumer preferences.

(e) Non-price competition tends to stifle product innovation and improvement.

EXERCISE

What is 'product differentiation'? Are consumers better or worse off from product differentiation?

Answers on page 247.

Monopoly and oligopoly

This chapter completes the analysis of market structures with an examination of monopoly and oligopoly. While the standard analysis of a profit-maximising monopoly firm indicates that resources are inefficiently allocated to the detriment of the consumer we need to be cautious in applying this conclusion to real-world monopolies, particularly in framing policies towards them. Monopolies may be more efficient than competitive firms while the threat of competition may force down monopoly prices. In oligopoly (an industry with only a few firms) the behaviour of firms can vary widely from outright competition between them to the formation of cartels. It is difficult therefore to reach general conclusions about price and output under oligopoly.

7.1 INTRODUCTION

The competitive markets discussed in the last chapter both involve competition among many firms, none of which has significant market power. This kind of **atomistic competition** is found in many real-world markets, but in a large proportion of industry we also have a high degree of **concentration** where supply is dominated by just one or by a handful of firms each with a significant share of total sales. The type of analysis developed for competition amongst the many cannot be easily applied to these situations of monopoly or oligopoly. For example, in neither case is there a simple supply curve which tells us how the firms will react to changes in demand (and price).

Also, the assumption of profit maximisation may be less reasonable. In most industries with a high level of concentration, the individual firms are themselves very large. If they operate in the private sector they are likely to be **public limited companies** with many shareholders and there may be a conflict of interests between shareholders, who want maximum profits, and the managers, who may be more concerned with maximising the growth of the company and with their own rewards. Similarly, in nationalised industries, controlled ultimately by the government, profit maximisation may be secondary to other political goals such as maintenance of employment and holding down prices. In cases of industrial concentration therefore we need to apply a different analysis. Let us begin with monopoly.

7.2 MONOPOLY

A monopolistic industry can be defined simply as one in which there is a single supplier of a product with no close substitutes. This definition may not match up with what are often referred to as 'monopolies' in practice. In Britain, for example, a company can be referred to the **Monopolies and Mergers Commission** when it has more than 25 per cent of the market for a product. Many such cases are therefore of firms in oligopolistic markets with several producers. Monopoly models may still be relevant since the firms may form cartels and behave like a monopoly. If they don't, we need to use the models of oligopoly discussed in the next section. Also, firms with an apparent monopoly for their products may in fact be subject to strong competition from others producing more or less close substitutes. A monopoly supplier of gas—like British Gas—is constrained in the prices it charges by competition from electricity, oil and coal. An oligopoly model could once again be more relevant, or, if there are a large number of competing products, we might do better to use the model of monopolistic competition of Chapter 6.

7.2.1 Profit-maximising monopoly

If we assume that a monopolist aims to maximise profits, the analysis of the firm's equilibrium position is essentially the same as in monopolistic competition. Thus, a monopoly by definition faces the market demand curve for its product. For simplicity, we assume it is a straight-line demand curve as shown in Figure 7.1, but there is no reason to suppose that demand is relatively elastic at the relevant outputs as we did with the imperfectly competitive firm. In fact, since the monopolist's product has no close substitutes, demand will be inelastic at some prices, so that marginal revenue is negative (see the analysis of MR in Chapter 6). This occurs in the lower half of our demand curve at output greater than OF—an increase in output results in a fall in total revenue. It follows that a profit-maximising monopoly cannot be in equilibrium when demand is inelastic since it can then increase revenue and profits by reducing output. The profit-maximising output must occur where demand is relatively elastic and marginal revenue positive, somewhere in the top half of the demand curve.

FIGURE 7.1   **A profit-maximising monopoly's equilibrium price and output**

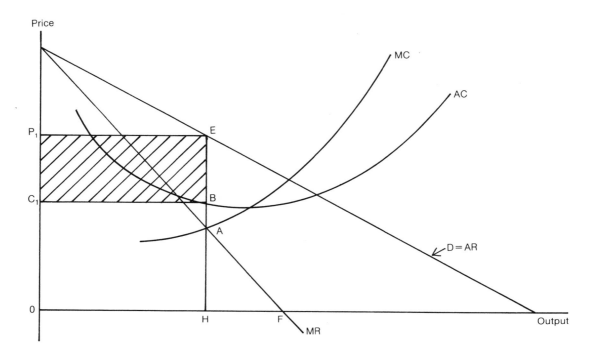

The precise profit-maximising output can be found by drawing in the monopolist's average and marginal cost curves. The curves can be interpreted as representing the firm's short run or long run costs. The analysis will then give us the short run or long run equilibrium position. So long as the AC curve lies below the AR curve at some outputs the monopolist can make super-normal profits. The general condition for profit maximisation (that MC equals MR) applies. The optimum output is where the MC curve cuts the MR curve at A or output OH. In turn, by extending HA vertically upwards to meet the demand curve at E we find the price, P_1, at which the output can be sold. The profit per unit of output is equal to P_1 (average revenue) minus the average cost of producing OH. The firm is at B on its AC curve so that AC equals C_1. The unit profit is thus C_1P_1; multiply that by the number of units of output, OH, and total profits are measured by the shaded rectangle, C_1P_1EB.

Since the normal return on capital is included in costs, the monopoly is making super-normal profits, more than sufficient to keep the firm in business. These surplus returns can be earned so long as there is some output at which AR is greater than AC. The limiting case is like that in equilibrium in monopolistic competition, when the AR or demand curve is just tangent to the AC curve so that the firm can at best make only normal profits. If demand then fell the monopolist would go out of business. Super-normal profits will attract new firms into the industry and can only be maintained therefore if the monopolist can keep out potential competitors with effective **barriers to entry**.

7.2.2   Barriers to entry

There are a number of possible barriers against the entry of new firms:

1 **Legal barriers** Some monopolies are legal monopolies. Most nationalised industries, such as British Coal, British Rail and the Post Office in Britain, have near-monopolies in supplying their particular products. Sometimes, privately-owned firms have sole legal rights of production—British Gas and British Telecom largely retained their monopoly positions when they were 'privatised' in the 1980s. They are now **regulated private monopolies** where competition is largely excluded by law but the companies' ability to charge monopoly prices is restricted by setting up special regulatory bodies to monitor both the price and quality of their products or services. Private firms can also acquire temporary monopolies in new products or processes by taking out **patents** and **copyrights**.

2 **Economies of scale** If economies of scale (see Chapter 5) obtain up to very high levels of output we may have a **natural monopoly** because the market is too small to support more than one firm. The first firm to expand its scale of output will have lower costs and therefore be able to drive competitors out by undercutting their prices. In Figure 7.1 this would occur if the minimum point on the long run AC curve lies to the right of the demand curve. Any potential competitor can be kept out with an actual or threatened price cut. The electricity, telecommunications, gas and water supply networks are good examples of natural monopolies in most countries, because the capital cost of setting up the national (or international) distribution system is very high, while the marginal cost of providing services to customers from the established system is very low.

3 **Artificial barriers** If there are no legal or natural barriers to entry the monopolist may try to erect artificial ones to deter competitors. For instance, the firm may ward off a potential entrant by temporarily lowering its price as a warning that the interloper will make losses in a price war if it dares to intrude. This is sometimes known as **predatory pricing**. Alternatively, the monopoly may deliberately invest in over-capacity which it can use to swamp the market to cut prices and force a new firm out of business. Another possibility is to engage in product differentiation either by advertising to establish brand loyalty, by producing a range of products with real physical differences or by investing in research and development (R&D) to ensure a stream of new products to keep one step ahead of potential rivals. Yet again, the monopoly may buy up or 'tie' retailers and other distribution outlets to its products so that new producers will have to set up their own distribution facilities. The aim of all these strategies is to raise the costs of entry for newcomers to prohibitive levels.

7.2.3 Barriers to exit

A recently developed theory of industrial competition shifts the emphasis from barriers to entry into a monopolist's market towards **barriers to exit**. This apparently novel idea is found in the theory of **contestable markets** put forward most prominently by American economist, William Baumol, in the 1980s. Baumol argues that monopoly power in a market is not so much threatened by low costs of entry into the industry but by low, even zero, costs of leaving the industry. He gives the example of an airline with a present monopoly of a particular route. The airline operator may not be able to charge monopoly prices because of the continual threat of competition from other aircraft owners. Any attempt to raise the price above the competitive level and to make super-normal profits will immediately attract a new firm to fly over that route. Assuming there are no legal barriers to entry, such as the need to acquire a licence, the new firm's cost of entry is zero because it already has planes which it can divert from other routes. More important for Baumol is that, having made super-normal profits, even if only briefly, the raiding firm can then exit from the route at zero cost, simply by moving the planes elsewhere.

The point of this example is that the newcomer has no **sunk costs** which cannot be recovered on leaving the industry. The possibly high cost of investing in the plane is not relevant so long as it retains its market value and the cost can be recouped on leaving the industry. For Baumol, therefore, the threat of competition is a function of the level of sunk costs or the costs of exit. If these are very small even a monopoly will be forced to behave like a competitive firm and will earn only normal profits. We have what Baumol calls a 'contestable market'. If sunk costs are large, as they might be in, say, investing in a rig to produce oil, new firms will be deterred from entering. How important these ideas are to our understanding of the workings of actual markets and to the framing of industrial policy is being hotly debated among economists. The traditionalists believe that Baumol has simply redefined what they have long called a barrier to entry as a barrier to exit. Baumol disciples claim contestable markets as an exciting innovation in industrial economics. For the present, we reserve judgment.

7.2.4 Monopoly and welfare

Monopolies are often seen as imposing a cost on society by raising price and lowering output relative to the levels under perfect competition. We can see the basis for this conclusion in Figure 7.2. Assume first a perfectly competitive industry with an upward-sloping long run supply curve formed by adding the long run marginal cost curves of the firms in the industry (LRS = ΣLMC). In equilibrium the price is P_C and output Q_C given by the intersection of the supply and demand curves. We saw in Chapter 6 that this position at G can be viewed as giving an optimal allocation of resources.

FIGURE 7.2 **Welfare comparison of monopoly and perfect competition**

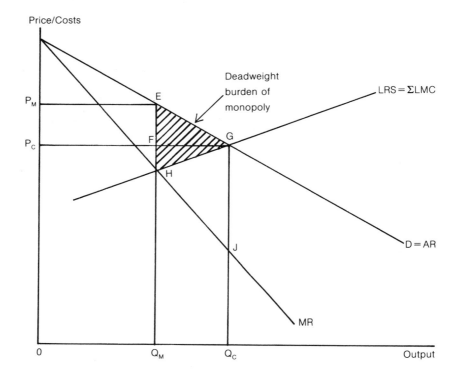

Then, suppose the industry is monopolised. The LRS curve is now the monopoly's long run marginal cost curve. The demand curve is the firm's average revenue curve but there is now a separate MR curve. As we have seen, the monopoly maximises profits where MR equals MC at the higher price P_M and a lower output Q_M. This is a sub-optimal position because at the output Q_M, the value of marginal utility at E on the demand curve is greater than the marginal cost at H. An extra unit of output will thus add more to utility than to costs. The distance EH measures the increase in net social benefit or welfare from an extra unit of output. As output is expanded the vertical gap between the demand and MC curve gets smaller, but there is a net benefit from raising output till we reach the optimum position at G. The shaded triangle EGH is therefore a measure of the social cost or loss of welfare from the monopolisation of the perfectly competitive industry. This cost is often referred to as the **deadweight burden** of monopoly.

We can make the same analysis of social costs in all industries, not just monopolies, where in equilibrium marginal benefits exceed marginal costs. Some economists have actually tried to calculate them for real-world economies and have come up with estimates of the costs ranging from as low as 1 per cent of national income to as high as 7 per cent. One reason for the large discrepancy is that the higher estimates try additionally to calculate the costs of erecting artificial barriers to entry, especially in wasteful ways such as creating unneeded spare capacity and advertising. The stifling of competition may therefore impose quite substantial costs on society, while the analysis ignores the super-normal profits earned by monopolies at the expense of consumers. The total burden on consumers from the higher monopoly price is measured by the loss of consumer surplus, equal in the diagram to the area P_MEGP_C (see Chapter 4). Part of the loss is redistributed to the owners of the monopoly in super-normal profit and the rest contributes to the deadweight social cost. The ability of monopolies to extract super-normal profits by raising prices might be regarded as an inequitable redistribution of income justifying action against abuse of monopoly power irrespective of the deadweight burden imposed.

However, the comparison of monopoly with perfect competition is unlikely to be a good guide to the framing of policy towards monopolies. The welfare conclusions suggest that there will be social gains from breaking up monopolies into a large number of small firms, but it is clear that in the majority of cases this is simply not a practical option. It is naive to think that big natural monopolies, like those in gas and telecommunications, can be broken up into smaller units without a significant increase in costs. If so, the social losses from the rise in costs could more than offset any gains from introduction of competition. Thus, in Figure 7.2, economies of scale under monopoly might lower the marginal cost curve so that it cuts the MR curve to the right of J. If so, it can be seen that the monopoly's equilibrium output will be higher and its price lower than under perfect competition.

The realistic option is to break up a monopoly into a few firms, that is, to create an oligopoly. There may still be losses of scale economies while, as we shall see in the next section, there is no guarantee that oligopoly will bring a move towards the optimum competitive position. Also, we cannot presume that fragmenting a monopoly brings gains in greater product innovation. While competing firms may have an incentive to innovate in order to make super-normal profits, at least in the short run, we have already seen that a monopoly may use heavy spending on R&D and product innovation to create barriers to entry. The comparison, moreover, assumes that the monopoly is a profit-maximiser, but we have noted that large companies in monopolistic positions may have alternative goals because of the **divorce between ownership and control**. The shareholders seek profits, but effective control is in the hands of directors and managers whose main interest is increasing their own remuneration and other rewards. These in turn may be a function of variables like the number of subordinate employees and the assets of the firm. Profits, especially when distributed to shareholders, may even be viewed as a cost by managers. The point is that we can't be sure what price, costs and output will be when the monopoly pursues other goals.

A related cost of monopoly may arise from a failure to maximise technical efficiency. When there are effective legal or natural barriers to entry, the absence of both actual and potential competition may lead to a lack of concern among managers and directors about minimising costs. For the sake of a quiet life they may collude in overstaffing and turn a blind eye to lax quality and financial control, to poor standards of customer service and to employees' long lunch breaks and unpunctuality. This excessive use of labour and other inputs or the failure to maximise both the quantity and quality of output from given inputs has been called **X-inefficiency** giving rise to **organisational slack**. Some economists believe this to be a more important source of social costs from monopoly than the allocative inefficiency discussed above. Any gains from economies of scale may be outweighed by the increased costs from X-inefficiency.

7.2.5 Price discrimination

A further qualification is that firms with monopoly power can often practise **price discrimination**, which we introduced in Chapter 4. We saw there that a firm might be able to increase its revenue and profits by taking advantage of consumer surplus which results from the willingness of consumers to pay more for the first units consumed of a good. Suppliers can gain either by varying the price to individual consumers, for example, by giving quantity discounts, or by charging different prices to different consumers, for example, by offering lower prices to old age pensioners or students. However, price discrimination of either kind is impossible if people who can buy at the lower price can freely resell it to others who are being charged higher prices. In some cases, especially with personal services, resale is ruled out or very difficult. A patient who has been charged a low price for an operation cannot resell it to another paying a higher price!

In other cases, suppliers will often attempt to prevent resale. Producers of personal computers, for example, offer discounts to students and teachers and try to stop resale (not always successfully) by restricting purchases to one per privileged customer and insisting on proof of the buyer's status. Much preferable for the supplier is for the government to make resale illegal. Gas and electricity companies, for instance, can prosecute customers who try to avoid the fixed charge by connecting their premises to their neighbour's supply and it is illegal to travel on the railway or by air with someone else's discounted ticket.

When resale can be prevented, price discrimination is likely to be profitable because of differences in the price elasticity of demand (PED) among consumers which reflect their willingness to pay. Because detailed price discrimination is costly to administer and enforce, producers usually practise it only among broad groups of consumers. Suppliers of computers, for example, have presumably deduced that educational users typically have a more elastic demand than business customers. So long as the marginal cost of the extra sales to students and lecturers is less than the price charged, the suppliers' profits are increased. When discrimination is possible, therefore, producers will gain by segmenting the market, charging lower prices where the PED is high and higher prices where the PED is low.

Price discrimination clearly leads to a loss of consumer surplus for those who have to pay higher prices and there is an overall social cost when the price is set above marginal cost. This is certainly true when the costs of supplying different consumers is the same. However, there are cases where apparent price discrimination may be justified on grounds of differing costs. For example, the railways and other transport suppliers commonly charge lower fares for off-peak and low season travel to **all** passengers. It is therefore arguable whether this represents price discrimination at all while it can be justified by the much lower marginal cost of providing services at off-peak times when the rail or other transport system is operating below capacity.

Finally, a case can be made for discrimination when the demand or AR curve lies below the AC curve. Charging a uniform price will clearly result in losses. But it is possible that total willingness to pay (the area beneath the demand curve) exceeds total cost for some range of outputs. Consumers therefore will benefit if the supplier is able to capture sufficient of the consumer surplus by price discrimination to cover costs, otherwise the product or service will not be offered. A doctor, for example, might have to give up his or her practice when charging uniform fees but might survive by extracting bigger fees from rich patients. All the patients, including the rich ones, are better off compared with the alternative of no doctor at all.

7.3 OLIGOPOLY

Oligopoly, an industry dominated by just a few producers, is found in many real-world markets. Examples are the steel, chemical and motor car industries, the distribution and marketing of oil, and, in Britain, banking and life insurance. Also in Britain there are only two major producers of washing powder or detergent, an example of **duopoly** which is a special case of oligopoly. In these industries, the number of producers is so small that each one, in deciding its own competitive behaviour, must take into account the possible reactions of each of the others. If, for example, there are four firms each with 25 per cent of the market, a change in output by any one will have a significant effect on total output and price. If one is considering a cut in price it must assess the likely response of each of the other three to estimate the effect on its profits. This **interdependence** of firms in oligopoly therefore gives an added dimension of uncertainty and risk to the firms' competitive strategies. Simply, they can never be sure how their rivals are going to behave.

7.3.1 Cartels

The uncertainty of oligopoly makes it difficult to reach general conclusions about the equilibrium price and output in oligopolistic industries. The actual outcome can range between the two extremes of **collusion** and **competition**. In order to avoid outright competition which may drive profits down to the normal level, firms in oligopoly have a strong incentive to collude with each other and to form cartels in which they agree price and total output and carve up the market among themselves. The cartel thus effectively becomes a monopoly. If we assume, reasonably, that the firms aim to maximise their joint profits, the analysis of profit-maximising monopoly in the previous section becomes relevant. Joint output will be set where MR equals MC and the firms together will make super-normal profits. Price will exceed MC so that the cartel imposes costs on society.

Despite the clear attractions of cartels to producers, there are a number of practical difficulties in forming and maintaining them. One obvious problem is that, with a few exceptions, formal cartels are illegal in most countries. Important cartels which are allowed and in fact are promoted by governments include IATA, the airline cartel discussed in Chapter 2, and the steel industry in the European Community. In these and other cases, governments have rightly or wrongly been persuaded that a cartel is necessary to protect profits and employment in their own national industries. More widely, although formal cartels are prohibited, it is difficult for governments to detect and prosecute informal collusion between producers. Even if a cartel is possible producers will find other obstacles in reaching agreement on price and output and then in enforcing the agreement.

Certain general considerations point to the main requirements for a successful cartel. Firstly, there is clearly more chance of agreeing on price and output the fewer the number of firms involved. Various attempts to form lasting cartels by producers of primary commodities, such as coffee and cocoa, have almost invariably foundered because of the large number of producing countries. This makes it difficult to agree on market shares or 'quotas' and costly to enforce and police any agreement, for example, to prevent individual producers exceeding their quotas. OPEC, by contrast, was highly successful in the 1970s, partly because of the relatively few big producing countries in the cartel. Secondly, the market demand for the product should have a low price elasticity. If demand is inelastic output need be restricted only by a relatively small amount to bring a proportionately large rise in price and revenue. Conversely when demand is elastic, a cartel is unlikely to be formed in the first place since a cut in output will lead to a fall in revenue. Profits, of course, may increase but the potential gains may be too small to offset the costs of forming and running the cartel itself.

A third condition is obviously that all major producers should be members of the cartel and a fourth that new entry into the industry should be difficult or costly. If a cartel succeeds in raising price and generating super-normal profits for its members, new producers will be attracted into the industry. Without legal or natural barriers to entry the cartel is likely to set up artificial barriers of the type discussed in the previous section, but the relative severity of the conditions necessary for a successful cartel suggests that most, if not all, are unlikely to survive without government legal backing.

7.3.2 The kinked demand curve

If cartels never get off the ground or break down firms in oligopoly must compete with each other. If the product is homogeneous price competition is the only option and we can expect the price to be driven down to the normal profit level of the marginal or highest-cost producer as in perfect competition. But with product differentiation the outcome is uncertain because of the interdependence of firms. This is illustrated by the **kinked demand curve model** described in Figure 7.3.

FIGURE 7.3 **The kinked demand curve model**

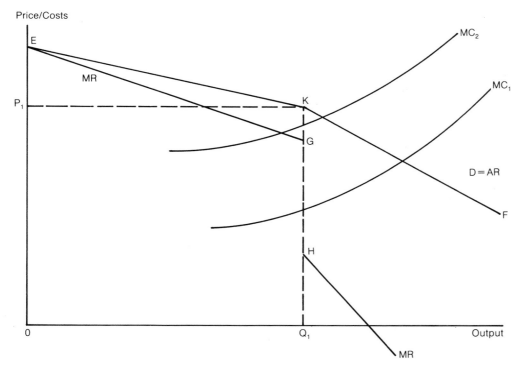

Suppose firm A in an oligopoly is considering altering its price. In the diagram, point K indicates the firm's current price, P_1, and output, Q_1; K must therefore be a point on the firm's demand curve. The remainder of the demand curve, however, is uncertain because the effect of a change in A's price on the quantity demanded of A's output depends on the reaction of other firms to the price change. For instance, A might predict that, if it raises its price, the others might well not follow suit in the hope of gaining market share at A's expense. For a price increase, therefore, A might expect a relatively large reduction in its sales—from K upwards it may perceive a relatively elastic demand curve like EK in the diagram. But if firm A reduces its price it may expect the others to make a corresponding price cut to prevent A gaining in market share. If so, the increase in sales will be proportionate to the rise in combined sales determined by the market demand curve. Demand will be less elastic for a price reduction than for a price increase—the perceived demand curve from K downwards might be like KF, less elastic than AK.

The demand curve as perceived by A is therefore EKF with a 'kink' at point K. We can then construct the related marginal revenue curve. This has two parts. First, there is EG which relates to the section EK on the demand curve. Since we have assumed EK is relatively elastic, MR is positive but falling along EG. However, the abrupt reduction in demand elasticity at K means that there is a correspondingly sudden drop in MR at the output Q_1. MR is given by point G for price increases but it slumps to H for price reductions. In the diagram, MR at H is shown as positive and then falls away to become negative. In short, the MR curve has a break or discontinuity in it, shown by the dotted line GH. If we now add in the MC curve, firm A will hold its price constant as long as the MC curve such as MC_1 passes through the discontinuity. If it is right about the other firms' reactions, A can only reduce its profits by a price change in either direction; it cannot increase them.

If the discontinuity in the MR curve is a large one, then, with a given demand curve, there may have to be a substantial change in A's costs to induce it to alter its price. The MC curve must rise above G to, say, MC_2 before A will raise price and to below H to bring a price reduction. The model may thus help to explain the relative stability of prices in some oligopoly situations—the uncertainty about competitors' reactions to price changes may lead firms to presume the worst outcome and to reluctance to engage in price competition. A big shift in costs or in demand may be necessary to induce one firm to take the initiative in raising or lowering price. Also, a price change might be seen as irreversible, at least within a given time span. Producers under oligopoly may therefore prefer to engage in forms of non-price competition such as advertising, since an increase in the advertising budget can quickly be reversed if it fails to have the desired impact on sales without the antagonism from customers which frequent price changes might arouse.

The kinked demand curve model, however, has severe limitations. In particular, it doesn't explain how the original price and output came about. The general theoretical problem with oligopolistic competition, particularly when there is product differentiation, is the indeterminacy of the equilibrium outcome from the virtually infinite range of competitive strategies and counter-strategies which the firms can follow. A large number of models have been devised which give us valuable insights into oligopoly behaviour but none allows us to make general predictions of price and output. The outcome may vary between the monopoly solution when a successful cartel is operated and one approximating to that under perfect or imperfect competition when the oligopolists engage in competition. Each real-world oligopoly therefore needs separate analysis.

SUMMARY

A profit-maximising monopoly will make super-normal profits so long as its AC curve lies below the demand or AR curve. These profits are dependent on the maintenance of effective barriers to entry of new firms. Barriers may be legal ones or may derive from economies of scale leading to the emergence of natural monopolies. Otherwise, the monopoly may have to rely on artificial deterrents to entry such as predatory pricing and creation of surplus capacity. Other things being equal, the equilibrium price and output of a profit-maximising monopoly is sub-optimal relative to perfect competition and imposes a deadweight burden on society, but the comparison with perfect competition may be unrealistic, especially if the monopoly is able to exploit scale economies not available to small competitive firms. The main feature of oligopoly is interdependence of firms illustrated by the kinked demand curve model. This and other models provide insights into oligopoly behaviour, but none can offer general predictions of price and output under oligopoly.

SELF-TEST QUESTIONS

1 **Referring to the diagram of a profit-maximising monopoly in Figure 7.1, which one of the following statements is wrong?**

(a) The monopolist can make super-normal profits so long as the demand curve lies above the AC curve at some output.

(b) The monopoly's maximum profit per unit of output is measured by the distance BE.

(c) The monopoly's optimum output will always be at a point like E on the demand curve where demand is relatively inelastic.

(d) If the firm had zero marginal cost its optimum output would be OF.

(e) If the AC curve shifts upwards to become tangent to the AR curve at E the firm will continue to produce OH but make only normal profits.

2 **Which one of the following statements is correct?**

(a) Legal barriers to entry are unimportant because the government always sets up regulatory bodies to prevent legal monopolies from charging excessive prices.

(b) A natural monopoly is one where there are economies of scale in producing natural products such as tin and coal.

(c) Predatory pricing and investment in surplus capacity are methods by which a monopolist may try to deter potential competitors.

(d) A contestable market is one in which entry costs are small but sunk costs are high.

(e) A firm with a legal monopoly on a bus route cannot make super-normal profits because of the threat of competition.

3 **Referring to the comparison of monopoly and perfect competition in Figure 7.2, which one of the following statements is correct?**

(a) The marginal social benefit of an expansion of the monopoly's output from Q_M is measured by the distance EH.

(b) The deadweight burden of monopoly is

shown by the increase in marginal cost from H to G.

(c) The social cost of monopoly measured by the triangle EGH is equivalent to the monopoly's super-normal profit.

(d) The monopoly can no longer make super-normal profits if economies of scale lower its MC curve to cut the MR curve at J.

(e) The social cost of monopoly arises from a transfer of income equal to triangle EFG from consumers to the monopolist.

4 **Which one of the following statements is correct?**

(a) Breaking up natural monopolies into smaller competing firms will bring a more efficient allocation of resources.

(b) Divorce between ownership and control in large firms ensures that they operate with maximum efficiency.

(c) Price discrimination is possible so long as consumers can resell at higher prices.

(d) The railways profit from charging lower prices to pensioners because their demand is less elastic than that of other passengers.

(e) Price discrimination may help a monopoly to stay in business when charging a uniform price results in losses.

5 **Referring to the kinked demand curve model in Figure 7.3, which one of the following statements is wrong?**

(a) The oligopolist believes that a rise in price above K will bring a large relative fall in sales.

(b) The MR curve has a discontinuity because the demand curve from K downwards is less elastic than from K upwards.

(c) So long as the MC curve lies below K the firm will hold price constant.

(d) A shift of the MC curve to MC_2 will induce the firm to raise its price.

(e) If firm A cuts price below K and firm B follows suit, A's sales will rise broadly in proportion to the increase in quantity demanded in the market.

EXERCISE

'Monopoly results in a misallocation of resources compared with competition. Monopolies should therefore be broken up'. Do you agree? Give your reasons.

Answers on page 249.

Factor markets and income distribution

We are concerned here with the way in which the national income is distributed between households in a market economy. Since income largely derives from selling the services of factors of production owned by a household, we need to consider the determination of factor prices such as wages, rent, interest and profits in factor markets. Although we can use the basic analytical tools of supply and demand, we find that both the supply of and demand for factor services have special characteristics. Since the majority of households derive most of their income from selling labour on the market we pay particular attention to the labour market and examine how far imperfections in the market can explain the differences in people's earnings.

8.1   INTRODUCTION

A major dimension of the general problem of resource allocation in any economy is the way in which the national income is distributed between households—the question of who gets what is produced. In a centrally planned economy, the issue is resolved by the government laying down criteria for income distribution. It might decide, for example, that as nearly as possible all households should have the same income with adjustments for the size of the household, the number of elderly dependants and children, and for people with special needs such as the sick and disabled. In this case, the guiding principle would be one of **equity**—the notion that the fairest way to divide income is to give everyone an equal share while recognising that some people have extra needs.

While equity as a basis for income distribution is no doubt appealing to many people, any government which relied on it entirely would almost certainly encounter problems in having goods and services produced efficiently or even at all. If all individuals could rely on receiving the same income as everyone else, irrespective of their contribution to producing that income, there would clearly be little incentive to work. 'Work' which people like doing, like composing and playing music, would still be carried out but many jobs which involve disutility for the worker might not be unless people were given incentives to do them in the form of wages. Thus, even in socialist economies such as that of the Soviet Union, the need for incentives to work is recognised with wages and with higher rates of pay for the more irksome jobs or for those requiring higher skills and greater responsibility.

Income distribution therefore raises a fundamental political issue of **equity versus efficiency**. Equity may only be achieved at the expense of efficiency; maximum efficiency at the sacrifice of equity. Inevitably, there has to be a compromise and people's political views decide which principle dominates over the other. There is a normative question here which goes beyond the scope of this book. We focus instead on the explanation of the distribution of income—a positive rather than normative question. Also, we concentrate on income distribution in a predominantly market economy in which households derive their income from selling the services of the factors of production which they own but before we do so we should be clear what we mean by 'income' and its relation to wealth.

8.1.1   Income and wealth

Income is received by households as a **flow** over time, so much a week or month or year. If we ignore **transfer payments** (transfers of income, particularly those such as pensions paid by the government) a household's income derives from its **wealth.** Wealth is measured at a point in time as the value of the household's **stock** of assets. These will clearly include all the various kinds of **financial assets** owned by the household such as deposits in banks, building societies and other institutions, equity shares in companies, interest-bearing bonds, and so on. All these assets constitute claims to a stream of income in the form of interest and dividends. In turn, households own property—land, buildings, houses. They may derive an income in rent from letting it or, more likely, they receive a notional rental income from living in the houses which they own. Ownership of durable goods like cars and washing machines generates a similar notional return equal to the rental value of the goods.

Most important for the majority of households is their income in wages and salaries for selling their labour services on the market. The capitalised value of the future stream of labour incomes constitutes the household's **human capital.** (The notion of capitalising income streams is taken up in Chapter 13.) The value of human capital, as we have seen, can be increased by investment in education and training and for most households human capital or labour power is the most important constituent of its total wealth. It is different from other types of wealth in that, with the almost universal abolition of slavery, human capital cannot usually be bought and sold as an asset (although there are exceptions such as the sale of footballers between clubs). Normally, the individual can only sell labour, the services of human capital, in return for a wage or salary.

If income derives from wealth, then the ultimate determinant of income distribution is the distribution of wealth between households. We shall take wealth distribution as given and focus on the determination of the prices of factors. Obviously, given the quantities of the different factors such as labour, land and capital, which the household has to sell, its income depends on the prices it can obtain for them—the level of wages, rent, interest and profits. In examining how factor prices are determined in markets we can apply the same analytical tools of supply and demand as in the study of other markets. We find though that factor markets have some special characteristics which need separate attention.

8.2 THE DEMAND FOR FACTORS

Let's first consider the demand for factors of production in general. The services of factors are mostly purchased not for their own sake but for their contribution to the production of final goods and services. The demand for labour, land and capital is a **derived demand.** Firms hire them to assist in production of goods which they sell and the quantity of factor services demanded is thus primarily a function of the factor's contribution to the revenue of firms. If firms aim to maximise profits then the optimum level of employment of labour or any other factor is found by equating the extra revenue obtained by employing one more unit with the price of the factor. This is the basis of the **marginal productivity theory** of demand for factors.

To understand this we return to the product curves that we drew up in Chapter 5 in order to construct a firm's short run cost curves. We assumed that labour was the variable factor and that, as it was applied in increasing amounts to the fixed factor (capital) diminishing returns eventually set in to produce a decreasing marginal physical product of labour (MPP_L). The MPP_L, remember, is the addition to output from employing one more unit of labour:

$$MPP_L = \frac{\Delta Q}{\Delta L}$$

The value of the MPP_L is determined by the price of the final product. If our firm producing table tennis bats can sell them for £2 each and the MPP_L is 10, the value of the MPP_L to the firm is clearly £20. This addition to the revenue of the firm from employing one more unit of labour is called the **marginal revenue product** (MRP) of labour. It is found quite simply by multiplying the MPP_L by the marginal revenue, in this case, the price of the product (P):

$$MRP_L = MPP_L.P$$

Similarly, APP_L is the output per worker (Q/L) and the average revenue product (ARP), the revenue produced per worker, equals the APP_L times P:

$$ARP_L = APP_L.P$$

Thus we can very easily transform the physical product curves we drew up in Chapter 5 into revenue product curves by multiplying MPP_L and APP_L at each employment level by the price of the product. If the product price is given we end up with identical curves; all that changes is that we now measure the money value of the product on the vertical axis instead of the physical product itself. This is done in Figure 8.1.

FIGURE 8.1 **The revenue product of labour**

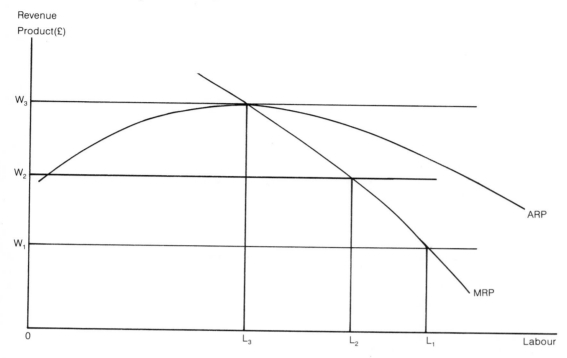

The firm's demand curve for labour is given by the MRP curve where it lies below the ARP curve. For example, if the wage is W_1, it pays the firm to employ another worker so long as the addition to revenue (the MRP) is greater than the marginal cost of labour which is equal to the wage. Since MRP is greater than W_1 up to a level of employment of L_1 and is less for employment beyond L_1, the optimum level which maximises profits must be L_1. If the wage rises to W_2 the optimum employment level is L_2. In short, the firm, in order to maximise profits, must employ labour to the point where the wage equals the MRP of labour. The MRP curve therefore constitutes the firm's demand curve for labour. However, if the wage rises above W_3, equal to ARP at its maximum, the average revenue earned by each worker is less than the wage or average cost of each worker. The firm cannot cover its labour costs and will go out of business. This is the same as saying that if the firm cannot cover its variable costs it should close down even in the short run (see Chapter 5). If the wage rises above W_3 therefore the firm's demand for labour is zero and it is only that part of the MRP curve below the ARP curve which is relevant.

For a profit-maximising firm, the optimum employment of every factor, not just labour, is found where the MRP of the factor is equal to its marginal cost. Thus, physical capital, such as machines and other fixed assets, should be installed to the point where the percentage rate of return on the last machine is equal to the marginal cost of the last unit of investment which is measured by the interest rate paid by the firm on loans or other finance for its investment (this will be taken up again in Chapter 13). A farmer should use fertiliser until the extra revenue from using one more sack equals the price (the marginal cost) of a sack of fertiliser. The principle then is a general one.

We have assumed that the price of the firm's product remains constant as the firm varies its demand for labour with changes in the wage. This is reasonable if only the one firm adjusts its employment and output after, say, a rise in the wage from W_1 to W_2. But if all firms producing table tennis bats respond in the same way to an increase in labour costs by cutting employment from L_1 to L_2 there will be a corresponding shift to the left of the supply curve for bats. Depending on the elasticity of demand for bats, the price of bats will rise and both the ARP and the MRP curves will shift upwards in proportion to the higher price of the product. The MRP or demand curve for labour shifts up and to the right because of the rise in the price of bats. This increase in the demand for labour (a shift to the right of the MRP curve) will partly offset the fall in employment from the movement up and along the original MRP curve. As a result, the industry's demand curve for labour will be less elastic than the MRP curve of the individual firm drawn up on the assumption of a constant product price.

8.2.1 Elasticity of demand for factors

There are in fact several general influences on the price elasticity of demand (PED) for factors of production. **The demand for any factor will be more elastic**:

1   **the more elastic the demand for the product.** Thus, suppose the demand for table tennis bats is perfectly elastic. When wages rise, the supply curve for bats shifts to the left but the price of bats remains the same. The firm's MRP curve is therefore unaffected and employment is cut as shown in Figure 8.1. At the other extreme, if the demand for bats were perfectly inelastic the producers could pass on the whole of the increase in wage costs in a higher product price. The MRP curve would shift up and to the right to keep employment constant at the higher wage and the demand for labour would be perfectly inelastic.

2   **the easier it is to substitute other factors.** Just as the demand for goods is more elastic the greater the availability of substitutes, so will be the demand for factors. For example, if machines can easily be substituted for labour, a rise in wages may bring a relatively large fall in employment.

3   **the more important the factor's contribution to the firm's total costs.** This is similar to the income effect of a change in the price of a good. If wages account for most of the cost of producing bats a wage rise of 10 per cent will have a bigger effect on the price of bats than a 10 per cent increase in the price, say, of materials. Other things being equal, the demand for labour will therefore be more elastic than the demand for materials. (Note though that there is a theoretical exception where the reverse is true, when labour is a kind of 'inferior factor' analogous to an inferior good in the markets for final products.)

4   **the more elastic the supply of substitute factors.** As firms substitute machines for labour after a rise in wages the increase in demand for machines will push up their price. This discourages substitution and checks the fall in demand for labour, but the size of the effect depends on the elasticity of supply of machines. If supply were perfectly elastic, machine prices would stay constant and the effect would be zero.

8.3   THE SUPPLY OF FACTORS

If all factor markets were free and perfectly competitive and all the owners of factors aimed at maximising the rewards from selling factor services, then the quantities of factors supplied in different employments would be related to the relative returns offered. We would always tend to move towards a general equilibrium position in which the price of any factor of a given type and quality would be the same in all employments. Suppose, for example, that accountants are a homogeneous group of labour, each one with exactly the same skills and productivity as every other. Imagine also that they are all indifferent about where and for whom they work and that there are no costs in moving from one employment to another—accountants are **perfectly mobile**. Then, if one employing firm needed to take on more accountants it would bid up salaries to attract some from other employers. A temporary salary differential would result but it would quickly be eliminated since other firms would have to bring their salaries into line to retain their own accountants. In other words, competition will ensure uniform wages not just for accountants but for all homogeneous labour groups. The same would apply to land and capital—land of the same quality would fetch the same price and capital would earn the same returns wherever it was employed.

8.3.1   Equal net advantage

In practice, though, uniform factor prices clearly do not prevail and there are various reasons for this, often related to imperfections in factor markets. But, even with perfect mobility and homogeneity of factors, we would still find differences in earnings of factors which are explained by **the principle of equal net advantage**. The rewards from employment are not measured in monetary terms alone.

Accountants, for instance, can take a variety of jobs each with **non-monetary advantages and disadvantages**. Setting up in private practice is more risky than taking salaried employment in, say, the civil service and we might expect the monetary rewards to reflect this. An accountant who takes a lecturing job in a polytechnic trades off the likely lower earnings against the non-monetary advantages of long vacations and freedom to do research. The same goes for all other occupations. Jobs with net advantages like security, good pension arrangements and perks (free meals, company cars and other benefits in kind) will tend to have offsetting lower monetary rewards. Conversely, those with disadvantages—working unsocial hours, short holidays, work involving accident or health risks—will tend to attract higher monetary returns.

Thus, in free and competitive factor markets the net advantages of different occupations would be equalised. All labour of the same kind would receive the same rewards when these are adjusted for the market valuation of the non-monetary advantages and disadvantages of different occupations. The monetary returns to capital would vary in the same way; lenders expect to earn higher returns on risky investments than on safe ones. The level of returns will differ from industry to industry depending largely on the degree of risk perceived by investors. Similarly, land and property prices will reflect the relative advantages of different locations—house prices and rents are higher in areas well served by roads and public transport and with a more pleasant environment.

8.3.2   Earnings differentials

Equal net advantage may explain some of the observed differences in rewards to factors but by no means all of them. With labour in particular we find sometimes large earnings **differentials** which cannot be explained simply by non-monetary advantages and disadvantages. Some of these are explained by non-economic factors. The income of, say, a head of state or an ambassador is determined politically to reflect their status and hardly at all by supply and demand. This applies also, though in less degree, to the pay of top civil servants, judges, chief executives of large companies, admirals, generals and so on. But as we move down the status ladder we find that earnings are more and more influenced, if not determined, by the supply and demand for labour. Yet there are still large differentials in the earnings of people with similar skills, experience and qualifications. An electrician lucky enough to have a job in a TV company in Britain may earn several times more for less work than another in the building industry. A highly-qualified maths teacher may earn a fraction of the rewards of a young stock market trader with only a basic education. In a market economy this kind of differential can be explained by **barriers to mobility** which prevent people moving into occupations earning the highest returns.

BARRIERS TO MOBILITY

Keeping the focus on labour, there is a wide range of obstacles to the movement of people into higher earning jobs:

1   **Non-competing groups** Labour is not a homogeneous factor. People partly inherit their physical and mental make-up and, as we have seen, they develop their particular abilities, skills and talents through their upbringing, education, training and experience. The labour market is therefore made up of a large number of overlapping sub-markets for manual workers, school teachers, accountants, lawyers, plumbers and so on. In large degree, people compete for jobs in just one or a few closely related sub-markets—labour supply is divided into largely **non-competing groups**. The limited supply of certain types of labour, say, tax advisers, in relation to demand may push up their earnings relative to other groups who, in the short run at least, cannot take advantage of the higher pay because of their lack of the necessary expertise in taxation. Some individuals—musicians, sports personalities, TV chat-show hosts, top business managers—may have unique talents in high demand which enable them to earn very high incomes. Each constitutes a non-competing group of one!

2   **Human capital** Acquisition of human capital by education and training will normally put people into a new non-competing group or groups with higher potential earnings. That, of course, is one of the basic motives for engaging in training with, very often, the sacrifice of current earnings. Higher earnings of tax experts may induce accountants to take courses in taxation. The rational accountant will weigh up the cost in terms of the loss of current income

D

and the course fees against the discounted value of the future stream of increased earnings. In the long run, the non-competing groups formed by investment in human capital do not conflict with the principle of equal net advantage. Any differential earnings which remain after accountants have trained as tax advisers will simply reflect the compensation required for the cost of the extra training. In long-run equilibrium, the higher lifetime income of people in any occupation requiring training such as accountants, doctors, engineers and so on represents the minimum or normal return necessary for people to make the initial investment in human capital.

3   **Restrictions on entry** In many occupations, trade unions and professional bodies restrict the supply of labour and force up the earnings of their members. In Britain, for instance, unions in some industries have been able to operate 'closed shops' so that all the workers in a plant or firm must be union members. Legislation in the 1980s substantially curbed the ability of unions to regulate the supply of labour in this and other ways but unions are still strong in some sectors of industry and are often able to push wages up above the competitive level. Moreover, restrictions on entry remain prevalent in the professions. This can sometimes be justified by the need to maintain minimum standards (that's why you have to pass exams to become an accountant) but other restrictive practices, such as the split between solicitors and barristers in the legal profession, are less easy to defend.

4   **Geographical barriers** Moving from one part of the country with unemployment and low pay to another where there are jobs and higher earnings may involve substantial costs—travel, renting temporary accommodation while looking for a job, expenses in buying and selling houses, and so on. These costs may result in regional pay differentials while workers in any case may be reluctant to leave places in which they have family and friends or children at school. These barriers will be still more pronounced when pay differentials exist internationally. People in low-wage countries wishing to emigrate usually have higher costs than those moving domestically but have to contend also with language and cultural barriers. Even then, immigration controls in the rich countries may be an insurmountable barrier resulting in the maintenance of sometimes huge income differentials internationally.

5   **Discrimination** Discrimination against particular social groups on grounds of race, colour, sex, class and religion can be a potent source of pay differentials. It may be difficult to enter certain professions such as medicine without the 'right' social background and education. In Britain there is still more than a vestige of the notion that certain jobs, like nursing and teaching, are 'women's jobs' and becoming a doctor or a judge is largely reserved for men.

8.3.3   Economic rent

We have seen that when firms earn super-normal profits they are earning more than the minimum necessary for the owners to retain their capital in the business. The owners therefore are receiving a **surplus** or what economists have come to call **economic rent**. Normally, of course, we think of rent as the return to owners of land and property. The use of the word in the broader sense of surplus earnings of any factor of production evolved from the analysis of land rents by the English economist David Ricardo (1772–1823). He treated land as in perfectly inelastic supply with the result that rent or the price of land was determined purely by the demand for it. Thus, in Figure 8.2, when the demand curve shifts up and to the right the only effect can be to increase rent. Landowners therefore obtain a proportional rise in their property income measured by the rectangle beneath the demand curve. Moreover, if landowners are prepared to bring land into productive use for any rent, however small, the whole of their rental income is an unearned surplus. A rise in rent has no economic function in bringing more factors into use; it simply redistributes income to landowners.

The same analysis can be applied to any factor in less than perfectly elastic supply. In the extreme case, supply may be virtually perfectly inelastic as in Figure 8.2. Successful rock groups, singers, TV stars, footballers and snooker players all constitute their own non-competing group and the supply of their services is highly inelastic. The greater the demand for their services the higher their earnings, which are nearly all in the nature of a surplus or rent. Owners of tourist attractions like the Eiffel Tower or the Grand Canyon again receive economic rent.

The less extreme case is where the supply curve of the factor is upward-sloping. Thus, suppose Figure 8.3 represents the supply and demand curves for tax advisers. G is the minimum wage, say, £12,000 a year, necessary to induce the first person to train as a tax adviser. Each successive entrant

FIGURE 8.2 **Rent as a surplus**

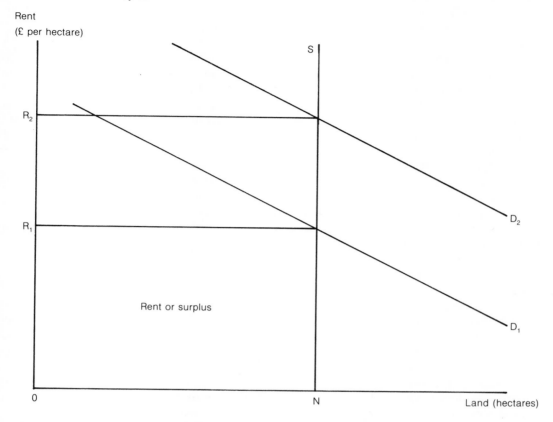

requires a higher minimum—the second might want £12,010, the third £12,020 and so on. This minimum payment necessary to attract people into the profession is exactly analogous to normal profits. When the concept is applied to factors generally we call it the factor's **transfer earnings**—the minimum necessary to attract the factor into and to keep it in the particular occupation. In the diagram the equilibrium wage of tax advisers is W. If W equals £30,000, all the tax advisers with transfer earnings less than £30,000 are earning a surplus or rent. The first to enter needed only £12,000 and thus earns a surplus of £18,000. The last to enter—the marginal

FIGURE 8.3 **Transfer earnings and economic rent**

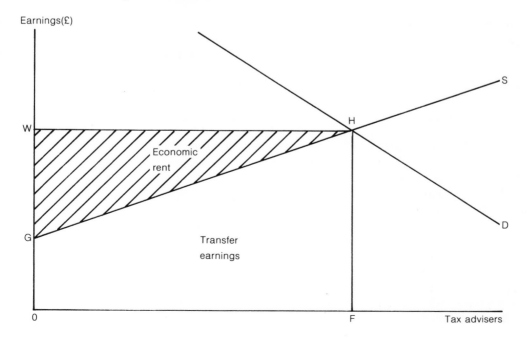

entrant—has transfer earnings of just £30,000 and therefore earns zero rent. The total earnings of tax advisers are measured by the rectangle OWHF. This is divided between transfer earnings of OGHF (the area beneath the supply curve) and economic rent equal to the triangle GWH.

The rent element of total earnings will be greater the less elastic is the supply curve. Since supply is usually less elastic in the short run than in the long run it is possible to have substantial short run rent which shrinks in the long run. For example, suppose the demand curve for tax advisers shifted to the right. The short run supply of trained tax experts is likely to be highly inelastic and their wage will rise steeply. This induces more people to invest in training; as they come into the profession the wage drops back and the rent element is reduced. These short run rents are referred to as **quasi-rents**.

It should be stressed that the notion of rent as a surplus is generally applicable. Super-normal profits are a rent; under competition only intramarginal firms with lower costs can earn permanent rents and short run quasi-rents are competed away as new firms are attracted into the industry. Rents earned by a monopoly or by people in occupations with restricted entry can be maintained by entry barriers. Since the rent component in any factor's earnings serves no economic function it is often argued that rent can be heavily taxed without affecting the supply of factors. That may be so but, except in the more obvious cases, it is difficult in practice to separate the rent element from transfer earnings for most factors.

8.4   WAGES

Much of our general discussion of factor supply and demand has been in terms of labour and the price of labour, wages. In large degree, the labour market as a whole and the sub-markets for non-competing groups can be analysed with the ordinary tools of supply and demand, but the labour market is clearly far from competitive. There are imperfections because of the various barriers to mobility already discussed and because of trade unions which are able to exert varying degrees of monopoly power in the supply of labour. Unions may contribute to relative inflexibility of wages after changes in the demand for and supply of labour. If labour demand falls, for example, and workers, both unionised and non-unionised, resist the wage reductions needed to restore equilibrium, unemployment may result. This possibility and the whole question of wage rigidity is taken up in later chapters in discussing the causes of general unemployment.

8.4.1   Minimum wages

The markets for many groups of labour are highly competitive, especially in private sector industries with only a low degree of unionisation, such as agriculture, retail distribution, hotels and catering, the construction industry. If wages are being held up above their equilibrium level in the unionised sector the excess supply of workers will be forced to look for jobs in the competitive non-union sector. The supply curve of, say, cleaners in hotels is pushed to the right and their wages are depressed. Large parts of the non-unionised labour market, especially for unskilled and semi-skilled workers, are characterised as a result by very low wages which have led in many countries to **minimum wage legislation**.

The effects of minimum wages can be examined with the analysis of minimum price controls in Chapter 2. If the minimum wage for cleaners is fixed above the market-clearing level (there is no point in fixing it below) an excess supply of cleaners will emerge; more people will want to work as cleaners at the higher wage than employers are willing to hire. It is debatable therefore whether a minimum wage solves the problem of low pay. Workers who keep their jobs are certainly better off. Those who don't either become unemployed or are forced to take other jobs, say, as domestic cleaners where wages are not controlled. But, of course, they now add to the supply of domestic cleaners and depress their wages. Either way, they end up worse off than they were without the 'protection' of the minimum wage. This might also lead to a kind of black market in labour. Employers in hotels have an incentive to avoid the minimum wage while workers threatened with losing their jobs may be willing to collude with employers by accepting wages below the legal level. Payments are then usually made in cash to avoid detection by the tax authorities. These transactions form part of the **black economy** (see Chapter 11); workers might actually be better off by avoiding tax and other deductions but they may lose their rights to welfare and other benefits such as compensation for accidents at work.

8.4.2 Collective bargaining

In many industries wages are determined by **collective bargaining** between trade unions on the one side and employers on the other. Here, a number of different outcomes is possible, depending in large degree on the relative bargaining strengths of the two sides. Thus, assume first that the union is able to operate a closed shop and has a virtual monopoly in the supply of labour. Employers on the other hand are numerous and badly organised so that there is effectively a competitive demand curve for labour. The position can be seen in Figure 8.4. Without the union the market-clearing wage would be W_1. The union though can behave in some respects like a monopolist in being able to regulate the supply of labour to push the wage up, for instance, to W_2.

FIGURE 8.4 **Wage determination with a trade union**

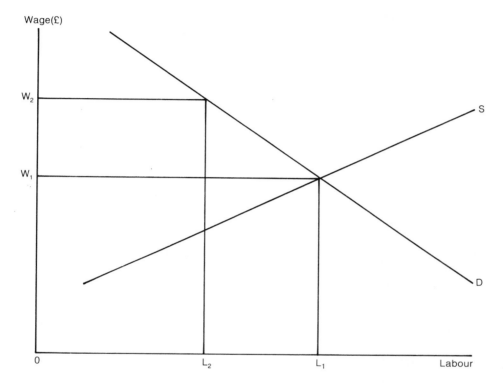

However, we can't predict how far the union will force up wages. If it negotiates a wage of W_2, the supply of labour effectively becomes perfectly elastic at that wage and employers will reduce employment from L_1 to L_2. The wage rise is won at the cost of some workers losing their jobs and the union losing members. For any given wage rise the reduction in employment is greater the more elastic is demand for labour. We discussed above the determinants of elasticity of demand for factors and they can be applied here. The general point is that the union has less of a problem in trading off higher wages against unemployment the less elastic is the demand for labour. Even so, a downward-sloping demand curve for labour can be an effective constraint on the union's ability and willingness to raise wages.

Suppose we now go to the other extreme where the unions are weak and disorganised but the employers are well organised so that they are effectively a **buyers' cartel** or **monopsony** (from the Greek for 'one buyer'). The situation is shown in Figure 8.5. The supply curve represents for the employers the wage or average cost per worker at each level of employment. If it is upward-sloping, however, the marginal cost of labour is greater than the average wage since, in order to attract more workers, employers will have to pay a higher wage not just to the extra ones employed but to all the existing workers as well. The marginal cost of labour is the increase in the total wage bill from employing one more worker and that will increase faster than the wage or average cost. This is shown by the curve for the marginal cost of labour drawn above the supply or average cost curve.

W_1 is the wage in a competitive market but with the formation of the employer's monopsony wages are likely to fall. This is because the optimum level of employment for the employers is L_2, where the marginal cost of labour (MCL) is just equal to the MRP of labour (which is, remember,

FIGURE 8.5 **Wage determination under monopsony**

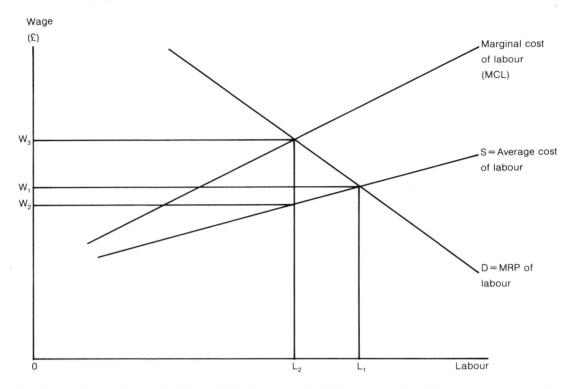

given by the demand curve for labour). Each extra unit of labour up to L_2 adds more to revenue than to costs because MRP is greater than the MC of labour. Beyond L_2 the cost of extra labour rises faster than revenue so that L_2 is the most profitable level of employment. But to hire that many workers the employers only have to pay a wage of W_2 as given by the supply curve. Under monopsony therefore the wage is likely to be pushed down below the competitive level.

Finally, if we now imagine we have a monopoly union bargaining with a monopsony employers' association, the solution becomes indeterminate. If we start with the monopsony position in Figure 8.5 and a union is then formed, the union may now be able to negotiate a wage up to W_3 without reducing employment in the industry. Alternatively, it could push the wage back to the competitive level, W_1, and increase employment compared with the monopsony position. The overall conclusion is that, in the presence of unions and employers' associations, it is impossible to predict either wage or employment levels in different industries and occupations. Certainly, a union is likely to raise wages above competitive or monopsony levels but by how much depends on the union's own goals and on factors like the elasticity of demand for labour which influence the union's bargaining power.

Note that we have assumed that the demand curve for labour remains unchanged when a union is formed. In practice, unions may influence labour productivity and shift the demand curve. If unions insist on restrictive practices, productivity may be lowered. But, equally well, negotiation by unions of better working conditions, training schemes, and so on may raise productivity and shift the demand curve upwards and to the right to the benefit of both employers and workers.

8.4.3 The supply of labour

A comment should be made about the supply curve for labour. We have assumed so far that the supply curve is upward-sloping. That may be reasonable for the supply of workers to particular industries and occupations—higher wages have to be paid to attract workers from alternative employment and to induce them to retrain or move home. In the economy at large we might also expect a general increase in real wages to increase the **participation rate**—the percentage of the potential working population who are willing to become active members of the labour force and to accept jobs. But, for individual workers, a rise in wages could quite plausibly reduce their willingness to work, because a wage rise has income and substitution effects of the kind discussed in Chapter 4.

For example, suppose my wage rate goes up from £10 to £20 an hour and at the old wage I worked for 10 hours a day leaving, say, 5 hours a day for leisure. My income was therefore £100 a day which I could spend on goods and services. But with the wage rise I can now have the same income from working only 5 hours and can take another 5 hours of leisure. What I do depends on my relative marginal valuation of leisure and other goods. The opportunity cost of leisure has doubled and the pure substitution effect will cause me to work harder and to take less leisure. But if leisure is a normal good (and there is no reason to suppose it isn't) the income effect works in the opposite direction. If the income effect is more powerful than the substitution effect I end up working less after a rise in the wage rate. A rise in wages has a disincentive effect!

This means that the supply curve of labour for an individual could be negatively sloped or **backward-sloping**. In turn, this could dominate increases in the participation rate after a rise in wages to produce a backward-sloping aggregate supply curve. The possibility needs to be considered by governments when they make changes in income tax rates or unemployment benefits. The effects on work incentives could turn out to be quite different from what was expected. This is discussed further in Chapter 17.

8.5 INTEREST AND PROFITS

8.5.1 Interest rates

We shall comment only briefly on interest rates since they are dealt with more fully in Chapter 15. Interest rates are essentially the reward for saving and lending money, that is, for deferring present consumption. Rates vary quite significantly depending on the term and riskiness of the loan. Normally, we expect interest rates to rise the longer the term of the loan since lenders will usually want a higher return for committing their funds for longer periods. But there are situations, when interest rates generally are expected to fall in the future, in which long-term rates may temporarily fall below short-term rates. Also, lenders such as banks will charge higher interest rates to, say, personal borrowers where they see a greater risk of default on the loan.

Although interest rates differ, economists, as we shall see, often refer to '**the** rate of interest' to mean the average or general level of interest rates. An important point here is that this normally means the **real** rather than the **nominal** interest rate. If you are charged a nominal rate of 15 per cent on a loan to be repaid after one year but there is 10 per cent inflation over the year, the real value of the amount to be paid back will have dropped by 10 per cent. The lender effectively has received only 5 per cent in real interest. The real interest rate therefore can be found approximately by deducting the inflation rate from the nominal interest rate. The real rate of interest in the economy is determined, on the one hand, by the supply of funds from savings and, on the other, by the demand for funds to finance real investment and other spending on goods and services by firms, households and the government. However, another view of the determination of the rate of interest—by the supply of and demand for money—is dealt with in Chapter 15.

8.5.2 Profits

We have already seen that profits can be regarded as the reward to the owners of a business for their 'enterprise' or for putting their financial capital at risk. Normal profits, remember, are treated as a necessary opportunity cost for a business and it is only super-normal profits or rent which constitute **pure profit**. The economist's concept of profit may differ quite sharply therefore from the accountant's, particularly when calculating a company's tax liability. The tax inspector will probably not be amused if you report a zero profit because you have treated the normal profits made as part of the firm's costs.

SUMMARY

Factor markets require separate analysis because of the special characteristics of the demand for and supply of factor services. The demand for these services is derived from the demand for final products. For any one factor the most profitable level of employment is found where its price is equal to marginal revenue product. In free and competitive markets, factors will move to their most profitable employments and equalise returns in terms of net advantage. Differences in rewards in different employments are explained largely by barriers to mobility of factors while factor owners normally earn at least part of their rewards as a surplus or rent. Wages in competitive labour markets may be depressed by high wages in unionised markets. Legal minimum wages will help only those who retain their jobs. Others may become unemployed or be forced to accept even lower wages or to take jobs in the black economy. Unions are likely to be able to raise wages for their members but at the possible cost of a drop in employment. The outcome of collective wage bargaining is indeterminate since it depends on the relative strength of unions and employers.

SELF-TEST QUESTIONS

1   Which of the following best describes how a profit-maximising firm determines the level of employment of labour in a competitive market?

(a)   Workers are hired until the revenue per worker is at its maximum.

(b)   The firm increases employment to the point where the MRP is at its maximum.

(c)   Employment is increased to the point where total revenue is maximised.

(d)   More workers are hired until the revenue produced by the last one is equal to the average revenue product of labour.

(e)   Workers are employed to the point where the extra revenue from employing one more is equal to the extra cost of employing one more.

2   Which of the following best describes or illustrates the principle of equal net advantage?

(a)   The market for accountants is in equilibrium when all accountants have the same earnings.

(b)   Doctors earn more than nurses because of restrictions on the numbers entering medical schools.

(c)   An economics lecturer who values long summer holidays rejects the offer of a much higher paid job with a stockbroker.

(d)   Printers on a newspaper negotiate the same salaries and perks as journalists.

(e)   Equal opportunities legislation lays down that women should be paid the same as men for equal work.

3   The demand for labour will be less elastic:

(a)   the easier it is to substitute machines for labour.

(b)   the easier it is for producers to pass on an increase in labour costs in a higher product price.

(c)   the greater the share of labour costs in total costs.

(d)   the more elastic is the supply of machines.

(e)   the less elastic is the supply of labour.

4   Which of the following statements is wrong?

(a)   Most of the pay of unskilled manual workers consists of transfer earnings.

(b)   When land is in perfectly inelastic supply the return to landowners will consist entirely of economic rent.

(c)   The more elastic the supply of a factor the greater is the element of transfer earnings in the returns of the factor.

(d)   Minimum wage regulation is designed to increase the earnings of low-paid workers by fixing the minimum wage above the market-clearing level.

(e)   The more elastic the demand for labour the less is the constraint on unions' ability to raise wages without reducing employment.

5   Which one of the following statements is correct?

(a)   The supply of labour becomes perfectly inelastic at the wage agreed in collective bargaining.

(b)   For a monopsony buyer of labour the marginal cost of labour is less than the wage.

(c)   In bargaining between a monopoly union and a monopsony employer the wage is invariably settled at the competitive level.

(d)   A wage rise will lead to a reduction in hours worked if leisure is an inferior good.

(e)   The real rate of interest is the nominal rate adjusted for the expected change in the general level of prices.

EXERCISE

Why are trade unions apparently more successful in raising wages in some industries than in others?

Answers on page 251.

Market failure and government intervention

In this chapter, we are concerned with ways in which the free market system may give rise to various types of inefficiency, usually termed 'market failures'. Our focus is on **micro**economic problems, and we distinguish public goods, externalities, questions of market power and undesirable patterns of income distribution. In each case, we indicate some of the types of government intervention in markets which are claimed to be necessary to deal with these problems. We emphasise that governments may intervene in different ways to remedy market failure. The choice between methods may not always reflect objective evaluation of the alternatives, for political pressures may favour some types of intervention rather than others. Furthermore, as we shall see in Chapter 10, the costs of government intervention may sometimes outweigh the benefits from it; 'government failures' may be at least as significant as market failures in some areas.

9.1   INTRODUCTION

In Chapter 1 we briefly contrasted two types of economic system: the free market economy where decisions were taken by individuals, households and firms, and the planned, or command, economy where a planning ministry or other government body determined production and income distribution. We argued that each system had strengths and weaknesses, and that in practice most 'real world' economies were a blend of the two approaches.

In the succeeding chapters we have largely concentrated on the operation of the market system; this is justifiable because the economies of most countries where students are likely to read this book are dominated by private enterprise (the public sector only produces a minority share of output), and even where this is not the case, as in Eastern Europe and some less-developed countries, market forces nevertheless have a profound impact. Now, however, we must turn to consider those areas in which, even in capitalist market economies, we commonly find government intervention. These are areas where **market failures** arise, where market forces alone tend to produce an inefficient outcome and it is believed that government intervention can improve matters.

In attempting to evaluate the efficiency of markets, we should, as far as possible, try to avoid letting our political prejudices intrude. Some people are totally opposed to the market system on ideological grounds. They regard the pursuit of self-interest and private profit as something to be deplored as immoral and destructive of social cohesion. The rewards offered to successful individuals in market economies are seen as unjust and arbitrary, while the costs of failure are unacceptably high. On the other hand, there are extreme 'economic liberals', often associated with parties of the political right, who argue that any government intervention in the economy is to be resisted, for governments are necessarily tyrannical and destructive of personal freedom, as well as wasteful and inefficient in their use of taxpayers' money.

We suspect that few of our readers can be classified simply into one category or the other. In practice many socialists accept that the market has an important role to play, while political conservatives are willing to accept a significant amount of government involvement in the economy. The real debate is about the appropriate mix of government and private enterprise. Here the economist can be helpful in analysing the efficiency with which market forces and government intervention operate. (In approaching examinations in economics, students are well advised to pay attention to *economic* analysis, for few marks are awarded to those who simply express political opinions.)

We have seen that in many circumstances the market is viewed by economists as an efficient means of allocating resources to the production of goods and services which are desired by consumers. Firms seeking profits are forced by competitive pressures to use resources efficiently in the production of those commodities which are in demand, using techniques which minimise costs.

However, there are several areas in which the market, left to itself, may produce outcomes which economists regard as inefficient. We list them here, and then proceed to examine them in separate sections:

1   In the production of **public goods**
2   In cases where there are **externalities** (external costs or benefits) in the production or consumption of goods and services
3   Where there is **market power** or an absence of sufficient competition (this has already been discussed to a limited extent in Chapter 7)
4   In the **distribution of income** (discussed in Chapter 8)
5   When there is **insufficient aggregate demand** (this takes us into the field of **macroeconomics** and is discussed at length in Chapter 12).

9.2   THE PROVISION OF PUBLIC GOODS

Until now, virtually all our discussion has concentrated on private goods and services, those purchased and consumed by individuals and households. These commodities include everything we buy in shops and other retail outlets, such as clothes, food, TV sets, carpets, haircuts, restaurant meals and so on. We have already seen that in a competitive market economy such private goods and services are produced and traded to the mutual benefit of producers and consumers and, other things being equal, the market works adequately.

However, there is a class of goods where things are not so simple. These goods are known as **public goods**. It is important to stress here that the fact that a good is produced by a government-owned enterprise or a government does *not* make it a 'public good' in the sense we wish to use the term. A motor car produced by a publicly-owned car firm and an illustrated guidebook sold by a government-owned museum are both examples of private goods. The distinguishing feature of a public good is that the benefits it provides (the utility it gives) are not confined to one individual or household. Many goods and services may have this characteristic of 'publicness' to some degree—for instance I may get pleasure from seeing you with new clothes and a stylish haircut. What distinguishes a pure public good from a private good is its possession of two economically relevant attributes:

1   **Non-rivalness** This means that consumers are not in competition with each other; if one person benefits from the provision of the good, this doesn't stop somebody else benefiting. This contrasts with a private good, such as a banana; if I eat it, you can't! An example of non-rivalness is street lighting. Once it is provided we can all benefit.
2   **Non-excludability.** This means that once the good is provided you can't prevent anybody from getting the benefit. Again, street lighting is a good example.

We should emphasise that it is the possession of *both* these characteristics which is necessary to define a pure public good. For example, a seat in a cinema is non-rival so long as the cinema isn't full; we can both enjoy the movie. But cinema operators can of course exclude people if they don't pay for their tickets.

Economists argue that in the case of pure public goods there arises what has been called the **free rider** problem. Selfish people will reason that, if the public good is provided by somebody else, they will be able to get the benefits without paying. Let that somebody else pick up the bill, we will take a free ride. Many of us will have experienced such behaviour in everyday life. If enough people think like this, the public good will not be provided because firms will not find it profitable to produce if people who don't have to aren't willing to pay.

In such circumstances, the market may be seen to have failed, for individuals can't get the quantity of good they would wish to have if everybody paid a fair share. Take the case of street lighting; to put street lights throughout a town would be beyond the resources of all but a tiny number of individuals, but many would be prepared to pay a fair share of the cost if they could be sure everybody would do the same. If in such circumstances the government intervenes to provide streetlighting and forces individuals to pay through taxation, it seems likely that the outcome will be preferable to that which the free market would produce. However, in the absence of unanimity, we can't be sure of this. Some people may not have wanted street lights. Should you, for instance, tax blind people to pay for them?

Take another example which is often quoted: defence. Clearly it would be very difficult to defend a country against external aggressors if we all purchased our own private soldiers. This seems to be a very strong case for taxation and government provision of the 'public good' in question. However, there are always large numbers of people who object to any particular defence policy a government adopts: nuclear disarmers, pacifists, defence experts who disagree with the government's methods and so on. Should they be forced to pay for policies with which they disagree?

The public good argument is actually a rather dangerous one, for it tends to offer scope for politicians and civil servants who claim to know what is best for the public. Recently economists have become rather sceptical of it. It has been pointed out that public goods problems may not always require government intervention. Private philanthropy, for example, may lead to the supply of some public goods such as parks and museums. Voluntary organisations such as clubs may be able to organise the provision of, for example, sporting facilities which have public goods characteristics. Or, very importantly, businesses may be prepared to pay for or sponsor the provision of public goods.

For example, the transmission of radio broadcasts seems at first to offer a non-rival and non-excludable service, thus offering a justification for government-provided broadcasting paid for out of taxation or licence fees. However, it is clear that an alternative is to have radio financed by advertising or programme sponsorship. Moreover, technical change opens up new possibilities; nowadays it is possible to 'scramble' radio and TV signals in such a way that the viewer or listener has to hire special equipment from the broadcaster in order to receive them. Thus the non-excludability problem disappears.

Even if, on balance, it is seen to be appropriate for the state to intervene to secure provision of public goods, there are different ways in which this can be done. The government does not have to supply the good or service directly. Instead, it can invite private sector firms to tender for a contract to supply it. For example, in the United Kingdom, a number of local authorities have contracted-out their refuse collection and street cleaning. In this way it is hoped to obtain the public good of tidy streets more cheaply than would be the case if local government employees were involved. This is part of the privatisation process discussed in Chapter 10.

9.3 EXTERNALITIES

Externalities are the positive or negative effects which the activities of production and consumption can have on **third parties**. Where these effects are positive and beneficial they are termed **external benefits**. Where they are negative or detrimental, we call them **external costs**.

9.3.1 External benefits

Public goods, which we have just examined, are an extreme case of an external benefit. If my neighbour and I agree to install a street light outside our house, we not only obtain private benefits but also confer benefits on third parties—passers-by who have their way home illuminated. The **social benefit** is the private benefit plus the external benefit. Wherever social benefit exceeds the private benefit there is the possibility that the good or service will be underprovided by the market and there may be a case for government intervention to bring its supply up to the optimal level.

As we indicated earlier, there are many commodities which have some element of publicness without being a pure public good—these are likely to be the types of good or service where the social benefits exceed the private benefits. An example might be public transport, which in most countries makes commercial losses and is subsidised by the government. This is clearly not a pure public good, for people can be excluded from buses and trains if they don't pay, but there may be a justification for subsidies if there are external benefits; the social benefits of travel by public transport are greater than the private benefits (which of course determine what individuals are prepared to pay). For example, buses may be more efficient users of road space than private cars. People who travel by bus contribute to the reduction of traffic congestion and the speeding up of journeys, benefits which are shared by all road users.

Other important examples of external benefits are often said to arise in education and health care. Education provides private benefits, for instance by raising an individual's earning capacity, but society as a whole may also gain from mass education. Employers will find it easier to train workers for specific tasks, there will be better communication if the whole population can read and write, advertising and marketing will be easier (thus lowering costs of production indirectly), and so on.

Similarly, although health care clearly gives private benefits to individuals whose lifespan and quality of life are improved, there are also external benefits to society from a generally healthy population. One important example is immunisation against infectious diseases: if an individual is protected from the disease, his or her likelihood of transmitting the disease to somebody else is reduced. Current campaigns to prevent the spread of AIDS can be justified in this way, too.

Of course, arguments like this apply to certain aspects of education and health care but not to others. The external benefits from all-round primary and secondary education may be substantial, whereas those from a PhD programme in mediaeval Latin literature (or, for that matter, in some of the more obscure branches of economics) may be less obvious. Similarly, we can accept the need for some government subsidies for health care without accepting that there are overwhelming social benefits from, say, certain types of cosmetic surgery.

Furthermore, we must again emphasise that, even where we accept the need for some government intervention to remedy the deficiency of markets and to stimulate production and consumption of some good or service, this does not necessarily mean that the government should directly provide the commodity in question. In education, for example, the government may subsidise fees for students while leaving the provision of schools and colleges to the private sector. In health care, the government may subsidise and enforce private medical insurance schemes rather than operate a health service itself. We shall explore alternative types of market intervention shortly.

9.3.2 External costs

Let us turn now to cases where there are significant external costs, such that the free market tends to *over*provide the good or service in question. A frequently-cited example is environmental pollution resulting from many production and consumption activities. Motor cars driven in towns emit fumes and cause congestion. Aircraft taking off and landing cause a noise nuisance. Prostitution and sex shops in a residential area can create considerable annoyance. People on beaches leave enormous quantities of litter. Many modern manufacturing and processing industries have particularly unpleasant by-products.

Suppose we take the case of oil refineries. There are the private costs of production—crude oil and other raw materials, labour, machinery, storage space etc—which will be taken into account by firms deciding on their most profitable level of output, but they may also impose costs on third parties (ie, neither the producers nor the consumers of the product) by polluting the atmosphere, discharge of waste materials into rivers or the sea and disfiguring the landscape. Some of these external costs may be immediately apparent—destruction of fish or other wildlife, discoloration of and damage to buildings and so on; some may take longer to emerge, such as a higher incidence of cancer and other diseases. Some of these costs are easy to evaluate, some much more difficult.

FIGURE 9.1 **External costs resulting in overproduction**

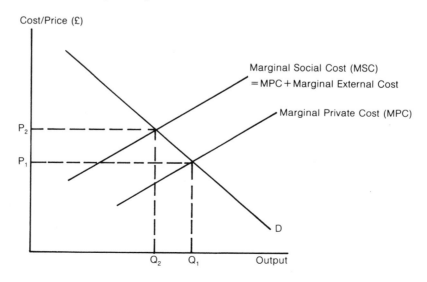

We show the overprovision of the product in relation to the level which is socially desirable in Figure 9.1. For simplicity, the oil-refining industry is assumed to be perfectly competitive; so equilibrium is reached where the demand curve cuts the supply curve (the supply curve is constructed from the marginal **private** cost curves of refineries). The price-output combination resulting from an uncontrolled free market would therefore be P_1, Q_1. However the social optimum would be where the marginal **social** cost (the marginal private cost plus the marginal external cost) is equal to the marginal social benefit (assumed to be equal to the marginal private benefit or marginal willingness to pay; as we have seen in earlier chapters, this is shown by the demand curve). We have drawn a marginal social cost curve lying above the marginal private cost curve; it cuts the demand curve at a price-output combination of P_2, Q_2. Thus if the pollution costs were taken into account by producers, they would produce a smaller output. Overproduction of $Q_1 - Q_2$ is occurring.

(Such a diagram, incidentally, could have been used to show **under**production in the case of external benefits, and students might find it instructive to draw one. In such a case you would have a marginal social benefit curve lying above the demand curve.)

9.3.3 Types of intervention

While there appears to be a strong case for government intervention where externalities occur, there are grounds for dispute over the *methods* of intervention used. The main methods are:

1   **Persuasion** This is a common and relatively cheap method of attempting to deal with both external costs and benefits. Governments often run publicity campaigns to persuade people to do things which they wish to encourage (join training schemes, protect property from theft) and not to do things which they regard as undesirable (drinking and driving, smoking). Although such campaigns can be successful if properly researched, targeted and funded, economists tend to be rather sceptical of them, arguing that tastes and preferences are not easily manipulated in this way.

2   **Production by the government** Governments may undertake production directly through publicly-owned enterprises. In many countries governments directly supply tax-financed education, health care, police and defence, and sell services such as postage, tele-communications and transport to the public. However, as we shall see in Chapter 10, such methods of intervening in the economy seem to be declining in popularity.

3   **Regulation and controls** The government can legislate to prohibit the production of certain goods which are thought to impose serious external costs, for example dangerous drugs. It can also impose requirements on people that they purchase certain commodities, for example motor vehicle insurance. However, outright prohibitions or requirements may not be appropriate. For example, it would not be sensible to ban air transport completely because of aircraft noise; instead noise standards may be laid down. Similarly, to prohibit all discharges of chemical by-products into rivers may be excessively costly; instead acceptable levels of discharge may be determined by the government. Again, danger from machinery, radiation and natural hazards may be impossible to exclude in certain types of production, but acceptable levels of risk can be defined which are less than those that the free market would choose.

   Such **regulation** may be costly to administer, for it will require expert knowledge, research, and the resources to monitor implementation. Economists would suggest that such administrative costs are likely to be minimised if there are heavy penalties attached to breaking regulations.

4   **Taxes and subsidies** The use of fines to motivate behaviour is only one example of the way in which economists attempt to structure incentives and disincentives in order to deal with externalities. For many years they have argued the case for using taxes or charges and subsidies rather than direct intervention by the government. In the case of external costs, as in the case illustrated in Figure 9.1, a tax on producers equivalent to the marginal external cost would shift the supply curve upwards to the marginal social cost curve. This would mean that the external cost would be 'internalised' by producers, leading them to choose the socially optimal price-output combination P_2, Q_2. The same principle can be applied to virtually any case of external costs—airlines can be taxed for flying noisy planes, motorists charged more for driving in towns and causing congestion, and so on.

In the same way, the underprovision of goods and services the consumption of which produces external benefits can be corrected by the provision of subsidies (a form of 'negative taxation') to producers or consumers. This would lower prices and increase consumption in the desired manner.

Note that taxes or charges and subsidies may be **alternatives** in some contexts. For instance we could attack congestion in towns **either** by taxing motorists **or** by subsidising public transport.

5   **Assignment of property rights** Many problems of pollution and other external costs arise because some land, water and so on are owned communally; and the atmosphere is not 'owned' at all. Where land is privately owned, its owner can in principle sue polluters which damage it and claim damages from them. This is one reason why firms do not normally use your front garden as a rubbish dump. One possible solution, therefore, is to assign or sell property rights over the environment, preferably in such a way that all those affected can combine to launch legal action against polluters. Then the solution to the problem can be left up to those directly involved, with the courts adjudicating or (more likely) with some sort of deal being struck between the polluter and those who suffer from the damage. Although this solution is attractive in principle, because it minimises the cost of government action, its application may prove difficult in practice.

9.4   MARKET POWER: MONOPOLY AND IMPERFECT COMPETITION

The inefficiencies resulting from monopoly have already been discussed in Chapter 7, and we will consider some aspects of them further in Chapter 10. Nevertheless there are some points which need to be made here.

For a socially optimal allocation of resources it is necessary that marginal cost equal the marginal benefit of output in all markets. We have already seen that under perfect competition this basic condition for optimality is met in long-run equilibrium. Under monopoly, oligopoly and imperfect competition, by contrast, there is a presumption that the marginal conditions will not be satisfied; the profit-maximising monopolist, for example, produces at a level of output where the price (reflecting the marginal benefit) exceeds the marginal cost of output. As with the externalities discussed in the previous section, there is a presumption that there is a need for government intervention.

The general problem is that, as with the case of external benefits, there is underproduction of goods and services with monopoly, cartels and other forms of 'producer power'. The aim of policy here will be to lower price and increase output to reach the social optimum. There may also be **equity** or distributional problems posed by monopoly and oligopoly. They obtain super-normal profits, which are a form of economic rent (see Chapter 8), at the expense of consumers. It may be appropriate to tax these away.

9.4.1   Policies to reduce monopoly power

Once again, we have to stress that there are alternative ways of dealing with this type of market failure. In this case we can distinguish the following:

1   **Measures to increase competition** Where monopoly is the result of artificial barriers to entry the government can clearly enact measures to remove or reduce them. The same applies to formal and informal cartels, restrictive agreements and other 'anti-competitive practices'. Thus in the United Kingdom the Office of Fair Trading (OFT) has powers to investigate such restrictions on competition and take cases to the Restrictive Practices Court. As we have previously indicated, the Monopolies and Mergers Commission has the power to investigate firms producing 25 per cent or more of a market's output and can examine mergers which seem to threaten competition. The European Commission also has power to investigate concentrations of power in markets where trade takes place amongst countries in the European Community.

2   **Nationalisation** Government ownership of monopolies was often considered in the past to be a means by which concentrations of market power could be brought under social control. In the

United Kingdom from the late 1960s onwards nationalised industries were required, wherever possible, to equate price to marginal cost, thus replicating the outcome of a perfectly competitive market. However, there are great problems with such a policy. For one thing, it is impossible to monitor, for outside observers cannot effectively judge whether costs are being accurately reported. For another, if there is a continuously-declining long run average cost curve, as in the case of so-called **natural monopolies** this implies that at a price equal to marginal costs the enterprise must make a loss. We shall discuss nationalised industries and enterprises in Chapter 10.

3   **Regulation** Instead of nationalising a monopoly or breaking up concentrations of market power, the government can use its powers to lay down rules about prices charged, output levels, rates of return and other aspects of firms' activity. This has commonly been the way of dealing with these problems in the United States and it has become more common in the United Kingdom recently. For example Oftel (the Office of Telecommunications) has been set up to regulate the privatised British Telecom.

4   **Taxes and subsidies** One possibility is to grant a production subsidy to a monopolist, thus lowering marginal cost and inducing the firm to raise output to the optimal level. This however would, other things being equal, increase the monopoly's profits. This might be dealt with by imposing special **lump sum** taxes (ie, a fixed amount, say £xm), or proportional taxes on the monopoly's profits. For example, the United Kingdom government has in the past imposed a 'windfall' profit tax on banks when interest rates (as a result of government policy) have been abnormally high, and it operates special profits taxes on oil companies operating in the North Sea and on commercial TV companies.

9.4.2   Monopsony

A type of market power discussed in Chapter 8 in relation to the labour market is **monopsony**, a situation where there is only one **buyer** of a product (as opposed to one seller, the case of monopoly). By analogy, **oligopsony** defines a market with a few buyers.

Monopsony or oligopsony firms are in a position to use their market power to force the prices of goods and services below those which a competitive market would determine. As a consequence, output and price diverge from their optimum values and resources are misallocated. Examples of this sort would arise where a firm or small group of firms are the sole employers of labour in a town; or where a car firm is the sole purchaser of components from a supplier, or where monopoly electricity generating companies are the monopsony buyers of power stations and generators. In principle, governments have the power to investigate such situations and use policies analogous to those outlined above to deal with monopolies.

9.5   INCOME DISTRIBUTION

Government intervention to influence the distribution of income is normally justified on grounds of **equity** rather than the efficiency considerations which we have so far emphasised. A market economy inevitably produces inequality in the distribution of income between individuals, households and social classes. As we saw in the previous chapter, market-determined incomes (as opposed to intra-family, charity and other transfers) depend on the ownership of factors of production and the valuation placed on the services of these factors. As people are born into families with different levels of wealth, inequality is passed on from generation to generation. Although of course individuals, either by their own efforts or luck, can rise from humble backgrounds to positions of wealth and power (and, conversely, individuals can fall in status and economic position), inheritance and background still count for a great deal.

If the distribution of income produced by a free market is felt to be unacceptably unequal, the government may intervene in markets to alter this position. This involves value judgments or opinions about equity on which it is difficult for the economist to comment *as an economist*, though naturally we all have our own views as citizens.

9.5.1   Equity and efficiency

Despite this, as we have pointed out in Chapter 8, we cannot totally ignore the effects of income redistribution on the efficiency with which the economy operates. Too much redistribution may produce serious motivational problems. It is argued, for example, that the prospect of higher incomes encourages young people to undertake education and training and gives an incentive to work harder in business and take on greater responsibilities. This is almost certainly true to some extent; as we argued before, an economy where everybody received exactly the same income would probably be one where it was difficult to get individuals to put very much effort into work. However, it is possible (as we shall see in Chapter 17) to exaggerate this effect. People work for a variety of motivations as well as the incomes they receive; and their work effort may not be very sensitive to changes in pay over quite wide ranges.

There is also an argument that unequal incomes lead to higher average savings. As we shall see in Chapter 12, people with higher incomes tend to save more on average than poorer people. Equality of income would therefore reduce overall savings. For example suppose we have two individuals, one with an income of £20,000 and saving £5,000 while the other has an income of £6,000 and saves nothing. Total savings are £5,000. If income were instead split equally, each would have £13,000 out of which each might save, say, £2,000. The result would be total savings of only £4,000. Greater equality would result in lower savings, with lower investment and probably slower economic growth.

However, both these arguments are rather tenuous. Although there is something in them, it would be very difficult on these grounds to support a case for maintaining the vast disparities in income and wealth which the free market produces. Certainly the 'have-nots' are unlikely to agree that the free market distribution of income is completely desirable, and in modern democracies they have the voting power to demand some degree of redistribution via government intervention. Accordingly, we find that most governments intervene to reallocate income. As with other forms of market failure, government intervention can take a variety of forms, for example:

1   **Progressive income tax** A progressive income tax is one where the proportion of income paid in tax increases with the level of income. Progression in various degrees has been typical of the income tax system of many countries, though its importance has substantially diminished in recent years. Making the better-off contribute more than the poor is a form of redistribution (as compared with making everybody pay the same); it also in principle enables the government to raise a larger sum in taxation than would otherwise be the case.

In a progressive income tax system, the **marginal tax rate** rises with income. The proportion of extra income earned which the individual can spend falls as income rises. As we have seen, this may have some disincentive effect. Surprisingly, this disincentive effect may not always be greatest on the richest members of society. In the United Kingdom, for example, marginal income tax rates combine perversely with the effects of the welfare benefits system to produce very high effective tax rates on poorer people, because many welfare benefits may be linked to income. Thus when a low paid worker gets an increase in pay, he or she may lose entitlement to some welfare benefits. This, coupled with the extra tax paid on the higher income, may mean that the worker is little better off (indeed, in some cases may actually be **worse** off) as a result. In such circumstances we may well be concerned about the efficiency effects of the tax-benefit system.

In order to avoid such a problem (which has been called the **poverty trap**), many economists have argued for a long time in favour of a reform of the tax-benefit system with the introduction of **negative income tax**. This would extend the concept of progression backwards so that once income (from whatever source) falls below a certain level, the individuals would automatically receive an income supplement which would increase the lower the level of income. The aim would be to secure low effective marginal tax rates at all income levels and thus to restore adequate work incentives for the lower-paid.

2   **Cash-grant transfers** Negative income tax is a system which would replace the rather messy system in the United Kingdom and elsewhere which involves special cash grants to individuals or households in specific circumstances. Such systems are complex, expensive to administer and confusing to claimants, as well as generating the poverty trap. Whatever their deficiencies, however, economists generally prefer them to **transfers in kind** or **direct market interventions**.

3   **Transfers in kind** This means giving assistance to the poor in the form of free or subsidised goods and services—for example, free school meals, food stamps (as in the United States), free transport and telephones. The major objection to transfers in kind is that it is unlikely that the item provided free would be that which the recipient would want to buy if he or she were given a sum of money equivalent to the cost. Would you prefer to be given a cheque for £100 or a food parcel with an ostensible value of £100? Benefits in kind are generally a very inefficient means of redistributing income to the poor.

4   **Government intervention in markets** The last comment applies perhaps even more to this approach to redistributing income. Here the government intervenes in the markets for goods and services to hold down the prices of goods on which the poor spend a large part of their income. For example, rents may be controlled, food prices may be held down or the price of gas and electricity reduced by subsidies from the taxpayer. We have seen in Chapter 2 how such policies distort the workings of markets, and it should be clear that the methods of 'helping the poor' are the least efficient of all. For one thing, it is badly targeted; cheap electricity benefits those who use a lot of electrical appliances (unlikely to be the poorest section of the population); rent controls benefit existing tenants who may be much better off than those looking for homes and unable to find them.

5   **Redistribution of wealth** Perhaps a more fundamental approach would involve attacking the existing distribution of wealth, in particular the way in which rich parents are able to pass on their accumulated wealth to their children. Taxes on inheritance have been used to some effect in many countries, though their yields have sometimes been disappointing as the very rich can afford to devise elaborate schemes to avoid death duties. It has been pointed out recently that in the United Kingdom the big rise in owner-occupied housing among today's middle-aged will cause a large increase in the numbers of people inheriting significant wealth in the 1990s and beyond; governments are likely to see this as an important area for taxation in the future.

9.6   INSUFFICIENT AGGREGATE DEMAND

Our focus so far in this book has been on **micro**economics and we have yet to consider the working of the economy as a whole. Implicit in our analysis has been the assumption that the economy is fully employed, that all workers who wish to obtain jobs are able to do so and that capital equipment and other resources are being fully utilised. In other words, we are on the production possibility curve illustrated in Chapter 1. However, it will be clear to readers that in many countries there are large numbers of people unemployed and resources lying idle. In such circumstances, many would claim, the government has an obligation to step in and increase the level of **aggregate demand** in the economy, that is the total amount of spending planned by the private and public sectors. We cannot adequately discuss this without entering the field of **macro**economics, and so we leave discussion over until Chapter 12.

9.7   GOVERNMENT FAILURE

Our emphasis in this chapter has been on the ways in which the mechanism of the free market may produce economic efficiency or social injustice. Such market failures may serve as a justification for government intervention in the economy.

However, before we conclude that there is necessarily a major role for the government to play in the economy, we need to make a few observations. First, we have seen that there are alternative *potential* policies which can be adopted to deal with the market failures we have examined. Some of these involve the government's playing a major role in the economy, employing large numbers of people and intervening in detail in markets. Other policies, however, may involve a much more limited government involvement. To take one example, pollution control can involve detailed and expensive regulation and control of industry at one extreme, or setting up a system of property rights (where the government leaves interested parties to determine acceptable levels of pollution) at the other. We cannot assume that the existence of market failure necessitates a very large role for the government in the economy.

The choice between different policies may not always be made on rational grounds of cost efficiency. Instead, governments may be lobbied by various interest groups who prefer one approach to another on grounds of their own self-interest. Specialists and professionals in a field may prefer solutions which allow for detailed regulation of an industry, with lots of scope for increasing the demand for their services (economists and accountants are not immune to this). Unionised workers may prefer a monopoly to be nationalised rather than broken up into competing enterprises. Civil servants will, other things being equal, prefer larger government bureaucracies; politicians like to be popular with their civil servants. So we cannot assume that the policy chosen will be the optimal policy.

Furthermore, even if a policy does seem sensible and appropriate, we cannot assume that it will be efficiently and effectively carried out. In practice markets are not the only institutions which can fail; so can **governments**. It may be the case that the costs of government intervention are greater than the benefits to be achieved from it. In the 1980s people in many countries have become much more sceptical about the virtues of government intervention in the economy. This has led to attempts to reduce the role of the public sector. In Chapter 10 we explore two aspects of this disenchantment with governments, when we examine **privatisation** and **deregulation** policies.

SUMMARY

In this chapter we have examined the way in which markets can sometimes produce outcomes which are economically inefficient or socially undesirable. We have looked at a range of alternative policies which may be used to improve matters. There may well be a need for a substantial degree of government involvement in the economy; however we should be sceptical of the view that governments always 'get it right'. If markets can fail, so can governments.

SELF-TEST QUESTIONS

1 Lighthouses are often held to have 'public good' characteristics. Is this because:

(a) Lighthouses are always provided by governments.

(b) There are external costs in constructing lighthouses.

(c) Once a lighthouse is built, ships can make use of the light to navigate even if their owners haven't contributed to the building cost.

(d) Lighthouses are non-rival in use but you can exclude people from their benefits.

(e) Lighthouses are a natural monopoly.

2 Which of the following is incorrect?

(a) If a commodity is a public good, the government must produce it.

(b) Education provides private benefits to individuals.

(c) Education provides social benefits.

(d) The demand curve for a good may not indicate marginal social benefit.

(e) Where marginal social benefits exceed marginal private benefits production will be less than the social optimum.

3 Which of the following is correct?

(a) Governments should subsidise the production of goods where there are substantial external costs.

(b) An oligopsony market is one where there are just a few suppliers of a good.

(c) Street lights cannot be considered as public goods because they could be purchased by householders.

(d) Traffic congestion is an example of the external benefits of motoring in London.

(e) Not all goods with the characteristic of non-excludability are public goods.

4 If a high marginal rate of income tax leads high income-earners to emigrate, this is an example of which of the following?

(a) The poverty trap.

(b) Negative income tax.

(c) A wealth tax.

(d) The disincentive effect of taxation.

(e) A market failure.

5 Economists argue that transfers in kind are inefficient because:

(a) They allow the recipient freedom of choice.

(b) They are expensive.

(c) They are valued by the recipient more highly than by the donor.

(d) Recipients might prefer an equivalent sum of money.

(e) Everybody is treated equally.

EXERCISE

'The existence of externalities means that free markets are often inefficient and justifies substantial government intervention.' Discuss.

Answers on page 253.

Current microeconomic issues

In this chapter we look at two closely related policy issues which have come into prominence in the last few years in many countries: **privatisation** and **deregulation**. We have seen in Chapter 9 that weaknesses in the functioning of the private sector give rise to market failures; in this chapter we consider the consequences of malfunctioning of the public sector. Advocates of privatisation argue for the selling off of public enterprises and property, and the contracting-out of various services which have been supplied by government employees in the past. Many critics of government intervention also argue for deregulation, claiming that governments have often attempted to control private industry to such an extent that the costs vastly outweigh the benefits. These arguments are considered in detail.

10.1 INTRODUCTION

In Chapter 9 we examined some of the ways in which 'real world' market economies may diverge from the conditions necessary to maximise economic efficiency—where externalities, public goods problems or imperfect competition occur—or provide an equitable outcome. We saw that government intervention of various types may be justified on these grounds. In practice, however, claims of market inefficiency or inequity may be exaggerated on political grounds, and government intervention can actually occur in pursuit of the sectional claims of particular groups, rather than in promotion of the national interest. Moreover, government involvement in the economy, whether through direct production or indirectly through regulation of markets, can itself be inefficient or inequitable. In the late 1970s and 1980s many influential economists, business people, commentators and politicians came increasingly to the view that the costs of much government intervention exceeded the benefits to be expected from it. This is the case we now have to consider.

10.2 PRIVATISATION

Privatisation is a broad term. Most people will be aware of one aspect of it, namely the sale of shares in previously-nationalised enterprises. New privately-owned companies, such as British Telecom, British Airways and British Gas, have been 'floated' on the United Kingdom stock market, and their shares have been eagerly purchased by millions of small investors as well as by the large financial institutions which hold the bulk of company shares. This has been a particularly important aspect of the economic policies of Mrs Thatcher's government in the United Kingdom. Plans in the late 1980's commit the United Kingdom government to raising £5bn pounds per annum through sales of this sort (and also the sale of some assets directly to other private sector companies) for the next few years. Similar programmes of asset sales have begun in other developed countries such as Japan, France, Canada and Italy. Moreover, in many less-developed countries there have been moves towards selling off factories and plant to the private sector and to foreign investors, although direct company flotations have been less common because few LDCs have active stock markets.

However, this is only one aspect of privatisation. In Britain another is the sale of publicly-owned housing to tenants at substantial discounts and a third is the sale of surplus land and property to the private sector. Then there is the 'contracting-out' of public sector services to the private sector, briefly mentioned in Chapter 9. Such services continue to be paid for out of taxation, but instead of being performed by public sector employees they are provided by private-sector firms in return for a fee. Usually contracts are put out to tender, under which a detailed specification of the job to be done is set out, and firms are invited to submit schemes for carrying out the work, including cost estimates. Other things being equal, the cheapest estimate will be chosen (although in some cases there may be other considerations which are relevant, such as the experience and reputation of the firm).

Contracting-out of this kind has been applied in the United Kingdom to hospital cleaning and catering, local authority housing maintenance and roadsweeping, building security and so on. In other countries the range of such practices is greater; one interesting example is the privatisation of prisons in some American states.

Finally, privatisation can take the form of the governments simply abandoning the provision of certain types of service which it previously offered free or at reduced cost to taxpayers, leaving individuals to purchase these services at market prices from the private sector. For example, the United Kingdom government in 1987 stopped providing cheap spectacles on the National Health Service.

10.2.1 Public enterprise in practice

Let us begin by looking at the privatisation of nationalised enterprises, that is those government-owned 'firms' which produce output for sale to the public. It is these enterprises which have been sold off to shareholders, and which have attracted most publicity in the last few years. As we saw in Chapter 9, a case can be made for certain types of productive enterprises to be owned and controlled by the government where market failures occur. Examples are where major externalities exist, or where there are problems of excessive market power. The latter case is particularly significant. As seen in Chapter 5 some industries are **natural monopolies**. This means that economies of scale are so pronounced in such an industry that there is only room for one efficient producer. A firm which was producing at the lowest possible long-run average cost would have to be producing the entire industry's output. A private sector firm in such a position will clearly be tempted to abuse it, and raise prices to the customer.

However, market power can in principle be controlled through regulation rather than nationalisation, and in any case there are very few cases of clear-cut natural monopolies. Indeed, the **economic** case for public ownership of many nationalised enterprises is sometimes difficult to find. More often, enterprises were nationalised for political reasons. This might involve a deliberate commitment, as when the United Kingdom Labour Government of the 1940s nationalised the coal industry, or might occur as a result of a sudden crisis, for instance when Mr Heath's Conservative government of the 1970s nationalised Rolls-Royce to save it from bankruptcy. In France after World War II, many firms were taken into public ownership because their owners had collaborated with the Nazis. In many less-developed countries foreign-owned firms were nationalised in an attempt to assert independence from former colonial powers and, more recently to increase government revenue.

Thus it can be seen that the nationalised sectors in many countries grew for a variety of reasons. Firms could remain in the public sector long after any plausible case for nationalisation had vanished. To give an extreme example: during World War I, the British government nationalised public houses in Carlisle, where there was an important munitions industry, in an attempt to stop workers drinking too much and detracting from the war effort, but in the event the pubs remained nationalised until nearly sixty years later.

By the 1970s, public enterprises had a major role in the economies of many Western countries (with the significant exception of the United States, to which we will refer later). In the United Kingdom, for example, they accounted for nearly 10 per cent of output and employment. In this decade, the economic performance of many countries faltered and growth rates were much lower than in the 1950s and 1960s. The United Kingdom fared particularly badly, and increasingly attention focused on the nationalised sector as one possible source of the problem.

Over the 1970s, the United Kingdom nationalised enterprises compared unfavourably with the private sector in relation to such measures as labour productivity, growth, and rate of return on capital. Many nationalised industries and firms were making substantial losses which had to be paid for out of taxation at a time when public spending generally was rising rapidly. A similar problem was seen in other countries: in Italy nationalised industries were notoriously overstaffed and inefficient, and in France and Japan, where in engineering terms the nationalised railway systems were improving dramatically, this was only at the cost of an enormous increase in subsidies.

10.2.2 Weaknesses of public enterprise

Critics of nationalised enterprises have pointed to a number of reasons why their performance record was not very good:

1 **Monopoly power** It has been pointed out that some (but by no means all) nationalised enterprises enjoy monopoly positions which may lead to inefficiency, lack of innovation and restriction of consumer choice.

2 **Trade union power** In many countries, nationalised industries show high levels of trade union membership and considerable union influence over staffing and working practices. It has been alleged that this is a major cause of the poor productivity performance of this sector.

3 **Confusing objectives** Often the legislation setting up nationalised industries and firms offers little clear guidance on what objectives the enterprises should pursue. It is often felt, especially where enterprises are monopolists, that it is inappropriate to maximise profits. But what is the alternative? In the United Kingdom in the 1940s nationalised industries were instructed to act 'in the national interest' and to 'break even, taking one year with another'. This seems to imply setting prices equal to average costs, but this policy doesn't offer clear guidelines. It certainly doesn't provide much incentive to keep costs down.

4 **Difficulties in monitoring performance** In the 1960s and 1970s, United Kingdom nationalised enterprises were told to equate marginal cost to price wherever possible (and thus to simulate the outcome of perfect competition), and to evaluate new investment programmes by requiring them to produce a rate of return comparable to that obtained in the private sector. This policy proved difficult to monitor however, because only the nationalised enterprises were in possession of the information needed to check claims of efficiency.

5 **Lack of incentives** The private sector provides incentives to promote efficiency. If managers do not perform satisfactorily, they may lose their jobs; if they do particularly well they may be promoted or share directly in the company's profits through bonuses and share options (opportunities to obtain company shares on favourable terms). Such incentives are frequently missing in the public sector, where jobs have often been secure and where career advancement may not be directly linked to economic performance.

6 **Government interference with management** Even where managers have clear objectives and are properly motivated, nationalised enterprises may often suffer in unpredictable ways from government interference in pursuit of some current policy not directly related to the enterprise. For example, public enterprises are often forced to buy from domestic suppliers rather than cheaper foreign sources, they may be required to keep prices artificially low in periods when the government is concerned about inflation or to raise them when the government wants to increase revenue without putting up taxes or they may be forced to keep factories open in areas where unemployment has risen and the government faces an important election! Such arbitrary interference with the running of enterprises demoralises management and makes it difficult to meet performance targets.

10.2.3   Objectives of privatising nationalised enterprises

Against this backround, it is not surprising that interest in privatisation should have grown so rapidly in the 1980s. Privatisation can be seen as a means of increasing the efficiency with which the economic system operates. However, just as we saw that political considerations play a role in the expansion of the public sector, they are also present in the privatisation process, for privatisation can involve a number of conflicting objectives. Let's consider some of these:

1 **Promoting competition** This is particularly important where a nationalised enterprise was previously a monopoly. By opening the market up to new competition when deregulation accompanies privatisation it is hoped to stimulate the enterprise to improve its performance.

2 **Developing a market for corporate control** As we shall see in Chapter 14, a vital role is played by the Stock Exchange in making it possible for shares to be sold by those who are dissatisfied by a firm's performance and bought by those who think they can improve it by getting rid of the existing management and putting in a new team. Thus the sale of shares in a privatised firm makes the continuation of the existing management's control dependent on the maintenance of adequate performance. Notice that this advantage of privatisation does not depend on the firm being faced by much competition in its product markets. However it will be of less significance if the government retains a 'golden share' or some other arrangement which prevents takeovers, or if the privatised firm is so large (eg British Telecom) that an attempt to purchase enough shares to take it over would be prohibitively expensive.

3   **Reducing the Public Sector Borrowing Requirement (PSBR) or taxes** Selling off public enterprises raises funds which can be used to reduce the amount the government has to borrow or raise in taxation to finance its activities.

4   **Reducing the power of trade unions** As we have seen, trade union power is particularly concentrated in the public sector. Reducing trade union power can be seen as a means of promoting greater efficiency, or can be seen as an end in itself; the latter is the case with some politicians who see trade union influence as inherently unwelcome.

5   **Promoting wider share ownership** Again there is a mixture of economic and political motives. Some may see it as inherently desirable to spread share ownership in order to create a 'property-owning democracy'. Others may see it as a means to an end: if increased shareholding encourages individuals to take a more adventurous attitude towards investment and the formation of new businesses, and teaches them to be more appreciative of the problems of business, a new 'enterprise culture' may develop. In such an environment, the economy is likely, it is claimed, to be more successful.

It is clear that some of these objectives can be in conflict. For example, if your prime objective is to raise a large sum of money to reduce PSBR or taxes, it will be easier to do this if the privatised enterprise is sold off with considerable monopoly powers which will guarantee high earnings for shareholders. The possible efficiency gains from competition will be reduced. Similarly, share flotations may be cheaper and raise more money if shares are sold to big financial institutions rather than to millions of small shareholders. Or again, selling off an enterprise with considerable market powers is unlikely to force it to get tough with its unions; rather managers may prefer a quiet life where they coexist peacefully with trade union restrictive practices.

These and other conflicts have emerged in the UK and other countries where privatisation has been put into effect. This suggests that the process of privatisation is likely to be almost as muddled in its objectives and execution as was the original process of nationalisation. Moreover, it is clear that some of the gains supposedly resulting from privatisation could in principle be achieved with enterprises remaining in the public sector. For instance, competition could be encouraged between previously-protected nationalised enterprises and the private sector by deregulation without denationalisation taking place, or large, unwieldy nationalised industries could be broken into smaller segments, competing with each other while remaining in public ownership. In this context it is interesting to see that the performance of those United Kingdom enterprises still in the public sector has improved dramatically since the early 1980s as a result of a more consistent set of objectives, more dynamic management and a reduction in trade union power. At the same time, complaints have grown about the behaviour and efficiency of some privatised enterprises, notably British Telecom. It appears that the transfer of ownership is neither a necessary nor a sufficient condition for greater efficiency.

10.2.4   Welfare and other public services

Another area where privatisation has been advocated is the provision of those services which have been directly provided by local or national government and financed by taxation. The rationale for the existence of such services is, like that for the nationalised industries, obscure and complex. Although it is possible to put a case for many of them by reference to the theory of public goods discussed in Chapter 9, this theory cannot explain the form of provision adopted. Anyway, as we saw earlier, many public goods can in some circumstances be provided by the private sector.

In relation to health and education, the argument usually relates to income distributional problems which may prevent poorer people having access to adequate medical care and schools. However if this was all there was to it, we could simply redistribute income via the tax and welfare benefit system and let people buy health care and education in the market.

Economists have sometimes argued that people do not have full information (for example about health needs) or adequate foresight (in the case of education), particularly where parents make decisions on behalf of their children. In such circumstances, consumption of the service in question may be less than is in the long-term interests of individuals. These categories of expenditure are sometimes described by economists as **merit goods**, where increases in consumption over free market levels are held to be desirable. The normal assumption that the consumer is sovereign is dropped, and it is thought appropriate to substitute the judgment of 'experts' for that of ordinary people.

This is a view which has been increasingly challenged in recent years. It has been claimed that putting decisions about health, education, housing and other services in the hands of planners has led to restrictions of choice, queues for popular services and the substitution of planners' views (for instance an irrational preference for tower blocks over low-rise housing) for those of the public.

Furthermore, it has been claimed that the form in which public provision has been made has concentrated power in the hands of large bureaucracies and public sector trade unions. Competition from the private sector has been deliberately excluded and consequently organisations have become inefficient and costly to operate, while providers of services have become indifferent to the wishes and feelings of the people they are supposed to serve.

Finally, it is said that taking choice out of people's hands has smothered initiative and created an expectation that the government will always provide. When consumers get services 'for free' (actually, paid for from taxes) they do not consider the costs they are imposing, and they make unnecessary demands on services. Moreover, because individuals have to pay taxes to finance government health care, for example, they do not seek out potentially more attractive private insurance schemes.

There is also the argument, discussed in Chapter 17, that the provision of welfare services free of charge to the unemployed and low paid may act as a disincentive to seeking employment or better-paid work.

10.2.5 Methods of privatising services

This seems a formidable indictment. If it is accepted that these inefficiencies occur, what remedies are advocated?

1   **Cuts in services** One answer is just to cut services completely and leave provision up to individuals. Although this is economically feasible in some areas (eg the provision of libraries), such cuts are often highly unpopular with the public (and even more so with the providers of the service) and there are many areas (such as the provision of home helps to the elderly and handicapped) where it is difficult to see how privately organised and funded services could work effectively.

2   **Encouraging private provision** Governments can maintain basic services for the population as a whole while trying to encourage as many people as possible to 'opt out' and provide for themselves. Tax concessions for those paying for their own private health care or those sending their children to private schools offer one way of doing this. The problems here are that opting-out is only likely to appeal to a minority and that the services offered to those left to rely on the public service are likely to decline further in quality as the richer (and hence more articulate) consumers leave and staff are enticed away to the private sector by better pay and conditions.

3   **Reorganising the method of payment** Altering the method of paying for a service while still maintaining public sector funding can alter people's behaviour. For example, the United Kingdom's National Health Service is free at the point of use; people do not have to pay when they are admitted to hospital. An alternative approach is to organise payment on the basis of an insurance scheme, where people have to pay for services but can claim it back through government-provided insurance. Such a system operates in France. Such a scheme makes people much more aware of the costs they impose on the system, and can make doctors think more carefully about the costs of treatments which they arrange. It also offers the possibility of development into a partially private-funded system at some later stage. It is, however, costly to administer and there is no *direct* incentive to minimise costs of treatment.

4   **The creation of internal markets** Various schemes have been suggested to make public services behave rather like markets. One example is the **educational voucher**. Here parents would be given vouchers entitling their children to free education at a government-funded school of their choice. These vouchers would be handed over to the school. Successful schools, with lots of vouchers, would be able to expand; those schools which could not attract sufficient pupils would eventually have to close. Thus an 'internal market' is created within the education service. In this way efficiency would be promoted and schools would have to respond to parental choice. However, although such schemes have been much discussed, governments have not been eager to experiment. It is felt that the costs of adjustment to changes in parental preferences could be quite substantial, and that public sector education might become polarised

as better-off parents organised themselves to get children into good schools while poorer parents lagged behind. It is also possible that such polarisation might occur on socially-damaging racial or ethnic lines.

5 **Contracting-out** As we have indicated earlier, contracting-out of services may be seen as a way of reducing costs and increasing competition and innovation in the public sector. However, there are some difficulties with contracting-out. Typically, contractors tender to take over a specified range of services for a given period. There are dangers in this. One is that, in essence, a monopoly is granted for a given period and there may be difficulties in monitoring and enforcing the terms of the contract. One temptation is to offer short-term contracts so that unsatisfactory contractors can quickly be replaced but this gives rise to the problem that this may discourage long-term investment and commitment by contractors.

So, although there are many ideas for privatising services currently under discussion, there seem to be drawbacks to these schemes. It is perhaps not surprising, therefore, that privatisation in this area has not proceeded as rapidly or been as popular with the public as the privatisation of nationalised enterprises has been. Although Mrs Thatcher's administration in the United Kingdom, for example, is strongly critical of many fields of public service provision, it has yet to make any radical impact in this area.

10.3 DEREGULATION

As we saw in Chapter 9, governments have a range of options open to them to deal with perceived market failures. They can nationalise industries or provide tax-financed services directly to the public and in the previous section we have seen that in recent years there has been a movement away from this as a result of privatisation.

An alternative to direct government control is regulation, where the government or its agents lay down rules of various kinds affecting the behaviour of firms and individuals. Regulation has historically been of particular significance in the United States, where government ownership of industry has been very limited and where direct public provision of services has not reached the levels found, say, in Western Europe (for instance, the United States has never had an equivalent of the United Kingdom's National Health Service). This relatively low level of direct state involvement in the United States' economy has a number of explanations including the strong political support for free enterprise and the lack of a significant socialist party, the separation of powers between the President and Congress and between the States and Federal Government and the vast size and diversity of the country. However, the American economy **has** been characterised by a high degree of regulation at Federal, State and local levels. A bewildering variety of bodies—for example the Federal Communications Commission, the Food and Drug Administration, the Interstate Commerce Commission, the Securities and Exchange Commission, the Civil Aeronautics Board—has interfered in industry and commerce in various ways.

This is not to say that regulation has been unimportant in other countries; far from it. In the United Kingdom, for example, rules and regulations affect most areas of economic life. Indeed, in some areas regulation has increased recently as a result of privatisation. For example, bodies known as Oftel (Office Of Telecommunications) and Ofgas have been set up to regulate and supervise the newly-privatised telecommunications and gas industries.

However, in the United States, United Kingdom and several other countries, regulation has been looked at with an increasingly critical eye since the mid-1970s. It has been claimed that regulation (like more direct government involvement in the economy) brings costs as well as benefits. **De**regulation has increasingly been advocated by those with a strong belief in the virtues of the free market. It has been argued in the United Kingdom, for example, that privatisation should be accompanied by substantial deregulation if the benefits of greater competition are to be realised.

10.3.1 Types of regulation

Before we discuss regulation and deregulation any further, we need to be aware of the different forms of regulation found in mixed economies. One distinction to make is between regulation which has an impact right across the economy, sometimes called **social regulation** and that which affects a particular industry, profession or market. Examples of social regulation include health and safety at work legislation, anti-pollution laws and equal opportunities programmes. These will affect firms across the economy, altering their output decisions, methods of production, employment policies and so on from those which they would otherwise have adopted. By contrast a body such as the United Kingdom Oftel has powers limited to the telecommunications field, although they are in principle extensive within this area. This is an example of **market regulation**.

When the government is regulating particular markets, there are a number of means by which it may choose to do this. It can employ a variety of **regulatory bodies**, of which the commonest are:

1 **Government ministries or departments** may lay down detailed regulations in particular areas. For example, in Britain the Department of Education and Science lays down rules about who is able to teach in schools and colleges. The Bank of England (in effect under ministerial control) regulates the commercial banking system.

2 **Local government** at State (for example in the United States, West Germany and Nigeria) or municipal level often possesses considerable power to regulate businesses. In the United Kingdom, local authorities can control opening hours of shops and give planning permission for businesses and new buildings.

3 **Semi-independent regulatory bodies** may be set up by governments. They are given a broad set of rules, but are able to apply these in detail at their discretion. Often they are controlled by a board of appointees intended to represent a broad cross-section of the population; they have a fair degree of independence and cannot usually be dismissed at the will of the government. Examples would include the Independent Broadcasting Authority and the Securities and Investment Board in Britain, the West German Bundesbank and the US Securities and Exchange Commission.

4 **Self-regulatory bodies** have in the past been particularly significant in the United Kingdom, though their position has come under attack recently. Here the government allows a market or a profession to regulate itself, rather than installing an outside body for the task. For example, the legal and accountancy professions have traditionally been regulated in this way, whilst recent legislation has led to the creation of several Self-Regulatory Organisations (SROs) in the financial sector. It is often argued that self-regulation offers advantages in that members of a group are better able to understand the nature of any abuses which are occurring, and have a common interest in rooting out these abuses. Critics assert, however, that such arrangements can lead to 'cover-ups' to protect the reputation of a profession or group, and can exclude competition which would benefit the consumer.

Market regulation may involve a detailed control over the behaviour of firms and individuals. It may involve the determination of the level and structure of prices charged (for example, the United Kingdom Oftel currently stipulates that the price of domestic telephone calls in the United Kingdom cannot rise faster than the increase in the Retail Price Index minus 3 per cent), rate of return on capital, who is allowed to enter a market, entitlement to supply (for example, British Telecom is normally obliged to provide telephone services to anyone who wants them) and so forth.

10.3.2 Regulation in practice

According to critics, regulation has in practice often produced rather undesirable results. For example, rules to define who should be allowed to practise a profession (justified originally by the apparent need to protect consumers against incompetent or dishonest practitioners) have served to **restrict competition**, discourage innovation and keep up earnings for a privileged group. An example of this might be English barristers, who are protected from competition with solicitors. Price regulation—for example, insisting that utility producers (water, gas, electricity) or transport systems should charge similar prices to different customers—may involve **inequitable cross-subsidisation**, with poorer city dwellers paying higher prices to subsidise richer suburbanites. In the United Kingdom, unlike the USA, local telephone calls (predominantly private) are expensive relative to long-distance calls (predominantly business) as a result of restricted competition under a regulatory framework.

Regulation of rates of return on capital, as practised by market regulators in the United States, often has perverse results. If you lay down that a firm can make, say, a maximum 10 per cent return on any investment, but allow it to set prices to cover costs, a firm with a secure monopoly (protected by regulation) will have an incentive to overinvest. Industries subject to this type of regulation are likely to operate with an **inappropriate (excessively capital-intensive) technology**.

Moreover, where a regulatory body is set up to oversee an industry, there is a tendency for it to be **captured by the industry**. Because regulators and the industry must work together, they are likely to develop an unhealthily close relationship. The industry will be the major source of information to the regulators, and may indeed be a source of recruitment for it; who better to regulate a market than somebody who has worked in it? This can work the other way round, too, with firms recruiting staff who have worked for the regulators. Over a period of time, the regulators and the industry may come to have interests in common which do not necessarily coincide with those of the public.

As for social regulation, a lot of attention has focused on the **costs of implementation** of many regulations. For example, as we suggested in Chapter 9, the cost of pollution control can sometimes be excessive in relation to the perceived gain and labour market regulation (for example, employment protection legislation or sexual discrimination laws) can improve the conditions of those in work at the cost of reduced employment opportunities for those who are seeking jobs.

It is not surprising, therefore, that there has been recently a feeling amongst some economists and politicians that regulation should be subject to much more critical appraisal than has been the case in the past, and that deregulation, in appropriate areas, may offer significant efficiency gains.

10.3.3 Examples of deregulation

1 **Financial deregulation** In many countries, recent years have seen significant deregulation of the financial sector, offering greater competition and increased innovation. For example, in the United Kingdom abolition of exchange controls in 1979 made it much easier to transfer funds between Britain and other countries, thus increasing the competition which British banks, financial institutions and commercial and industrial firms faced from abroad. Legislation and relaxation of regulations have made it possible for building societies and other non-bank financial intermediaries (see Chapter 14) to compete with the commercial banks, offering chequebooks and other facilities. In October 1986 there occurred **Big Bang**, the name popularly given to the reform of the United Kingdom Stock Exchange. Minimum scales of commission were abolished, boundaries were eliminated between the traditional functions of stockbroking and stockjobbing, and membership restrictions were relaxed to allow large companies, both British and foreign, to participate in the stock market directly. These developments were stimulated by technical change (such as computer and satellite technology) which make possible enormous gains in speed and coverage of financial deals, but these advances could not have been properly exploited without financial deregulation.

2 **Broadcasting** Radio and television have been tightly regulated in most countries since their inception. Governments usually controlled these media because they were fearful of the immense power which ownership could place in the hands of those who wished to undermine accepted moral standards and political ideas. This may have made some sense in the past, when there was a very restricted range of frequencies available, and when the viewing and listening public was unused to choice. Nowadays, however, technical advance has made it possible to use existing wavebands more effectively and has introduced competition from satellite broadcasting, cable networks and videos. It is now widely recognised that there has been a fundamental change in the nature of broadcasting, which is now much more like newspaper and book publishing with a wide choice, specialist markets and little justification for old-style controls. Accordingly, broadcasting deregulation is occurring or being contemplated throughout the Western World.

3 **Air transport** Some sort of regulation of air transport is universal because there is a need for safety standards and of coordination and control of air traffic within and between countries, but regulation has frequently and unnecessarily been extended to price and competition. The International Air Traffic Association (IATA), see Chapter 2, is a well-known example of this; it has restricted entry to routes and kept prices artificially high, behaving in effect like a cartel. In some countries, however, internal deregulation has progressed considerably. The most notable example is the United States, where prices for journeys within the country have fallen substantially, and route maps and services have altered considerably as a result of increased competition and the ending of cross-subsidisation.

4   Labour markets Governments have always intervened in labour markets to alter working conditions, rates of pay, pension provisions and so on. As we shall see in later chapters, many economists have argued that these interventions may have had the effect of making labour markets less flexible, less able to adapt to changed demand and supply conditions. Increased labour market intervention by governments in the 1960s and 1970s has been held to be one of the reasons why unemployment is so much higher than it was in the first 25 years after World War II. Consequently some governments, notably that of the United Kingdom, are trying to deregulate labour markets, by repealing laws protecting trade unions, reducing the scope of minimum wage provisions and so on. More is said on this subject in Chapter 17.

Note, however, that despite the distinct trend towards deregulation in most Western economies there are still strong pressures for more, not less, regulation in many spheres. In Britain, for instance, the Financial Services Act of 1987 introduced a comprehensive regulatory system over the financial sector which some think will undo much of the earlier deregulation under Big Bang. The power of interest groups to lobby for and to obtain new regulations should never be underestimated.

SUMMARY

We have pointed out in this chapter that the last few years have seen a decline in confidence in the abilities of governments to intervene effectively in the market. This has led to a reduction in the public sector's direct role in the economy—privatisation—and a related movement towards deregulation. These changes do not mean that in future the government will have no role to play, but they do suggest that there is going to be an increasingly critical attitude taken to the view that governments should automatically intervene whenever there appears to be some form of market failure.

SELF-TEST QUESTIONS

1   Which of the following could not be an objective of privatisation?

(a)   Promoting competition.
(b)   Reducing taxes.
(c)   Spreading share ownership.
(d)   Reducing market pressures on management.
(e)   Reducing government borrowing.

2   Which of the following statements is incorrect?

(a)   Putting the maintenance of public parks and gardens out to tender is an example of privatisation.
(b)   The existence of a market for corporate control facilitates takeovers.
(c)   Nationalisation has sometimes been carried out by Conservative governments.
(d)   All nationalised industries are monopolies.
(e)   It is difficult to monitor performance in nationalised industries.

3   Which of the following statements is correct?

(a)   A merit good is a commodity which the private sector cannot provide.

(b)   Educational voucher schemes involve parents paying directly for their children's education.
(c)   Managers in the private sector usually face confused and conflicting objectives.
(d)   Nationalisation has been much more common in the United States than Europe.
(e)   Deregulation can assist in achieving some of the objectives of privatisation.

4   Which of the following is least likely to be a valid reason for regulating an industry?

(a)   To reduce pollution.
(b)   To promote competition.
(c)   To protect consumers' health.
(d)   To restrict excessive profits resulting from monopoly.
(e)   To lay down performance standards.

5   Which of the following is least likely to result from deregulation?

(a)   A reduction in cross-subsidisation.
(b)   An increase in innovation.
(c)   An increase in supernormal profits.
(d)   An increase in consumer choice.
(e)   A reduction in trade union power.

EXERCISE

What benefits have been claimed to result from privatisation?

Answers on page 255.

National income, output and employment

In this chapter we move from microeconomics to macroeconomics, the study of the economy as a whole. We examine the concept of the circular flow of national income, and show how national income can in principle be measured in three different ways. We then discuss in detail some refinements of national income concepts and the theoretical and practical problems associated with conventional national accounts. Finally, we indicate the relation between national income and aggregate employment, and some of the difficulties associated with ideas of full employment and unemployment.

11.1 INTRODUCTION

So far in this book we have been concerned with **micro**economics, the study of the behaviour of individual households and firms in particular markets—the market for potatoes, the market for sliced bread, the market for microcomputers. We now turn to examine the way in which markets interact to determine aggregate levels of income, output and employment and the general level of prices. This is the subject matter of **macro**economics.

Macroeconomic analysis, as a distinct subject, is a product of the last fifty years or so. In earlier periods there was little systematic collection of data about the economy as a whole to stimulate theorising. Economists since the days of Adam Smith in the eighteenth century had concentrated on microeconomic reasoning, and assumed that the lessons drawn from the study of individual markets could be generalised to the economy as a whole. For example, if the quantity of potatoes supplied exceeded the quantity demanded at a given price, the market could be cleared and excess supplies sold if the price was lowered. The price mechanism, left to itself without government intervention, would tend to produce a situation where supply was equal to demand throughout the economy. Resources would be fully and efficiently employed.

As we have seen, there are some qualifications to microeconomic analysis of this kind; there are situations where market failure can occur. But in most individual markets the analysis has a lot of plausibility. However, its application to economic policy in the 1930s in the United Kingdom and other countries seemed to many people unhelpful. The early 1930s were characterised by falling levels of output and rising levels of unemployment. The economies of most countries were experiencing a major **recession** (or slump, as it was more commonly described at the time).

Cycles of boom and slump had been common in the nineteenth century, and economists had put forward hypotheses to explain them. The consensus was that such fluctuations in economic activity were caused by fluctuations in financial conditions such as the availability of credit, but it was believed that the free market economy was self-correcting—slumps would not last for long; prices of raw materials would fall to make it cheaper and more profitable to produce goods and similarly wages would fall so that the unemployed would find it easier to obtain work. It was widely believed that periodic boom and slump were inevitably associated with dynamic economies, part of the natural order of things. They might be deplored but they had to be accepted as a fact of life.

This suggested that governments could do little to improve matters in recession. Many economists advised them to behave as prudent households would be doing; they should cut spending and make whatever savings they could. They should encourage 'realistic' behaviour of firms and workers, who had to realise that market forces must be allowed to operate as freely as possible to assist the process of recovery.

The recession of the 1930s did not turn rapidly to recovery as a result of these policies. It seemed to get worse. This led to a great deal of rethinking about the relationship between individual markets and the economy as a whole. Was it true that we could understand the behaviour of aggregates simply by a study of their parts? After all, many areas of science suggest this is doubtful. The behaviour of water is very different from that of its component elements, hydrogen and oxygen. With

E

humans, too; anybody who goes to football matches will recognise that the behaviour of a crowd will often be very different from the behaviour of the individuals who make it up.

The key figure in this rethinking was the English economist John Maynard (later Lord) Keynes (1883–1946). In his most famous book, *The General Theory of Employment, Interest and Money,* published in 1936, Keynes developed a new type of analysis which started from propositions about the economy as a whole, rather than starting with individual markets. It was Keynes' work which was mainly responsible for the development of the distinct study of macroeconomics. Although, as we shall see, his ideas have been strongly challenged in the last twenty years, Keynes was to leave an indelible mark on economic theory.

11.2   THE CIRCULAR FLOW OF NATIONAL INCOME

Before we can examine Keynes's approach in detail, we need to understand a number of key ideas. In *The General Theory* Keynes was primarily concerned with the determination of the level of **national income** in relation to the productive capacity of an economy. We must therefore start by exploring the meaning of national income.

In a given period of time, such as a year, an economy generates incomes for those who take part in production of goods and services. These incomes may derive from different types of productive contribution (as we have seen earlier in the book), but they all give rise to purchasing power.

Incomes result from the sale of output of goods and services. In turn they provide spending power necessary to buy that output. An implication of this is that there are three different ways of measuring national income—by looking at the value of total incomes, total output and total spending. This can be clarified by looking at Figure 11.1, which shows the **circular flow of income and expenditure**.

FIGURE 11.1   **The circular flow of income and expenditure**

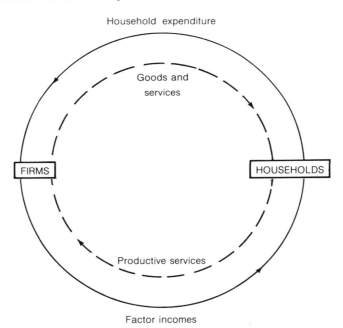

The diagram shows a highly simplified economy with no government, no foreign trade and where households spend all their incomes in consuming goods and services—there is no saving. There are only two types of institution. These are households, which own all the factors of production (land, labour and capital), and firms. Households supply the services of factors of production to firms, which organise the productive process.

In the diagram, there is a 'real' flow of productive services from households to firms, indicated by a dotted line. In return for these services households receive a 'money' flow of payments—wages and salaries, interest, rents and dividends (collectively known as factor incomes) indicated by an unbroken line. Firms also provide a real flow, the output of goods and services, again indicated by a dotted line and they receive a money flow of payments for these commodities, a flow arising from household expenditure.

Because we have assumed that there are no savings, household income (usually written Y) is just equal to consumption expenditure (C). There is no reason why the circular flow shown here should not continue indefinitely; in each period all the output is sold and all income is spent. Firms receive enough income from sales to employ the same productive resources as before, and households can afford to buy the same amount of output.

11.2.1 Leakages

This is clearly unrealistic. More generally we recognise that not all household income is automatically passed back to firms as in Figure 11.1. There are **leakages** from the circular flow of income. The important ones to distinguish are:

SAVINGS (S)

In modern economies, many people have incomes considerably in excess of their current consumption needs. They may therefore wish to save a proportion of their incomes, holding cash or (more importantly) building up financial assets such as building society deposits, pension funds, company shares and so on. Note, too, that firms can save by retaining profits rather than distributing them to shareholders in the form of dividends. In either case, some spending power **leaks** from the circular flow of income and is not passed back round the system.

TAXATION (T)

The payment firms make for factors of production is not necessarily the same as the incomes households receive. In the real world governments exist, and they impose taxes. Such taxes may be **direct**, such as income taxes or corporation taxes (on the profits of firms) or they may be **indirect**, such as value added tax. Taxation is a second leakage from the circular flow, for it means that some of the incomes created by productive activity are not passed back round as spending.

IMPORTS (M)

A third major leakage arises when we have an 'open' economy—one that trades with the rest of the world—rather than the 'closed' economy shown in Figure 11.1. This is because some spending goes on foreign goods and services (imports), and is therefore not passed back to domestic firms.

11.2.2 Injections

If this were all there were to it, the existence of leakages would mean that income would get less and less from period to period, for as firms received less back in payment for sales than they had paid out in incomes, they would have to cut production and employment would fall. Incomes would be less. If leakages continued, incomes would again fall. But fortunately leakages are compensated for by **injections** into the circular flow. Injections are forms of spending on domestic output which come from outside the household sector. There are three important types, which correspond to our categories of leakages:

INVESTMENT (I)

This is spending on capital goods, such as machinery and equipment. It is undertaken by firms, the productive institutions in our analysis (we are ignoring physical investment undertaken by households, such as do-it-yourself home improvement, as it is not purchased in the market). An important distinction to which we shall refer shortly is that between **gross** and **net** investment. Gross investment is the total of all investment spending in a period, net investment allows for the fact that existing capital assets wear out and have to be replaced. Some gross investment is therefore needed to cover depreciation:

$$\text{Net investment} = \text{Gross investment} - \text{Depreciation}.$$

GOVERNMENT SPENDING (G)

The government buys goods and services from firms—roads, buildings, computers. It also employs people—civil servants, teachers, nurses, police. Government spending on goods and services is clearly an injection into the circular flow. Note, though, that government spending on **transfer payments** such as social security benefits and old age pensions is not included. What happens here is that the government transfers spending power from one group of people—taxpayers—to another—welfare recipients. The government gets nothing in return: no output is created and there is no addition to national income. The recipients of transfer payments spend them, and their spending counts as part of consumer expenditure. If the amount the government spends on transfer payments counted as an injection there would therefore be double counting. Transfer payments should be treated as negative taxes to be deducted from total taxes in calculating the leakage T.

EXPORTS (X)

In open economies, goods and services can be sold to foreign residents as well as domestic households and firms. Payments received for exports constitute another injection into the circular flow.

Figure 11.2 incorporates some of these complications, although it concentrates on the money flows and omits the real flows of Figure 11.1.

FIGURE 11.2 **Circular flow with leakages and injections**

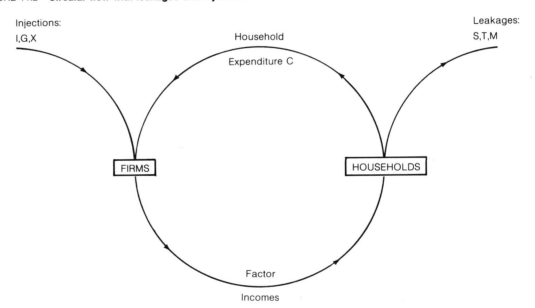

From this more complex picture a question naturally arises: do the planned injections and leakages balance? If they do—if the sum of I, G and X is just equal to the sum of S, T and M—we have a situation which is essentially the same as in our simpler model. With injections just equal to leakages, there is no reason why the same level of income cannot be maintained period after period. Economists say that there is **equilibrium in the circular flow of income**.

However, if the money value of the expenditure which households, firms, governments and foreign customers decide on is less than the value of the output produced, national income will tend to fall from period to period until it reaches a new equilibrium. Conversely, if spending exceeds planned output, national income will rise. We can make an analogy with a reservoir. When the water flowing in exceeds that flowing out the water level stays the same. If we raise the dam and allow more water to flow out, the level drops. If more flows in, the level rises.

11.3 NATIONAL INCOME EQUILIBRIUM

Before Keynes wrote *The General Theory*, most economists held views which implied that there were automatic forces which tended to bring the circular flow into equilibrium. These were the familiar mechanisms of microeconomics, essentially variations in price which would bring demand and supply into balance. If leakages temporarily exceeded injections, the value of planned spending would be less than the value of output, so goods would be unsold, but prices and wages would fall until equilibrium was restored. Further, it was argued that the equilibrium level of income to which the economy tended was one at which existing resources of land, labour and capital were fully employed.

Keynes disagreed with this. He argued that the mechanisms by which supply and demand were brought into balance were rather different from those emphasised by his predecessors. Conclusions drawn from microeconomics were misleading when applied to the economy as a whole. For example, if some workers were unemployed in a particular market it made sense to argue that a fall in wages (the 'price' of hiring labour) would bring supply and demand into balance, thus disposing of unemployment. However, if unemployment was widespread throughout the economy such a prescription might not work. Cuts in wages for all workers (and you couldn't just cut those offered to the unemployed, of course) would reduce aggregate household income and spending. Not only would spending be directly affected by incomes being reduced, but there would also be secondary effects. Expectations about future incomes would be lowered, and firms and households would respectively reduce planned investment and spending on consumer durables such as cars and household goods.

Keynes claimed that such cutbacks in planned spending could set off a downward spiral in national income, output and employment. Adjustments in output rather than prices and wages would be the major effect of injections and leakages getting out of line. The process would not continue indefinitely, for Keynes argued that eventually equilibrium would be reached when savings and other leakages had fallen to match the lower level of injections, but the new equilibrium might be one at which output was well below the economy's potential.

11.4 MEASUREMENT OF NATIONAL INCOME

We look at Keynes's reasoning in more detail in Chapter 12. Before we can usefully discuss it, though, we need to explore further some of the concepts which we use in macroeconomics. In particular, we have to look at national income.

As we saw from our consideration of the circular flow, national income can be measured in three ways:

11.4.1 The income method

This approach involves adding up the flow of **pre-tax** incomes accruing to owners of factors of production (wages, salaries, rents, dividends, interest payments, undistributed profits) which are generated in a given year or other relevant period. Notice that **factor incomes** arise from the sale of productive services of various kinds. This means that we must take income figures before tax, for if firms are prepared to pay these amounts they must value factor marginal products at least as highly. It also means that we must therefore exclude from national income any transfer payments, such as social security benefits. We saw earlier that these do not arise from the provision of a service. Were we to include them in national income as well as the pre-tax incomes which pay for them, we would have an absurd result. It would imply we could increase national income simply by increasing both taxes and benefits to transfer more and more from those in work to those not in work.

If no adjustment has been made to profits for depreciation, the sum of factor incomes is termed **Gross National Income (GNY)**. This is not an ideal measure of national income, as it does not tell us what level of income could be sustained over time. In order to know this we must subtract the cost of maintaining the existing capital stock. We then have **Net National Income (NNY)**:

$$NNY = GNY - Depreciation$$

11.4.2 The output method

Factor incomes arise from the sale of goods and services produced in the economy, so another method of calculating national income is to add up the value of all output created in the relevant period, mainly for sale in the market. When measured in this way the national income is usually referred to as the **national product**. Normally this value is measured by the supply price of output, ie, the price a firm receives for its product (supply price can differ from the price to the consumer if there are indirect taxes or subsidies).

However, some output is not sold in the market, for example, goods and services produced by households for consumption in the home. This is not included in national income (though we shall say something about it in 11.5). But we *do* include services produced by the government, even though they are not sold to the public in the conventional sense. For instance, the government may provide free education to school students or free medical care to the sick. Resources are used in the production of these services and factor incomes are created. For the purpose of national accounts, it is conventional to impute the value of such output by reference to the values of the inputs used. In principle, this is straightforward but in practice there are problems. The input value of government-provided services may seriously under- or over-estimate their value when sold in a free market.

Again, a distinction must be made between Gross and Net National Product:

$$NNP = GNP - Depreciation$$

There is a potentially serious problem of double-counting when calculating the national product. The value of output created by a firm will include within it the value of raw materials and intermediate goods purchased from other firms, for instance, the value of the output of a motor manufacturer will include the value of the steel used in vehicle production and the value of components such as sparking plugs bought in from outside suppliers. If we simply added the value of vehicles sold by the firm to the value of the steel and components produced by the supplying firms we would have an absurd result. It would imply that national income could be increased by a firm buying parts rather than making them for itself.

We must therefore concentrate on the **value added** by labour and capital employed in firms at each stage of production. This is found for each firm by deducting its purchases of materials, components and services from the value of its total output. This is not just some strange theoretical concept—many students will be aware that it is the basis of **value added tax** (VAT), an important source of tax revenue in the United Kingdom and many other countries.

11.4.3 The expenditure method

Spending of all kinds provides the incentive to supply output and thus create factor incomes. Adding up all that is spent on a country's output is the third way of calculating the national income; it gives us what is called **expenditure on the national product**.

A particular problem here is that the country's total expenditure exaggerates the value of incomes and output if there are indirect taxes (like VAT) and underestimates it if the government pays subsidies for the production of various goods and services. In either case, the price to consumers does not reflect the real cost of using the resources necessary to produce the commodities in question. Once again, this could lead to absurdities: national expenditure at market prices (and therefore income) would appear to be raised by increasing indirect taxes, or lowered by subsidising output. We therefore need to adjust national expenditure figures by the difference between prices charged in markets and the real cost of employing factor services:

$$NP \text{ at factor cost} = NP \text{ at market prices} - indirect\ taxes + subsidies$$

Figures for expenditure are often broken down into the broad components listed earlier: consumption expenditure (C), investment spending (I), government expenditure on goods and services (G) and exports (X). Because each of these includes spending on imports (for example, even goods a country exports may have been produced using raw materials, energy and intermediate goods imported from abroad), we need to deduct imports (M) from total expenditure to arrive at an aggregate which corresponds to the other measures of national income:

$$Expenditure \text{ on } NP = C + I + G + X - M$$

Yet another complication should be briefly mentioned; you will often see references to **gross** domestic product (GDP). This is the value of income generated by output produced within a country, as opposed to the value of all incomes received within a country. The difference arises because of property and investment incomes (profits, dividends, rent and interest) received by the country's residents from abroad. Of course, overseas residents also receive some of the incomes generated within the country. We must therefore concentrate on **net** property and investment income from abroad:

GDP = GNP − net property and investment income from abroad

For many countries the difference between GNP and GDP is substantial; for others inflows and outflows of property incomes roughly cancel out. For our purposes we shall largely ignore the distinction.

We see, then, that the calculation of national income aggregates is quite complicated. If there are three different ways of calculating national income, there are also numerous alternative measures of each aggregate. For instance, Figure 11.3 shows eight different national product aggregates and the connection between them. Similar measures exist for income and expenditure figures.

FIGURE 11.3 **Eight different national product aggregates**

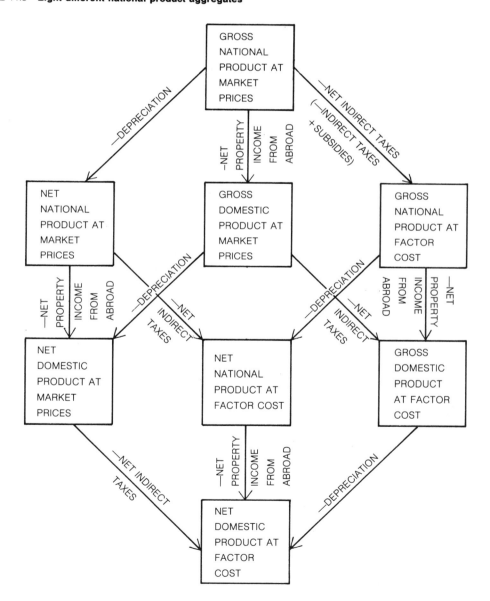

But these complications should not confuse you because the different ways of measuring national income are logical and straightforward once you understand the basic principle involved—

that we are trying to measure how resources are used to produce goods and services available for consumption and investment in a period.

Do bear in mind, though, that the collection of data to calculate these measures presents a lot of difficulties. In theory our income, output and expenditure figures should all give the same total. In practice they don't because the data are collected in different ways. For instance, income data are largely collected through income tax returns, while much of the expenditure data is collected from (voluntary) household surveys. Not surprisingly, people seem to be much more honest in giving details of their expenditure than in reporting their incomes! Even when questions are answered honestly and replies correctly reported, there will be many omissions from the data (for instance, those who quite legitimately don't pay tax because their incomes are too low) and estimates will have to be made. Published figures therefore have to include 'residual error' items to account for the difference between the various estimates.

11.5 PROBLEMS IN USING NATIONAL INCOME STATISTICS

Nowadays nearly all governments attempt to measure national income, with most Western economies making use of conventions of the sort described above (socialist countries employ slightly different conventions which use the Marxist distinction between productive and unproductive labour, though it is possible to make these figures roughly commensurate). Estimates of national income are used to measure economic growth, to provide a measure of average living standards (income per capita), or to compare one country with another. When using figures in these and similar ways we need to be aware of some of the pitfalls which face the unwary user:

COMPARING LIKE WITH LIKE

In addition to the data collection problems touched on above, it should be remembered that methods of collection and reliability of data change over time, and between countries. For instance, it is unlikely that data on incomes from the United Kingdom Inland Revenue collected in the 1950s are strictly comparable with that collected in the 1980s. Tax rates are different, changing the incentive to under-report, and different proportions of the population are required to pay tax because exemption levels have altered. It is also the case that revenue collectors and statisticians are much better equipped than in the past, and so the accuracy of their figures is likely to have changed. A similar problem arises when comparing data between countries. Data produced in a poor economy with an inefficient bureaucracy and few statisticians are unlikely to be as reliable as those from a rich country with a competent tax administration, a sophisticated statistical service and access to the latest computer technology.

INFLATION

Comparisons over time are difficult as a result of price changes. Initial data will be in terms of current money values. As well as the adjustments necessary to turn values from market prices to factor cost, as soon as we compare income in one year with that in another we must correct for **inflation** (the rise in the general level of prices). Then we can compare **real national income** in the two years. In order to do this we need an index of the general level of prices. Suppose that we know that national income per year in 1980 was £150,000m (in **current prices**, ie, those of that year), and that in 1985 it was £250,000m. However, between those years, prices had risen. Suppose that an index of prices has a value of 100 in 1980, and 150 in 1985. Then, to express 1985 national income in **constant** (ie, 1980) prices we must multiply by 100/150, thus:

$$\frac{100}{150} \times £250,000m = £166,667m$$

Those of you with a statistical background will realise that there is a whole set of theoretical and practical problems associated with the choice and construction of an appropriate index, but we cannot go into this subject here. We shall just note that in this context the index economists prefer to use is one called the **national income deflator**, which is found in the example by revaluing output in 1985 at 1980 prices.

NON-MARKETED GOODS

We mentioned earlier that goods and services produced for consumption in the home are excluded from national income figures. In less-developed countries, this is often a major omission. Subsistence farming may occupy a large part of the population so that national income per capita figures alone will give an unrealistically low indication of living standards: where families produce virtually all of their own food, cash incomes have a rather different significance from that which they have in developed economies. Within rich countries, domestic production is mainly confined to 'do-it-yourself' home improvements (a fast-growing activity in countries like the United Kingdom), cooking, cleaning, child care and other forms of housework. These activities *are* important in determining the quality of life and their exclusion from national income does produce anomalies. If a man marries his housekeeper, or a woman marries her gardener, measured national income falls even though they may continue to perform the same tasks for their new spouses: because they are no longer paid, their output isn't counted. These may be trivial examples, but there is an important principle involved. Since the 1950s in the United Kingdom, the United States and many other countries, there has been a big increase in the number of married women who go out to work. National income has risen accordingly, but many would argue that this overestimates the gain to the economy. The opportunity cost of the extra marketed output may have been a fall in domestic production. However, the practical and conceptual difficulties of valuing housework preclude us from making an allowance for this.

THE 'BLACK' ECONOMY

We have already seen that national income figures cover transactions in the 'official' economy, ie, those recorded for tax purposes. A common feature of most economies, however, is a significant sector of economic activity which goes unreported officially. This will include work by people who are trying to avoid income tax or VAT such as those who work for 'cash in hand, no questions asked', the sale of smuggled goods, or the sale of price-controlled products at higher prices than those which can be charged officially and the sale of goods and services which are illegal. All this activity is described as the 'black', 'informal' or 'unofficial' economy. In making comparisons between national income figures over time, we should be aware that this activity, as a proportion of recorded, official activity, may be rising or falling—perhaps in response to changes in laws, taxes, and regulations (including those concerned with eligibility for social security benefits) which alter the incentive pattern facing individuals, and there is a good deal of evidence to suggest that the extent of the black economy varies considerably from country to country. A study by the Organisation for Economic Cooperation and Development (OECD), for instance, concluded that, while the United Kingdom and the United States had black economies of around 4 per cent of GDP in the early 1980s, that of Italy (unofficial champion of the developed world) was around 30 per cent of GDP!

DEPRECIATION

We saw earlier that we need to remove depreciation from GNP to get NNP. The difficulty here is that we have no certain way of distinguishing new from replacement investment. In a constantly changing economic environment we rarely want to replace worn-out machines by identical new ones. Technology, demand patterns and the relative costs of different methods of production will have changed over the working life of the old machine. For accounting and tax purposes allowances are made for depreciation (so that firms are not paying out as dividends, or paying taxes on, funds which are needed to replenish the capital stock). These are used as the basis for national income calculations. But this is rather an arbitrary approach because accounting conventions and tax laws differ from period to period and from country to country. Accordingly, although we would sometimes prefer **net** figures, when making comparisons economists often rely on **gross** measures of national income or product.

INCOME DISTRIBUTION

Where figures for national income per capita are used for comparisons they can often be misleading indicators of general economic welfare. Two countries might have the same national income per head, despite the fact that in one country most people have approximately the same income, whereas in the other there are a large number of very poor people and just a few rich people who pull up the average. The first country has a more equal distribution of income than the other. Because of this problem, comparisons between countries are better done (where data allow) in terms of **median** income (a statistical term meaning that income where 50 per cent of the population have less than this figure, and 50 per cent have more) rather than mean (or average) income.

CONSUMPTION AND PRICE STRUCTURES

Patterns of consumption and the relative prices of goods differ such a lot from country to country and over time that comparisons of living standards are very difficult. Products which are available cheaply in one country may be unavailable or very expensive in another. Varying tastes and cultural attitudes may make a product which is widely appreciated and consumed in one country (beef in the United States) seem unattractive in another (India). Consumption of coal and oil to keep warm in a cold country is not even necessary in a hot one. Over a period of time, new products such as videos and personal stereos emerge which previous generations could not have envisaged and old products like red flannel petticoats and stagecoaches disappear. Consequently, we should be very wary when we make comparisons between living standards of different populations using national income figures.

EXCHANGE RATES

Comparisons between countries have to be made in terms of common currency, usually the US dollar. Unfortunately, the fluctuations of a country's exchange rate against the dollar can be enormous in a relatively short period of time, and such fluctuations may reflect special factors which have little to do with the underlying national income or changes in price levels. Moreover, some countries operate artificially high fixed exchange rates against the dollar—most Eastern European countries, for example—which bear no relation at all to the underlying 'purchasing power parities' (see Chapter 19).

Thus we see that there are very great difficulties involved in the use of national income statistics as indicators of economic welfare. Apart from these technical objections, some people may raise ethical or philosophical objections to taking money values as a guide to levels of human happiness. In recent years these objections have often been allied to belief that economic growth has had harmful side effects or externalities (see Chapter 9) which are rarely paid the same attention as are national income data. For example, it is argued that the state of the natural environment has deteriorated as countries have become richer in monetary terms and the **quality of life** in our crowded cities and ever-spreading suburbs has worsened.

Nevertheless, national income statistics *are* widely used as indicators of macroeconomic activity in forecasting and policy-making and we need to be clear about their construction and significance and the pitfalls in using them.

11.6 EMPLOYMENT AND UNEMPLOYMENT

Keynes's examination of the determination of national income, which we are going to look at in detail in Chapter 12, was ultimately stimulated by his desire to understand the determination of **employment**. As we have seen earlier in this book, changes in output in the short run (Keynes's concern) are associated with changes in employment of the variable factor of production, labour. So if we understand the determination of output, we know what determines employment.

In the sort of presentation of Keynes's ideas we are going to undertake, it is useful to refer to the idea of a 'full employment' level of national income and output. Below this level, increases in aggregate expenditure have the effect of increasing **real** national income, output and employment. Above the full employment level, however, increases in expenditure can have no effect on output and employment—they simply serve to drive up prices and generate inflation. Thus we have a rise in **money** national income but employment remains unchanged.

11.6.1 Full employment

In reality, things are not quite this clear-cut. For one thing, Keynes recognised that, rather than there being a clear distinction between less-than-full and full employment, there is in practice a more gradual movement from a situation where **most** of an increase in aggregate expenditure goes to create extra output, and only a small part is dissipated in higher prices, to one where most of the impact is on prices and very little on output.

For another, we need to be aware that **full employment** does **not** mean that every single adult in the population is employed. There will of course always be individuals who are physically or mentally incapable of normal work, those who are ill, those who have retired and those in full-time education. Excluded, too, are full-time homemakers and those lucky people who have private property incomes sufficient to enable them to live a life of leisure.

So we have to define full employment in relation to the **working population** or **labour force**—those willing and able to work. This still presents us with problems, since in principle many of those not currently in the working population can work and in certain circumstances will work. For example, in World War II many retired people returned to the labour force; in 'sheltered' conditions, many disabled people are capable of productive employment; at sufficiently attractive wage rates and given the availability of childminders many mothers with young children seek jobs. In addition changes in the availability of higher education are another factor which affects the **participation rate**, ie, the proportion of the population in the labour force. Thus the full employment level of output is something which we can only define in the short run for a particular size of labour force.

How do we measure the size of the labour force? One approach, used in official statistics in the United Kingdom, is to count all those people who are in employment or self-employed, those in government training schemes and those registered as seeking work (ie, unemployed). In the United Kingdom this last category is mainly made up of those who are claiming welfare benefits because they are unemployed. Some economists argue that many of this group should be excluded from the labour force as they are not *genuinely* seeking work but deliberately living off state benefits with no intention of getting a job, at least in the formal economy (although they may be engaged in the 'black economy'). If we follow this line of reasoning, we should reduce both the number of unemployed *and* the labour force shown in official government figures.

Another approach, used in the United States, is to survey a sample of the adult population of working age and ask them whether they are in work or would like to work. This will often pick up a larger number of unemployed (and a larger number of potential workers) than does the United Kingdom method, because in the UK many active job-seekers do not register as unemployed if they are not entitled to benefits.

Not surprisingly, therefore, the question of the size of the labour force and the number of the unemployed is one of intense political controversy. We shall return to it in a later chapter.

11.6.2 Types of unemployment

Economists recognise that, even ignoring the problem of the 'work-shy', there will always be some members of the labour force who will be unemployed at any particular time. A number of categories have been distinguished:

FRICTIONAL UNEMPLOYMENT

First, there are workers who, although currently unemployed, are genuinely 'between jobs' having left one job to take another which is starting shortly or are currently choosing between a number of offers. Although technically unemployed, they do not constitute a significant social problem, nor do they mean a real loss of output to the economy, as their period of **search** in the labour market may actually be a productive use of time. If they 'shop around' for the best offer, they are likely to end up in jobs where they are more productive than they would have been had they taken the first offer they received.

SEASONAL UNEMPLOYMENT

Frictionally unemployed people could be described as **voluntarily** unemployed. Another group sometimes classed in this way are the **seasonally** unemployed. For some types of worker—ski instructors, tourist guides, professional cricketers—demand is concentrated in one part of the year. For the rest of the year jobs may not be available, and the workers will be unemployed. Nevertheless, if people continue in these occupations, they can be said to have 'voluntarily' accepted their temporary unemployment.

STRUCTURAL UNEMPLOYMENT

Structural unemployment exists because of a 'mismatch' between workers and jobs. This may be geographical (for example jobs are currently available in the southeast of Britain while workers are unemployed in the north) or occupational (jobs are currently available for computer programmers while steelworkers are unemployed). In principle, unemployed workers could move from area to area (geographical mobility) or retrain (occupational mobility). To the extent they don't do so, they could be said to 'choose' not to do so, and thus their unemployment is 'voluntary'. This view is, not surprisingly, a controversial one. In practice, there may be economic and social barriers to mobility, for example, lack of suitable housing, high costs of moving and retraining and reluctance to leave friends and relocate family. There are certainly strong grounds for arguing that government intervention is required to improve the situation of the structurally unemployed, for example by reform of the housing market, relocation of industry, retraining schemes etc, but the point is that such measures are essentially **microeconomic** in nature because they alter the pattern of incentives facing individuals and firms. Structural unemployment cannot be dealt with by raising the level of aggregate demand in the economy. This point is taken up again in the discussion of supply-side economics in Chapter 17.

Frictional, seasonal and structural unemployment will always exist in a dynamic economy. Although their level can be reduced, there is an irreducible minimum. Thus Keynesians recognise that full employment will always involve a certain amount of unemployment. At the end of World War II, Keynes believed that full employment would be compatible with 'voluntary' unemployment of about 5 per cent of the labour force. In the 1950s and 1960s it was clear that for that period he had probably been too pessimistic—for a long time the unemployment rate in the United Kingdom and other developed countries was kept down to 2 per cent or even less. However, for a variety of reasons discussed later in the book, it seems likely that the feasible 'full employment' rate of unemployment today is much higher than in the early postwar period.

Keynes's analysis was not really concerned with 'voluntary' unemployment, which he took as given. Rather he was concerned with **involuntary** unemployment. This occurs when people wish to work, are prepared to accept wages currently being obtained by employed workers, are willing to be mobile and are properly qualified, but nevertheless cannot find jobs. In Keynes's view this situation may exist because there is insufficient aggregate demand or planned expenditure. His solution, as we shall see, is for governments to expand aggregate demand, primarily through increasing public expenditure.

For Keynes full employment would have to be defined as a situation where there is a no **demand-deficient** unemployment. We shall take this as our point of reference in Chapter 12.

SUMMARY

In this chapter we have introduced the idea of the circular flow of income, output and expenditure. We have seen that injections and leakages of various kinds affect this flow. We have seen how national income figures are obtained, and examined some of the conceptual and practical problems involved in their use. Finally, we have linked this discussion to levels of employment and unemployment, and have tried to make clear the use to which the idea of 'full employment' is put in Keynesian economics.

SELF-TEST QUESTIONS

1 **Other things being equal, which of the following would not lead to an increase in the equilibrium level of income in an economy where there are unemployed resources?**

(a) A fall in imports.
(b) A cut in government spending.
(c) A fall in savings.
(d) A rise in the budget deficit.
(e) A cut in taxation.

2 **Which of the following statements is not correct?**

(a) The value of the output of the United Kingdom's National Health Service is included in its national income.

(b) Goods purchased by do-it-yourself enthusiasts are included in national income.

(c) The existence of value added tax is one

reason why GDP at market prices differs from GDP at factor cost.

(d) If a good is produced for export sale only, it doesn't enter GDP.

(e) A rise in social security payments has no direct effect on measured national income.

3 How do you obtain a figure for GDP at factor cost?

(a) GDP at market price plus subsidies minus indirect taxes.

(b) GDP plus net property income from abroad.

(c) GDP at market prices minus depreciation.

(d) NDP at market prices minus indirect taxes.

(e) GNP at market prices plus subsidies.

4 Which of the following statements is correct?

(a) Two countries with the same national income must have roughly the same living standards.

(b) Real national income figures are unreliable because they ignore the effect of inflation.

(c) There is never any opportunity cost when homemakers re-enter the labour force.

(d) Income per head is always a better measure of a country's living standards than median income.

(e) We often use Gross rather than Net National Product figures because it is difficult to calculate the amount by which the capital stock depreciates in a period.

5 If skilled engineering workers lose their jobs because their industry declines and they cannot find work despite a high level of employment in the economy as a whole, how are they best described?

(a) Seasonally unemployed.

(b) Geographically mobile.

(c) Workshy.

(d) Structurally unemployed.

(e) Frictionally unemployed.

EXERCISE

How useful are national income accounts in making comparisons of living standards between countries?

Answers on page 257.

Introducing the Keynesian model

Having explored the meaning of the circular flow of national income, we now look in some detail at Keynes's analysis of the factors determining the level of aggregate demand in the economy. Assuming that there is excess productive capacity and that the aggregate level of wages and prices remain unaltered, changes in aggregate demand lead to changes in total output and employment in the economy. In Keynes's view, the level of aggregate demand generated in a free market economy may frequently fall below that required to produce full employment. In such circumstances increased injections into the circular flow lead to multiplied increases in output, but because such increased injections may not arise spontaneously governments should, through aggregate demand management, step in to remedy the market's deficiencies.

12.1 AGGREGATE DEMAND

Before setting out our 'Keynesian' model, we must stress that Keynes himself is not easy to read. The question of what Keynes really meant is one which has bemused two generations of commentators. What we present here is just one interpretation of Keynes; but it *is* an extremely common one, on which much of economic policy has been based since World War II.

We saw in the last chapter that one way of defining national income equilibrium was in terms of **injections** into the circular flow being equal to **leakages** from that flow. Another, absolutely equivalent, way of defining equilibrium is 'that level of national income at which aggregate planned expenditure (or **aggregate demand**) is equal to aggregate income and output'.

As we saw before, aggregate demand or expenditure is made up as follows:

$$AD = C + I + G + X - M$$

Now if Y stands for national income (or national product, for the terms are equivalent at the aggregate level), then national income is in equilibrium when:

$$Y = C + I + G + X - M$$

In an accounting sense, this statement is simply a tautology, true by definition. Nothing is said about what causes the level of income and expenditure to be what they are, but Keynes's claim is that aggregate demand **determines** the equilibrium level of real income, output and employment. How?

Think of an economy in the short run, when the total stock of capital equipment is fixed. Assume there is enough labour available to produce at full employment (as defined in Chapter 11) a maximum output worth £5bn per week. In short, we could say full employment income is £5bn per week. But if aggregate demand falls to less than this, say, £4bn per week, then firms will have to reduce their output to this level, otherwise they will be accumulating undesired and unsaleable stocks of goods. In reducing output they will reduce employment.

Notice that this ignores the possibility that firms react to deficiencies in demand by cutting prices and that workers react by accepting lower wages. As we saw in the previous chapter, Keynes tended to play down the significance of wage and price adjustments at the aggregate level. Keynesians tend to argue that there are factors operating in real-world economies to induce a certain amount of wage and price 'stickiness'. For instance, there may be costs associated with frequent price changes—relabelling goods, transmitting information to branch offices and shops, loss of consumer loyalty—and wage cuts may be resisted either by workers organised in trade unions or as a result of widely-held notions of fairness which inhibit employers from short-term profit maximisation. As a result, Keynes and his followers have stressed that a new equilibrium would be reached through

quantity rather than **price** adjustments because output and employment would fall as workers become involuntarily unemployed as a result of a deficiency in aggregate demand.

The determination of aggregate demand, then, is of crucial significance in Keynes's analysis. To bring this out more clearly, consider a closed economy (X and M are both zero) where there is no government rôle in the economy (G and T are zero). This is only a simplification and makes no difference to the principle involved, as we shall see.

In such a model, then, we have only one leakage from the circular flow, savings (S) and only one injection, investment (I). There are only two components of aggregate demand—consumption and investment:

$$AD = C + I$$

12.2 THE CONSUMPTION FUNCTION

We start by looking at the determinants of aggregate consumption in any period. What households plan to spend on consumption goods and services will depend on many factors. Obviously, household income (Y) will be one; another is the rate of interest (r). The interest rate reflects the opportunity cost of current consumption in terms of higher consumption which today's savings make possible in the future: higher interest rates make it more attractive for households to save. It also shows the price of borrowing to finance consumption today. In practice, interest rates charged to borrowers are higher than those paid to lenders, but since they move up and down together we can ignore this point.

Further influences on planned consumption include the quantity of highly liquid assets (LA), such as bank deposits, held by households; and the size of other wealth holdings (W) in less liquid assets such as bonds, company shares, housing and so on. **Liquidity**, which will be dealt with in detail later, means the ease with which assets can be converted into cash.

The relationship between planned consumption and its determinants can be conveniently expressed in a **consumption function** (a function, remember, is a mathematical relationship between a **dependent** variable—here, consumption—and one or more **independent** or **explanatory** variables). Concentrating on those factors we have mentioned, we could write a function like this:

$$C = f(Y, r, LA, W)$$

To simplify further, Keynes argued that one of these factors had the predominant influence on planned consumption—the level of current real income—other factors could effectively be ignored. Although economists since Keynes have broadly agreed that income is a very important consideration, they have sometimes argued for rather different interpretations of income. One view is that an individual or household's **relative income** (ie income relative to past experience, or relative to the income of other people) is of more significance. Another is that the appropriate concept is **permanent** income (a sort of average of expected future income, allowing spending to be maintained from period to period), a concept particularly associated with Professor Milton Friedman and discussed briefly in Chapter 15.

Returning to Keynes: his consumption function concentrates simply on the relation between consumption and current income with other influences on consumption held constant:

$$C = f(Y)$$

In fact, Keynes goes on to suggest that this function would have a particular form. Notice that in this simplified economy household income is either consumed or saved, ie Y = C + S. The proportion of income spent is called the **average propensity to consume** (APC):

$$APC = C/Y$$

Correspondingly, we can write the average propensity to save:

$$APS = S/Y$$

Because households only either spend or save, it must be true that:

$$APC + APS = 1$$

Keynes reasons that poorer households will spend a large proportion of their incomes so the average propensity to consume will be close to 1. Indeed it may in some cases be greater than 1. Households may spend more than their current income by **dissaving** (financing the excess by running down their assets or borrowing). However, as income rises, a smaller proportion is spent and a higher proportion saved, the average propensity to consume falls and the average propensity to save rises. Keynes's generalisation about behaviour, which he argued to be a 'fundamental psychological law' would be compatible with (amongst others) a consumption function of this type:

$$C = a + bY$$

Here a is a positive constant (representing an irreducible minimum level of consumption financed if necessary by dissaving), and b is a positive fraction showing the proportion of **extra** income which is consumed. Keynes calls this fraction the **marginal propensity** to consume (MPC) and he argues that it will be less than 1. An example of such a function would be:

$$C = 1,000 + 0.5Y$$

If we plot such a function on a graph, as in Figure 12.1, we observe that it is a straight line. In this case the term a is 1,000. This gives us the point where the line crosses the consumption axis. Perhaps less obviously, the b term (in this case 0.5) indicates the gradient of the line. You should be able to see that for each extra pound of income, consumption rises by 50p.

FIGURE 12.1 **The consumption function**

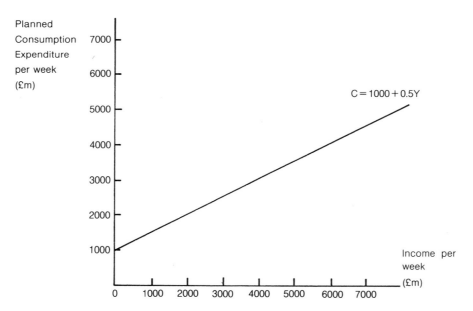

From the graph we can see the level of consumption associated with each level of income, and use this information to calculate the average propensity to consume. This declines as income rises and, correspondingly, the average propensity to save rises. Table 12.1 shows this for various income levels. Remember, though, that the **marginal** propensity to consume, and its counterpart, the **marginal** propensity to save, remain constant.

To clarify these relationships, look at Figure 12.2. In the upper part of the diagram we again show a line representing our consumption function, but this time with the addition of a line drawn at 45 degrees to the origin. Along this line planned consumption expenditure is equal to income. The 45 degree line crosses the consumption function at an income level of £2,000m. Below this income level, it should be apparent that consumption exceeds income so that savings are **negative**; above this income, consumption is less than income so that we have positive savings. In the lower part of the diagram we emphasise this by plotting savings against income.

TABLE 12.1   **Values of average propensity to consume and average propensity to save when C = 1000 + 0.5Y**

Y (£m)	C (£m)	S(£m)	APC (=C/Y)	APS (=S/Y)
0	1000	−1000	(∞)	(−∞)
1000	1500	−500	1.5	−0.5
2000	2000	0	1.0	0
3000	2500	500	0.83	0.17
4000	3000	1000	0.75	0.25
5000	3500	1500	0.70	0.30

FIGURE 12.2   **Consumption and savings**

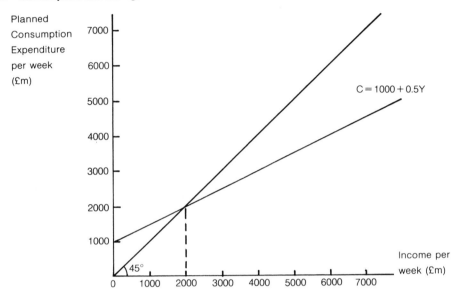

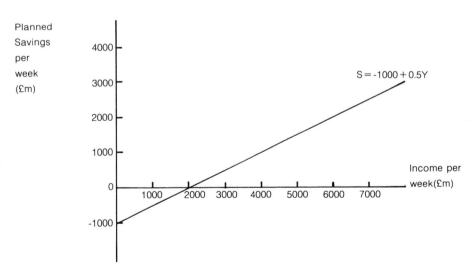

Note that the line relating savings to income represents a **savings function.** Where there is only the one leakage from the circular flow of income, as in this example, the savings function can be derived thus:

$$S = Y - C$$
$$\text{and} \quad C = a + bY$$
$$\text{therefore} \quad S = Y - (a + bY)$$
$$S = Y - a - bY$$
$$\text{or} \quad S = -a + (1 - b)Y$$

12.3   INVESTMENT

Like planned consumption, planned investment spending by firms is likely to be affected by a range of factors, two of the more important of which will be the **interest rate** (which measures both the cost of borrowing to the firm and the opportunity cost of its own funds) and the **level of business profits**. Profits in turn will be related to the level of national income. However, when making decisions about investment, we are inevitably looking to the future, so it is not so much current national income which influences investment spending decisions, but rather the **expectations** about the future growth of national income held by entrepreneurs and business executives.

If firms' decision-makers are optimistic about the future, expecting sales and profits to rise, they will want to install more capital equipment. If they are pessimistic—perhaps thinking that their productive capacity is already more than enough to meet likely demand—they will not want to carry out new investment even if interest rates are low and current profits adequate. They may not even wish to replace existing machines and plant as they wear out (remember the distinction between new investment and replacement investment that we introduced in Chapter 11).

Keynes argues that expectations and the state of 'business confidence' are crucial in determining the level of planned investment. As a result, although a fall in interest rates *with a given set of expectations* might be expected to make investment more attractive, it might have little impact if, simultaneously, expectations are deteriorating, so he thought that falling interest rates (a special case of the price flexibility which orthodox economics held to be so important) in periods of economic recession would have little effect in stimulating investment. We examine this argument further in the next chapter.

For the moment we simply observe that Keynes's emphasis on intangible and unobservable expectations led him to argue that planned levels of investment were largely independent of economic variables such as interest rates, profits and, importantly, current income. So although investment is clearly a component of aggregate demand, for the purpose of setting up our simple Keynesian model we can treat it as **exogeneous** or **autonomous**. In other words we shall just assume there is a particular level of investment demand—say, £1,000m a week—without specifying how this is determined.

12.4   EQUILIBRIUM INCOME

Bearing this in mind, we can modify our consumption function diagram to illustrate the determination of equilibrium income. To do this we construct an aggregate demand function, represented by the line AD_1 in Figure 12.3. This shows aggregate demand (consumption **plus** investment) at every

FIGURE 12.3   **Determination of equilibrium income**

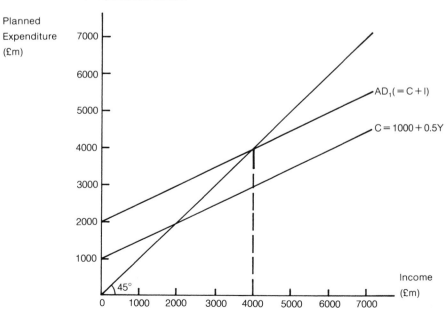

level of income. It is simply the consumption function of the earlier diagrams shifted upwards by £1,000m (the amount of investment we have assumed). We have again drawn in the 45 degree line. The income level at which this line cuts our aggregate demand function is significant: here planned expenditure (aggregate demand) is equal to income, which as we we saw in 12.1, is the **equilibrium level of income**. We can see from inspection of the diagram that equilibrium income on these assumptions is £4,000m per week. We can also reach this conclusion algebraically. Call the equilibrium income Y. We know that this must be equal to planned expenditure, C + I. We then substitute into the equation what we are assuming about C and I:

$$Y = C + I$$
therefore $\quad Y = (1,000 + 0.5Y) + 1,000$
$$Y = 2,000 + 0.5Y$$
$$Y - 0.5Y = 2,000$$
$$0.5Y = 2,000$$
therefore $\quad Y = 4,000$

Remember the meaning of equilibrium income. At all other values of Y there is either excess demand (driving up income and thus output) or insufficient demand (pulling income down). You should check this by calculating aggregate demand for income levels other than £4,000 million. Another way of understanding the conditions for equilibrium income is to remember that, in equilibrium, planned injections equal leakages. In our simplified model this means savings equal investment. Figure 12.4 illustrates this. The level of investment (£1,000m) does not change with income and can therefore be represented by a line parallel to the income axis. At the income level where this cuts the savings function, derived from Figure 12.2, we have savings equal to investment.

FIGURE 12.4 **Savings, investment and equilibrium income**

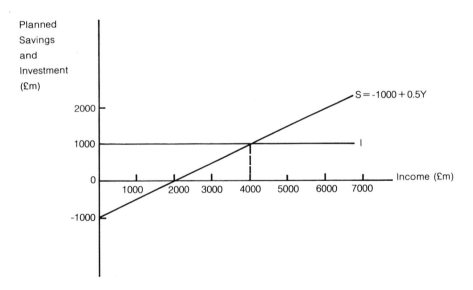

12.5 THE MULTIPLIER

Keynes argues that the equilibrium level of income at which the economy settles may be less than the full employment level of income (in the sense discussed in Chapter 11). In these circumstances, increases in aggregate demand can be expected to boost aggregate output as unemployed resources (equipment and plant as well as labour) are brought back into use. Furthermore, he argues—using an idea developed by his colleague Richard (later Lord) Kahn—that an increase in injections into the circular flow will produce an increase in national income and output greater than the increase in injections which set it off. How is this apparently miraculous result achieved?

Look at Figure 12.5. As in Figure 12.3, we show an aggregate demand function AD_1 on the assumption that consumption (C) is equal to (1,000 + 0.5Y), and that investment (I) is equal to £1,000m per week. In these circumstances, equilibrium income is £4,000m. Now suppose that investment (an injection) increases by £500m per week, perhaps as the result of an upsurge in business confidence. In Figure 12.5 this means that there is an upward shift of the aggregate demand function from AD_1 to AD_2.

FIGURE 12.5 **The effect of an increase in aggregate demand on equilibrium national income**

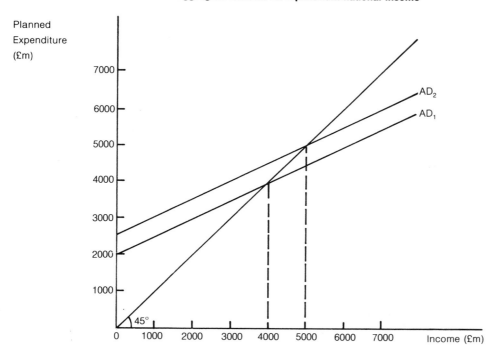

The equilibrium level of income is now determined where AD_2 cuts the 45 degree line. As we can see from the diagram, this is at £5,000m. So, as a consequence of an increase in investment of £500m, equilibrium income has risen by £1,000m. So much for the diagram. But what is the economic process involved? The initial increase in investment spending by firms of £500m leads to an increase in output in the capital goods industry. More workers are taken on, and therefore more wages are paid. In addition increased profits are made, and dividends paid to shareholders. Households therefore obtain incomes £500m per week greater than before.

We have assumed that the marginal propensity to consume is 0.5. This means that half of the extra household incomes is spent, and half saved. Thus there is an extra £250m of consumer spending. This creates more demand for labour and capital and gives rise to a further £250m of wages and profits. Households receiving these incomes consume half (£125m) and save half. This extra spending again gives rise to higher output and income and so on.

Each rise in household income therefore induces further increases in spending and income. However, at each stage the induced spending is getting less and less, until eventually the increases become negligible and the accumulated increase in income per week since the beginning of this process reaches a limit. In this example, the limit it reaches is £1,000m:

$$500 + 250 + 125 + 62.5 + 31.25 + \ldots = 1,000$$

Notice that there is also a series of induced increases in savings which again reaches an upper limit:

$$250 + 125 + 62.5 + 31.25 + \ldots = 500$$

The sum of induced savings is £500m, exactly the same amount as the increase in investment which set the process off. This is not an accident, because in equilibrium injections must equal leakages. Thus if injections increase, the level of income will rise until leakages have risen by just enough to bring leakages and injections back into balance.

The process we have just seen is called the **multiplier process**, and it is important to note that it can work in reverse, with **decreases** in injections leading to a multiplied **decrease** in income.

The ratio between the initial change in injections, in this case the increase in investment, (ΔI), and the ultimate change in equilibrium income resulting from this process (ΔY) is known as **the multiplier** (k):

$$k = \frac{\Delta Y}{\Delta I}$$

In this particular case, the multiplier's value is:

$$k = \frac{1,000}{500} = 2$$

In general, the value of the multiplier will depend on what proportion of households' extra income goes back round the circular flow as an increase in consumption. In other words, the larger the marginal propensity to consume, the larger the multiplier. This is shown in a simple expression for calculating the value of the multiplier in our kind of model, where there is, remember, no government and no foreign trade:

$$k = \frac{1}{1 - mpc}$$

In our case:

$$k = \frac{1}{1 - 0.5}$$

$$= \frac{1}{0.5} = 2$$

Suppose the marginal propensity to consume were higher, say 0.75. Then k would be $1/(1 - 0.75)$, which is 4. Thus an increase in injections as a result of a rise in investment would ultimately lead to an increase in equilibrium income of four times the amount of extra investment.

12.6 THE SIGNIFICANCE OF THE MULTIPLIER

The multiplier plays a crucial role in the policies advocated by Keynesians. Look again at Figure 12.5. Suppose the level of national income and output associated with full employment is £5,000m per week. Currently, however, aggregate demand is insufficient to achieve this. The aggregate demand function is AD_1, which cuts the 45 degree line at an income level of £4,000m. In equilibrium, therefore, there is a deficiency of aggregate demand. In order for the economy to reach full employment it is necessary for the aggregate demand function to be shifted up to AD_2.

Keynes argues that in the depths of a recession it is unlikely that the free market, left to itself, will generate a sufficiently large increase in aggregate demand. For instance, although a fall in the interest rate (one likely result of a depressed economy) will have a tendency to stimulate investment *other things being equal*, in practice this effect (as we suggested earlier) will be small as long as business expectations about the future remain depressed. So Keynes argues that it is necessary for the government to boost aggregate demand directly by increasing its own spending (G) on goods and services. For instance, the government might build more hospitals, schools and roads.

In our model so far we have, of course, assumed away the existence of the government; but let's now introduce it into our picture. Given the aggregate demand function AD_1 shown in Figure 12.5, what is the appropriate amount for the government to spend in order to generate full employment? At first glance it would seem to be the difference between £4,000m and £5,000m, ie, £1,000m per week, but this is not the case. All that is necessary is for the government to spend an extra £500m without imposing an equivalent amount of taxation, that is by running a **budget deficit** (borrowing the money).

This additional £500m of spending will be **multiplied** by the process described earlier. Government spending of £500m will have the same effect as the increase in investment spending analysed in the previous section. There is a **government spending multiplier** exactly comparable to the investment multiplier:

$$k = \frac{\Delta Y}{\Delta G} = \frac{1,000}{500} = 2$$

Another way of thinking about this is to look again at Figure 12.5. We see that there is a vertical gap between AD_1 and AD_2 which measures the increase in spending necessary to restore full employment. This is known as the **deflationary gap**, which is, as we can see, smaller than the increase in income and output which will result from the increased injections.

12.7   LIMITATIONS OF THE MULTIPLIER

Keynes and his followers used the concept of the multiplier in order to strengthen their argument for government spending to boost their economy. They were able to point out that the government spending on 'public works' would have a **pump-priming effect**—it would stimulate further spending by the private sector. So, although the role of the government in the economy would grow, it would not be at the expense of the private sector; instead the private sector would also grow. This was an important element in the case for a 'mixed' economy.

So the multiplier is a useful analytical device. But it has a number of limitations which need to be stressed:

1   **It is only relevant in an economy with demand-deficient unemployment**
The multiplier effect we have examined shows the way in which *real* output and income are stimulated by a boost in spending, but this only works if unemployed labour (and other resources) can be brought into use. We are assuming that there is demand-deficient unemployment. If this is *not* true, then the only result of extra spending will be to drive wages and prices up as firms and consumers compete for a limited supply of goods and productive resources. Excessive (as opposed to deficient) demand may thus be a cause of inflation. Just as we had a **deflationary gap** showing the amount by which planned aggregate spending would have to be increased in order to generate full employment, so we can define an **inflationary gap** which is the amount by which planned aggregate spending would have to be *reduced* in order to avoid inflation. We explore this idea further in Chapter 16.

2   **There may be a long period of adjustment**
The multiplier deals with changes in equilibrium income and output, but the process of movement between one equilibrium and another may take considerable time. It may be many months or even years before the full multiplier effects of an increase in spending work their way through the economy and in that time economic conditions may have altered in some way that will affect national income. So it may not be possible, therefore, to forecast the result of changes in planned spending as precisely as our example seems to suggest.

3   **The consumption function may be unstable**
The value of the multiplier depends, as we have seen, on the value of the marginal propensity to consume. If this changes, so will the multiplier. Although Keynes thought that the MPC was stable in the short run, empirical evidence about consumer spending since he wrote *The General Theory* suggests some volatility. Those factors influencing consumer behaviour which Keynes played down—such as the interest rate—may have more of an effect than he thought. To the extent that they do, the multiplier is unstable and the results of macroeconomic policy are less predictable.

4   **Multiplier effects may be weak in practice because of additional leakages from the circular flow of income**
The simple model we have examined treats savings as the only leakage from the circular flow, but taxation and spending on imports are further leakages which reduce the size of the proportion of extra income that feeds back into the circular flow. The United Kingdom, for example, has a high **marginal propensity to import** and a relatively high **marginal tax rate**. These extra leakages mean that the value of the multiplier is reduced; it has been calculated that the value of the United Kingdom multiplier is less than two.

12.8   THE EXTENDED KEYNESIAN MODEL

However, developing the simple model to recognise the existence of the government and foreign trade does not fundamentally alter the conclusions of Keynesian analysis.

We have two additional injections into the circular flow, and two additional leakages. For equilibrium in the circular flow it is now necessary that the **sum** of injections equals the **sum** of leakages:

$$(I + G + X) = (S + T + M)$$

but it is no longer necessary that S should equal I in equilibrium, for these are only particular components of leakages and injections. For instance, suppose investment was £800m, government spending was £1,700m and exports brought in £650m. This would be quite compatible with a national income equilibrium where savings were £900m, the government took £1,500m in taxation and imports were £750m in value:

$$(800 + 1,700 + 650) = (900 + 1,500 + 750)$$

(Here we would have what are technically known as a **private sector financial surplus (S > I)**, a **budget deficit (G > T)** and a **balance of trade deficit (X < M)**.)

In the extended Keynesian model, the aggregate demand schedule now has two extra components, G and X. An increase in either government spending or exports—just like an increase in investment—will shift the aggregate demand function upwards and equilibrium income will rise. We have already seen that there is a government spending multiplier $(\Delta Y / \Delta G)$; there is thus also an **export multiplier** $(\Delta Y / \Delta X)$.

Similarly, additional leakages—taxation and spending on imports—will have an effect on the value of the multiplier, and thus on the position and **gradient** of the aggregate demand function (remember, this reflects the marginal propensity to consume). Figure 12.6 shows this: in part (**a**) we show how an increase in government spending, other things being equal, raises equilibrium income, while in part (**b**) an increase in the marginal propensity to import lowers equilibrium income, in this case because import spending makes the AD function flatter.

FIGURE 12.6   **Effects on equilibrium national income of: (a) Government spending and (b) an increase in the marginal propensity to import**

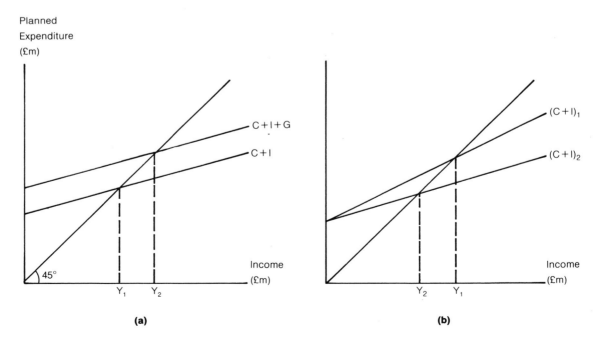

(a)   (b)

SUMMARY

In this chapter we have looked in some detail at the way in which variations in aggregate demand produce changes in equilibrium income and output in the context of a Keynesian model. Particular emphasis has been placed on the way in which changes in injections and leakages produce multiplied changes in income. This analysis provides the theoretical basis for the policies of demand management which are associated with Keynesian macroeconomic policy. We note, though, that the usefulness of the analysis depends on a set of assumptions about economic behaviour which are debatable. Demand variations are assumed to be reflected in income and output rather than wage and price changes; unemployed resources are assumed to be available; the consumption function is assumed to be stable. We shall see later in the book that these assumptions have been challenged.

SELF-TEST QUESTIONS

1   According to Keynes, which of the following occurs as income rises?

(a)   The average propensity to consume rises.

(b)   The marginal propensity to consume rises.

(c)   The marginal propensity to consume is greater than the average propensity to consume.

(d)   The average propensity to consume falls.

(e)   The marginal propensity to save falls.

2   In an open economy, with a government sector, which condition is necessary for equilibrium in the circular flow?

(a)   Investment must equal savings.

(b)   Government spending must equal taxation.

(c)   Exports plus government spending must equal imports plus taxation.

(d)   Government spending plus investment must equal savings plus taxation.

(e)   None of the above.

3   In an economy with no government sector and no foreign trade, the consumption function is found to be $C = 2000 + 0.75Y$. Investment is £1,500 million. The full employment level of income is £16,000 million. Which of these statements is not true:

(a)   Equilibrium income is £14,000m.

(b)   In equilibrium, savings are £1,500m.

(c)   The marginal propensity to save is 0.25.

(d)   There is a deflationary gap of £2,000m.

(e)   The value of the multiplier is 4.

4   A depreciation of a country's currency makes imports more expensive and tends to lower the marginal propensity to import. Which of the following effects do you predict?

(a)   The value of the multiplier will increase.

(b)   The value of the multiplier will decrease.

(c)   The value of the multiplier will stay the same.

(d)   The value of the multiplier will increase or decrease depending on the country's ability to export.

(e)   None of the above.

5   Multiplier effects may be quite small in practice for which of the following reasons?

(a)   Income may fluctuate considerably.

(b)   The marginal propensity to save is small.

(c)   There are other leakages from the circular flow as well as savings.

(d)   There is a great deal of unemployment in the economy.

(e)   There is a deflationary gap.

EXERCISE

What do you understand by the 'multiplier' effect of an increase in injections? How useful is this idea to policy-makers.

Answers on page 259.

Investment and the business cycle

In this chapter we discuss the role of investment in the economy in detail. We examine some of the likely determinants of investment, and we show how investment plays a major role in the business cycle. One simple model of a business cycle is developed. This makes use of the **accelerator** principle of investment determination, in conjunction with the multiplier process which we introduced in the previous chapter.

13.1   INTRODUCTION

In our outline of a Keynesian model in Chapter 12 we focused on the determinants of consumption and treated investment as autonomous, that is given from outside the model. We considered the effects of changes in investment, but did not spell out in a formal way what might bring such changes about. However, we did note a number of factors which might influence investment: the rate of interest (the cost of borrowing or the opportunity cost of a firm's own funds); the level of business profits; and the state of expectations about the future growth of sales and output. Investment is a very important component of national income, and one which is highly volatile: it varies much more from period to period than does consumption. We must now therefore look at investment in more detail.

Investment in the present context is expenditure undertaken in one period in the hope of generating revenue in the future which will more than cover the cost of investment and thus produce a profit. There is a strong case in economic theory for including a great deal of spending under this heading, for example, expenditure by individuals and government on education and health care, which contributes to the accumulation and maintenance of 'human capital' (see Chapter 8). However, in macroeconomics we tend to take a rather narrower view, concentrating on what national income figures refer to as **fixed capital formation**—expenditure by firms and governments on machinery, buildings and equipment which are used to produce goods and services—plus investment in **inventories** or stocks of raw materials, semi-finished goods and finished products.

Note particularly the second element, inventory or stock holding (something often neglected in discussions of investment). This meets our definition of investment, because expenditure is incurred today in return for benefits in the future. One reason for holding stocks is that firms are enabled to take advantage of any unexpected increase in demand for their product. Otherwise sales might be lost to their rivals.

We must stress again a point which we have touched on earlier in the book: the purchase of already-existing assets (for instance a firm buying second-hand machinery) or financial claims (such as company shares) is not our concern here. Although such activities constitute investments by the individuals or firms involved, from the point of view of the economy as a whole they are simply transfers of the ownership of property, and do not constitute an injection into the circular flow of income.

13.2   THE MICROECONOMICS OF INVESTMENT

13.2.1   Fixed investment

It is helpful to start by thinking of investment expenditure at the level of the firm. Consider first the case of investment in new fixed capital. Economists argue that a rational profit-maximising business will want to invest in a project (a car firm considering the construction of a new factory, a newspaper going over to new printing technology) if it expects that the revenue resulting from the investment will exceed the costs of the project. This should be obvious but what is perhaps less immediately obvious is that the business needs to ensure that its calculations take into account the **timing** of costs incurred and revenues received. A cost of £1,000 today is not adequately compensated for by a revenue of £1,000 to be received in five years' time, for if we had £1,000 available today we could turn it into a larger sum five years from now simply by leaving it on deposit, risk-free, with a bank or other financial institution. In order to make proper comparisons between costs and revenues we need to express them in terms of their value at the same time, today. Accountants talk of **discounting** sums of money at future dates to **present value** terms. There is a simple formula which enables us to do this. The present value of a sum of money A_t to be spent or received t years from now is given by:

$$PV = \frac{A_t}{(1+i)^t}$$

where i is a **discount rate** measuring the opportunity cost of capital—the rate of return on the next-best alternative investment available elsewhere in the economy (in the formula, it is expressed as a decimal or fraction rather than in percentage terms: ie, 10 per cent is written as 0.1). In the simplest case, this may be the rate of interest on a bond or bank deposit.

We thus have a formal criterion for investment: go ahead if the discounted present value of the revenues exceeds the discounted present value of the costs associated with the project. Or, more simply, invest if the **net present value** (NPV) is positive.

If we assume for the moment that the appropriate discount rate to use is the interest rate, then we can see how variations in the latter will, *ceteris paribus*, affect the level of planned investment, for the higher the interest rate, the greater will be the effect of discounting on the present value of future revenue. Using the formula above, students should be able to show that a sum of £1,000 to be received five years from today has a discounted present value of £784 when the interest rate is 5 per cent (0.05), but a PV of only £621 when the interest rate is 10 per cent (0.1). Thus a rise in the interest rate causes the attractiveness of investment projects (for which, remember, the justification is future returns) to decline, and so planned investment falls.

The matter may be slightly more complicated than this; in the real world different firms have access to capital funds on different terms and thus face different effective discount rates, but the inverse relation between the interest rate and planned investment in fixed capital seems soundly based in microeconomic reasoning.

13.2.2 Inventory investment

Holding stocks can, of course, be an unplanned and undesired response to a sudden fall in demand because goods which are produced cannot be sold as anticipated. However, even if firms are currently selling the amount they had predicted, they will always hold some stocks, of materials and components as well as finished goods. Planned inventory investment also seems likely to be inversely related to the interest rate. Stockholdings may arise because of a speculative motive: firms may believe that prices of raw materials are going to rise, and hope that by stockpiling copper or tin now they will have lower raw material costs in the future than they would otherwise. Or the motive may be more of a precautionary one; the possession of stocks gives firms more room for manoeuvre in the event of unforeseen increases in demand. Stocks of finished goods enable them to increase sales rapidly, while stocks of raw materials, components and semi-finished products make it easier to increase production rapidly.

So there are clear potential benefits from stockholding. However, there are costs involved. Resources devoted to producing goods for stocks, or accumulating inventories of raw materials, have an opportunity cost. In the simplest case, we can again assume that this is the interest rate. At any particular interest rate there will be an optimal level of stockholding, where the marginal benefit of an extra unit of the good is equal to its marginal cost (determined by the interest rate). As the interest rate falls, the marginal benefit of an addition to inventories now exceeds the marginal cost of that addition, and the optimal level of stockholding rises, so investment in inventories will take place.

13.3 MACROECONOMICS OF INVESTMENT: THE MARGINAL EFFICIENCY OF CAPITAL

In introducing the idea of the net present value of an investment project, we saw that this depended on the discount rate (assumed to be the interest rate): the higher the discount rate, the lower the NPV. Another way of thinking about the attractiveness of an investment opportunity is to consider the discount rate is such that the NPV is zero, so that the project is just on the margin of acceptance or rejection. This discount rate is known as the **internal rate of return** of investment.

All this is at the level of the firm. In *The General Theory* Keynes used the idea of the internal rate of return (although he didn't use this term) in a discussion of investment in the economy as a whole.

Assume that we know all the potential investment projects available in a period (given the existing stock of resources, technology and—very importantly—expectations about the future). We can rank all these alternatives according to their internal rates of return (IRRs). A few projects will have very high IRRs, more will have lower IRRs. Starting from a position of zero investment, we can define what Keynes called the **marginal efficiency of capital** (MEC). This is the rate of return on each additional unit of investment. When investing, an efficient economic system would first go for the project with the highest IRR, then the next highest and so on. The marginal efficiency of capital would therefore decline as investment increases. Figure 13.1 shows an illustrative marginal efficiency of capital schedule.

FIGURE 13.1   **Marginal efficiency of capital**

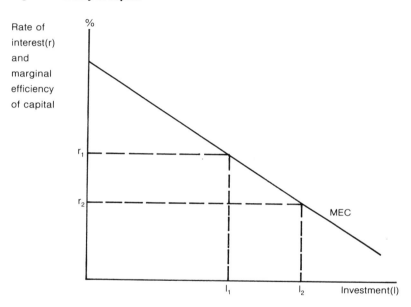

The MEC schedule is in effect, Keynes claims, a demand curve for investment. For if we show the interest rate (r) on the same diagram and bear in mind that the interest rate is the opportunity cost of capital, it is clear that investment will take place up to the level where the marginal efficiency of capital is equal to the interest rate. Thus if the interest rate is r_1, planned investment in the economy will be I_1. If the interest rate falls to r_2, planned investment will rise to I_2.

It should be noted that this analysis is not strictly correct, as commentators writing after Keynes have pointed out, for the IRRs which underly the MEC schedule are based on *ceteris paribus* assumptions. But consider what is likely to happen when there is an increase in investment in the economy as a whole. Firms will be competing for a limited supply of capital equipment and this will tend to drive up the price of capital goods. When this occurs, the cost of any individual investment project will tend to rise, and its IRR to fall. It has been suggested that a schedule be defined which would take account of this effect; this schedule is called the **marginal efficiency of investment** schedule. It would lie to the left of and be steeper and less elastic than, the MEC schedule, as in Figure 13.2. This is not fatal to Keynes's analysis; rather, it tends to support his position. For Keynes argued, as we saw in the last chapter, that investment depended overwhelmingly on expectations about future economic conditions. In these circumstances interest rate changes would be unlikely to have much impact on perceived IRRs (which, because the future is unknowable, can only ever be informed guesses, strongly influenced by the general business climate of optimism or pessimism). The MEC schedule was therefore likely to be fairly steep; if the appropriate demand curve for investment is the even steeper MEI schedule this only confirms Keynes's view that cuts in interest rate cannot of themselves have much impact on planned investment.

In short, the MEI schedule is likely to be **interest-inelastic**. **Shifts** in the demand curve for investment, as a result of changes in expectations, are likely to be of much greater significance than

FIGURE 13.2 **Marginal efficiency of capital and marginal efficiency of investment**

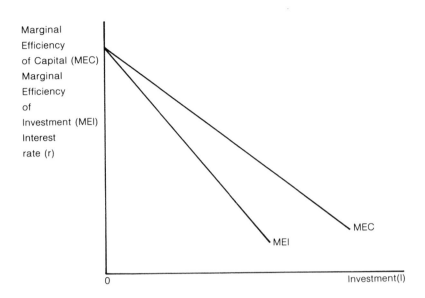

movements along such a curve. Not surprisingly, in view of the difficulties of analysing the process of forming expectations and because of the volatile nature of business confidence, simple Keynesian analysis usually tends, as we have seen, to treat planned investment as autonomous.

13.4 THE ACCELERATOR PRINCIPLE

However, although followers of Keynes accepted his view that expectations were the key to understanding fluctuations in the level of planned investment, they were unwilling to accept that economists could say little about them. They sought to develop models which would enable us to link planned investment to observable economic variables which affect expectations.

For example, models were developed which linked investment to **changes in profits**. It can be argued that current profits act as indicator of future business prospects. An increase in profits therefore raises expectations. It also increases the internal funds available for business expansion. In either case, an increase in profits may be thought to stimulate future investment.

But the most widely known of such extensions of Keynesian analysis is the **accelerator** principle. This links the level of planned investment to *changes* in national income. The principle can be traced back for over seventy years, but in its modern form the idea was developed more or less simultaneously in the late 1930s by two British economists, Roy Harrod (a close associate of Keynes and his first biographer) and John Hicks (later a Nobel prizewinner), and an American, Paul Samuelson (author of the most successful economics textbook yet written). What follows is a simplified outline of this approach, drawing on elements of the work of each of these writers.

13.4.1 The capital stock adjustment principle

The key assumption made is that firms aim to maintain a constant ratio between their output and their productive capacity, which in turn is held to be related to their stock of capital equipment. When aggregate demand in the economy increases, it is claimed that firms will plan to increase output *if they expect the higher level of demand to continue*. This is an important point for, remember, it is expectations which are important. Planned increases in output require increases in the stock of capital equipment; thus planned investment increases.

Suppose that we are in a Keynesian economy where an increase in aggregate demand last year leads to an increase in planned output of £1,000m in the coming year. We are assuming that firms will want to maintain a fixed ratio between planned output and the capital stock. For example, this ratio (the **capital-output ratio**) might be 3. What this means is that firms will on average want to maintain a capital stock equal in value to three times the value of current annual output (we should note that there are conceptual difficulties in valuing capital, but we shall ignore them here).

In order to adjust the capital stock to its new desired level, new investment must take place (in addition, of course, to replacement investment which is continually taking place as the existing capital stock wears out). In this example, assuming that all the new investment takes place within the year, investment will rise by £3,000m. Investment therefore **accelerates** or rises out of proportion to the rise in demand for output; this helps to explain the volatility of investment.

13.4.2   The accelerator coefficient

In general, if I_{nt} is planned new investment in the current period t, Y_{t-1} and Y_{t-2} are aggregate output (= national income) in periods $t-1$ and $t-2$ respectively, and v is the desired capital–output ratio, we have:

$$I_{nt} = v(Y_{t-1} - Y_{t-2})$$

Thus, new investment in the current period depends on the change in income in the previous period. We have assumed that all of the planned new investment takes place in the current period. In such a case, we can call the desired capital-output ratio, v, the **accelerator coefficient**.

This is a highly simplified model. If there are **lags** in completing planned new investment (factories take time to build, machinery takes time to order and install), such that planned investment takes more than one period to complete, then the accelerator coefficient (the ratio of current new investment to the change in output) will be smaller than the desired capital output ratio. Econometric forecasters using models based on the accelerator routinely build lags of this kind into their approach. They also recognise that capital-output ratios differ from sector to sector in the economy and make allowances for this.

But these, in principle, are relatively minor refinements. Like other aspects of Keynesian analysis, the accelerator theory of investment depends crucially on some basic assumptions. In this case they are:

1   That the desired capital stock bears a fixed relationship to output, a position which ignores the possibilities of capital-saving technical progress and the substitution of labour for capital in currently known technologies; and
2   That expectations about future output are simply based on output in the previous period, a doubtful proposition which conflicts with assumptions made in other areas of macroeconomic theory (see Chapter 16).

Nevertheless, the accelerator principle remains an interesting attempt to understand the volatility of investment behaviour. It shows how new investment reacts disproportionately to an increase in national income. It should be pointed out that the principle also implies that investment falls very sharply when there is a fall in aggregate demand. The existing level of the capital stock is now seen as excessive and so even replacement investment may be cut back. The model outlined above certainly suggests that in a recession no **new** investment will take place, though it must be pointed out that we are assuming that all parts of the economy behave the same. In reality, there is always likely to be some new investment, for even when aggregate demand is falling, some industries and firms will be increasing their share of the market at the expense of others; they will find it profitable to increase their plant and equipment.

Next we will show how a stylised Keynesian model of a **business cycle** can be constructed using the accelerator principle and the multiplier process discussed in Chapter 12.

13.5   THE BUSINESS CYCLE

Investment plays a key role in the business cycle (sometimes known as the 'trade cycle'). This is the pattern of fluctuations in activity in market economies which has been observed since the early nineteenth century. A range of economic indicators shows a cyclical movement of expansion and contraction in economic activity over a period of time. Some of these indicators rise in periods of expansion (rate of growth of output, rate of growth of prices, job vacancies, investment), others fall (unemployment, bankruptcies), but a pattern is discernible. Over the long run, of course, economies usually display an underlying positive rate of growth. For example, this has averaged about 2 per cent per annum in the United Kingdom this century, but in some years growth has been much faster, while in other years it has been much slower. Indeed, in some years (for example in the early 1980s) growth has actually been **negative**, ie, national income and output in real terms have fallen.

Economists have distinguished various types of cycles. There are short-run cycles which seem to be connected with variations in inventories. These stock cycles have been estimated to last (from peak to peak) between eighteen and forty months. Then there are medium-term cycles which have a duration of eight or nine years, the type with which we are primarily concerned and the form of which is shown in Figure 13.3. The diagram shows the phases of this type of cycle. Finally, some economists have claimed to observe very long cycles of fifty years or so duration which are associated with major technological changes such as the application of steam power, the development of the internal combustion engine, and (currently) the revolution in microelectronics. These cycles are sometimes called Kondratiev cycles after the Russian economist who wrote about them in the period between the two World Wars.

FIGURE 13.3 **A medium-term business cycle**

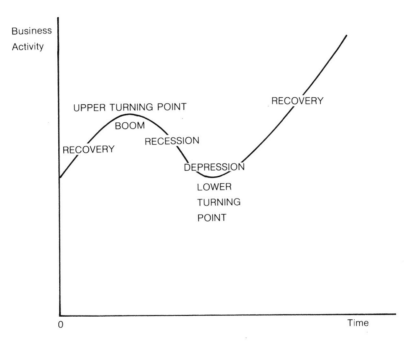

It is the medium-term cycles which are of most concern here because they seem most amenable to government macroeconomic policy. Indeed, it was widely felt in the 1950s and 1960s that 'Keynesian' macroeconomic policies had effectively removed the problem by 'stabilising' the economy—using government spending in particular as a means of smoothing out the ups and downs of aggregate demand in the business cycle. More recently, however, the big fluctuations in economic activity in the 1970s and 1980s have revived interest in cycle theory.

13.6 MULTIPLIER-ACCELERATOR INTERACTION AND THE BUSINESS CYCLE

Without committing ourselves to a view about the ultimate causes of business cycles, it is possible to show how the multiplier process of the previous chapter, coupled with the accelerator principle we have looked at here, can produce a cyclical pattern of economic activity in the medium-term. Suppose we begin on the rising or **recovery** phase of the cycle. A rise in aggregate demand occurs (as we said, we are not offering a view why this might happen). This rise in demand leads, according to the reasoning in 13.4, to a rise in the desired capital stock. New investment therefore takes place in order to bring the capital stock up to its new desired level. This is the accelerator principle in action.

The increase in new investment is an injection into the circular flow of income. It gives rise to new incomes for households (wages, dividends etc); these new incomes are, in part, spent and go on to create further incomes elsewhere in the economy. The multiplier process is at work. In turn, the increase in aggregate demand brought about by the multiplier leads to a further rise in the desired capital stock, a further increase in investment and thus a further increase in incomes .... and so on. A **boom** occurs.

Eventually, however, the economy reaches an **upper turning point** as it approaches the full employment ceiling. Output and real income can rise no further (although money or **nominal** national income can continue to rise if prices are driven up by an excess of spending power). Once the capital stock has reached its required level, new investment falls away and the process goes into reverse. Lower investment means lower incomes, which in turn leads to still lower investment. The economy is now in **recession**.

However, output does not fall indefinitely in this model. Suppose gross investment fell to zero—in other words not even replacement investment was being undertaken (a highly unlikely situation in peacetime). This would be a lower limit or **floor** to the cycle, for at this level of investment, savings and investment would now be equal at zero and (in the simple model with no government and foreign trade) injections are equal to zero and the economy is in equilibrium. However, in a more realistic model, it is clear that the floor to the cycle would occur long before gross investment fell to zero. When changes in aggregate demand affect different firms and industries differently, there will always be some new investment taking place, and in an economy with government spending and exports as injections it is very likely that increases in these forms of expenditure will after a time counteract the fall in private sector investment.

Once the floor of the cycle has been reached and national income has reached its minimum, the desired capital stock will be constant. This means that machinery will again be replaced when it wears out and replacement investment will lead to increases in income, magnified through the multiplier process and again leading to further increases in investment. The recovery process has begun again.

This is a very schematic outline of how the multiplier and the accelerator interact. Although it is an interesting approach, the student should not be misled into thinking that real world cycles are as simple as this. Remember that the theory underlying both the accelerator principle and the multiplier process is based on a number of assumptions which may not necessarily be valid in all circumstances.

SUMMARY

In this chapter we have looked in detail at the determinants of aggregate investment. In Keynesian thinking, as we have indicated, the role of the interest rate is played down, with emphasis being placed on the state of expectations. Changes in expectations shift the marginal efficiency of capital and marginal efficiency of investment schedules. Later writers following Keynes tried to link expectations to the capital-stock adjustment principle, and this led to the accelerator theory of investment. The accelerator can be used together with the multiplier to generate a simple model of the medium-term business cycle.

SELF-TEST QUESTIONS

1 **Which of the following investments results in an injection into the United Kingdom circular flow of income?**

(a) The purchase of shares in a newly-privatised company.

(b) A British firm buying shares in, and taking over, an American company.

(c) A British firm taking over a British company.

(d) A redundant worker using savings to purchase second-hand printing machinery to start a small business.

(e) An increase in stocks of components because a firm plans to increase production.

2 **A firm is considering the reequipment of its factory with new machinery. Which of the following is likely to increase the net present value of this investment project to the firm?**

(a) A rise in the interest rate.

(b) A fall in the cost of the raw materials the firm uses in its production process.

F

(c) A fall in the price of second-hand machinery of the type the firm is considering purchasing.

(d) A fall in the price of the good which the firm produces.

(e) A rise in the price of the new machinery.

3 The marginal efficiency of investment schedule lies below the marginal efficiency of capital schedule because

(a) Investment fluctuates a great deal in response to changes in expectations.

(b) An increase in investment tends to raise the price of capital goods and make investment less attractive to firms.

(c) Net present value of an investment becomes zero at high interest rates.

(d) The capital-output ratio is unstable.

(e) There is a floor below which investment cannot fall.

4 The accelerator coefficient will be greater

(a) The shorter the lag between a change in planned output and the completion of the induced investment.

(b) The greater the possibility of substituting labour for capital in the production process.

(c) The smaller the capital-output ratio.

(d) The higher the value of the multiplier.

(e) In a boom rather than in a depression.

5 If the capital-output ratio is 2, an increase of planned output of £1,000m will induce extra investment of

(a) £2,000m.

(b) £1,000m.

(c) £1,000m x the value of the multiplier.

(d) Zero

(e) More than £1,000m, but we can't say how much without further information.

EXERCISE

What determines the level of investment in an economy?

Answers on page 260.

Money and banking

In this chapter we examine the development of money from its earliest form as 'commodity' money to the sophisticated banking system of today. We outline the functions which money serves, and show how these functions are performed in different monetary environments. We look at the process of deposit creation by the banking sector, and this leads us on to modern definitions of the money supply. Finally we briefly discuss the role of non-bank financial intermediaries and the working of the money and capital markets.

14.1 INTRODUCTION

So far our macroeconomic analysis has effectively been conducted in terms of **real** variables: real income (purchasing power over goods and services), real output (the production of goods and services) and employment (inputs of labour and other resources into the productive process). In the exposition of the simple Keynesian model and our analysis of investment we have largely assumed that prices remain constant. Thus an increase in aggregate demand in money terms (say, £1,000m per week) means an increase in spending in real terms. But if the general level of prices alters, the value of a given sum of money changes. One of the most important issues in modern macroeconomics is the extent to which increases in aggregate demand **in money terms** are reflected in an increase in real output or simply dissipated in inflation. In order to be able to consider this question, we need to understand money in some detail.

14.1.1 Meaning and origins of money

In developed economies, most market transactions involve the use of money. It is rare for goods and services to exchange directly. In order to obtain a copy of this book, it is most unlikely that you went to the bookshop and offered to dust the bookshelves or clean the carpet for the proprietor in exchange for it. Similarly, the publishers didn't offer two hundred books in exchange for the authors' services. In both these cases, the conventional way to handle transactions is to pay for them with money. This has not always been the case: in primitive societies direct exchange of one commodity for another, **barter**, may be more common. It is still not quite extinct in developed economies: schoolchildren swap toys, grownups exchange homes for holidays. But in modern conditions the range of different occupations has become so wide and the goods and services we purchase so varied that barter is not a practical option for most transactions.

For barter to be feasible, there must be what economists call a **double coincidence of wants**. For instance, if I go to a restaurant for a meal, my demand for food would have to be matched by the restauranteur's demand for something I can offer, perhaps a lecture in economics. The chances of our striking such a mutually agreeable bargain are remote. If, however, I get paid for my economics lecture in money, I can take that money to the restaurant and buy a meal.

Money therefore gives **generalised** purchasing power and means that we no longer have to bother searching for a double coincidence of wants. We can devote time and resources to other uses. Money facilitates the division of labour, and therefore promotes economic advance. It is one of the human race's greatest inventions. We tend to take it too easily for granted. Yet it is a mysterious and puzzling phenomenon. When things go wrong with money, as happens when there is **hyperinflation**, an extremely rapid acceleration in the general price level of the order of thousands per cent a year, the consequences are frightening.

14.1.2 What is money?

A standard definition of money is **anything generally acceptable in payment of a debt**, a debt being an obligation incurred when a transaction takes place. But what makes money acceptable?

Obviously the use of money is based on convention; its acceptability varies over time (£1 notes, perfectly acceptable in the United Kingdom twenty years ago, are no longer used), from place to place (French francs are not acceptable for purchases in the United States) and in relation to the nature of the transaction (you cannot buy a house with a large sack of 50 pence pieces and few newspaper vendors will accept a £50 note in payment for an evening paper). Some of these conventions are based in law (in the United Kingdom, the term 'legal tender' means that there is a legal obligation to accept currency in specified circumstances); others are based on contractual guarantees (when you use a bank cheque card to support a personal cheque); still others on the reputation or plausibility of the individuals involved. In order to understand the conventions underlying the use of money we have to know something of its historical development.

14.2   FROM COMMODITY MONEY TO BANKNOTES

The first stage of progress from simple barter is to adopt one or more of the most frequently traded goods as 'money'. Such **vehicle commodities** have in the past included cattle and salt (our word 'pecuniary' comes from the Latin for cattle, and 'salary' from the word for salt). Ornaments and shells have also been important monetary forms in different cultures in the past. In modern conditions, there are sometimes situations—such as arise in prisons—where 'official' money is irrelevant or unavailable, and vehicle commodities take over. Tobacco, for instance, has frequently played such a role. Where a vehicle commodity is generally acceptable, individuals will sell their product and receive in exchange some of the vehicle good even though they have no particular need for it; they know they can exchange it for something else they value.

As trade increased and money transactions became more common in ancient Europe and the East, certain types of vehicle commodity came to predominate. These were precious metals, notably silver and gold, particularly when stamped into coins of specified weight and purity. The reasons why they became popular can be understood when we consider the attributes which an ideal commodity money should possess:

DURABILITY

Money has to pass through many different hands during its working life. Precious metals became popular because they do not deteriorate rapidly in use, as we can see when we visit museums where ancient coins are displayed.

STABILITY OF VALUE

Some commodities—for instance, agricultural products—fluctuate widely in value as supply conditions alter. By definition, precious metals are scarce and the current level of output will only ever be a small proportion of the accumulated stock of the commodity. Of course, demand fluctuations can still have a big effect on the value of gold and silver, but this is true of all potential vehicle commodities.

UNIFORMITY

Each unit of money should (as far as possible) be identical to all others. This is possible with precious metals, rather more difficult with cattle.

DIVISIBILITY

Monetary transactions may involve large or small sums. Metals have the advantage that they can be divided into very small units. Clearly this is not true of cattle.

PORTABILITY

As economies become more complex, trade is likely to involve larger distances between some buyers and sellers. Money therefore must be easily transportable.

The possession of these desirable attributes explains why gold and silver became the most frequent forms of commodity money. The need for uniformity and stability of value explains the early involvement of the monarchy or other political authority in controlling currency. Gold and silver are capable of being debased, that is mixed with other, cheaper, metals in such a way that it is difficult to tell adulterated coinage from the real thing. It has been argued by some economists, notably Nobel Prizewinner Professor Friedrich von Hayek, that in principle the private sector could devise ways of regulating and controlling the currency; in practice this has rarely occurred. In the past, the king's head on a coin was both a guarantee that the coin contained a specified proportion of the precious metal and a warning to would-be counterfeiters. Dire penalties were meted out to those who dared to forge or debase the coinage, and even today such crimes are considered very serious. Considering the chaos and economic and social costs which result when people lose faith in a currency, this may not be unreasonable.

Despite the advantages of precious metals as a form of money, they have some disadvantages. Precious metals are scarce because they are costly and difficult to obtain. This means that the economy's resources are diverted from the production of other goods and services. In modern economies, commodity money has fallen out of use. In the UK, for example, although gold and silver coins have circulated within living memory, they have now been completely replaced by cupro-nickel coins, of little intrinsic value, which are much cheaper to produce. Such coins are an example of **token money**, which is of use only because people have faith in its value. Moreover, coins are now in use only for small transactions. Nowadays we make more use of another form of token money, banknotes.

14.2.1   Banknotes

Historically, banknotes first appeared in Europe as receipts issued by goldsmiths who contracted to store and protect large quantities of gold and other valuables deposited with them (because they worked with precious metals, goldsmiths needed to take careful security measures themselves, and so were able to offer such facilities to other merchants and tradespeople). These receipts would often carry a promise to pay back on demand the sum deposited. Banknotes issued by the United Kingdom's central bank, the Bank of England, still carry such a promise, although it has now lost its meaning. It is interesting to observe that these banknotes promise to pay 'the bearer' of the note, not the original depositor. This points us to the next stage of the development of banknotes, their circulation from hand to hand.

If merchants wished to make a payment for goods or services received, it was time-consuming (and involved a certain amount of risk) to take their gold out of the goldsmith's vault and transport it to the workshop or house of their trading partners: particularly if the latter then simply took it back to deposit it with the goldsmith. It was far simpler to hand over the receipt, which could then be used at a later date either to reclaim the gold or to pass it on in turn to somebody else in payment of a debt. So long as there was complete confidence in the ability of goldsmiths to repay on demand, their notes were, literally, 'as good as gold'. And so the notes came to function as money.

As the practice of note issue grew, banking (the word actually derives from the benches on which Italian money-lenders sat to conduct their business) became a specialist function, increasingly separated from the profession of goldsmith. In the course of time, widespread acceptance of banknotes meant that less and less notes were redeemed, and deposits of gold remained untouched for years. In these circumstances, bankers could be confident that, provided they kept a 'prudential reserve' of gold sufficient to meet likely withdrawals, they could issue notes in excess of the gold remaining in their vaults. They could make loans, at a rate of interest, to individuals and companies. This was a much more profitable business than simply acting as caretaker for other people's wealth.

The note issue thus came greatly to exceed in value the amount of precious metals nominally backing it. The system worked well, and enabled banks to play a useful role in helping to finance business during the Industrial Revolution in Europe. However, it did depend on bankers being able to guess correctly the appropriate level of gold reserves to maintain. Inevitably some bankers overstepped the bounds of prudence. They lent too much; when customers wanted to withdraw their deposits, they were unable to do so. Banks collapsed.

Recurrent banking crises in many countries led to controls being placed on the activities of bankers. For example, the Bank Charter Act of 1844 led to restriction of the power to issue banknotes in Britain to the government-controlled Bank of England and a few Scottish banks. There had never been a bank collapse in Scotland, and so the prudent Scottish bankers were allowed to keep the privilege of issuing their own notes—a privilege they still retain today. However, this freedom is a rather limited one, as the total size of the note issue is controlled by the Bank of England. In modern economies, note issue is a monopoly of government-controlled—or owned central banks (see 14.5) throughout the world. Moreover, today's banknotes are no longer backed by reserves of gold or other precious metals, but rather by government securities of various kinds. In other words, they ultimately depend on the power of the government to tax its citizens.

14.3   THE CREATION OF BANK DEPOSITS

A repeated pattern in the history of monetary development is the way in which banks and other financial institutions react creatively to government restrictions. If governments make it impossible for certain types of money to be issued, or loans to be offered, profit-maximising banks will find ways of offering another type of service to potential clients.

Restrictions on note issue gave a stimulus to the development of the **chequing system**. A cheque is a piece of paper on which a person who holds a bank account transfers a right to payment to somebody else. It is not a claim issued by the bank, as in the case of a banknote, but it performs much the same purpose. It is, indeed, a much more flexible means of transferring spending power than a banknote because it can be made out for any value; and it is rather more secure because it can normally only be cashed by a named individual or firm. Cheques have a very wide acceptability in modern conditions, and account for a far greater value of transactions than is accounted for by notes and coins. In the last few years, their domination has been challenged by further innovations such as direct debits and credit cards, but so far they remain preeminent.

Cheques, like banknotes, are promises to pay, and depend for their acceptability on confidence in the banking system. Just as confidence in banks enabled them to expand their note issue beyond the deposits of precious metals they held, so today's banks are able to lend to customers by 'creating deposits' on which customers can draw cheques even though they have not previously deposited equivalent sums of currency. So long as a prudential reserve of notes, coins and other liquid assets (those assets which can easily and cheaply be turned into cash) is maintained, an enormous structure of credit can be erected to facilitate economic activity. In this sense, banks can 'create money'. How does this work?

14.3.1   A model of deposit creation

Consider what happens when a banking system starts up from scratch with a bank accepting deposits of notes and coins to a value of £100m. Its **assets** are the cash and its **liabilities** (what it owes) are the deposits. We can set out a simple balance sheet as follows:

ASSETS	£m	LIABILITIES	£m
Cash	100	Deposits	100

The bank's **cash reserve ratio** (its ratio of cash to deposits) is 100 per cent. It may obtain a small income for keeping the cash safely, but otherwise its cash assets are idle. Now suppose that over time the bank finds by experience that its customers never want to withdraw more than 10 per cent of their cash at a time. It can therefore be sure of meeting its obligations, being able to pay out cash on demand, so long as it maintains a cash holding of £10m. The other £90m of cash assets can be lent to individuals and firms. Its balance sheet now looks like this:

ASSETS	£m	LIABILITIES	£m
Cash	10	Deposits	100
Loans	90		
	100		100

The bank's cash ratio is now at its desired level, 10 per cent. But this is only a temporary position. The extra £90m spending made possible by the loans means that individuals and firms supplying goods and services to these borrowers receive cash. Suppose they pay this cash into their bank accounts or pass it on to other people and firms who have bank accounts. On the assumption that all the cash eventually finds its way back into the bank, the balance sheet will end up looking like this:

ASSETS	£m	LIABILITIES	£m
Cash	100	Deposits	190
Loans	90		
	190		190

The bank's cash ratio has now risen again, to more than 50 per cent. It will once more wish to reduce this ratio by making further loans. This time it would need to make loans of £81m to reduce the ratio to 10 per cent. If the cash lent was again redeposited, further loans of £72m could be made...and so on. Each extra round of lending is nine-tenths of the previous one. The process continues until the following position is reached:

ASSETS	£m	LIABILITIES	£m
Cash	100	Deposits	1000
Loans	900		
	1000		1000

The bank ends up, therefore, with total deposits ten times as large as those with which it began. The example is oversimplified, but the point is clear. The bank has effectively 'created money', if we include in our concept of money deposits in the bank on which cheques can be drawn which are virtually as widely acceptable as notes and coins.

14.3.2   The bank credit multiplier

The process by which an original deposit of cash leads to much larger final total deposits has similarities to the income multiplier process discussed in Chapter 12. We can therefore define a **bank credit multiplier** (also known as the deposit creation multiplier). If ΔR is the change in cash deposits and ΔD the change in total deposits at the end of the process, the bank credit multiplier can be shown (by reasoning similar to that in Chapter 12) to be:

$$\frac{\Delta D}{\Delta R} = \frac{1}{\rho}$$

where ρ is the cash ratio which the bank maintains. This is 0.1 (ie 10 per cent) in our example, so the bank credit multiplier is 10.

The basic principle of the bank credit multiplier is not modified by the introduction of more than one bank into the economy, for the banking system as a whole behaves rather like one big bank in this context. However we should note that the deposit multiplier is not as large as is suggested by this example, for two reasons.

First, banks find it necessary to maintain a further prudential reserve of liquid assets, such as deposits with the central bank and Treasury Bills (to be explained shortly) which give an implicit rate of interest and thus contribute to bank profits, but are easier to turn into cash than long-term loans to firms and individuals. Second, the model outlined above is based on the assumption that all cash lent is ultimately returned to the banking system. In practice, the public will wish to hold a proportion of its spending power in cash form, or else on deposit with **non-bank financial intermediaries** (such as building societies in the United Kingdom or thrift associations in the United States) or in government-owned savings banks (see 14.5).

Suppose that c is the fraction of the public's money holdings which it wishes to hold outside the banking system. The bank credit multiplier is reduced as a result of this 'leakage', from $1/\rho$ to $1/(\rho + c)$. Suppose c is 0.2, for example: the value of the bank credit multiplier in the case considered above falls from $1/0.1$ to $1/(0.1 + 0.2)$, ie from 10 to 3.33.

14.4   THE MONEY SUPPLY

From the discussion so far, it is clear that the scope of our definition of money has changed over time. What is generally acceptable in payment of a debt has changed as the monetary system has evolved.

And as this process of evolution is a continuing one (indeed, it has accelerated in the last decade) it is apparent that a rigid specification of what counts as money is likely to be misleading. Yet, as we shall see in later chapters, some indication of the size of the money stock (or **supply of money**) is often considered very important for economic policy purposes. What should we include? Some people would argue for a very narrow definition of the money supply, mainly notes and coins; others would include bank deposits. Some would make a distinction between different types of deposits, for instance by including **current accounts** (or **sight** deposits), which pay only a low interest rate (or no interest at all) are instantly accessible (via cashpoints, for example) and are used mainly to pay for day-to-day expenses, but excluding **time deposits**, which carry a higher interest rate, may require giving some notice before withdrawal, and are used to some extent as savings accounts. Others may want to widen the definition still further to include deposits with other types of financial institution, such as building societies in the United Kingdom.

14.4.1 Monetary aggregates

The significance of these different categories has changed considerably in recent years as a result of increasing competition between financial institutions and rapid innovation, particularly in the development of new financial instruments and in the electronic transmission of money. As a result, the monetary aggregates which governments concentrate on have altered. A few years ago, governments such as those of the United Kingdom and United States tended to concentrate on 'broad' measures of money; nowadays the focus is on 'narrow money', particularly MO, the **monetary base**. This consists of what is sometimes called 'high-powered money', which is directly under the control of a country's central bank. In the case of the United Kingdom, MO consists of currency (notes and coins) plus deposits held by the commercial banks with the Bank of England. Table 14.1 shows the United Kingdom monetary aggregates currently monitored by the Bank, and the size of these aggregates in November 1987. Although definitions differ slightly, similar aggregates are calculated for most other developed countries.

14.4.2 Determination of the money supply

The model of bank deposit creation sketched above points to the crucial significance of the commercial banks' reserves of cash and liquid assets to the determination of the total level of deposits and thus of the wider monetary aggregates. So what determines these reserves?

An important influence is the level of government borrowing. If the government runs a budget deficit (ie, spends more than it receives in taxes), it must borrow. The resulting **Public Sector Borrowing Requirement** (PSBR) can be financed in two ways. The government can borrow direct from households and firms in the private sector. In the United Kingdom this is done by selling long-term government bonds ('gilt-edged securities'), national savings certificates, premium bonds etc. However, the larger the amount the government wishes to borrow by this means, the higher the interest rate it will have to offer to attract sufficient lenders. Higher interest rates are not very popular with firms and households which are borrowing money, so an alternative method of raising finance is by borrowing from the commercial banking sector via the Bank of England.

One way in which this happens is that the government draws cheques on the Bank of England, cheques which are then presented by their recipients to the commercial banks. In turn, this enables the commercial banks to increase their holdings with the central bank. As we have seen, these are part of the monetary base and are thus functionally equivalent to an increase in cash holdings. The banks experience an increase in their liquidity and are in a position to increase their lending; total deposits rise through the multiplier process. Thus government borrowing from commercial banks has led to an increase in the money supply.

This is only one way in which the government can affect the size of the money supply. It can do so, too, through **open market operations** (see Chapter 16) and by altering the rules and regulations constraining banks. However, there are other influences on the money supply over which the government has less control. One is inflows of funds from abroad, which tend to swell the domestic money supply. Another is variations in the size of the bank credit multiplier, as a result (for instance) of changes in the proportion of wealth held in cash or changes in the size of the non-bank financial sector (both of these, incidentally, are likely to be influenced by the level of market interest

TABLE 14.1 **UK Monetary Aggregates, November 1987**

		£m
Narrow money		
M0		
Notes and coin in circulation with the public		15,548
plus banks' till money		
plus banks' operational balances with the Bank of England		
M1		
Notes and coin in circulation with the public		92,572
plus private sector sterling sight bank deposits		
M2		
Notes and coin in circulation with the public		186,085
plus private sector non-interest-bearing sterling sight bank deposits		
plus private sector interest-bearing retail sterling bank deposits		
plus private sector holdings of retail building society shares and deposits and national savings bank ordinary accounts		
Broad money		£m
M3		
M1		
plus private sector sterling time bank deposits		183,456
plus private sector holdings of sterling bank certificates of deposit		
M3c		
M3		
plus private sector holdings of foreign currency bank deposits		214,339
M4		
M3		
plus private sector holdings of building society shares and deposits and sterling certificates of deposit		299,374
minus building society holdings of bank deposits and bank certificates of deposit, and notes and coin		
M5		
M4		
plus holdings by the private sector (excluding building societies) of money market instruments (bank bills, Treasury bills, local authority deposits), certificates of tax deposit and national savings instruments (excluding certificates, SAYE and other long-term deposits)		314,311

Sources: Bank of England Quarterly Bulletin; Economic Trends

rates). There are differences in opinion about how far governments can control the money supply in practice. Some **monetarist** economists (discussed in Chapter 15) take the view that governments can and should control the money supply by reducing budget deficits and thus the need to borrow. However, the experience of the 1980s, when governments in many countries tried to follow this policy, has suggested that this is difficult to do.

14.5 THE BANKING AND FINANCIAL SYSTEMS

In this final section we give a brief outline of the banking and financial systems. Although our description and analysis is mainly concentrated on the United Kingdom, the main categories of institution are comparable in most developed economies.

14.5.1 The central bank

At the centre of the system is the **central bank**, which in the United Kingdom is the Bank of England. Founded in 1694 in order to lend money to the government, it remained nominally in private hands until it was nationalised in 1947. For many years previous to this, though, it had been effectively under government control. The Bank of England is one of the oldest central banks in the world (by contrast the American equivalent, the Federal Reserve System (the 'Fed'), was not set up until 1913). Its current role is the culmination of hundreds of years of experience of regulating banking and finance and carrying out the monetary and exchange rate policies of the government. To be more precise, the Bank of England, like other central banks, has the following functions:

BANKER TO THE COMMERCIAL BANKS

In the United Kingdom the commercial banks (see below) maintain accounts with the Bank of England. These accounts are used to settle inter-bank indebtedness.

'LENDER OF LAST RESORT'

The Bank of England has to ensure the solvency of the banking system by standing ready to lend to banks which are experiencing large unanticipated withdrawals or other problems. Such assistance is, however, usually provided at a penal cost, to discourage banks from excessive lending. In the United Kingdom the 'lender of last resort' function is, uniquely, carried out indirectly via the **discount houses** which invest in short-term assets with funds borrowed largely from the banks; the mechanism need not concern us here.

BANKER TO THE GOVERNMENT

Government departments maintain accounts with the central bank and day-to-day financing is carried out through these accounts. In the UK a related function is the management of the **National Debt**, the total stock of accumulated government borrowing.

ISSUER OF BANKNOTES

As we saw earlier, this is nowadays the monopoly of central banks.

TO OPERATE MONETARY POLICY

Central banks aim to influence the supply of money and credit and to influence the interest rate, the 'price' of credit. In this role, the Bank of England buys and sells in various financial markets—the **money market** (in which short-term financial assets are traded), the **'gilt-edged' market** (for government bonds) and the **foreign exchange market**. It may also intervene from time to time to impose direct controls of various kinds—on bank lending or foreign exchange transactions—in line with government policy. However, in recent years the Bank of England has chosen not to make much use of such powers, in line with the trends noted in Chapter 10 towards deregulation of financial markets.

TO REGULATE OTHER FINANCIAL INSTITUTIONS

By regulating, licensing and exercising 'prudential supervision' over banks and other financial institutions, the central bank tries to ensure that they operate on sound financial principles—for instance in relation to minimum reserve ratios. Again, however, in the last few years the Bank of England has used regulatory powers sparingly. We shall see in a later chapter how financial deregulation has been a feature of the 1980s.

14.5.2 The commercial banks

Commercial or deposit banks are institutions which are licensed to make loans and accept deposits, including those against which cheques can be written. In the UK over 600 banks are allowed these privileges, but the most important of these are the **London Clearing Banks**—so called because they cooperate to 'clear' cheques drawn on each other through the London Clearing House. Of these the 'big four' (Lloyds, Barclays, National Westminster and Midland) control 90 per cent of the deposits.

These banks are one of a much wider class of **financial intermediaries**; that is, they stand between ultimate lenders and ultimate borrowers of funds. They compete (and competition has increased considerably in the last few years) with non-bank financial intermediaries for the savings of individuals and firms which they lend to finance investment, consumer spending, house purchases and so on.

Commercial banks have historically had balance sheets with a characteristic structure setting them apart from other financial institutions, although distinctions have become more blurred recently. On the **liabilities** side, apart from capital and reserves, the majority of items consist of deposits: sight (or current) deposits and time deposits and certificates of deposit, a special form of deposit with a fixed term. On the **assets** side, the balance sheets of commercial banks reflect the need to maintain a balance between **profitability and liquidity**. In general, the liquidity of an asset tends to be inversely related to its rate of return. As profit-seeking enterprises, commercial banks aim for maximum profitability compatible with the ability to make funds available to depositors who wish to withdraw their money. As we saw earlier, this means that prudential reserves have to be maintained. In order of decreasing liquidity, commercial banks' typical asset holdings in the United Kingdom include:

CASH

This includes both cash in tills and balances held with the central bank and which can be drawn on instantly. Nowadays this accounts for less than 2 per cent of bank assets.

MONEY 'AT CALL AND SHORT NOTICE'

Banks lend money on a very short-term basis (literally overnight) to other financial institutions operating in the **money market**. Some interest is paid, but obviously very little as the loans are highly liquid.

BILLS

These are essentially a form of IOU, normally of a relatively short 'maturity': repayable in ninety days. The British government makes great use of one type of bill, the **Treasury Bill** (similar financial instruments are found in other economies). Short-term commercial bills are issued by private institutions and are held by commercial banks. Bills are issued at a discount; that is a bill which is worth £100 on payment in three months' time will be sold for, say, £98. Thus if a bank holds such a bill to maturity it makes an implicit rate of interest on it (in this case, an 'annualised' rate of around 8 per cent). Bills are profitable assets for commercial banks—but are also very liquid, as there is a very active market where they can be sold before maturity if this is necessary.

SECURITIES

Banks hold a small proportion of (mainly government) bonds with up to five years to maturity.

ADVANCES

These are loans to customers; this is where the highest returns are to be made, and not surprisingly 60–70 per cent of commercial banks' assets are advances. Interest charges on most loans are linked to the **base rate**, the rate which banks themselves have to pay if they borrow funds in the money market. Borrowers pay margins over this depending on the nature of the loan and their credit-worthiness. Despite the attractiveness of this type of lending to banks, it does have the drawback of being a relatively illiquid form of asset.

14.5.3 Non-bank financial intermediaries

The distinguishing feature of commercial banks used to be that their deposit liabilities were generally considered to be money, and monetary policy was therefore often particularly directed at them. However these banks are just one part of the total capital market which brings together borrowers and lenders. Nowadays the distinction between banks and **non-bank financial intermediaries**

(NBFIs) is more difficult to maintain. In the United Kingdom, for example, as a result of legislation in the 1980's, some building societies now offer chequebooks and cashcards which directly compete with those of banks. Moreover the commercial banks themselves have been moved in new directions, for instance to involvement in the lucrative **Eurocurrency market**, where deposits are taken and loans are made in currencies held outside their country of denomination. Such lending, very loosely regulated by the Bank of England, now constitutes over 25 per cent of the assets of London Clearing Banks.

Some of the more important NBFIs operating in the United Kingdom are:

MONEY MARKET INSTITUTIONS

As we have seen, the money market deals in bills and other short-term securities. The main institutions involved, apart from the commercial banks, are the **discount houses**, which specialise in this type of activity. Buying and selling in the money market enables institutions to adjust their liquidity position on a day-to-day basis. The Bank of England is also an active market participant as it can use its sales and purchases to influence the liquidity positions and hence the lending policy of the commercial banks.

BUILDING SOCIETIES

These compete directly with the commercial banks for the funds of the small saver. Their lending is almost entirely directed to house purchase, and because of this and their peculiar organisational structure (they are legally owned by their depositors), they possess certain legal privileges which are not available to other institutions. This may be changing as building societies seek new areas of business and access to capital and may be willing to forego these privileges in exchange for new opportunities. Building society retail deposits in total are much bigger than those of the commercial banks, although they are much more widely dispersed amongst hundreds of smaller institutions. As most of their deposits can be withdrawn at short notice, there is a case for including them in money aggregates. As we can see from Table 14.1, these deposits are included in 'broad money' measures, M4 and M5.

LIFE ASSURANCE AND PENSION FUNDS

These raise large sums from the personal sector and on-lend them to the government (by purchasing bonds) and to companies by buying shares. An increasing proportion of their investments is in foreign securities.

THE STOCK EXCHANGE

This is the secondary (or resale) market for longer-term securities issued by government and the private sector. Trading is in securities issued in the past and thus does not directly provide new finance. However, the trading decides the market value of existing securities and thus helps determine the terms on which the government and the private sector can raise long-term finance by making new issues. Moreover the Stock Exchange plays a most important role as a **market for corporate control**. Because shares are freely traded, an unsuccessful firm will experience a fall in the price of its shares. When this happens, outside entrepreneurs may be tempted to acquire control of the firm by buying its shares cheaply, dismissing the existing management and replacing it by a better team which will improve the firm's performance. The fear of this occurring may be a powerful spur to incumbent management to improve performance. There is much more which could be said about the rapidly-changing financial system in the United Kingdom and other countries. Some discussion of the effects of the recent deregulation of financial markets is provided in Chapter 20.

SUMMARY

In this chapter we have explored the meaning of money and outlined the historical development of the sophisticated monetary system of today. We showed that in modern conditions money is largely bank deposits, and we presented a simple model of how banks could create deposits. This led on to a discussion of the money supply. We showed how various different definitions of the money stock are used. Finally we examined the role of banks in the wider financial system.

SELF-TEST QUESTIONS

1 Which of the following statements is not true?

(a) A useful commodity money must not wear out easily.

(b) Banknotes first began as a form of receipt.

(c) Restrictions on the issue of banknotes helped stimulate the development of the chequing system.

(d) Any UK commercial bank can issue banknotes.

(e) Today's coins are an example of token money.

2 Which of the following statements is true?

(a) A profitable bank will aim to maintain a 100 per cent cash reserve ratio.

(b) The larger the cash reserve ratio, the greater the size of the bank credit multiplier.

(c) The smaller is the fraction of their money holdings which people hold outside the banking system, the smaller is the bank credit multiplier.

(d) Loans are a liability on a bank balance sheet.

(e) Cash is an asset on a bank's balance sheet.

3 Which of the following statements is not true?

(a) Sight deposits pay a very high rate of interest.

(b) The monetary base includes notes and coins in circulation with the public.

(c) An increase in the PSBR may lead to an increase in the money supply.

(d) Monetarists believe that reducing the budget deficit will help to control inflation.

(e) An inflow of funds from abroad can lead to an increase in the domestic money supply.

4 Which is the best description of a non-bank financial intermediary?

(a) An institution which comes between final borrowers and final lenders.

(b) An institution which is a lender of last resort.

(c) An institution which borrows and lends but whose liabilities cannot be directly used to make payments.

(d) An institution offering life assurance.

(e) A discount house.

5 Which of the following statements is true?

(a) Modern central banks are usually privately owned.

(b) A gilt-edged security is one which is backed by gold.

(c) Banknotes constitute a large proportion of M2.

(d) The market for corporate control operates through the purchase and sale of treasury bills.

(e) The existence of the money market increases the liquidity of the banking system.

EXERCISE

What is the relationship between the PSBR and the domestic money supply?

Answers on page 262.

The demand for money

In this chapter we examine the evolution of the theory of the demand for money. Starting with the 'classical' quantity theory of money, we lead on to the Fisher equation and the idea of the transactions demand for money. This then requires us to examine the functions which money performs, and the way in which Keynes differed from his predecessors by emphasising money's function as a store of value. The Keynesian analysis of liquidity preference is examined, together with its implications for money's role in macroeconomics. We then look at the revival of classical ideas in the 'New Quantity Theory' associated with Milton Friedman.

15.1 INTRODUCTION

In the last chapter we showed what money is, how it developed over time and how the money supply is affected by government policy. In order to gain a fuller understanding of the role of monetary factors, however, we need to analyse the factors determining the **demand for money**. This involves examining the motives for holding money in some detail and is actually a rather odd procedure. Some people would argue that we can discuss the determinants of the demand for money without asking why people hold money. In analysing the demand for apples, it may be pointed out, economists concentrate on such factors as their price, the price of other fruits, consumers' incomes and so on, without concerning themselves with the nature of apples. However, the case of money is rather different. For an apple is clearly a commodity which gives its consumer utility; consumption is an end in itself. By contrast, money is only a means to an end. In itself (especially in its modern forms, discussed in Chapter 14) money gives no direct utility. So why do people want money?

One commonsense answer, which largely satisfied the 'classical' economists (those economists writing from about the time of Adam Smith in the second half of the eighteenth century to the early years of this century) was that people wanted money to enable them to buy goods and services while avoiding those costs (discussed in Chapter 14) associated with barter. Another way to put this is to say that money was needed to **finance planned transactions**. The demand for money was thus linked to the level of planned transactions and the price at which those transactions took place. Note the emphasis on the price of transactions, for this was where the emphasis was placed by the classical writers.

15.2 THE QUANTITY THEORY OF MONEY

As long ago as 1690, the English philosopher John Locke traced a connection between changes in the amount of money in circulation and changes in the general price level. In the 1760s David Hume, the Scottish philosopher who was a friend of Adam Smith, produced a sophisticated analysis of the causal mechanism involved. The insights of these and other early writers were refined and improved throughout the 19th century, and became known as the **Quantity Theory of Money**.

Its best-known version was developed by the American economist Irving Fisher, who first presented it formally in his book *The Purchasing Power of Money*, published in 1911. His approach is summarised in the **Fisher equation**, also known as the **Equation of Exchange**:

$$MV = PT$$

Here M stands for the stock of money in existence (in modern terms, one or other of the money supply aggregates described in Chapter 14); V is the **velocity of circulation** of this money stock, which means the average frequency with which a unit of money changes hands in a given period; P is the average price at which a transaction takes place; and T is the number of transactions taking place in the period concerned (we should note that a transaction is defined as the exchange of a commodity for money).

This 'equation' is, as it stands, a **tautology**; that is, it must be true because of the way Fisher defined the terms. In a given period, a number of transactions take place. Their money value in total must clearly be PT, the average price at which a transaction occurs multiplied by the number of transactions. But in order that these transactions can take place, money must change hands. If the total money stock is M and V is the average number of times each unit is used, MV is also the money value of total transactions. The two sides of the 'equation' are simply two different ways of defining the same thing.

But the Fisher equation was given more content by the addition of some further assumptions. First, it was claimed that V, the velocity of circulation, was roughly constant. In the view of Fisher and earlier writers, V was determined by the institutional characteristics of an economy at a particular time, such as the frequency with which people are paid (whether daily, weekly or monthly), the stage of development of its banking system, the average period for which trade credit is granted, and so on. As these characteristics changed only slowly (particularly in the eighteenth and nineteenth centuries), it was argued that V could be treated as approximately constant.

More contentiously, it was claimed that the level of transactions was closely related to the level of national income and output. These in turn would be led by market forces to their 'full employment' levels. This, as we saw in Chapters 11 and 12, was a common assumption made by economists up to the time of Keynes.

Now the Fisher equation could be given a sharper interpretation. For if V was constant and T was at its maximum (full employment) value, there must be a simple relationship between M and P. If the money stock—the Quantity of Money—rises, *ceteris paribus*, the price level will have to rise to keep the two sides of the equation in balance. Increases in the general level of prices—inflation— were thus blamed on increases in the money supply. There was certainly a good deal of historical evidence to support this view. The influx of precious metals into Europe following the conquests by the Spanish in South America, for example, had set off a long period of rising prices.

15.2.1 Transactions and final output

This version of the quantity theory concentrates on the total amount of transactions taking place in an economy. There is a slightly different version of the equation of exchange which makes a direct link between money, prices and the level of national income or output. In this version we write:

$$MV = PY$$

In this case Y is the level of real output or income in the economy. M is defined as before, the money stock. V and P, however, have slightly different meanings. V is now the income velocity of circulation; it is the number of times money changes hands in a period to purchase final output. P is the average price at which **final output** is sold.

The reason for these distinctions is firstly that, as we saw in Chapter 11, in complex economies there will be many intermediate transactions before final output is produced and sold; therefore the value of final output is less than the value of all the transactions which have been involved. Secondly, in any period much trading concerns the sale and purchase of goods and financial assets created in previous periods—secondhand cars, houses, company shares etc. These clearly don't enter into final output in the current period.

As we have seen, the ratio of the total value of transactions to the total value of current output (ie, money or nominal national income) was assumed to remain constant. This implies, amongst other things, that the degree of **vertical integration** of production (ie, the extent to which firms produce their own components and other intermediate goods rather than buying them from other firms) remains constant. Thus, excessive increases in the quantity of money would *ceteris paribus* mean increases in the average price of final output as well as the average transaction price.

15.2.2 Transactions demand for money

This second version of the Equation of Exchange is particularly useful, as it enables us to link up with a number of other theories of the demand for money. One is the approach used in the cash balances equation developed at the University of Cambridge in the early years of this century by such economists as Alfred Marshall and AC Pigou. Their approach is of particular interest, as it was the way in which the Quantity Theory of Money was taught to the young JM Keynes. Although we have not so far stressed the monetary aspects of Keynes's work, he was a great monetary theorist and his thinking in this area was largely a response to the Cambridge version of the quantity theory.

The Cambridge tradition saw the quantity theory not so much as a way of explaining variations in the price level, although of course this aspect was recognised, but rather as a special case of the theory of demand in general.

The Cambridge economists saw money as a special commodity, but one which nevertheless was subject to the laws of supply and demand and could be analysed accordingly. It was pointed out that holding money has an opportunity cost for individuals and firms. Instead of holding money in the form of notes, coins and non-interest-bearing bank deposits people could invest in interest-bearing assets. If they chose to hold 'cash balances' it could only (assuming they were rational utility-maximisers) be because they needed cash to finance planned transactions, purchases of goods and services.

So the demand for money was a **transactions demand**. It was argued that this was a constant proportion, k, of their money income, PY. Rather as in the case of the velocity of circulation, k was held to be determined by the institutional characteristics of the economy at a particular time. We therefore have the Cambridge cash balances equation:

$$M_d = kPY$$

M_d stands for the *demand* for money. Suppose that the supply of and demand for money are initially in equilibrium ($M_d = M_s$) and the economy is fully employed. If the money supply is now increased, there will be an excess supply of money in the hands of the public. The free market acts, as elsewhere, to restore equilibrium. Individuals and firms with excess cash balances will run these balances down. They can do so either by spending more on goods and services (in which case, given full employment, prices will be driven up), or by purchasing larger holdings of financial assets. If they do the latter, they drive up the price of financial assets and therefore drive down the interest rate (see 15.4). The lower interest rate encourages increased investment by firms and increased spending by households. Again prices are driven up. This is the classic case of 'too much money chasing too few goods'.

So we have a similar result to that emphasised by Fisher's reasoning. Their similarity is more clearly brought out when we consider that the value of k in the Cambridge equation is equal to 1/V where V is defined as in the second version of the equation of exchange: in both cases the underlying assumption is that no institutional change takes place to alter patterns of payment and debt settlement.

15.2.3 'Classical' monetary policy in depressions

Both the Fisher and Cambridge approaches assume that the economy is fully employed, so that the only effect of money stock changes is on money prices. In this view of the market economy, *real* levels of output, income and employment are determined by *real* factors such as the production technologies open to the economy and consumer preferences. Money values have no impact on these things; as Pigou used to say, money is simply a 'veil' drawn over the functioning of the real economy.

However, this is only the case when the economy is in equilibrium. These economists did admit the possibility that there might be *short run* situations where resources were temporarily less than fully employed. Here monetary expansion might have a real impact. If cash balances were increased beyond the levels individuals and firms had planned to hold, extra spending would be stimulated. In so far as resources were not fully employed, this extra spending could bring forth new output rather than simply forcing up prices. In terms of the Fisher equation, an increase in M might stimulate an increase in T and Y. There would seem to be scope for the monetary authorities to increase employment by 'printing money'.

However, many of these economists would have rejected this suggestion as dangerous and unnecessary. For one thing, the notion of full employment is difficult to define, as we have already seen and will consider further. Much unemployment would have been characterised as 'voluntary' rather than 'involuntary' by pre-Keynesian economists. For another, even if it were to be agreed that there was a genuine problem and that monetary expansion could cure it, there was thought to be an alternative solution.

Quantity theorists argued that if prices and wages were allowed to fall freely in response to unsold goods and unemployment, as the market would appear to dictate, the **real** value of the money supply would rise (with a fall in prices and wages, a given money supply buys more in real terms). Thus you could have the same effect as increasing the money supply without relaxing banking orthodoxies and ideas of 'sound money'. To put this again in terms of the Fisher equation, if MV remained the same but P fell, T and Y must rise to compensate.

As we have seen earlier in the book, Keynes was profoundly critical of this 'laissez-faire' attitude to unemployment. He developed a different approach to monetary theory which showed, he claimed, that the classical approach to monetary policy in depressions was wrong. In order to see why he made this claim we must examine his argument in detail, but we first need to make a slight detour to think a little bit more about the reasons why people hold money.

15.3 THE FUNCTIONS OF MONEY

As we have seen in the last chapter, money is a complicated and rather mysterious phenomenon. In an attempt to understand it, and to see why people hold monetary balances, economists have traditionally distinguished a number of functions which money serves:

A MEDIUM OF EXCHANGE

We discussed this in Chapter 14, when we outlined money's role in reducing the costs associated with barter. In concentrating on the transactions demand for money, the classical writers clearly placed most emphasis on this function.

UNIT OF ACCOUNT

By enabling us to have a common measure of the value of commodities, money makes rational economic calculation easier. It is the basis for keeping accounts, costing, measuring assets and liabilities and estimating profit and loss. We should point out that money's efficiency in this function depends on two things. One, the prices of goods and services should be free to adjust to market forces of supply and demand; if we have non-market-clearing prices (as in many planned economies), money costs and prices will be misleading. Two, despite the fluctuations of *relative* prices, the *average* price level should be as stable as possible. In conditions of rapid inflation, for example, rational calculation becomes much more difficult.

STANDARD OF DEFERRED PAYMENT

Much economic activity involves making future commitments such as contracts to supply goods and services at some future date, in return for a payment at that time, and the existence of money makes borrowing and lending easier; this facilitates the efficient allocation of resources and long-term investment. In each case, we again emphasise the need for the value of money (or, equivalently, the average price level) to remain stable in order for it to fulfil this function successfully.

STORE OF WEALTH

Individuals, households and firms have purchasing power which they do not always want to use immediately. For example, you may wish to save a proportion of your salary rather than spend it. This purchasing power can be held in the form of financial assets (such as stocks and shares), and in real assets (such as residential property). Although these stores of wealth bring returns in one form or another, they have the disadvantage that, if spending power is needed urgently, it may take time to liquidate them, to turn them into cash. Moreover, as assets like these fluctuate in value over time as a result of supply and demand conditions, there is the possibility of a capital loss—that the asset will be worth less in monetary terms when you come to sell it. In this context, we can see that money itself can be a store of wealth, competing with other assets. It has two advantages, **perfect liquidity** and **constant nominal** value (although it can vary in real value, like other assets, as a result of changes in the general price level), to offset the disadvantage that it does not in normal conditions offer any rate of return to the holder. Because money has some attractive features as an asset, this suggests that there will be some demand for it in this function. Money will not simply be held for transactions purposes. This is an important insight, on which Keynes was to build his monetary theory. It distinguishes him from the classical writers, who largely neglected the asset demand for money.

15.4 KEYNES AND THE DEMAND FOR MONEY

We have seen that Keynes believed that it was possible for resources to lie idle—workers to be unemployed, factories empty and machines unstaffed—as a result of a deficiency in aggregate demand. By contrast, classical quantity theorists believed that the economy was self-correcting. If prices and wages were allowed to fall, the real value of money would rise and spending increase, as we indicated in 15.2. However, this assumes that extra real money balances are spent by households and firms, which in turn implies that money is used only for transactions purposes.

If, however, people do *not* use all their purchasing power (either in buying goods and services or real or financial assets), but instead hold **idle balances** of money, it is clear that the automatic self-correction of the market will be much more difficult.

It should be clear, then, that Keynes's emphasis on the 'store of wealth' function of money dovetails neatly with his analysis of aggregate demand. Idle resources are the physical counterpart of the idle balances of money held by firms and households. We now turn to examine Keynes's monetary theory in some detail.

15.4.1 Motives for liquidity preference

Keynes uses the term **liquidity preference** for the desire to hold cash balances rather than other assets. There were, in his view, three motives for holding money. One was the **transactions motive** previously discussed, but in addition there were the **precautionary** and **speculative** motives, both deriving from money's function as a store of wealth. Keynes argued that the classical writers had ignored these motives because they had failed to recognise the importance of **uncertainty** in economic decision-making.

If the consequences of all our actions were known with absolute certainty, the quantity theorists would have been right to argue that money would only be held for transactions purposes. Individuals and firms would know their future incomes and the future course of prices (including the prices of assets) and thus their future consumption and investment patterns. They would only hold that amount of cash which they planned to spend in a particular period. Any current excess of income over spending would be used to purchase income-yielding assets allowing higher consumption levels in the future. In such circumstances, money would not be held as a store of wealth, for its special attributes would be redundant. Liquidity and certain nominal value would be no advantage in a world where all movements of prices could be predicted, and therefore an optimal asset-holding plan could be devised which ensured that purchases and sales of assets were appropriately timed to give a positive rate of return.

But of course in reality the world is dominated by uncertainty. In consequence, despite the opportunity cost of holding money (the rate of return on other assets), precautionary balances will be held in case there is a need for unplanned expenditure, eg, to pay the repair bill after a car accident or breakdown. This might be catered for in the spirit of the quantity theory approach by simply assuming that people hold precautionary balances in proportion to their planned transactions (say, for instance, a margin of 20 per cent over what they plan to spend in a period). In such a case, the values of V in the Fisher equation and k in the Cambridge equation would be different, but otherwise the quantity theorists' analysis would hold.

The speculative demand for money cannot be so easily disposed of—it is at the heart of Keynes's criticism of the classical writers. Keynes argues that the speculative demand for money is sensitive to changes in the interest rate, implying that Fisher's V and the Cambridge k are unstable. As we have seen, the predictions of the quantity theorists hinge on the assumption of stability in k and V.

15.4.2 The speculative demand for money

Keynes argued that, when interest rates are low, holding money as an asset will be a more attractive proposition than when they are high. Suppose, to take a highly simplified case, that there are just two stores of wealth available—money and a financial asset. Let us further assume, as did Keynes, that this is an undated bond, that is, a fixed-interest bond with no specific repayment date. For example this might be a bond, with a nominal value of £100, paying a fixed interest payment of £5 per year.

Although the bond has a nominal value of £100, its actual price will be determined by demand and supply conditions in the bond market. Other things being equal, its price will vary with the market interest rate prevailing in the economy, because with the interest payment fixed the price of existing bonds will have to vary in order for the return on bonds to be equalised throughout the market. Thus if a bond originally sold at £100 with a fixed £5 being paid in interest, the bond's price would have to fall to £50 if the interest rate on new bonds rose to 10 per cent. Why? Because nobody would be prepared to pay £100 for an old bond paying £5 per year when new bonds pay £10 per year. Only when the price falls to £50 will the rate of return (£5 on £50 = 10 per cent) be competitive.

Against this background, Keynes claimed that the demand for bonds of this type—and therefore the demand for the alternative asset, money—would depend on the relationship between the current interest rate and that rate which was expected to be maintained in the long run, the 'normal' interest rate.

If the current interest rate was thought to be exceptionally high and bond prices, therefore, thought to be exceptionally low, the expectation would be that the interest rate would fall and bond prices rise. Keynes argued that in these circumstances individuals and firms would want to buy bonds in the hope of making a **speculative gain** when their price rose. They would therefore be unwilling to hold idle balances of money, preferring to buy bonds instead. Conversely, if bond prices were thought abnormally high, and interest rates abnormally low, people would be unwilling to hold bonds (and face a likely capital loss) and would hold money instead. There would therefore be a considerable speculative demand for money when the interest rate was low.

On the assumption that all individuals and firms had slightly different views on what the 'normal' rate of interest might be, they would switch from holding bonds to holding money (and vice versa) at different market interest rates. Such variations in expectations (and remember, this is a world of uncertainty, so expectations can differ) generate a smooth downward-sloping demand curve for idle cash balances as shown in Figure 15.1.

FIGURE 15.1 **Speculative demand for money**

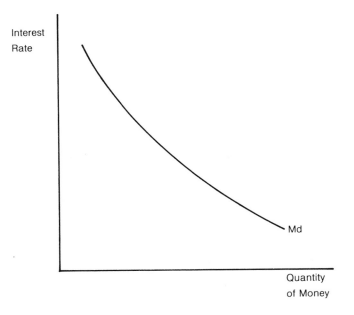

15.4.3 A theoretical possibility: the liquidity trap

Keynes claims, then, that the demand for money is **elastic** with respect to the interest rate (to remind yourself of the meaning of elasticity, refer back to Chapter 3). This is by contrast with the quantity theorists, whose belief is that the demand for money is perfectly interest-inelastic.

Indeed, Keynes argued that in some circumstances the interest-elasticity of demand for money might become infinite. That is to say, at a sufficiently low rate of interest **everybody** might prefer to hold idle balances of money rather than bonds. As Keynes put it, liquidity preference would become absolute. In such circumstances (known as the **liquidity trap**, and shown in Figure 15.2) it would be impossible to sell new bonds to finance investment and thus increases in savings would not be matched by increases in investment. As a consequence, unemployment could persist for long periods.

FIGURE 15.2 **The liquidity trap**

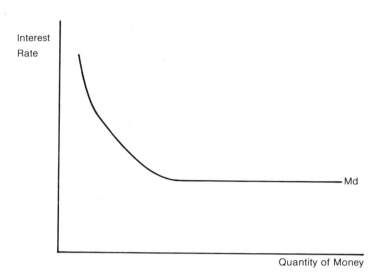

However, it would be unwise to lay very much emphasis on the idea of the liquidity trap except as a theoretical extreme case of the interest-elasticity of the demand for money. Most monetary economists nowadays do not believe that a perfectly elastic section of the demand curve for money has ever been, or is likely to be, observed. However, most would agree with Keynes that the classical assumption, amounting to the belief that the demand for money is completely **in**elastic with respect to the interest rate, is equally implausible. In practice, the demand curve for money slopes downwards; debate tends to focus on the steepness of the curve.

15.4.4 Post-Keynesian developments in the theory of the demand for money

Keynes's basic insight into the interest-responsiveness of the demand for money has been confirmed by theoretical developments since his death. For one thing, it has been argued that the transactions and precautionary demands for money are themselves likely to be interest-sensitive, for when the interest rate rises, the opportunity cost of holding money increases and firms and households will attempt to economise on holdings of money. For instance, by lengthening the period before you pay bills (something which the quantity theorists assumed to be institutionally determined), you can reduce your average holdings for transaction purposes. Similarly, at a higher interest rate you are likely to reduce your precautionary balances; even though this involves an increased risk that you will not be able to cover unplanned expenditure from your cash holdings, this is compensated for by the higher interest payments received.

For another, Keynes's analysis of the speculative demand for money has been refined and extended as a result of insights drawn from **portfolio analysis**.

Keynes's original approach is now seen as unsatisfactory for two reasons. First, it seems to imply that individuals will only hold one type of asset at a time. If an individual thinks that the current interest rate is above the normal rate, he or she will only hold bonds; if it is thought to be below the normal rate, only money will be held. In practice, many individuals hold bonds *and* idle balances of money.

The second problem with Keynes's presentation can be seen if we think back to Chapter 14. Here it was argued that money cannot be clearly demarcated from other financial assets; rather there is a 'spectrum of liquidity'.

Modern Keynesians, then, present the argument rather differently. They think of wealth holders as possessing a **portfolio** of different assets. This means a combination of assets which range from highly liquid cash and time deposits to less liquid long-dated stocks and equity shares. Generally speaking, the less liquid an asset, the higher its rate of return—but also the greater its 'riskiness' in terms of the variability of the return (*on average* investment in shares may give you a higher rate of return than deposits with a building society—but remember you may make a capital loss if you have to sell at a time when share prices have fallen).

Given this, individuals will have to weigh up the advantages of various ways of storing wealth. There is no one asset which is clearly superior (as there was, or subjectively appeared to be, in Keynes's model) and individuals will commonly 'diversify their portfolios' and spread their risks by holding a variety of different assets simultaneously.

In these circumstances, a rise in interest rates leads people to redistribute their wealth away from the liquid asset end of the spectrum towards less liquid assets, but this is a shift of emphasis rather than a complete movement out of money into other assets; a gradual movement rather than a discontinuous one. In portfolio analysis, therefore, the **individual's** demand curve for money slopes downwards as in Figure 15.1. Interest-elasticity characterises the individual's demand curve, and not just that of the market.

15.4.5 Money in a Keynesian economy

Whether in its original form as put forward by Keynes, or in its later refinements, it is clear that the Keynesian view of the demand for money is rather different from that of the quantity theorists. There are four features of the Keynesian view of money which should be particularly emphasised:

1 **Money as a store of wealth** As we have seen, the focus on this function of money is central to Keynes's analysis.

2 **Indirect transmission mechanism** The quantity theorists believed that excess cash balances would largely be spent on goods and services. However, in the Keynesian picture the impact on the economy is indirect. The **transmission mechanism** by which monetary changes affect the economy is through the interest rate. An increase in the money supply reduces the rate of interest, **ceteris paribus**. This is shown in Figure 15.3: a shift of the money supply from M_{S1} to M_{S2} reduces the interest rate from i_1 to i_2. It is this fall in the interest rate which has a stimulating effect on the economy; it makes borrowing for investment or consumption cheaper.

FIGURE 15.3 **Money supply expansion**

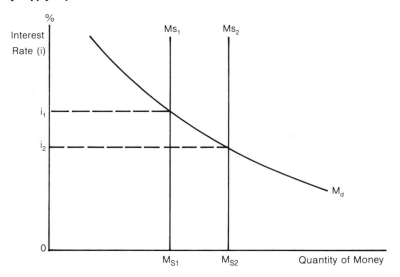

3 **Weak effect of monetary expansion** Keynes argued that this indirect expansionary effect could be very weak; this is one reason why he opposed attempts to remedy unemployment by monetary means alone. For one thing, in the theoretical case of the liquidity trap outlined earlier, changes in the money supply would have no impact at all on the rate of interest, and

thus there would be no expansionary impact. This is shown in Figure 15.4, where an increase in the money supply leaves the equilibrium interest rate unchanged.

FIGURE 15.4   **Money supply expansion with the liquidity trap**

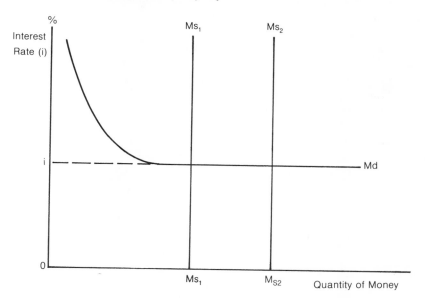

Even in the absence of the liquidity trap, however, Keynes thought that the fall in interest rates brought about by monetary expansion might have little effect on total spending, as we saw in Chapter 12.

4   **The supply of money and its control** If you refer back to the discussion of the money supply in Chapter 14, you should be able to see that much of that analysis fits happily into the 'quantity theory' tradition, for example, the bank credit multiplier. One thing which determined the size of this was the proportion of people's money holdings which they wished to hold outside the banking system, either in cash or on deposit with non-banking institutions. In order for the bank credit multiplier to have a stable value, this proportion must be constant, but we have seen in this section that Keynes's analysis implies that the proportion of people's wealth held in cash is not fixed, but depends on the interest rate. The implication is that the bank credit multiplier is unstable. It is thus difficult to predict the effect of changes in the monetary base on wider measures of the money supply, and difficult for governments to control the money supply with any great precision.

Indeed, Keynesians tend to see the whole process by which money is created as being more complicated than was suggested in Chapter 14. Essentially, the deposit creation process outlined there suggests that if banks want to increase their lending because their cash and other liquid holdings have increased, they can do so. Keynesians point out that the loans which banks make are not provided free; an interest rate is charged. To assume that all loans which banks wish to supply will be demanded, irrespective of the interest rate, seems implausible.

Moreover, the Keynesian emphasis on the substitutability of money and other assets at the margin also implies that the monetary authorities cannot permanently suppress a demand for loans and credit. If the existing commercial banks are unwilling to lend, or are not allowed to do so, other close substitutes for money will be developed by what are currently non-banking financial intermediaries, if the price is right. This was how our modern banking system emerged. In other words, in the Keynesian view the supply of money is partly demand-determined. This is a conclusion very different from that of the quantity theorists, and it makes it possible to argue that the Fisher equation, for example, can be reinterpreted: that increases in planned spending (PT or PY) may bring about increases in M, rather than vice-versa.

15.5   THE 'NEW' QUANTITY THEORY: FRIEDMAN'S MONETARISM

For many years after World War II, Keynesian ideas about the role of money in the economy were highly influential with governments, particularly in the United Kingdom, where a key document was the **Radcliffe Report**. Published in 1959, this government report expressly rejected the analysis of the old classical quantity theorists, and enshrined Keynesianism as the new orthodoxy. It was to maintain this position until the 1970s, when massive inflation throughout the Western world provoked another round of official rethinking.

The key figure in this rethinking was Professor Milton Friedman, then at the University of Chicago and later a Nobel Prizewinner and controversial public figure. Friedman is usually called a **monetarist**. His work derives from that of the classical quantity theorists; one of his most famous articles (published as long ago as the 1950s) is called *The Quantity Theory Restated*. His conclusions on monetary matters were essentially in agreement with those of Fisher and other classical writers. However, he went beyond the ideas of the old quantity theorists by incorporating some of Keynes's ideas and placing much more importance on empirical evidence.

Friedman's approach has evolved over time and its emphasis has altered. But there are a number of ways in which we can clearly distinguish the work of Friedman from that of his classical predecessors.

REAL BALANCES

For Friedman, the demand for money has to be understood as a demand for **real balances**, that is, nominal money holdings corrected for inflation. This means that normally we would expect a doubling of all prices and money incomes to necessitate a doubling of cash holdings. The Cambridge equation of 15.2 of this chapter could therefore be rewritten as:

$$\frac{M_d}{P} = kY$$

In other words, the demand for real cash balances bears a constant relation to the level of real income. This was of course implicit in the older approach, but Friedman makes it explicit.

PERMANENT INCOME

Like both Keynes and the classical theorists, Friedman recognises that income is a major determinant of the transactions demand for money, but he defines the relevant concept of income in a novel manner, which we briefly touched on in Chapter 12. He emphasises that actual income fluctuates significantly from period to period, but people's spending plans are more stable. They will base their consumption (and therefore their demand for money for transactions purposes) on their **permanent income** rather than their current income. Permanent income can be defined as that income which they expect to maintain on average over time. If current income is below permanent income, individuals will borrow or run down their savings to finance consumption; if it is above it, they will add to their savings or reduce their debts. This behaviour has clear implications for the transactions demand for money which are very different from those of the older approach. It implies, for instance, that the demand for money over the business cycle will be relatively constant, rather than varying in line with fluctuations in income.

TYPES OF WEALTH

Permanent income bears a close relation to the value of people's wealth or assets (which, as we saw in Chapter 8, are the ultimate generators of income). Remember that such assets can be physical (houses, machines) or financial (building society deposits, company shares) or human in form. Human capital—those aspects of skills and training which enhance productivity and earning power—is an increasingly important form of wealth in developed countries. However, it has the disadvantage that it cannot be sold outright like other assets; it is therefore **illiquid**. Consequently, Friedman argues, the larger the proportion of earnings which are derived from human capital, the greater will be the demand for cash balances held by individuals to compensate for this illiquidity. To make this clear, think of two individuals who both have the same permanent income. One, however, gets most of his income from property (dividends, interest and rents) while the other individual gets his income mainly from work. Friedman's claim is that the second individual will hold larger real cash balances.

OPPORTUNITY COST

Like Keynes, Friedman is aware that the opportunity cost of holding money will affect the demand for it. In line with his broader approach to the concepts of wealth and income, however, Friedman doesn't just concentrate on one single rate of interest, as does Keynes. Rather he draws on portfolio theory to note that different assets have different yields, reflecting such factors as the riskiness and liquidity of these different types of investment. Thus the rates of return on the many different types of financial and other assets may all influence the demand for money.

Friedman argues, then, that the demand for real balances is a function of the level of *permanent* income (Y_p). We can write this as:

$$\frac{M_d}{P} = f(Y_p)$$

The nature of this functional relationship is influenced by the factors discussed above—the rates of return on different types of asset and the proportion of wealth held as human capital. Leaving aside the distinction between permanent and current income, this amounts to saying that the k of the Cambridge equation, and therefore the V of the Fisher equation, are treated as something determined by economic variables, rather than as something given by institutional factors.

15.5.1 The monetarist transmission mechanism

An implication of Friedman's approach is that the transmission mechanism, by which monetary changes have an impact on the economy, is different from that described by Keynes. Keynesians argued that an increase in the money supply had its effect primarily through depressing the interest rate on bonds, and that this effect on the economy as a whole was likely to be rather limited. Friedman sees the impact of monetary expansion as being much greater. Because a very wide range of assets compete with money, including, it should be pointed out, many types of consumer durables, it is not only the bond market which is affected. An excess supply of money is diverted into spending in many different types of market. It is likely, Friedman claims, to have an expansionary effect throughout the economy, in essentially the same manner as the classical economists suggested. As we shall see in Chapter 16, Friedman believes that in normal conditions much, if not all, this effect is on prices rather than output.

15.5.2 Positive economics: Friedman's empirical work

Milton Friedman has always been strongly committed to the philosophy of **positive economics**, outlined in Chapter 1. This approach involves the belief that useful hypotheses must be amenable to testing. Thus his work on the demand for money contrasts with that of the classical writers, whose conclusions were derived from tautologies, given meaning only by making essentially untestable assumptions, and also with that of Keynes, who was largely concerned with demonstrating the *theoretical* possibility of holding idle balances (as an underpinning for his analysis of aggregate demand deficiency).

Having examined the theory of the demand for money, Friedman hypothesises that, of the factors discussed above, only variations in permanent income have in practice much impact. The other variables, *in theory* capable of having an impact, are in reality of little significance. The ratio of human capital to non-human assets alters rather slowly, and may be ignored. More controversially, Friedman claims that the 'opportunity cost' variables—rates of return on different assets which compete with money as a store of wealth—have little effect. These hypotheses, if true, lead us back to the classical conclusion. Despite the increased sophistication, Friedman's approach still amounts to the belief that there is a constant relationship between the demand for money and the level of money income, ie, that the velocity of circulation is stable (except for fluctuations over the business cycle when permanent income and current income temporarily diverge).

For Friedman, these hypotheses are testable. Over many years (culminating in 1982 in a book written by Friedman and Anna Schwartz called *Monetary Trends in the United States and the United Kingdom*) he has published many research studies which appear to support them. In the view of monetarists, these studies indicated beyond reasonable doubt that there existed a strong and stable relationship between the demand for money and the level of permanent income (measured as a weighted average of income over a number of periods), but that *no* reliable relationship exists between the demand for money and yields on other assets.

Unfortunately for those with tidy minds, however, the monetarists' view of these studies isn't universally accepted. Both Keynesians and less committed economists have expressed strong doubts about the methods used in these studies and the conclusions drawn from them. Moreover, the evidence of the 1980s, when the income velocity of circulation seems to have altered dramatically in a number of countries (partly, no doubt, as a result of the major changes in monetary and financial institutions occurring at this time) is difficult to square with the earlier results. More will be said on this in Chapter 16.

SUMMARY

In this chapter we have seen how Keynes's approach to monetary theory, with its emphasis on the interest-elasticity of the demand for money, conflicted with the older classical quantity theory. He argued that 'idle balances' of money were held, so that it could not be assumed that expansion of the money supply would have the effect of increasing economic activity or driving up prices. Friedman, however, has reformulated the quantity theory in more sophisticated terms, and his claims for the empirical relevance of this approach were given a great deal of attention in the 1970s when high rates of inflation were a serious problem in many economies.

SELF-TEST QUESTIONS

1   Which of the following statements is not correct?

(a) Using money is a way of reducing transactions costs.

(b) Money is demanded for transactions purposes.

(c) The classical quantity theorists thought the demand for money was relatively insensitive to interest rate charges.

(d) Keynes thought money was never demanded for transactions purposes.

(e) Friedman argues that the demand for money is a demand for real balances.

2   Which is the best definition of the income velocity of circulation?

(a) The frequency with which money is used for transactions purposes.

(b) The number of times a unit of money is used on average to purchase final output in a given period.

(c) The average frequency with which money is used to purchase goods in a given period.

(d) The money stock divided by the average level of prices.

(e) A function of the rates of return on different assets and the proportion of wealth held in the form of human capital.

3   The classical quantity theorists tended to assume that depressions were self-correcting because:

(a) Governments could always print money to stimulate demand.

(b) Falling prices and wages led to an increase in the real money supply, which in turn would stimulate increased spending.

(c) An unexpected fall in Y would stimulate an increase in M and P, therefore restoring full employment.

(d) Most unemployment was involuntary, and therefore monetary expansion could not cure it.

(e) The liquidity trap meant that the interest rate could not fall below a certain level.

4   Which of the following statements is correct?

(a) Keynes believed that the demand for money was interest-inelastic.

(b) According to Keynes, the speculative motive for money explains why the demand for money depends on the level of income.

(c) Because of uncertainty, according to Keynes, people hold money for transactions purposes.

(d) When interest rates are high, people will hold large amounts of money for speculative purposes.

(e) Portfolio analysis suggests reasons why individuals hold idle cash balances and bonds simultaneously.

5 **Which of the following is not a difference between Friedman's approach and that of the old quantity theorists?**

(a) Friedman stresses the distinction between current income and permanent income.

(b) Friedman makes use of empirical tests of his hypotheses.

(c) Friedman argues that an increase in the money supply will have an impact throughout the economy.

(d) Friedman does not assume that the velocity of circulation is determined by institutional characteristics of the economy.

(e) Friedman offers a theoretical explanation why the velocity of circulation varies over the business cycle.

EXERCISE

(a) Define money and its functions.

(b) Examine the monetarist view that a change in the supply of money which is greater than the rate of increase of real output must lead to inflation.

Answers on page 264.

Macroeconomic policy and the unemployment-inflation trade-off

In this wide-ranging chapter we examine the macroeconomic objectives which governments pursue, and the policies (particularly fiscal and monetary policies) which they use to pursue them. We show how there can be conflicts between policy objectives and how this led economists to argue that there could be 'trade-offs' between them. We then go on to examine the case of the relationship between unemployment and inflation. We look at the evolution of views about this relationship in the context of the Phillips Curve.

16.1   INTRODUCTION

In the last few chapters we have developed some basic ideas about the workings of the economy as a whole. We have seen how Keynes's ideas about aggregate demand for output and about the motives for holding money represented a challenge to the orthodox economic thinking of his day. Pre-Keynesian economists had placed great emphasis on the self-correcting tendency of the market mechanism and on the belief that governments should avoid involvement in the economy as far as possible. But after the Keynesian Revolution of the 1930s economists came to the view that the economy, left to itself, could slip into a slump where resources could lie idle for long periods and in order to avoid this, governments should intervene to maintain a high level of aggregate demand and to take whatever other measures proved necessary in order to deal with macroeconomic problems. Since the early 1970s, however, there has been a considerable reaction against this macroeconomic policy activism. In this chapter we explore the way in which thinking about macroeconomic policy has evolved over the last fifty years.

16.2   POLICY OBJECTIVES

In the United Kingdom at the end of World War II, all political parties committed themselves to the principle of **maintaining full employment** embodied in the White Paper on Employment Policy published by the coalition government in 1944. This principle was to be followed in a number of other developed Western economies as well. Later on, United Kingdom governments broadened the scope of their macroeconomic ambitions. At various times since the war, governments have explicitly made commitments to **maintaining stable prices, promoting a healthy balance of payments**, and **achieving maximum possible economic growth**.

Over a period of time, the emphasis has changed considerably. In the early postwar years full employment was particularly stressed, not surprisingly, for politicians and the public had recent memories of the depression of the interwar period. In the 1950s and 1960s economic growth was stressed, but this ambition was often thwarted by the need (or so it was believed at the time) to maintain a stable exchange rate between the pound and other currencies: this led to a concentration on the balance of payments. In the 1970s inflation came to be seen as a major problem and by the 1980s the restoration of price stability became the overwhelming objective.

This changing emphasis partly reflects changes in beliefs about the way in which the economy operates, as we shall see, and also reflects political and other value judgments—normative economics as well as positive economics. Apart from differences within economies, it is interesting also to note that different countries have emphasised different objectives. For example, West Germany (partly as a result of the memory of very high rates of German inflation in the 1920s, with their disastrous economic and political consequences) has in the postwar period attached much more importance to price stability than most other countries. Japan made economic growth the central concern. The United States, although its postwar policy problems and political debate have been broadly similar to those of the British, embraced Keynesianism much later (not until the 1960s) and abandoned it rather earlier than was the case in the United Kingdom.

A basic problem is that there are conflicts between macroeconomic objectives, and choices thus have to be made. Such choices necessarily involve an element of value judgment. This should become clearer as we consider the major policy objectives in concern.

16.2.1 Full employment

Unemployment is both an economic and a social problem. In economic terms, unemployment wastes resources directly (people and machines are not producing goods or services) and indirectly (resources which could be used for other purposes have to be diverted to support the unproductive unemployed: moreover the taxes or borrowing necessary to support the unemployed distorts incentives). In social terms, unemployment is divisive, disruptive of family and other relationships and has been shown to have adverse effects on the health of the unemployed and their families. More controversially, it has been argued to lead to crime and public disorder. All these social effects, incidentally, themselves have economic consequences, although they are sometimes difficult to quantify. Other things being equal, then, we would like to have less unemployment. However, as we have seen in earlier chapters, unemployment is a problematic concept. Official figures on unemployment do not give us much guide to the nature of the problem.

For Keynes, *full* employment was a desirable goal. But he understood this to mean a level of employment where there is no demand-deficient or involuntary unemployment. The achievement of full employment in this sense is quite compatible with considerable levels of 'voluntary' unemployment in the sense defined in Chapter 11, and further discussed in Chapter 17. Policy debate has therefore often centred on the proportion of recorded unemployment which can be considered involuntary, and thus amenable to treatment by the Keynesian remedy of government expansion of aggregate demand. In the 1970s Milton Friedman and other economists came to argue that most unemployment was better understood as 'voluntary'. Friedman, rather than talking of full employment, defined a 'natural rate' of unemployment which could only be reduced by using microeconomic policies to make unemployment a less attractive proposition to the unemployed.

16.2.2 Stable prices

There is widespread support for the view that governments should attempt to hold down the rate of **inflation** which can be defined as a rising trend in the average level of prices. However, the precise reasons why inflation is a bad thing are rarely spelt out. Most of us worry about the effect of inflation on our living standards, but if money wages rise as fast as prices (the experience of many, if not most, people), does this mean inflation is not a problem?

Economists point out that inflation has a number of effects on the economy. In analysing these effects, they have found it useful to make a distinction between **anticipated** and **unanticipated inflation.**

In an economy where inflation was fully anticipated—that is, where everybody knew that inflation was going to be, say, 10 per cent per annum—it would only present two relatively minor problems. First, spending power held in currency and non-interest-bearing bank deposits would have a higher opportunity cost (see Chapter 15). People would therefore try to economise by holding smaller cash balances. This would involve making more frequent withdrawals, writing more cheques and making more frequent visits to banks, building societies and other financial institutions: this is sometimes referred to as the **'shoe leather'** cost of inflation! Second, there would be resource costs as a result of the need to alter labels on goods and prices on restaurant menus—the **'menu cost'** of inflation. Both of these costs are likely to be small.

The problem is that inflation cannot be fully anticipated. Although we could in principle tie all our incomes, taxes, prices and so on to a price index and thus bargain in real terms, this is in practice likely to be difficult. There is no perfect index; different price indicators would have to be monitored and compared. This involves time and resources and offers many opportunities for dispute and contention. For example, when Mrs Thatcher's government came into power in 1979 it argued that the increase in prices shown by the Retail Price Index (RPI) exaggerated the extent of inflation and therefore led trade unions to push for larger wage increases than were necessary in order to maintain living standards. The government tried to popularise an alternative index, the Tax and Prices Index, which showed a lower inflation rate. However, this index later came to show more rapid price increases than the RPI and so emphasis on it was quietly dropped!

Even if an appropriate index can be chosen, the extent to which groups can protect themselves against inflation varies considerably. This means that a period of rapid inflation has considerable redistributive consequences. It takes real spending power away from some groups and gives it to others in a way which is under no conscious control or direction. For example:

1   **Relative prices are distorted** Because some prices are 'sticky' and don't rise with general inflation, often as a result of government controls (eg on rents and food prices), those who consume such commodities experience a gain in real income at the expense of those who supply them. If this persists, supply will be reduced as profits fall and thus potential consumers may lose as well (the effect of this was explained in the context of the housing market in Chapter 2).

2   **Income and wealth redistribution** Similarly, some incomes and asset values may lag behind inflation. Those on fixed incomes—eg, some occupational pensioners and owners of fixed-interest securities—clearly suffer a loss of real income. So do those workers who, possibly as a result of government wage controls, find their pay failing to keep pace with price increases. Conversely, other groups benefit from inflation, for example, workers with powerful union backing and owners of real assets such as houses. More generally, those who **borrow** at fixed interest rates gain at the expense of those who **lend** if inflation is greater than was anticipated when the loan was made.

3   **Redistribution from the private sector to the government** One major borrower is often the public sector. If inflation is greater than was anticipated, the government pays back less in real terms than was foreseen when the debt was incurred. Similarly, the income tax structure, if not constantly adjusted to allow for inflation, has a continual tendency to increase the government's 'take' of real resources. Tax allowances are worth less in real terms, and higher tax bands are reached at successively lower levels of *real* income. Governments are often very dishonest about this. They claim to have made huge tax 'cuts' when appealing to voters, when all they have done is to make some partial allowance for inflation while still taking a larger chunk of real resources!

4   **Exchange rates** If the exchange rate of the country's currency is fixed against other currencies a higher rate of inflation at home will lead to a loss of trade competitiveness with a decline of exports and a rise in imports. The balance of trade and payments may therefore deteriorate with an ultimate need for possibly painful correction (see Chapter 19). If the exchange rate is flexible higher inflation than overseas will result in a corresponding external depreciation of the currency. This may help to maintain trade competitiveness but the rise in import prices may be a factor in sustaining the inflationary spiral of rising wages and prices. Continual currency depreciation may also lead to **capital flight** if investors lose confidence in the value of domestic money.

Of course, if inflation were to get completely out of control, with prices rising daily or even hourly as was the case with the German **hyperinflation** of the 1920s or the Hungarian experience of 1947, money would lose its effectiveness as a store of wealth, unit of account, standard of deferred payment or even as a medium of exchange. Economies would revert to barter or the use of such vehicle commodities as cigarettes. Such a breakdown of money's usefulness imposes enormous costs on virtually all sections of the community.

However, such extreme experiences are rare. It is possible for communities to continue with very high but relatively stable rates of inflation for many years without taking off into hyperinflation: in recent decades, for example, countries like Israel, Brazil and Argentina have had rates of inflation of hundreds or even thousands per cent per year. The persistence of such an apparently undesirable state of affairs suggests that it is *possible* to tolerate inflation, but invariably governments are forced to take anti-inflationary austerity measures with distressing results for some sectors of the population. Inflation is difficult to eradicate because it actually has a tendency to benefit some powerful groups in a community.

16.2.3   The balance of payments

The balance of payments as a policy objective is dealt with in some detail in Chapter 19. It suffices to say here that to run either a persistent surplus or a persistent deficit on the balance of payments (the record of financial transactions with the rest of the world) is undesirable. A persistent deficit implies that a country is continuing to spend in excess of its income from abroad and its ability to attract long-term inward investment. Such a situation cannot persist indefinitely, for a country's reserves and its ability to obtain short-term loans will eventually be exhausted. But it should not be assumed that a persistent surplus would be a good idea, either. It would imply that a country is continually sending abroad resources greater in value than those it is importing, which is not sensible; building up of exchange reserves may also create problems for the central bank in controlling the money supply with possible inflationary consequences.

It seems to follow, then, that a long-run equality between inflows and outflows—a genuine 'balance' of payments—is the appropriate objective. However, short-term difficulties or fears about the future often lead governments to aim for surpluses. This policy, if pursued to the exclusion of other objectives, has substantial costs. One measure to improve the balance of payments, used frequently by United Kingdom governments in the 1960s, is deflation of domestic demand. This reduces expenditure on imports but also tends to lead to higher unemployment in the short run.

16.2.4 Maximum economic growth

Expanding a country's capacity to produce goods and services widens the areas of choice open to individuals and creates a potential for increases in living standards. No government is expressly against economic growth. However, its benefits are not unqualified. We should bear in mind that:

1   **Future growth has current opportunity costs** For instance, increasing investment (which increases productive capacity) involves diverting resources from consumption today. To take another example, increasing productivity in a country's industries may involve massive reorganisation of working practices, retraining, replacement of labour by machinery, relocation of businesses from one part of the country to another. The costs of such dislocation are high, and those who ultimately get the benefit from economic change are by no means necessarily the people who bore the cost. Many critics of the rapid change in the British economy since the early 1980s point out that much faster growth overall has not assisted the long-term unemployed whose jobs disappeared as a result of structural change.

2   **Growth from increased industrial activity may bring considerable external costs** As we have seen, such external costs as pollution, traffic congestion, and pressure on housing, other amenities and limited natural resources are likely to increase as economic growth proceeds. Moreover, as the late Professor Fred Hirsch observed, some aspects of growth are self-defeating. Hirsch argued that increasingly consumers value what he called **positional goods**, which display an individual's status relative to others. If I am the only person who possesses a Porsche in my neighbourhood, I enjoy an envied position. If everybody has one, the pleasure diminishes.

Despite these qualifications, governments are likely to continue to pursue economic growth wherever possible.

16.3 POLICY INSTRUMENTS

The problem with pursuing the several different objectives noted in the previous section is that they can often conflict. Thus, for example, attempts to promote faster economic growth may worsen the balance of payments; policies intended to lower unemployment may produce higher inflation. We speak of policy **trade-offs** where a little bit more of one objective means a little bit less of another. We shall explore one particular trade-off, that between unemployment and inflation, in 16.4. However, before we do this we need to know a little bit more about the types of macroeconomic policies which governments can employ.

16.3.1 Fiscal policy

Fiscal or budgetary policy consists of the deliberate manipulation of government spending and/or taxation to influence aggregate demand. The levels of government spending and taxation together determine the size of the **budget surplus or deficit**, which in turn is a major element in the determination of the **public sector borrowing requirement** (PSBR), introduced in Chapter 14.

The budget came into fashion as a macroeconomic policy instrument with the Keynesian theory of effective demand. It was believed that shortfalls in aggregate demand below the full employment level could be made up by reducing taxation (to put more spending power in people's hands) or by increasing government spending. In either case, the multiplier process was expected to amplify the initial increase in aggregate demand.

Keynesian policies tended to be associated with unbalanced budgets and government borrowing. Although Keynes himself had envisaged running budget surpluses in periods when aggregate demand was high, and thus balancing the budgets over an entire business cycle, in practice this did not happen. For example, until the late 1980s there had only been one year since World War II in which the UK government had **not** run a budget deficit.

In the postwar period, the idea developed of using fiscal policy to **fine-tune** the economy. This means managing the level of aggregate demand, through fiscal policy, to maintain the level of output at the full employment level, while avoiding excess demand and over-full employment, which would stimulate inflation. Thus in the United Kingdom the Treasury (or Finance Ministry in other countries) would estimate the level of national income necessary to maintain this state of **internal balance** (full employment without inflation). If forecast expenditure was less than this, the Chancellor of the Exchequer would budget for a bigger PSBR in order to boost demand. If predicted expenditure was too large, a smaller budget deficit would be planned in order to deflate demand.

This use of the budget as a fine-tuning mechanism, which came to be called **discretionary fiscal policy**, was a central feature of government policy in the United Kingdom and elsewhere in the 1950s and 1960s and appeared at the time to work fairly well. Unemployment rarely rose above $2\frac{1}{2}$ per cent of the workforce and inflation averaged around $3\frac{1}{2}$ per cent per annum in the United Kingdom at this time. However, the simultaneous rise in unemployment and inflation in the 1970s has led to much questioning of Keynesian fiscal policy. Some major criticisms include:

1   In practice, Keynesian fiscal policy, it is said, made budget deficits the norm and built an **inflationary bias** into the economy. Monetarists claim that this was the basic cause of accelerating inflation in the 1970s because the deficits were largely financed by the creation of money (see Chapter 14).

2   Excessive government borrowing also had the effect, it is argued, of raising interest rates. This resulted in the **crowding out** of private sector spending, particularly business investment which would have been forthcoming at lower interest rates. (Note that Keynes would probably have disputed this: as we saw in Chapter 13, he was inclined to the view that investment was relatively interest-inelastic.)

3   Because governments were not worried about financing their spending through taxation, over a period of time there was a considerable expansion of the share of public spending in national income. In the view of many critics this had an undesirable effect on the economy as a whole. It has been asserted that resources are inefficiently used in the public sector. As we saw in Chapter 10, this claim has led to the policy of privatisation.

4   Fiscal policy is intended to stabilise aggregate demand, but in practice it may sometimes have *de*stabilised it. One problem which we have not so far mentioned is that there are **time lags** involved in the use of discretionary fiscal policy. Suppose that the government decides (on the basis of information gathered and processed over a period of months, and thus inevitably somewhat out of date) that an expansionary boost to the economy is needed. It takes time to make new spending plans, get them approved and carried out. By the time the new spending actually occurs, the aggregate demand picture may already have changed considerably. If the economy is now expanding rapidly, for example, the extra government spending may have an inflationary effect, contrary to what was intended. These information and execution lags, together with other uncertainties about the ultimate effects of fiscal policy, make the budget surplus or deficit a crude and inexact instrument for fine-tuning aggregate demand.

For these reasons, many economists and politicians in the 1970s came to the conclusion that Keynesian fiscal policy was no longer (if it ever had been) effective in maintaining internal balance. Instead, increasing attention was paid to the use of monetary policy. Although monetary factors were not totally neglected in the 1950s and 1960s, they played a subordinate role in economic policy debates. This was to change dramatically in the late 1970s and early 1980s.

G

16.3.2 Monetary policy

Monetary policy consists of measures to regulate the supply of and demand for money and credit and its cost (the interest rate). Note that it is not possible for governments to fix these independently; if they fix the interest rate they have to accept that there will be a certain quantity of money which people wish to hold (see Figure 15.3 in Chapter 15), and that the money market will only be in equilibrium if that quantity of money is supplied. Similarly, a decision to supply a given quantity of money implies a particular equilibrium interest rate (although this does not mean, of course, that governments can predict with any precision what this will be).

In the 1950s and 1960s, when most emphasis was placed on fiscal policy, monetary policy played an essentially subordinate role in macroeconomic management in the United Kingdom, although some other countries—notably West Germany—behaved rather differently. At that time the Bank of England tended to emphasise the level of interest rates as the main indicator of monetary 'stance', that is to say whether it was operating an 'expansionary' or 'contractionary' policy. In particular, it emphasised **Bank Rate** (later, **Minimum Lending Rate**) the interest rate at which the bank lends to the banking sector. When the United Kingdom government wanted to reduce the rate of expansion of money and credit (usually, at this time, because the balance of payments position was deteriorating), Bank Rate would be raised, penalising commercial banks which, because their liquidity position had declined as a result of excessive lending, wished to borrow from the Bank of England; more generally it would signify the need for restraint.

At this time, too, the Bank had a range of direct controls which it could use to influence lending and credit creation. It could fix minimum reserve ratios, which determined the proportions of their reserves which commercial banks had to hold as cash or in other liquid forms. It could place ceilings on the volume of lending permitted for certain purposes (for example, consumer credit). It could require banks from time to time to place part of their assets on deposit with the Bank of England; these 'special deposits' could not be counted as part of their reserve assets, and so the banks would have to contract their lending to restore their reserve ratios.

However, in 1971 a number of measures known as **Competition and Credit Control** were undertaken to liberalise the Bank of England's system of regulation. Further measures were undertaken in the later 1970s, culminating in August 1981 with the abolition of the compulsory reserve asset ratio and the Minimum Lending Rate. Nowadays, the Bank of England prefers to make much greater use of the market mechanism rather than regulation. Moreover, the shift towards less direction to banks went together with an emphasis on monetary aggregates as an indicator of monetary stance as policy-makers became more and more influenced by the arguments of Friedman and other monetarists.

The primary method which the Bank of England (and similar monetary authorities elsewhere) now uses to influence the money supply is **open market operations**. For example, the Bank of England buys and sells gilt-edged securities (see Chapter 14) all the time. Suppose it wants to reduce the rate of increase of the money supply. It will increase its sales of gilts to the public. The buyers pay for them with cheques drawn on the commercial banks. One effect of this is that the banks experience a fall in their holdings with the Bank of England, which, as we have seen, form part of their reserves. In order to restore their reserves, they must cut back on the number of loans they are making. Consequently the rate of increase of bank lending (and thus the money supply) is reduced. A second effect is that the increased supply of gilts forces down their price; this (as we saw in Chapter 14) tends to raise the interest rate on new bonds. The higher interest rate deters borrowers and again the result is a reduction in the rate of increase of the money supply. In the 1980's the emphasis in open market operations has moved away from gilts towards buying and selling of bills in order to influence short-term interest rates.

The increasing stress on monetary policy in the late 1970s and 1980s stemmed, as we have suggested, from an increasing concern with inflation rather than unemployment as the key policy objective. It was also influenced by the belief of Friedman and other monetarists that it is impossible to 'fine tune' an economy. Monetarists do not believe in discretionary monetary policy any more than they believe in discretionary fiscal policy. Friedman has long advocated the **Friedman Rule**, that the money supply should be expanded at a constant rate equal to the underlying long run real rate of growth of the economy, with some allowance for any predictable changes in the velocity of circulation. It should not be altered sharply from year to year in an attempt to 'manage' the economy.

This was the thinking behind the adoption of the **Medium-Term Financial Strategy**

(MTFS) in the United Kingdom in the 1980s. Although this involved a change in the rate of growth of the money stock (which was supposed to fall from year to year) it was supposed to fall at a preannounced rate rather than fluctuate widely from year to year (in practice, it was not altogether successful in doing this).

A final point on monetary policy; in the heyday of Keynesianism it often seemed as if there was no necessary connection between fiscal and monetary policy—that a budget deficit need not always lead to an increase in the money supply. Government borrowing might, for example be accomplished by the sale of long-term bonds to the general public, and not involve any borrowing from the banking system. By contrast, some monetarists have tended to fear that government borrowing eventually, directly or indirectly, leads to monetary creation. Consequently they have argued for a reduction of budget deficits. In the United Kingdom a phased plan to reduce the PSBR was the fiscal counterpart of the MTFS. Although the experience of the 1980s in the United Kingdom and the United States suggests that the monetarist view that there is a simple relation between budget deficits and money supply is mistaken, there is now a wide consensus amongst economists that the monetary effects of fiscal expansion cannot be wholly ignored.

16.3.3 Prices and incomes policies

These consist of attempts to hold down increases in prices and factor incomes (particularly, though not exclusively, wages), either by legal controls or voluntary agreements such as the 'Social Contract' developed by the United Kingdom Labour Government in the mid-1970s. Such policies are intended to reduce inflation without cutting back aggregate demand. The Labour Government elected in 1945 started the first systematic set of controls in the United Kingdom, but successive administrations, whether Labour or Conservative, tried various approaches to prices and incomes policy until the late 1970s. Similar measures were used in many developed countries in the postwar period, most notably Holland and the Scandinavian countries. Even the United States, under President Nixon, tried this sort of policy.

Prices and incomes policies involve setting a 'norm' for rates of increase of prices, pay, and sometimes property incomes. Firms are supposed to adhere to these norms, although there is usually some provision for exceptional cases, for example, firms where productivity increases are exceptionally high may be permitted to offer higher-than-normal pay increases to their workers. Often a formal body may be set up to monitor the policy and to adjudicate on doubtful cases. For example, the National Board for Prices and Incomes was set up by the 1964–70 Labour Government for such a purpose.

Prices and incomes policies have rarely lasted for very long. They have had varying degrees of short-term success in holding down the rate of inflation, but each episode of incomes policy has tended to break down in a 'wage explosion' when the rate of inflation has accelerated rapidly. The point is that such policies at best suppress inflationary pressures while doing little to deal with the underlying forces generating inflation. Monetarist economists, who are convinced that the real cause of inflation is excessive expansion of the money supply, have been particularly scathing in their criticisms.

According to monetarists, apart from ignoring the real cause of inflation, prices and incomes policies do positive harm, as they interfere with the workings of the market mechanism. In a dynamic and properly-functioning market economy, they argue, changes in patterns of demand and changes in productivity are continually altering the pattern of equilibrium *relative* prices and incomes. Changes in actual prices and incomes are necessary to signal changes in profitability and to motivate the movement of resources out of declining areas into expanding ones. If price and income controls interfere with these changes in relativities, the economy functions more sluggishly. Over a period of time productivity will not grow as fast as it would in an unregulated economy.

To some extent, of course, these undesirable effects of controls are mitigated by individuals and firms finding ways round controls. For instance, firms may reclassify jobs in order to be able to 'promote' (and therefore pay more to) workers who are in short supply. Similarly, top executives may be rewarded by 'perks'—company cars, better pension schemes, subsidised meals and so on—rather than by pay increases. If prices are controlled, firms may lower product specifications to cut costs. To the extent that these ruses are successful, the effectiveness of prices and incomes policies in reducing inflation is diminished. Moreoever, such evasions of controls may breed cynicism and disrespect for the law which may have long-run adverse consequences for society.

Given the growing influence of monetarist ideas in the 1970s, and the spread of deregulatory enthusiasm in the 1980s (see Chapter 10), it is not surprising that prices and incomes policies have fallen out of favour. However, there are economists and politicians who retain enthusiasm for the use of some variant of these policies. For example, the Social Democratic Party in the United Kingdom (now merged with the Liberals) has advocated a **'tax-based' incomes policy** which would avoid formal controls, but would tax away pay increases above a norm. It is possible such a scheme might be tried in the future.

16.3.4 Exchange rate and commercial policy

This set of policy instruments is dealt with in detail in a later chapter. There, however, the focus will largely be on the use of these instruments for dealing with the balance of payments. Here we can just note that governments can use their power to manipulate exchange rates between currencies, and can impose various restrictions on trade (**commercial policy**) in order to affect the level of domestic output and employment.

For instance, a government can engineer a **depreciation of its currency** (ie, a fall in its exchange rate) in order to make its exports cheaper and its imports more expensive domestically. This diverts demand from foreign products to home-produced goods, stimulating domestic output and employment. Similarly, the imposition of **import controls** (various forms of restrictions on imports such as **quotas** and **tariffs**) diverts demand to home production. The boost to spending will directly raise employment and will also have multiplier effects in the same way as a rise in investment or government spending.

These **expenditure-switching** policies, however, are not costless: a fall in the exchange rate, for example, raises the costs of importing food, raw materials and intermediate goods and thus has an inflationary tendency. Import controls may invite retaliation from other countries, and protect domestic firms from the consequences of their own inefficiency.

For these and other reasons, different schools of thought tend to have different attitudes to exchange rate and commercial policy. Broadly speaking, monetarists (with their faith in free markets) dislike manipulation of exchange rates, which they argue cannot permanently produce an exchange rate out of line with that which the market dictates, and measures to restrict imports. Keynesians and those on the political left who take a more critical attitude to the market economy, are much more inclined to advocate these policy instruments.

16.3.5 Exchange rates and monetary policy

Finally, we ought to add that since the mid-1980's attention has been directed towards exchange rates as an indicator of monetary stance. It has been pointed out that excessive expansion of the money supply will tend to weaken a country's exchange rate relative to other currencies. An excessively 'tight' monetary policy, especially when associated with high interest rates, will tend to cause a country's currency to appreciate.

In the 1980s, the various measures of money supply outlined in Chapter 14 have behaved in an increasingly erratic manner. Following monetarist policies, the monetary authorities in the United Kingdom, the United States and elsewhere have tried to control various money aggregates. However, they have rarely managed to keep those aggregates which they have targeted (notably, in the United Kingdom, the sterling component of M3) within their 'target zones'. It has been suggested that there is a fundamental problem with controlling measures of the money supply: once you start to try to control a particular aggregate, that aggregate will start to behave differently (this proposition is known as **Goodhart's Law** after a well-known monetary economist, Charles Goodhart). People will react to controls by trying, in various ways, to get round them.

Given this problem, it has been suggested that instead of monetary targets we should have **exchange rate targets**; the government would be able to tell whether it should take action (through open market operations) to expand or contract the money supply by seeing what is happening to the exchange rate, rather than by monitoring particular monetary aggregates. However, this proposal remains controversial; for example in March 1988 it appears that there was a major difference of opinion within the United Kingdom government about the importance to be attached to the exchange rate in this context.

16.4 THE UNEMPLOYMENT-INFLATION TRADE-OFF

Governments therefore have a number of policy objectives and various policy instruments at their disposal. Policy instruments, such as the budget deficit, may have beneficial effects on one objective while worsening performance in relation to some other target. From this many economists have argued that there may exist some trade-off between objectives, and that the role of policy-makers is to choose between feasible combinations of outcomes.

Most obviously this question has been raised in relation to the possibility of a trade-off between unemployment and inflation. This has been the most important area for policy discussion and theoretical speculation for many years, and is likely to remain so for years to come. In this section we outline the development of ideas about the unemployment-inflation trade-off.

16.4.1 The Keynesian picture

As we have seen, Keynes's analysis in *The General Theory* was concerned with the effect of increases in aggregate demand when there existed considerable involuntary unemployment, or what was referred to in Chapter 12 as a 'deflationary gap'. However, Keynes later came to consider what would happen if the government expanded aggregate demand beyond the full employment level of output. His particular context for writing about this was the big increase in aggregate demand experienced by the British economy at the beginning of World War II. In his pamphlet *How to Pay for the War*, published in 1940, he predicted that aggregate demand would soon outstrip the productive capacity of the economy and in those circumstances further increases in spending power could only have the effect of driving up prices.

In order to remove what came to be called the **inflationary gap** (the difference between aggregate planned spending and that level of spending sufficient to generate full employment *without* inflation: see Figure 16.1), the government would have to raise taxes, or cut public and private spending. (In fact Keynes came up with an ingenious scheme for compulsory savings which would have reduced private spending without permanently depriving people of their spending power, but it was only adopted in a watered-down form.)

FIGURE 16.1 **The inflationary gap**

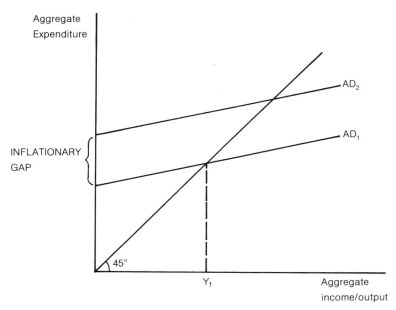

This is a highly simplified view, as Keynes recognised. It seems to imply that up to the full employment level of output (Y_f in Figure 16.1), increases in aggregate demand—for example, as a result of an increase in the budget deficit—boost employment but don't create inflation. Beyond this, however, a further boost in demand just drives up prices. In this framework, unemployment and inflation are never found together—you either have one or the other, so the idea of a trade-off doesn't arise.

However, in practice, as we have seen, the full employment level of output simply means that output level at which there is no involuntary unemployment. There will always be some unemployment, and simply by looking at the officially recorded figure we cannot judge whether full employment in the Keynesian sense has been reached. In any case, as we shall see in Chapter 17, Keynes himself admitted that the concept of full employment was a tricky one for another reason. There could, he noted, be excess demand for labour in one part of the economy while in other sectors there was substantial involuntary unemployment. The recorded unemployment rate is an average for the economy as a whole. Some industries or regions could be facing inflationary pressures even though elsewhere prices remained stable.

16.4.2   The Phillips Curve

The implication of these qualifications to the inflationary gap analysis is that the relationship between measured unemployment and inflation is a more subtle one. In the late 1950s this relationship was given a precise form in the work of Professor AW Phillips of the London School of Economics. He investigated the relationship which had existed historically between the rate of change of money wages and unemployment in the United Kingdom from 1862 to 1957 and claimed to find a stable relationship between these two variables. The original **Phillips Curve** therefore showed the rate of change of money wages on the vertical axis. It has become normal, however, to draw this curve as in Figure 16.2, with the rate of increase of prices on the vertical. This is reasonable, for wages account for 70 per cent or more of costs, and therefore the rate of wage inflation is a major influence on price inflation.

FIGURE 16.2   **The Phillips Curve**

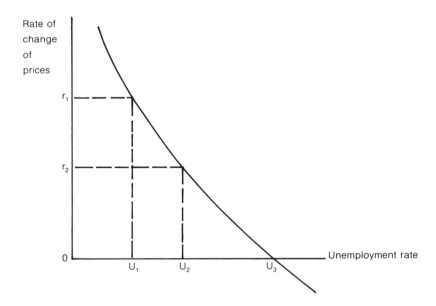

The curve is negatively sloped, showing that the lower the rate of unemployment, the higher the rate of inflation. At a very low level of unemployment, like U_1, we have a high rate of inflation r_1. When unemployment is higher, at U_2, the inflation rate is correspondingly lower, at r_2. At unemployment rate U_3, the rate of inflation has fallen to zero, and a further increase in unemployment is associated with *negative* inflation, ie, a *fall* in the general level of prices. Negative inflation, though rare in the postwar period, was common in the interwar years.

16.4.3   Cost-push or demand-pull?

It was claimed that the Phillips Curve showed the relationship which existed between unemployment and inflation. It did not of itself explain why this relationship existed. It was consistent with two broad types of explanation:

1 **Cost-push theories** These argued that the origin of inflation lies in increases in costs which can occur independently of demand conditions. The rise in oil prices in the 1970s, for instance, added substantially to industrial costs, which were then passed on to consumers in the form of higher prices for goods and services. Such price increases in turn provoked demands for higher wages to compensate workers. If granted, these wage increases added to labour costs, raising prices still higher and so on. The original rise in costs set off a **wage-price spiral**. It was sometimes argued that powerful trade unions could use their market power to set off such a process independently of any initial price increase. (Note however the important point that it is quite possible to believe that unions raise wages above the free market level without initiating inflation, which is a process of *continually* rising prices, rather than a once-and-for-all increase of union wages relative to those of non-union labour.) Other economists argued that unions were essentially reactive, rather than the initiators of inflation.

　　Whether or not union 'pushfulness' causes inflation, it was likely that firms would find it easier to pass cost increases—from whatever source—on to consumers if the level of aggregate demand was high, and unemployment correspondingly low. Thus inflation went with low unemployment, as shown by the Phillips Curve.

2 **Demand-pull theories** Here it was argued that the fundamental cause of inflation was excess aggregate demand. This resulted in a general rise in the price level and a rise in wages as the excess demand was transmitted to the labour market. A high level of demand implied a low level of unemployment, and we therefore had the relationship shown by the Phillips Curve. Opinions differed as to the source of the excess demand. 'Keynesians' looked to the different components of aggregate demand discussed in Chapter 13; they argued that increases in demand could occur irrespective of any changes in the money supply. Monetarists, however, followed Friedman's line that 'inflation is always and everywhere a monetary phenomenon' and so believed that the excess demand had to be traceable to over-expansion of the stock of money in the economy. This also implied a rejection of the view that 'cost-push' factors could have an influence on inflation. A rise in the price of oil, or an increase in wages for one type of labour, can only alter *relative* prices (the price of goods and services which use a lot of oil in their production will rise, while those using less oil will fall; union wages will rise while non-union wages fall) unless the money supply is being expanded.

16.4.4　Policy implications of the Phillips Curve

Whatever the causes of the Phillips Curve relationship were thought to be, the idea of a stable relationship between unemployment and inflation rapidly caught the imagination of economists and policymakers in many countries. It seemed to have two implications for macroeconomic policy.

　　First, it seemed to offer policy-makers a choice—they could trade off inflation against unemployment. In terms of Figure 16.2, there was no reason why economies should be confined to the zero-inflation level of unemployment U_3. If reducing unemployment was the priority, we could choose a lower level of unemployment—U_2 or even U_1, albeit at the cost of a higher rate of inflation. Thus governments were tempted to tolerate inflation.

　　Second, in order to reduce the inflationary pressures generated by the decision to keep unemployment down, governments tried to intervene directly in the labour market, via incomes policies, to alter the relationship between unemployment and inflation in effect to shift the Phillips Curve to the left. Consequently, in the United Kingdom from 1960 to 1979 there were only four years in which some form of incomes policy was not in operation; similar policies were used in many European countries and (more briefly) in the United States.

　　However, as the 1970s wore on, it became clear that these macroeconomic policies were not very successful. Inflation rose to what were very high levels compared with the earlier postwar period, peaking in the mid-1970's at 27 per cent in the United Kingdom, but this did not bring low levels of unemployment. Far from it; unemployment rose as inflation rose, something which seemed to contradict the Phillips Curve relationship, and incomes policies were widely seen to be ineffective, except in the very short run. This situation led to considerable rethinking by economists and politicians. Gradually more and more attention was paid to Milton Friedman's ideas about the relationship between unemployment and inflation, ideas which he had been developing since the late 1960s.

16.4.5   The expectations-augmented Phillips Curve

Friedman had never accepted the idea that there was a stable Phillips Curve. As a monetarist, he believed (like the classical writers we discussed in Chapter 15) that the economy was always likely to be close to its full employment level of output. Governments could therefore not boost aggregate demand (whether by fiscal or monetary means) to secure permanent gains in employment at the expense of higher inflation. For a time, this might work, but it could not last, so he was not surprised when, in the 1970s, unemployment and inflation both rose. He had an explanation ready made. This explanation caught on very rapidly, so that nowadays very few economists and even fewer politicians, believe in the Phillips Curve, at least in its original form.

Friedman makes use of a concept called the **natural rate of unemployment**. This is the rate of unemployment at which Keynesian involuntary unemployment is absent. There is only voluntary unemployment, the result of choices made by individuals not to accept work at given rates of pay. As we saw in Chapter 11, this includes frictional, search, seasonal and structural unemployment. Its level will depend on such factors as the extent of competition or monopoly in product markets, the strength of trade unions, the degree of regulation of the labour market, the effectiveness of job information services, the level of welfare benefits and so on; these factors are discussed in more detail in Chapter 17.

The natural rate will vary over time as its determinants alter. Friedman argues that it was higher in the 1970s and 1980s than in the 1950s and 1960s. However, at a particular moment there is a given natural rate at which the labour market is in equilibrium, in the sense that *those who are willing to accept* jobs can get them. Here there should not be any inflationary pressures, for with the supply of and demand for labour in balance there is no pressure to raise wages.

Suppose that the economy is originally at the natural rate of unemployment. This is shown in Figure 16.3 as U_n. It is the point at which the Phillips Curve T_1 cuts the unemployment axis: inflation is zero. If the government now decides that this rate of unemployment is too high, it may try to increase aggregate demand (by, for example, increasing the budget deficit). Friedman accepts that, temporarily, the government can succeed. The economy will move to a position like A, where lower unemployment is achieved at the cost of a positive rate of inflation. This is what is supposed to happen, according to the Phillips Curve.

FIGURE 16.3   **The expectations – augmented Phillips Curve**

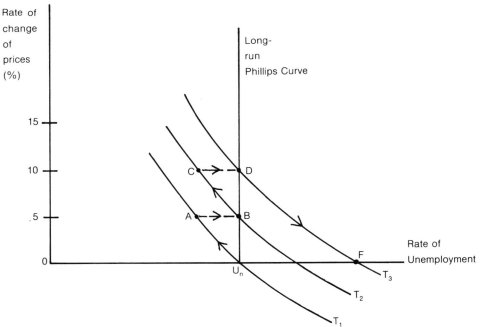

Friedman asks how this can happen. One explanation goes like this: the increased level of demand drives up money wages by, say, 5 per cent. Eventually, prices will have to rise in proportion, so workers will be no better off. There will be no incentive for them to alter their behaviour; if they were voluntarily unemployed before, they will remain so. However, if they do not understand what is going on, they may be temporarily fooled. They are **expecting** a zero inflation rate, and so interpret the money wage increase as a **real** increase in pay offers. They will be willing to take jobs they would previously have rejected; unemployment falls.

This cannot last, though. Eventually, workers' expectations **adapt** to the fact that there is a positive rate of inflation. Once their expectations catch up with reality, they will be aware that real wages remain what they were initially. Once this is the case, they will revert to the same pattern of behaviour as before. Unemployment will go back to its natural rate, only now this rate of unemployment will be associated with a positive rate of inflation of 5 per cent, as at B.

Suppose the government now decides to try to reduce unemployment again by giving a further boost to spending. Temporarily, it can again do so by boosting inflation (from 5 per cent to 10 per cent). If workers are expecting 5 per cent inflation, they will mistake a 10 per cent increase in money wages for an increase in real wages. Unemployment will fall. The economy will be at a position like C. We can draw a new Phillips Curve T_2, going through B and C: this curve represents the trade-off between unemployment and inflation **when 5 per cent inflation is expected**. Once expectations adapt, the economy again reverts to its natural rate of unemployment at point D. This point is on a **third** Phillips Curve, T_3, which shows the trade-off when 10 per cent inflation is expected.

There is therefore, in Friedman's view, a series of short run Phillips Curves, each associated with a different expected rate of inflation, although in the long run the Phillips Curve is **vertical** as in Figure 16.3. From this analysis of what has come to be called the **expectations-augmented Phillips Curve** a number of important points emerge for economic policy:

1   **The unemployment rate can only be kept below its natural rate by continually increasing the rate of inflation** The trade-off that exists is therefore one between unemployment and the rate of **increase** of inflation. This is why more recently the natural rate has been renamed the **non-accelerating inflation rate of unemployment** or **NAIRU**.

2   **Friedman's analysis suggests there is a temporary trade-off along the Phillips Curve.** The question arises as to how long the effect lasts. Friedman thought originally that it might last for a significant period, perhaps two or three years. He thought that it took quite a long time for people to become used to higher rates of inflation. In his view their expectations only adapted gradually. More recently, however, more extreme monetarists, usually known as **New Classical economists** have argued that expectations change much more rapidly than Friedman suggested. They point out that individuals who only alter their expectations of inflation gradually will always be lagging behind inflation if inflation is continuously rising. Such behaviour would be irrational, because workers would go on being fooled time after time. Instead, the New Classicals argue, people will form **rational expectations** based on all available information. If they see that the government is always pushing up the rate of inflation through excessive expansion of monetary demand, they will come to anticipate this and make allowance for increased inflation when money wages rise. If people behave like this, the government loses its power to trade off unemployment against inflation even in the short run. The implication is that New Classical writers believe that the economy is never likely to diverge significantly from its NAIRU *at all*. This is a much stronger argument against 'Keynesian' policies of demand management than that offered by Friedman.

3   **Reducing inflation may involve cuts in output and employment** Reverting to Friedman's position for the moment, an implication is that reducing inflation suddenly may be costly in terms of output and jobs. Suppose we have 10 per cent inflation that is fully anticipated: we are at position D in Figure 16.3. Suppose the government now decides it wants to reduce inflation to zero. It therefore cuts monetary demand back to a level which implies a zero rate of increase of prices and money wages. If, however, workers are expecting 10 per cent inflation, they will demand a money wage increase of 10 per cent. They won't get such an increase, so unemployment will rise. The economy moves to a position like F on Phillips Curve T_3, where unemployment is way above the NAIRU or natural rate. Only as expectations slowly adapt to the new situation will unemployment fall until the economy is back at U_n. Because Friedman argues that expectations only adapt slowly, he has always argued for **gradual disinflation**. New Classicals, by contrast, think that expectations can change very quickly, so governments

should get rid of inflation as quickly as possible; the cost in output and employment will be negligible.

4 **Both Friedman and the New Classicals argue against Keynesian demand management and in favour of 'Supply-side' measures** Friedman argues that increases in aggregate demand can only temporarily increase employment, New Classicals argue that there isn't even a short-run effect, but both are agreed that the sensible way to reduce unemployment (if this is thought desirable) is to try to influence the factors that determine the NAIRU. This involves microeconomic policies to alter the incentives facing workers and firms to supply or hire labour. This may involve policies to reduce the power of trade unions, schemes to retrain workers, restructuring the tax and benefit systems and so on. These are measures which affect the **supply side** of the economy and they are discussed in Chapter 17.

Monetarist and New Classical analysis and policies became highly influential in many countries by the early 1980s. However, it should **not** be assumed that these approaches are the only possible ones to take. Both assume that in the absence of inflation there would be no problem of involuntary unemployment. In other words, they assume that the demand for labour always matches the supply of workers willing to accept jobs. Keynesians and others still dispute this; they find it difficult to believe that millions of people in the 1980s have chosen in any meaningful sense to be out of work. They do not believe that the unfettered labour market would work as well as monetarists and New Classicals assert. The debate continues.

SUMMARY

In this chapter we have examined the most important aspects of macroeconomic policy since Keynes. We have seen that governments pursue a number of sometimes conflicting objectives using a range of policy instruments which have developed over the years. The great issue of the postwar period has been the nature of the relationship between unemployment and inflation and we have seen how views about this relationship, and the policy implications which follow from it, have altered dramatically over the years.

SELF-TEST QUESTIONS

1 **Which of the following is not a potential policy instrument?**

(a) Open market operations.
(b) Incomes policy.
(c) The exchange rate.
(d) The rate of economic growth.
(e) The budget deficit.

2 **Which of the following concepts is associated with the Keynesian analysis of inflation?**

(a) The natural rate of unemployment.
(b) The inflationary gap.
(c) Rational expectations.
(d) The expectations-augmented Phillips Curve.
(e) Supply-side policies.

3 **Which statement is incorrect?**

(a) Keynes believed in balancing budgets over the business cycle.
(b) Friedman accepts that there is a short-run trade-off between unemployment and inflation.
(c) Monetarists believe that attempts to 'fine-tune' the economy are likely to be ineffective.
(d) Keynesians sometimes favour incomes policy.
(e) New Classical economists believe that people are consistently fooled by government macroeconomic policy.

4 **The Phillips Curve shows which of the following?**

(a) A relationship which can only be explained by a 'demand-pull' model.
(b) A relationship between expected employment and inflation.
(c) A relationship between expected inflation and unemployment.
(d) Combinations of inflation rates and unemployment.
(e) Combinations of expected inflation rates and employment.

5   Which of the following is most consistent with Friedman's views?

(a)   The NAIRU is affected by changes in the level of welfare benefits available to the unemployed.

(b)   Governments should use incomes policies to control inflation.

(c)   Policy-makers can have lower unemployment in the long run if they are prepared to accept a high fixed rate of inflation.

(d)   Governments should alter the supply of money from period to period to keep the economy at its full employment level of output.

(e)   Trade unions are the main cause of inflation.

EXERCISE

Can governments reduce unemployment at the cost of a higher rate of inflation?

Answers on page 266.

Supply-side economics

In this chapter we introduce aggregate demand and aggregate supply curves and show how this diagrammatic technique can be used to show the points at issue between different groups of economists. We then go on to explore the idea of supply-side economics, which in recent years has been increasingly favoured by governments in preference to the demand-management ideas associated with Keynesianism. We look at a number of different types of policy which are aimed at improving the functioning of markets and thus stimulating the economy to supply more output.

17.1 INTRODUCTION

As the last chapter suggested, the principle of aggregate demand management which derives from Keynes's economics came under increasing attack in the 1970s and early 1980s. Many economists came to the conclusion that unemployment could not be pushed below its 'natural' level without rising inflation. The trade-off between unemployment and inflation apparently offered by the Phillips Curve was in any case argued to be only a temporary one and it was thought that governments should abandon attempts to use fiscal and monetary policy to reduce unemployment. If the rate of unemployment was considered unacceptably high, the correct policy to employ was one which altered the pattern of microeconomic incentives facing firms and households. Such a policy would operate on the **supply side** of the economy. In this chapter we examine the idea of supply-side economics by first developing the aggregate supply/aggregate demand framework and then considering examples of supply-side policies in some detail.

17.2 AGGREGATE DEMAND AND AGGREGATE SUPPLY

At this stage we introduce a type of diagram which builds on work we have done earlier in this book. In Figure 17.1 we show an **aggregate demand curve**. On the vertical scale we show the average

FIGURE 17.1 **The aggregate demand curve**

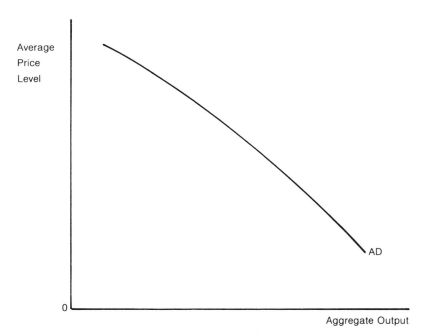

price level (most appropriately measured by the national income deflator introduced in Chapter 11). On the horizontal scale we show total output (in real terms) in the economy as a whole. The demand curve shows how the real demand for output varies, for a given level of the nominal money supply (eg, £10bn), as the price level alters. It slopes downwards for several reasons. One is that, as the price level falls, a given level of money income implies a higher real income. As real income rises, so does planned consumption and the demand for output. Another is that a fall in the price level means a rise in the *real* value of the money supply. As we saw in Chapter 15, this implies a lower interest rate in equilibrium, for an increase in the money supply will only be held by firms and households if the interest rate (the opportunity cost of holding money) falls. This lower interest rate may stimulate an increased demand for output (especially investment goods). In this type of diagram, an increase in injections on Keynesian lines (for example, an increase in government spending on goods and services) shifts the aggregate demand curve to the right (shown in Figure 17.2). This means that on any price level (for instance P_1), there is an increase in the demand for output.

FIGURE 17.2 **Shift in aggregate demand curve as a result of increased government spending**

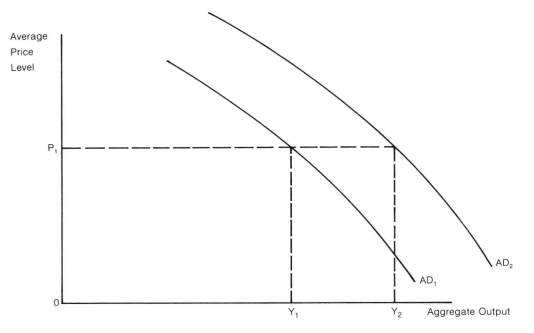

It may be helpful to think of this **macroeconomic** diagram in terms of the **microeconomic** demand curve for a particular good or service first encountered in Chapter 2. There, of course, we had the price of the commodity on the vertical axis; here we have the **price level**, ie, the average price of all goods and services. But just as we had an increase in the demand for one good as its price fell so we have an increase in demand for aggregate output as the **average price** of output falls, and just as an increase in the demand for a good at any particular price (as a result, say, of an increase in income for normal goods) could be shown by a **shift** in the demand curve for the good so an increase in aggregate demand at a given price level is shown by a shift of the AD curve.

Confusion sometimes arises between the aggregate demand curve and the aggregate demand function of Chapter 12. That function showed the relation between aggregate demand and national income with the price level held constant; the AD curve here shows the relation between aggregate demand and the price level with the money supply held constant.

We now turn to the aggregate supply curve. This shows the relationship between the price level and the total output which firms and households wish to supply. The shape of this curve depends on the assumptions we are making about the supply response of the economy. For example, think about the assumptions which underlay our simple Keynesian model of Chapter 12. Here we assumed that the only determinant of output was aggregate demand. If this increased, the economy could supply extra output without the price level rising, because unused resources of labour and capital could be brought into play. This amounts to saying that the supply of output is **perfectly elastic** at the existing price level, at least until full employment is reached. Then, as we noted, output reaches its maximum and no more can be produced; the aggregate supply curve becomes perfectly inelastic.

These assumptions are illustrated by the aggregate supply curve of Figure 17.3. As aggregate demand is increased, perhaps as a result of Keynesian policies, from AD_1 to AD_2, output can be increased, from Y_1 to Y_2, without prices rising. However, a further increase in aggregate demand to AD_3 serves only to increase the price level, from P_1 to P_2.

FIGURE 17.3 **Aggregate supply curve on the assumptions of the simple Keynesian model**

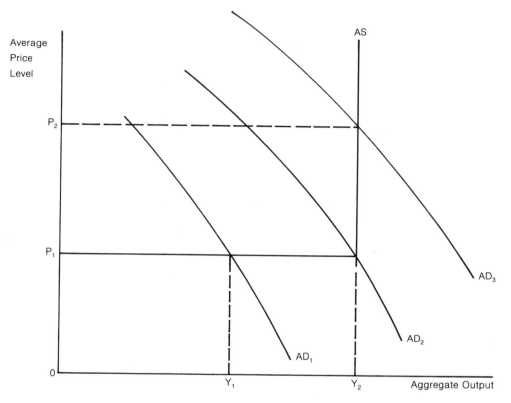

This represents a highly unrealistic view of the workings of the economy. Keynes himself argued that the relationship between increases in output and increases in the price level would be more subtle; the change from output increases to price increases would be more gradual. Full employment of resources might, for instance, be reached in some parts of the economy sooner than others. Therefore some prices would rise before others. Gradually more and more of the economy would be characterised by full employment, and the supply curve would slope upwards as shown in Figure 17.4. A shift in the aggregate demand curve from AD_1 to AD_2 increases output **and** prices. By way of a contrast with the Keynesian approach, we can illustrate the approach Friedman uses in his expectations-augmented Phillips Curve. Friedman argued that there is a natural rate of unemployment, from which increases in aggregate demand (as a result of Keynesian policies) can only temporarily shift the economy. When the economy is at this unemployment rate, there will be a **natural level of output** which is being produced. This is Y_n in Figure 17.5. In Friedman's view, an increase in aggregate demand from AD_1 to AD_2 will lead to a movement up the aggregate supply curve AS_1. Output rises. However, according to Friedman's reasoning as explained in the previous chapter, this rise in output (and the corresponding increase in employment) only occurs because firms and/or workers are temporarily 'fooled' by the increase in prices or money wages into thinking that their real position has improved. When they learn that all prices and wages have changed and that their real position is no better than it was, they will revert to their previous behaviour. The supply curve shifts to AS_2 (a higher price level is now required to bring forth any given output) and the economy reverts to the natural level of output.

Finally we show in Figure 17.6 how New Classical economists depict the effect of an increase in aggregate demand. In their view the economy is always at or close to its natural level of output. Because individuals and firms are assumed to be fully rational, they will be aware that aggregate demand expansion will raise prices and take this into account in their behaviour. If workers are offered a pay increase of 10 per cent, but are aware that prices are likely to rise by 10 per cent, they

FIGURE 17.4 **Aggregate supply curve on more realistic Keynesian assumptions**

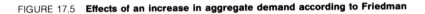

FIGURE 17.5 **Effects of an increase in aggregate demand according to Friedman**

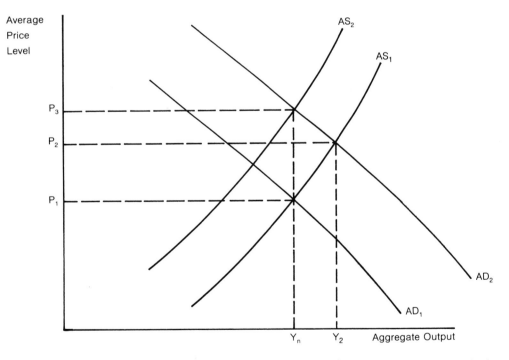

will not change their willingness to take jobs and the economy remains at the natural level of output. The only effect of demand expansion is to raise prices.

17.3 SHIFTING THE AGGREGATE SUPPLY CURVE

With the decline in support for Keynesian policies came the belief that increases in aggregate demand could either increase the level of output and employment only temporarily (Friedman) or not at all (New Classicals). If the level of output was nevertheless considered to be too low, what was needed instead was to shift the aggregate supply curve as in Figure 17.7.

FIGURE 17.6 **Aggregate supply on 'New Classical' assumptions**

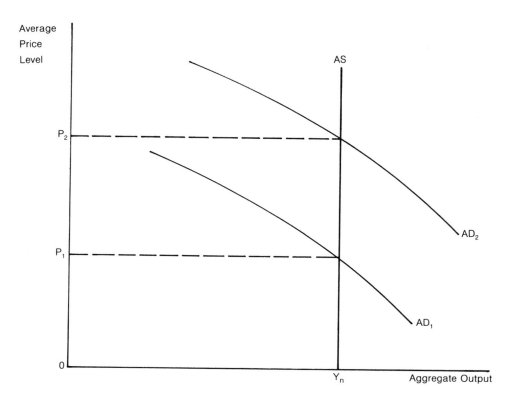

FIGURE 17.7 **Shifting the aggregate supply curve**

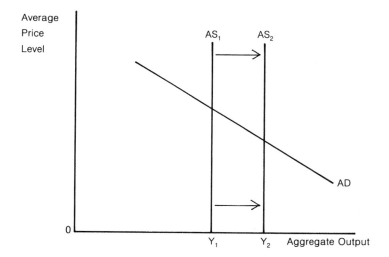

Supply-side economics is thus a shorthand expression for policies designed to achieve this effect. They are intended to operate on the incentives facing firms and individuals (making firms more willing to invest and to take on labour and workers more willing to take jobs and supply hours of labour), and to make markets more flexible and capable of rapid response to changes in supply and demand conditions.

The original 'supply-siders' were pro-free market economists in the United States who had a considerable impact on the then Presidential candidate Ronald Reagan in the late 1970s. But supply-side economics is also an appropriate description of many of the policies pursued by Mrs Thatcher's government in the United Kingdom and similar policies pursued by a variety of other governments. There is a regrettable tendency to assume that such policies are necessarily 'right wing' in political terms, but it is also possible, as we shall see later, to devise supply-side policies which are likely to appeal to people on the political Left.

17.4 TAX CUTS

One policy with which supply-siders have been particularly associated is that of cuts in income tax. President Reagan's two terms of office (1981–89) produced major reductions in Federal income tax, and in the 1988 Budget Chancellor of the Exchequer Nigel Lawson reduced the top marginal tax rate in Britain to 40 per cent (it had been 83 per cent less than ten years previously).

Tax cuts also play a part in 'Keynesian' demand management, for they increase disposable income and therefore have a tendency to boost aggregate expenditure. But it is not this effect on which supply-siders concentrate. Rather they focus on the supposed effect of cuts in the marginal rate of income tax (the proportion of the **extra** pound or dollar which goes in tax). Other things being equal, such cuts make paid work relatively more attractive in relation to leisure (or unemployment), and make savings (and investment) relatively more attractive in relation to consumption. As a result, it is argued, workers will be more willing to work, and firms to invest: aggregate supply should therefore increase.

However, such a conclusion does not necessarily follow. For example, take the case of the incentive to work. We saw in Chapter 8 that a wage increase (a cut in the marginal tax rate amounts to the same thing) gives rise to both income and substitution effects. Although the substitution effect is to make work a more attractive option, if leisure is a 'normal' good in the sense discussed, people will wish to consume more of it as income rises; they will therefore want to work less. Thus with the income and substitution effect working in opposite directions, whether or not the net effect of a cut in marginal tax rates will be to increase labour supply (and thus output) is unclear. What evidence we have on this suggests that for some groups of the population the net effect is to increase labour supply, while for others it is to reduce it. For instance it has been calculated in the United Kingdom that the lowest-paid 10 per cent of male workers increase their hours worked as a result of cuts in the basic rate of income tax, while the highest-paid 10 per cent reduce them. However, there are other dimensions of the supply of labour, such as effort, willingness to take on responsibility, attitudes to promotion, choice of occupation, on which there is little evidence.

Another aspect of supply-side analysis of tax cuts is their effect on the budget deficit. Conventional economics suggests that cuts in tax will lead (in the absence of matching cuts in spending) to increases in the budget deficit. However, some supply-siders have claimed that lower marginal tax rates may actually increase tax revenue, leading to a *reduction* in budget deficits. Why?

One reason is that lower tax rates reduce the incentive to underdeclare income for tax purposes. More importantly, it has been claimed that *if* the effect of tax cuts is to increase output and employment, the resulting higher incomes generated may lead to a higher amount being raised in tax, even though tax *rates* are lower. This may seem implausible, and indeed there is little evidence to suggest that it happened in the case of President Reagan's tax cuts. However, Professor Arthur

FIGURE 17.8 **The Laffer Curve**

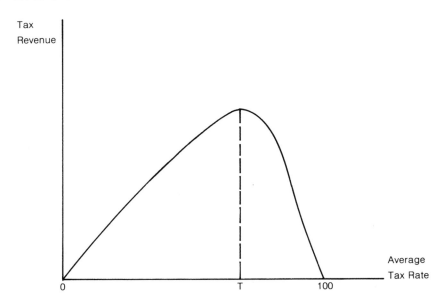

Laffer of the University of Southern California did demonstrate that there must be some range of tax rates over which cuts in tax would increase revenue. He made the point by drawing what has come to be called the **Laffer Curve**, shown in Figure 17.8. Laffer pointed out that tax revenue would (rather obviously!) be zero when the average tax rate was zero. Tax revenue would also be zero when the average tax rate was 100 per cent, for nobody would have any incentive to work (at least in the legal economy) if the government taxed all income away. But clearly at tax rates between 0 and 100 per cent some revenue could be raised. This implies that there is some tax rate at which tax revenue is maximised. In Figure 17.8 this average tax rate is T per cent.

Supply-siders like Laffer draw two conclusions from this. First, that if the average tax rate is currently above T per cent, cuts in the tax rate will increase government revenue. Second, the logic suggests a direct link between tax rates and national income. At a tax rate of 100 per cent measured national income and output would be zero (though presumably there would be an enormous black economy). As the tax rate fell, national income would rise, at least up to a point.

Some supply-siders therefore believe that to advocate tax cuts without government spending cuts (though ideally they would like these as well, as we shall see in 17.6) is not necessarily to be financially irresponsible. Moreover, lower taxes promote faster economic growth. However, as we have suggested, such beliefs rest on questionable assumptions. Certainly President Reagan's Laffer-inspired tax cuts were associated with economic expansion, but they also (when coupled with a large increase in defence spending) led to a massive increase in the American budget deficit in the mid-1980s. Some commentators argue that the expansionary effect of the Reagan tax cuts is rather more plausibly explained in Keynesian terms (the boost to aggregate demand) than in terms of supply-side analysis.

17.5 LABOUR MARKETS

As we have seen, supply-siders believe that economies tend to be close to their natural rate of unemployment (or NAIRU) most of the time. At this rate, remember, there is no tendency for inflation to accelerate or decelerate because all those workers willing to take jobs at the current wage are able to find them, and all wishing to employ labour at this wage can do so.

Almost all unemployment is therefore seen as **voluntary**, in the sense outlined in Chapter 11. Given the wage rate on offer, some workers 'choose' not to take employment. This may be because they are currently moving between jobs (**frictional** unemployment), currently engaged in active **search** for the best possible job compatible with their qualifications, **seasonally** out of work because of the nature of the job they have chosen or **structurally** unemployed because the pattern of demand for labour has changed and they have not yet adapted to the change. None of these categories of unemployment necessarily entails any moral blame on the individuals concerned but in all these cases, it is argued, workers have to an extent chosen to be unemployed; they *could* find some sort of work if they wanted to.

Nobody should necessarily complain about this—economics lecturers who become unemployed (no, it hasn't happened to us—yet!) cannot be expected immediately to take jobs in fast-food restaurants. It is rational for them to search for more appropriate jobs and better for the economy as a whole if they do. But the point that supply-siders make is that if we consider the NAIRU, which results from the choices of the unemployed, to be too high, the way in which to deal with this is by altering the incentives which individuals face. To take an obvious example, the level of welfare benefits will influence the amount of time for which the unemployed are prepared to search for better-paid jobs, and the availability of retraining schemes, and the cost of moving house from area to area will be important factors in determining the extent to which people are occupationally and geographically mobile.

Of course, in addition to these unemployed workers there will be some who are 'voluntarily' unemployed in the everyday sense of being 'workshy'—people who don't really want to work and prefer to exist on welfare benefits, plus those who are claiming benefits fraudulently while working in the black economy discussed in Chapter 11. There will also be some who are incapable of work for physical or mental reasons, yet who are nevertheless officially recorded as seeking work. Most labour economists would, however, argue that these categories of workers constitute only a small minority of those who are out of work.

The assumption that the unemployed **could** find some sort of work if they wished contrasts strongly with the Keynesian position that much unemployment results from deficiency in aggregate demand, and is thus **involuntary**, in other words, that even where workers are willing to work at or below wage rates currently on offer, they are unable to do so because jobs are not available. The implication, in terms of standard microeconomic analysis, is that for Keynesians wages may be above the equilibrium level.

Thus in Figure 17.9, with a wage rate of W, the quantity of labour workers wish to supply is N_2, while the quantity firms wish to hire is N_1. There is involuntary unemployment of N_2-N_1. In the absence of a fall in wages (the reasons for such wage 'stickiness' were briefly touched on in 12.1) unemployment can be removed by an expansion of aggregate demand, which would (it is assumed) shift the demand curve for labour to the right. (Notice that, on these assumptions, the unemployed labour could be 'mopped up' without raising the wage rate: so demand expansion need not boost wage inflation.)

FIGURE 17.9 **'Involuntary' unemploymment**

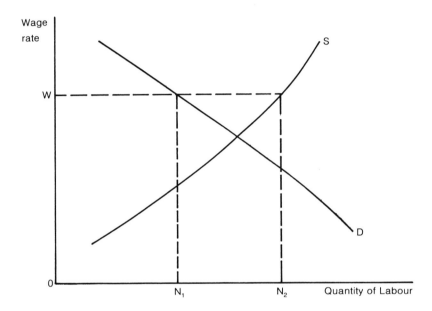

By contrast, supply-side economists would argue that the labour market is more adequately portrayed in Figure 17.10. This rather unusual diagram needs some explanation. In it is the familiar demand curve for labour, based on the value of labour's marginal product (see Chapter 8). The other curves are less familiar. The AJ curve shows the number of workers willing to Accept Jobs at particular wage rates. The LF curve, by contrast, shows the numbers of workers who would be in the Labour Force at these wage rates, whether or not they would actually be prepared to accept jobs. The horizontal difference between the two curves measures the numbers of those who are voluntarily unemployed in the sense discussed above. Supply-siders argue that the labour market is in equilibrium virtually all the time, in the sense that the wage rate just balances the demand for labour with the supply of **workers willing** to accept jobs (note the emphasis). No further workers could be obtained at this rate, as long as the pattern of microeconomic incentives remains unchanged. Thus demand expansion on Keynesian lines can only be inflationary. If the natural rate of unemployment [measured on the diagram as $(N_2-N_1)/N_2$] is thought to be too high, the answer is to bring the AJ and LF curves closer together by making it more attractive and easier for workers to accept jobs rather than remaining unemployed. As we have suggested, American supply-siders have placed great emphasis on tax cuts as a way of increasing incentives to work. Their United Kingdom counterparts, however, have stressed a number of other factors specific to the United Kingdom labour market.

For instance, the influential British New Classical economist Professor Patrick Minford has claimed that United Kingdom welfare benefits are particularly high by international standards in relation to the after-tax earnings of low-paid workers. Such workers, particularly if they have large families which entitle them to extra benefits, may thus choose not to seek work very diligently. Such a disincentive effect is implicitly shown in Figure 17.10, for the AJ and LF curves are further apart at lower wage rates, where the disincentive effect is at its greatest.

Minford's claim is part of a wider argument that the United Kingdom labour market is

FIGURE 17.10 **'Voluntary' unemployment**

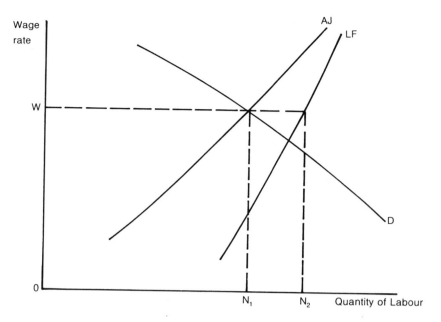

characterised by 'rigidities' of various types which discourage workers from actively seeking jobs, and employers from offering them. These rigidities are said to account for the very high level of unemployment experienced in the United Kingdom in the 1980s. They include such factors as:

1   **The power of trade unions to restrict entry into certain jobs and thus to keep wages artificially high** Professor Minford has claimed that there was a dramatic increase in such union power in the 1970s, and that we are still feeling the consequences of it.
2   **Distortions in the housing market** Because of subsidies to owner-occupation (such as tax relief on mortgage payments), house prices are artificially high; because of rent controls (see Chapter 2) rented accommodation is very difficult to obtain. These distortions make it costly and difficult for people to move around the country in search of work.
3   **Inadequate education, training and retraining facilities**
4   **Laws and regulations which raise the cost to the employer of hiring labour** Examples include minimum wages (discussed in Chapter 8) laid down by bodies called Wages Councils, which since 1909 have fixed minimum pay for certain groups of low-paid workers. Equal Pay and Employment Protection (enacted in the 1970s) may have rather similar consequences.

The policies of Mrs Thatcher's governments since 1979 reflect a broad acceptance of this diagnosis of the causes of unemployment.

17.6 PRIVATISATION AND DEREGULATION

Central to the supply-side analysis of governments on both sides of the Atlantic is the need for a reduction in virtually all aspects of the public sector's role in the economy. We have already seen that tax reductions, cuts in welfare payments and the reduction of 'interference' by the government and by trade unions in the labour market are all parts of this, but there is also the question of government policy towards industry in general. Here the emphasis is on privatisation and deregulation as a means of improving the performance of the economy. **Privatisation** is seen as a way of increasing incentives to managers and workforces, and forcing businesses to respond much more to the preferences of the consumer. It may also, by promoting wider share ownership, encourage a positive attitude to the 'enterprise culture' which is held by many to be essential to economic success. **Deregulation** will allow new firms to enter markets and supply output, and (it is hoped) encourage innovation.

These are clearly important aspects of supply-side economics which were covered in detail in Chapter 10.

17.7 ALTERNATIVE SUPPLY-SIDE POLICIES

Notice before we leave this subject that throughout this chapter we have concentrated on the ideas put forward by economists who see themselves as 'supply-siders' and consciously emphasise this approach to economic policy. Very largely these economists are associated with the political Right, with the Republican Party in the United States and the Conservative Party in the United Kingdom. This may be rather misleading, as we suggested in 17.3. For one thing, rather similar policies have been adopted by nominally socialist governments elsewhere, for instance in New Zealand and Spain. For another, there are other economists and politicians who regard demand management policy as ineffective in raising output and reducing unemployment, but who do not regard the reduction of government involvement in the economy as the answer to macroeconomic problems.

Thus many people in the Labour Party in the United Kingdom, the Democratic Party in the United States and most Social Democratic parties in Western Europe would argue, for instance, that positive interventions by governments in the workings of the economy are necessary in order to raise output and employment. In the 1970s, for example, the left-wing of the British Labour Party advocated an 'Alternative Economic Strategy' emphasising protection of, and government invest-ment in, key manufacturing industries which it was claimed were being inadequately resourced by the private sector. In the very different context of Japan, it has been claimed that much of the rapid growth of the economy has resulted from far-sighted government policies to direct resources into the new and expanding field of microelectronics. These policies could, without being misleading, be described as 'supply-side' in orientation. They involve the assumption that demand management is not enough to secure high levels of employment and rapid economic growth.

Moreover, even where there is a consensus amongst economists that the pattern of incentives is distorted by government interference, it is possible to devise alternative policies to deal with the problem. Take for example the combination of relatively high tax and national insurance contributions for low-paid workers, coupled with relatively generous welfare benefits to the unemployed which Professor Minford discerns in the United Kingdom. One solution to this is to cut benefits and make life unpleasant for the unemployed. An alternative would be to abolish income tax and national insurance contributions for low-paid workers, or, to go further, to give the low-paid an actual income supplement through a negative income tax (as discussed in Chapter 9).

The point we are emphasising here is that, although 'supply-side economics' is normally taken to relate to policies such as those adopted by the governments of Mrs Thatcher and President Reagan, in principle the term has a wider use. It may well be that future governments will continue to reject Keynesian demand management policies, but adopt very different supply-side policies from those currently in favour.

SUMMARY

In this chapter we have explained the use of aggregate demand and aggregate supply curves, and shown how the belief that expansions in aggregate demand will increase output has been comprehensively challenged by supply-siders. They argue that the economy is always at or close to its natural rate of unemployment or NAIRU. Thus lasting increases in aggregate output can only be brought about if the pattern of incentives to supply labour and output can be altered. This essentially microeconomic approach has implications for tax policy, for the labour market and for industrial policy. However, we should not make the mistake of assuming that the policies currently being put forward by the most prominent supply-siders exhaust the possibilities inherent in this approach to economic policy. Finally, we ought to add that at the moment it is difficult to form a final judgment on the usefulness of the supply-side approach; some people remain convinced that there is room for both demand management and microeconomic policies to make markets work better. We shall touch on this again in Chapter 20.

SELF-TEST QUESTIONS

1   Which statement is not correct?

(a)   An increase in government spending has, according to Professor Milton Friedman, the effect of permanently increasing aggregate output.

(b)   Keynes believed that an increase in aggregate demand would raise prices to some extent.

(c)   If the economy works less efficiently and more people opt to exist on welfare payments, the aggregate supply curve shifts to the left.

(d)   Supply-side economists do not believe in the effectiveness of fiscal or monetary policy as a means of stimulating output.

(e)   Supply-side policies inevitably mean a reduction of the role of government in the economy.

2   Which statement is correct?

(a)   A cut in tax rates must always reduce the revenue the government raises in taxes.

(b)   If leisure is a 'normal' good, people will always work less when the marginal tax rate is reduced.

(c)   President Reagan's tax cuts were associated with economic expansion; this proves that supply-side policies are successful.

(d)   A cut in marginal tax rates must increase the supply of savings.

(e)   The substitution effect of a cut in tax rates can be greater than the income effect.

3   Which is the best definition of voluntary unemployment?

(a)   A situation where the pattern of demand for labour has changed but workers have not yet adapted to this.

(b)   A situation where workers are actively engaged in looking for work.

(c)   A type of unemployment caused by variations in the level of aggregate demand in the economy.

(d)   A situation where individuals believe they are better off not working than they would be if they took jobs which they know to be available.

(e)   A type of unemployment associated with geographical immobility.

4   According to Professor Minford's diagnosis, which of the following would be expected to lead to a reduction in the NAIRU?

(a)   An increase in the legal protection given to trade unionists.

(b)   An increase in tax relief on mortgages for owner-occupiers.

(c)   The abolition of rent controls.

(d)   An increase in unemployment benefits.

(e)   A shift of the LF curve in Figure 17.10 to the right, other things being equal.

5   Which statement is incorrect?

(a)   Many supply-siders see deregulation as a way of stimulating competition.

(b)   Supply-side economics has not been proved to work better than demand management.

(c)   A policy which was successful in reducing the attractiveness of working in the black economy would be likely to lower the NAIRU.

(d)   The United Kingdom Labour Party's Alternative Economic Strategy was based on demand management.

(e)   A supply-side policy need not make unemployed people poorer.

EXERCISE

Supply-siders believe that governments cannot permanently reduce unemployment below its 'natural' rate by using fiscal or monetary policy. Does this mean that governments should do nothing about unemployment?

Answers on page 268.

International trade

We look here at the foreign trade of a country. The theory of comparative advantage indicates that countries can mutually benefit from trade based on differences in their comparative or opportunity cost of producing goods and services. Despite that, nearly all countries engage in protectionism which reduces the gains from trade. We shall see that most arguments for protection, if not fallacious, provide only weak justification for import controls on economic grounds and that the reasons for protection are commonly political. Examination of the concept of the terms of trade shows that an 'improvement' in the terms of trade is not always beneficial economically.

18.1 INTRODUCTION

So far in this book we have mostly treated the economy as if it were a **closed economy**—one with no foreign trade or other transactions with the rest of the world. Yet, all economies are **open economies**. They vary greatly in their openness; at one extreme exports and imports of the United States each account for a relatively small proportion of national income, in the order of 12 per cent. A smaller industrial country normally has much more involvement in trade—the United Kingdom, for example, sells over 30 per cent of its GDP overseas and a similar percentage of spending goes on imports. Very small primary producing countries, such as several of the oil producers, may export 90 per cent or more of their total output. Openness is thus loosely related to the size of economies. Big economies such as the United States tend to be relatively self-sufficient, producing most of what they want at home. Small ones tend to be specialised in production of a narrow range of goods and services much of which is exported in exchange for imports. Despite these variations trade is important for all countries; not even the United States relies on domestic production to satisfy all its needs and wants.

Trade is not the only way in which economies are involved internationally. There is substantial migration of labour between countries and, particularly in recent years, there has been a huge growth of international flows of funds and long-term capital. We shall look more closely at these investment flows in Chapter 19. Here, we focus on the causes and pattern of trade between countries. We shall look at the underlying forces which shape what a country exports and imports and the conditions necessary for countries to benefit from trade. An important question is why countries adopt measures to protect their domestic industries by restriction of trade. First, though, let's consider the basic principles of trade.

18.2 COMPARATIVE ADVANTAGE

The benefits of international trade are often quite clear. When a country, perhaps because of its climate, is unable to produce certain goods at home or can do so only at a very high cost it will have to import them from abroad and offer other goods which it does produce cheaply in exchange. Britain for instance can only produce tropical products such as bananas and pineapples at a prohibitively high **opportunity cost** by growing them in hot houses. Similarly, countries with no natural endowment of resources such as oil, coal and other mineral deposits must buy their requirements from overseas. But the basis for trade is less obvious when, say, the United States which can produce most goods more efficiently than the rest of the world, imports vast quantities of goods like motor cars, cameras, TVs and other electronic products from countries such as Japan and South Korea.

We find a general explanation of trade in the principle of **comparative advantage**. Credit for discovering the principle is usually given to David Ricardo (whom we encountered in relation to economic rent in Chapter 8) in a book published in 1817, although the idea was put forward by some earlier writers. Ricardo adhered to the **labour theory of value** which argues that the value of goods is proportional to the amount of labour embodied in their production. If it takes 2 hours to produce a chair and 4 hours to make a table, a table is worth twice as much as a chair. Or, we can say the exchange value of a table is 2 chairs. If, as Ricardo believed, labour was the only important factor of production the costs of production can be measured directly in terms of the labour hours required to produce a unit of any good.

However, we know that other factors, capital and land, are also significant in production. Suppose therefore we were able to calculate the output of a good from using a standard unit of resources—a given combination of land, labour and capital. We can then draw up an illustration of comparative advantage of the kind used by Ricardo. Take two countries, America (A) and Britain (B) which can produce the following amounts of two goods, food (F) and clothing (C), with one unit of resources:

	Output per unit of resources	
	America (A)	*Britain (B)*
Food (units)	240	80
Clothing (units)	60	40

We can see immediately that A's factors are more productive than B's in producing both goods. We say that A has an **absolute advantage** in producing both goods and B, obviously, an absolute disadvantage. Alternatively, if costs are measured in terms of the resources used to produce a unit of either good, A can produce both absolutely more cheaply than B. Writers before Ricardo would mostly have said that there is therefore no basis for trade between A and B. In particular, A will not be willing to import goods from B which it can produce more cheaply itself. However, Ricardo's contribution was to show that a sufficient basis for trade was a difference not in absolute costs but in relative or **comparative costs**. Country A is absolutely superior in both goods but to a different degree. A can produce three times as much food with a unit of resources but only one and a half times as much clothing. A is therefore comparatively better at producing food—country A has a **comparative advantage** in food. Similarly, although B is absolutely inferior in both goods, the inferiority is less in clothing than in food—B has a comparative advantage in clothing.

Ricardo went on to argue that each country could potentially gain from specialising in the production of and exporting to the other the good in which it had a comparative advantage. In exchange, of course, it would import the good in which it had a comparative disadvantage. How the gains arise can more easily be seen if we use the modern notion of opportunity costs in place of comparative costs. Suppose both countries have fully employed resources. Extra output of either good can only be achieved therefore by diverting resources from production of the other—the opportunity cost of food is the sacrifice of clothing needed to produce one more unit of food. This can be calculated from our figures. In country A an extra 60 units of clothing (60C) requires the switching of one unit of resources from food and thus a reduction of food output of 240 units (240F). Assuming constant costs, if 60C has an opportunity cost of 240F, 1C has an opportunity cost of 4F. Similarly, 1F has an opportunity cost of $\frac{1}{4}$C. We can calculate the costs in country B in the same way and, for both countries, express the costs as opportunity cost ratios:

Opportunity Cost Ratios	
A	*B*
1C:4F	1C:2F
1F:$\frac{1}{4}$C	1F:$\frac{1}{2}$C

Note that comparative advantage can now be expressed in terms of opportunity cost. A can produce food with a lower opportunity cost than B; B can produce clothing with a lower opportunity cost than A. Imagine now that trade opens up between them and that the two countries agree on an international exchange ratio or **terms of trade** of 1C:3F (1F:$\frac{1}{3}$C) (assumed for simplicity to be halfway between the respective opportunity cost ratios). Consider the effect in country A. Food producers who have been giving up 4F to obtain each unit of clothing now find they have to sacrifice only 3F to do so by importing clothing from B. In other words, the opportunity cost of a unit of clothing has fallen from 4F to 3F. A's food producers will therefore cease to buy clothing from the domestic industry. In turn, clothing producers with no demand for their output will switch resources into food production—country A will become completely specialised in food and will import all its requirements for clothing from B at a lower opportunity cost. A's consumers will benefit from the reduction in the cost of clothing.

Exactly the reverse will happen in country B; because B's cloth producers can now import food more cheaply at $\frac{1}{3}$F per unit of cloth instead of $\frac{1}{2}$F from domestic exchange, B becomes specialised in clothing and imports food. Thus, both countries can benefit so long as the terms of trade differ from their own domestic opportunity cost ratios. If so, they can each buy the imported good from the other at a lower cost in resources than producing it at home. International trade based on comparative or opportunity cost differences thus results in a more efficient division of labour between countries and an increase in world output and real income. What is in doubt is the division of the gains between countries. Each country will gain more the greater the difference between the terms of trade and its own opportunity costs. If country B, for example, could trade at or close to A's domestic ratio of 1C:4F it will be able to buy food even more cheaply.

A country's gains can be illustrated diagrammatically as in Figure 18.1. For simplicity, we have assumed constant internal opportunity costs in both countries (although we pointed out right back in Chapter 1 that increasing costs are more realistic). On this assumption, a country's production frontier is drawn as a straight line like JK which represents B's production possibilities supposing that it has, say, a million units of resources available per day. At the extremes, it can produce either 40 (million) units of clothing, 40C, at J or 80F at K. Before trade the production frontier is also B's consumption frontier—it cannot consume anywhere outside JK. Suppose it ends up halfway down JK at E producing and consuming 20C and 40F.

FIGURE 18.1 **How country B gains from trade**

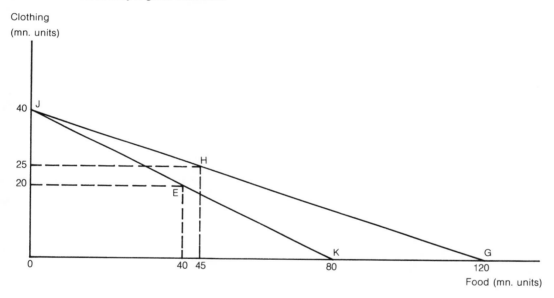

When trade opens up with a terms of trade of 1C:3F, B's production shifts from E to J—all resources are moved into clothing to produce 40C. But B's residents can now buy food from A—every unit of clothing sacrificed by exporting brings back in exchange 3 units of food. In principle, all 40 units of clothing could be exchanged for 120 units of food at G. JG is now country B's consumption frontier—B's consumers can now have any combination of goods along JG which (except for point J) lies outside the pre-trade consumption frontier. That means that B's residents can now have more of either good without any less of the other and there is a clear gain in real income. For instance, B's consumers might choose point H on JG where they have 25C and 45F. This is achieved by exporting 15C in exchange for imports of 45F. They now have 5 units more of each good than they had before trade at E. Wherever Britain ends up on JG, the important point is that trade has widened the country's consumption possibilities by the area JGK. Students should try drawing a similar diagram for America to show A's gains from trade.

18.3 PROTECTION

Ricardo's doctrine of comparative costs has stood the test of time in that it still provides the central economic argument in favour of **free trade** between countries. If relative prices of goods reflect the comparative or opportunity costs of producing them, countries stand to benefit if their residents are quite free to export and import goods and services to and from abroad. Even if the relationship between prices and opportunity costs is only approximate—as it will be in practice—there is a presumption that free trade will bring a more efficient allocation of world resources and income gains for virtually all countries. Yet we find that real-world trade is far from free. Governments of all countries intervene to restrict trade in varying degrees. Usually, the purpose of the intervention is to discriminate against foreign suppliers and in favour of domestic producers—to afford **protection** to home producers.

Protectionism has a very long history. In Europe, for example, it reached a peak in the seventeenth and eighteenth centuries when it was backed by the so-called **mercantilist** doctrine that countries should run export surpluses to enable them to import gold. Adam Smith was to attack mercantilism in *The Wealth of Nations* (1776). The assault was to be reinforced by Ricardo and this powerful intellectual support for free trade was to play no small part in the conversion of Britain to liberal trading policies in the second half of the nineteenth century, but the trend towards free trade was to be reversed in the run-up to World War I. Then, during the depression of the 1930s there was an escalation of protection as the industrial countries attempted to reduce unemployment in their own economies. Restoration of full employment after World War II led to a swing back towards liberal policies in the 1950s and 1960s but this has been followed by another return to protectionism since the recession of the mid-1970s. This latest wave of trade restriction is referred to as the **New Protectionism** because of the novel methods countries have introduced to shelter their home industries.

18.3.1 Methods of protection

Until recent years the main method of producing industries against imports was the **tariff**, a tax or duty on imports. Levels of tariffs reached their height in the 1930s but these were substantially reduced in the postwar years by international negotiations under the auspices of the **General Agreement on Tariffs and Trade** (GATT). GATT also banned direct control of imports by means of **quota restrictions** where a quantitative limit is imposed (for instance, 1,000 tons of steel a year). Thus, when pressures grew to increase protection in the 1970s governments were restrained by GATT from restoring tariff levels or imposing quotas. As a result, they have developed a battery of new protective measures which are usually called **non-tariff barriers** or NTBs. The more important NTBs include:

VOLUNTARY EXPORT RESTRAINTS (VERs)

To evade the legal ban on import quotas many industrial countries have negotiated VERs with foreign, particularly Japanese, suppliers. Under these, the suppliers agree to restrict exports to maximum levels; for example, Japanese motor car producers 'voluntarily' curb their sales in the United Kingdom to no more than 11 per cent of the market. Similar restrictions apply to a wide range of manufactured goods, especially consumer products such as TV sets, video recorders and photo-copiers where the Japanese and other Asian countries such as South Korea and Taiwan were threatening to capture the markets of the importing countries. A similar general arrangement exists under GATT to limit imports of clothing and textiles into the industrial countries from developing countries.

GOVERNMENT PROCUREMENT POLICIES

Governments of importing countries use their own market power in buying goods and services to discriminate against foreign suppliers. For example, a government might award a construction project or a contract for defence equipment to a home company even though it has tendered a higher price than foreign competitors. The government can also put pressure on nationalised industries and even private sector firms to discriminate in the same way.

DIRECT SUBSIDIES

Subsidies of various kinds to domestic firms allow them to compete against foreign producers both at home and in export markets. Subsidies can range from straight production subsidies to investment grants or loans at low interest rates. Exporters in most industrial countries can obtain cheap finance and insurance from government agencies.

CUSTOMS PROCEDURES AND VALUATIONS

In some countries the procedures and paperwork when imported goods pass through customs are made deliberately burdensome for the foreign exporter. In what has become a classic case in the 1980s, the French very successfully held down imports of video recorders to a trickle by insisting that each one had to be inspected at a customs post in Poitiers, many miles from the ports of entry. Another possibility is to give customs officers discretion in valuing imports in order to assess the duty payable. This can effectively increase the rate of duty paid if valuations are artificially high.

HEALTH, SAFETY AND TECHNICAL STANDARDS

Regulations to protect consumers, for instance, about food ingredients or to control exhaust emissions from vehicles, are sometimes more strictly applied to imports than to home-produced goods.

EXCHANGE CONTROLS AND EXCHANGE RATES

Imports can be kept out by controlling the amount of foreign currency which can be bought to purchase imported goods and services. Similarly, some countries have two or more exchange rates and may push up the price of certain imports by applying the least favourable rate to the foreign currency needed to buy them.

18.3.2 Cost of protection

Tariffs, quotas and NTBs have varying effects but when they are applied to restrict imports they almost invariably lead to a rise in the price of the imported products to the detriment of the consumer. Let's take a tariff as an example. In Figure 18.2 the curves S_D and D_D are the domestic supply and demand curves respectively for, say, bicycles. Suppose also that the domestic industry competes against imported cycles.

The importing country is assumed to account for only a small part of the world market for bicycles so that it can import as many as it wants at a constant price, W—the supply curve of imports, S_W, is therefore shown as perfectly elastic. Under free trade, therefore, consumers will be unwilling to pay more than W and total purchases are given by the demand curve as OQ at that price. Of that amount, the domestic industry produces only OJ and the rest of consumption, JQ, is supplied by imports.

FIGURE 18.2 **Effects of a tariff on bicycles**

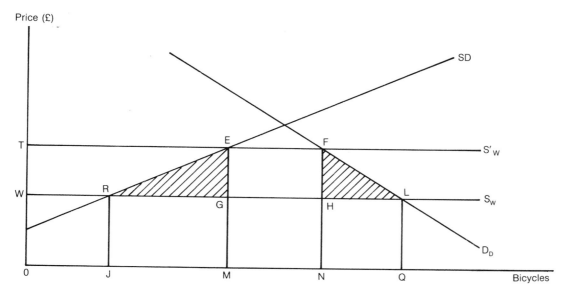

Suppose the home industry succeeds in demands for protection against imports and the government imposes a tariff equal to WT per imported bicycle. That effectively shifts the import supply curve up to S'w and the price of cycles from W to T. Because of the price rise consumers cut back their purchases to ON. Domestic producers, however, are now willing to produce OM cycles at the higher price. Imports therefore are squeezed from both sides and are reduced to MN from JQ. Note that a high enough tariff could squeeze out imports completely. That would be a prohibitive tariff; our example is of a non-prohibitive tariff. The effects of the tariff can be summarised as follows:

1   **Loss of consumer surplus** The rise in price puts a burden on consumers which can be measured (see Chapter 4) by the loss of consumer surplus equal to the area TFLW. This is typical of import controls generally; the major cost falls on consumers in higher prices.

2   **Increase in producer surplus or rent** We saw in Chapter 6 that even in a competitive industry (assumed here) intra-marginal producers can earn surplus profit or rent. The price rise increases these rents by the area TERW and this is a measure of the benefit the producers obtain from protection.

3   **Increase in government revenue** The government will raise revenue from the tariff equal to the reduced import volume, MN, times the tariff per bicycle, WT. This gives revenue equal to the rectangle EFHG. This is an indirect gain for taxpayers since the government could use the extra tariff revenue to cut other taxes.

If the burden on consumers is offset against the gains to producers and taxpayers it can be seen that there is still a net loss in welfare equal to the two shaded triangles. These measure therefore the net social cost of the tariff and we would find a similar cost from using other methods of protection. Some of these in fact may impose still heavier costs—a voluntary export restraint, for example, would raise no revenue and the foreign exporters might benefit by directly charging higher scarcity prices for cycles. The important point, though, is that protective measures nearly always impose costs on the importing country which denies itself the benefit of cheaper imports.

If protection results in self-inflicted costs, why do governments in both industrialised and developing countries alike engage so heavily in protectionism? The ultimate reason usually turns out to be political. Protection against foreign competition is sought by domestic **producer interests**— often a coalition of producing firms and workers in an industry in which profits and employment are being damaged by imports. The producer interest group may therefore put pressure on or 'lobby' politicians and government departments for protective legislation or regulation. Some pressure groups have more power than others. Farmers, for example, tend to have disproportionate voting strength in rural election constituencies and have exploited it to the hilt in securing a very high degree of protection in nearly all industrial countries. Politicians may similarly be inclined to try to buy votes by conceding protection to other interest groups.

The deciding factor in granting protection may be that producer interests are often well organised while consumers, who lose from protection, are usually not. Individual consumers may not be much affected by a single measure of protection such as the tariff on bikes and will often not even be aware that a rise in the price of a product may have been the direct result of a tariff or import restriction. This means that politicians can reap the political benefits of offering protection without having to worry unduly about the costs in terms of lost votes. Some pressure groups, moreover, are well placed to exploit the arguments used to justify protection.

18.3.3 Arguments for protection

Producer interests when seeking protection and politicians when justifying it commonly cite one or more **arguments for protection**. Some of the more frequently used arguments are:

UNEMPLOYMENT

The comparative costs model implicitly assumes continuous full employment. In the real world, that is unrealistic. Thus, suppose the domestic bicycle industry is suddenly subject to a surge of competitive imports from a **newly industrialising country** like Taiwan. In our analysis the home country gains from cheaper imports but we have ignored the social costs from workers being displaced in the domestic cycle industry—the costs of adjustment. If they can find jobs quickly in other industries in which the country has a comparative advantage then the social costs will be small. But if workers with skills specific to the industry are laid off there may be substantial costs in retraining or they are forced to take less well-paid jobs or they remain unemployed. Also, if there is geographical labour immobility and the cycle industry is regionally concentrated we may have a problem of long-term **structural unemployment**.

The case for protection here is that the social costs of adjustment would be alleviated by curbing imports. There would certainly appear to be a strong argument for at least temporary protection but there are possible objections. First, temporary protection often becomes permanent. It is politically difficult to remove protection once it has been granted because the loss of jobs which follows will then be blamed on the government. Second, if cheaper imports give overall benefits it might be more efficient to alleviate adjustment costs by subsidising retraining and providing cash grants to finance job search and removal costs and so on. Third, protection is likely to provoke **retaliation** from the exporting countries which are affected by it. Protection, once initiated, can quickly spread and escalate to the detriment of all countries.

Protection, in short, may be a **second-best** means of dealing with structural unemployment. The same applies to the arguments for protection to deal with general **deficient-demand unemployment**. The pressure for protection is especially great during recessions with large-scale unemployment—that is why the peaks of protectionism have come in the 1930s and again since the 1970s. The arguments for protection then have political appeal—import controls are needed to prevent foreigners depriving 'our' workers of jobs. General controls will divert spending from imports on to home-produced goods and the extra demand will be boosted by multiplier effects on output and employment. But protection by all countries to counter a recession is clearly self-defeating, as it was in the 1930s.

THE BALANCE OF PAYMENTS

Governments sometimes introduce import controls to curb outflows of spending and to try to reduce a deficit in the balance of payments (discussed in Chapter 19), but protection is once again a second-best measure. A balance of payments deficit will merely be suppressed by import restrictions; long-term adjustment, as we shall see, requires measures such as currency devaluation or monetary control depending on the source of the deficit.

UNFAIR COMPETITION

The argument here is that countries like, say, Taiwan and South Korea have an unfair advantage of low wages and 'cheap labour'. In general terms, this is a fallacious argument. Wages are lower in developing countries because of lower **absolute** labour productivity across the board. Thus, Britain in our comparative cost example will have lower real wages than America. Yet America can profitably trade with Britain because of the difference in comparative or opportunity costs.

The argument, however, may have substance if it can be shown that the foreign exporter is **dumping** goods overseas—getting rid of surplus output or using up spare capacity by selling goods overseas at prices below the cost of production. The European Community does this when it sells surpluses of butter at knock-down prices to the Soviet Union. GATT allows countries to take action against dumping but also requires proof of genuine dumping which can be difficult to establish.

INFANT INDUSTRIES

Developing countries in particular may justify protection of industries on the grounds that there are excess costs of establishing them, such as training and learning to produce a product in a new environment. These costs may deter private investment and justify at least temporary protection until the **infant industry** can stand on its own feet and is competitive in world markets. Similar arguments are used in developed countries for protection of established industries in which production technology is rapidly changing. Protection is required, it is said, to give the industry time to adapt and re-equip. But, while both types of arguments are sometimes valid, protection by means of import controls is once again second-best. Direct subsidies are a better solution but only if the protection is temporary and it can be demonstrated that the industry will become competitive without continued assistance.

ECONOMIC DEVELOPMENT

Many developing countries have used general import controls, particularly on manufactured goods, as a deliberate policy to diversify out of primary production and to stimulate domestic production of what the countries believe to be goods with more rapidly growing demand. The evidence on how far, if at all, protection stimulates economic development is mixed. Most observers, though, agree that import controls alone are likely to stifle rather than assist economic growth; the most dynamic economies in recent times have been those of countries such as Hong Kong and South Korea whose development has been based not on import restriction but on export growth.

THE TERMS OF TRADE

Large countries like the United States can use protection to improve their terms of trade by driving down the price of imports. They can do this because they have market power in international trade and therefore face an upward-sloping supply curve for imports (like a monopsonist discussed in Chapter 8). Imposition of import controls will drive foreign suppliers back down their supply curves and force them to reduce prices. The importing country can certainly benefit but only at the expense of exporters who in turn are likely to retaliate. If so, the total volume of trade may shrink and all countries, including the large one, may end up worse off.

TARIFF REVENUE

Governments sometimes claim the need to raise revenue from tariffs, but the argument is unconvincing, certainly in developed countries for which the potential revenue from tariffs is tiny compared with what can be raised from domestic taxes. Poor countries with a small domestic tax base, however, might have a more reasonable case for using tariffs as a revenue raiser.

NON-ECONOMIC ARGUMENTS

There are various political and social arguments for protection. Farmers, for example, often argue that agriculture needs to be protected to maintain rural communities and culture, to protect the environment and as an insurance against siege conditions in wartime. These arguments have varying degrees of validity but it is questionable once more whether goals such as environmental protection are best achieved by import controls.

Arguments for protection then clearly need to be treated with caution and even scepticism. Even when a good case can be made—for alleviating unemployment or helping an infant industry—it is nearly always a case not for protection through import restrictions but for **temporary assistance** by visible subsidies.

18.4 THE TERMS OF TRADE

In the comparative costs model the terms of trade were defined as the international exchange ratio between a country's export good and its import good. This is the **barter terms of trade** which measures the quantity of exports which has to be sacrificed to obtain a unit of imports and is easily calculated when there are just two traded goods. But in practice countries trade hundreds of different goods and services and the concept of the terms of trade becomes more complex. Estimates of the terms of trade are usually made by calculating an index of the price of the country's exports and dividing it by an index of import prices; this gives an index of the terms of trade:

Terms of trade index = (Export price index/Import price index) × 100

Thus, the price indices are essentially weighted averages of export and import prices. If these are set at 100 in some base year, say, 1988, then the terms of trade index is also 100. If in 1989 export prices rise by 10 per cent the terms of trade index will increase to 110. A 10 per cent fall in import prices would have approximately the same effect. A rise in the terms of trade index is usually described as an 'improvement' or as 'favourable' on the grounds that a rise in export prices relative to import prices theoretically means that a country can now buy the same quantity of imports for the sacrifice of less exports (or it can have more imports for the same volume of exports). Similarly, a fall in the terms of trade index is a 'deterioration' or is an 'unfavourable' movement.

These expressions, however, can often be misleading. Certainly, if a country's export prices rise or import prices drop it is better off, other things being equal, but we need to consider also the source of the price changes and their possible repercussions. Export price increases, for example, might simply be in line with general price inflation. With a fixed exchange rate the country's exports may become uncompetitive and a balance of payments deficit may emerge, reduction of which requires deflationary policies. The country may end up worse off after an 'improvement' in the terms of trade. On the other hand, if export prices fall because of increased productivity in export industries the terms of trade 'deteriorate' but the country may have a higher welfare because its enhanced competitive position gives a boost to export volume and domestic output and employment. We therefore need to take care in interpreting movements in the terms of trade and in the use of words like 'improvement' and 'deterioration' to describe them.

SUMMARY

Trade based on comparative cost differences between countries leads to a more efficient division of labour internationally and to potential gains in real income for the trading countries. There is a presumption therefore in favour of free or liberal trade policies. Despite this, all countries engage in some degree in protectionism by means of trade restriction. Tariffs and other trade barriers usually impose social costs which fall primarily on consumers and are only partly offset by gains to producers and in government revenue. Trade barriers are usually politically motivated and are justified by a range of arguments of varying validity. However, protection by means of import control is nearly always a second-best means of achieving the goals of protection, even when these are socially desirable.

SELF-TEST QUESTIONS

1   **Country A can produce 120 units of food (120F) or 30 units of clothing (30C) with one unit of resources; country B can produce 600F or 150C. Which of the following best describes the situation if trade is possible between the two countries?**

(a)   Country B is much more productive in producing both goods and will therefore be unwilling to trade with A.

(b)   Country A will specialise in food and export it in exchange for clothing.

(c)   The terms of trade will settle close to B's domestic opportunity cost ratio because B is the much larger country.

(d)   Despite the absolute cost differences there is no basis for trade because comparative costs are the same.

(e)   B will gain from specialising in clothing and buying food from A at a lower opportunity cost.

2   **Which one of the following statements is wrong?**

(a)   In Figure 18.1 country B's gains from trade are shown by the outward shift of the production frontier from JK to JG.

(b)   In the same diagram, B gains from trade because, compared with the pre-trade consumption at E, it can now have more of either good with no less of the other.

(c)   Trade is potentially profitable for a country so long as the terms of trade differ from the domestic opportunity cost ratio.

(d)   Protectionism tends to increase during periods of world recession.

(e)   Import quotas place an upper limit on the volume of imports in a given period.

3   **Which one of the following statements is correct?**

(a)   Voluntary export restraints put the onus on foreign suppliers to restrict their exports to an agreed level in a given period.

(b)   Government procurement policies usually discriminate in favour of foreign suppliers.

(c)   Exchange controls curb imports by limiting the amount of foreign currency which importers can sell.

(d)   Undervaluation of imports by customs officials is an effective method of deterring imports on which tariffs are levied.

H

(e) Cheap credit and insurance to importers is a type of NTB.

4 Referring to Figure 18.2, which one of the following statements is wrong?

(a) The shaded triangles measure the net social loss from the tariff.

(b) Because of the rise in price of bikes, imports contract from JK to EF.

(c) Taxpayers potentially benefit from the tariff revenue equal to the area EFHG.

(d) If the tariff were removed consumers would gain from an increase in consumer surplus equal to TFLW.

(e) Producers gain from the tariff through an increase in producer surplus equal to the area RGMJ.

5 Which one of the following statements is correct?

(a) Protection was a very effective method of reducing unemployment in the Great Depression of the 1930s.

(b) Import controls are the best method for securing a long-term improvement in the balance of payments.

(c) Developing countries can be shown to be dumping goods when they undercut prices of established industries in developed countries.

(d) Infant industries in developing countries should have permanent protection to enable them to learn the new technology.

(e) A rise in productivity in export industries may lead to price reductions and a worsening of the terms of trade.

EXERCISE

The principle of comparative costs shows that countries are likely to benefit from free trade. Why then is protectionism so prevalent in industrialised and developing countries alike?

Answers on page 269.

The balance of payments and exchange rates

Because different countries have their own currencies international trade and investment transactions usually require the buying or selling of foreign exchange at some point. Countries need therefore to maintain their ability to make payments overseas by avoiding persistent deficits in their balance of payments. The balance of payments accounts provide a record of foreign transactions. An overall payments deficit reduces a country's international liquidity and a chronic deficit must eventually be adjusted by appropriate monetary, fiscal and exchange rate policies.

19.1   INTRODUCTION

In considering trade in the last chapter we ignored the fact that foreign trade, like domestic trade, is carried out through the intermediary of money. Inside a country, money in the form of bank notes and deposits is nearly always acceptable as a means of payment. This is not so internationally because most countries have their own independent currencies. Money denominated in the currency of one currency cannot normally be used directly to settle debts in another country. A French shopkeeper is unlikely to accept British £10 notes and if I want to buy goods and services on holiday in France I have to exchange my pounds for francs at the bank. Conversely, if I do accept payment in, say, US dollars for teaching American students I will have to convert the dollars into pounds before I can spend them in Britain. The point is that most international transactions ultimately require the buying or selling of foreign exchange against the domestic currency. This in turn gives rise to international payments or monetary problems not encountered in domestic economies or in currency areas where two or more countries use a single currency (an example is the currency union between Belgium and Luxembourg).

The central monetary problem for a country internationally is to maintain its international liquidity—the ability of its residents to make payments overseas. If a country wants to import goods and services or wants to invest overseas it must in the long run receive enough foreign exchange from exports or from inflows of investment to cover its payments abroad. In the short run it may have reserves of foreign exchange or it may be able to borrow to finance an excess of payments over receipts—**a payments deficit**—but ultimately, when its reserves and credit facilities run out, it must take steps to remove the deficit. This is the problem of **payments adjustment**. Before considering that, let us first look at a country's balance of payments.

19.2   THE BALANCE OF PAYMENTS

The balance of payments accounts for a country are simply a record of all its international transactions over a period of time—the most detailed accounts are usually for one year and an example is given in Table 19.1. This shows the main items in the United Kingdom's balance of payments for 1986. Note that this is **not** a balance sheet, which would show the value of a country's foreign assets and liabilities at a **point** in time. In the balance of payments we record the **flows** of trade and investment transactions which give rise to changes in assets and liabilities over the period. The basis for presenting the accounts is the double-entry bookkeeping principle. A conventional distinction in the accounts is between **current** and **capital** items. Thus, the **Current Account** records flows of goods and services to and from abroad and other income flows and transfers. The **Capital Account** (now called 'transactions in United Kingdom external assets and liabilities' in the United Kingdom) shows changes in the country's foreign assets and liabilities in the period. Throughout the accounts credit items can be interpreted as giving rise to a potential inflow or supply of foreign exchange; debit items to an outflow or demand for foreign exchange. Let's look at the accounts in more detail.

TABLE 19.1 **United Kingdom Balance of Payments 1986**

£ billion

Current Account			
Visible trade			
Exports		72.8	
Imports		−81.3	
Visible Balance			−8.5
Invisibles			
1 Services:			
(a) Shipping, aviation, travel &	Credits	12.2	
government	Debits	−15.7	
	Balance	−3.5	
(b) Financial and other services	Credits	12.8	
	Debits	−4.4	
	Balance	8.4	
2 Interest, profits & dividends	Credits	47.3	
(IPD)	Debits	−42.6	
	Balance	4.7	
3 Transfers	Balance	−2.2	
Total Invisibles—	Balance		7.5
Current Account Balance			**−1.0**
Capital Account (Changes in United Kingdom external assets and liabilities)			
Long-term investment—	Outflows	−34.3	
	Inflows	13.6	
	Balance	−20.7	
Other identified capital flows (net)		13.3	
Capital Account Balance (Identified items)			**−7.4**
Balancing Item			**11.7**
Overall Balance or Balance for Official Financing			**3.3**
Increase in official reserves		−2.9	
Other official borrowing and lending		−0.4	
Total official financing			**−3.3**

CURRENT ACCOUNT

The current account is sub-divided between **visible trade** and **invisibles**. Visible trade simply consists of exports and imports of goods or merchandise and, for most countries, is the most important part of the current account. United Kingdom exports in 1986 amounted to nearly £73bn but imports were over £81bn to give a large **balance of trade deficit** of £8.5bn. The deficit measures the excess of spending on imports over receipts from exports; an excess of exports over imports is called a trade surplus. The UK's 1986 trade gap was exceptionally high (in 1985 it was only £2.2bn) because of the slump in the price of the country's oil exports. Before the 1980s, Britain used regularly to run a visible trade deficit but the development of North Sea oil and high oil prices in the early 1980s resulted in large trade surpluses. Trade turned back into deficit after 1983 with a decline in the competitiveness of non-oil industries and an associated deterioration in the trade balance in manufactured goods.

The return of trade deficits, however, is not necessarily a cause for concern because the United Kingdom normally runs a substantial surplus on the invisibles in the rest of the current account. The invisible items can be broken down into three main categories:

1 **Services** All countries trade services as well as goods. The most important categories are financial services (such as banking and insurance), shipping and aviation, and tourism or travel. Of these, financial services were easily the biggest earner of foreign exchange for the United Kingdom in 1986. Total earnings from sales of 'financial and other services' to foreigners—the earnings mainly of the **City of London**, the world's biggest international financial centre—amounted to a huge £12.8bn. Payments to foreigners were only £4.4bn to give a net surplus of £8.4bn, virtually offsetting the deficit on visible trade.

Other trade in services, however, was in deficit of £3.5bn. A major contributor to this was the United Kingdom government which regularly has a large deficit (£1.4bn in 1986) because of large military spending overseas as well as civil expenditure on embassies, trade missions and so on. Shipping and aviation were also in the red. Tourism showed an exceptionally big deficit of nearly £650 million in 1986 but this item tends to fluctuate from year to year since it is very sensitive to changes in exchange rates and income levels at home and abroad. In 1985, for example, foreign visitors to Britain spent £570 million more than the British spent on holidays and business abroad.

2   **Interest, profits and dividends** (IPD) This is foreign **investment income**. Because of huge accumulated investment overseas, British companies and financial institutions have a massive income amounting to £47bn in 1986. There was a large outflow of IPD to foreigners with investment in Britain but there was still a big surplus of £4.7bn. This surplus on IPD has been normal for many years but has grown in recent years with an upsurge of British investment overseas after the ending of government restrictions in 1979. Note that these investments are recorded in the capital account; only the income from investment is shown in the current account.

3   **Transfers** The final category of invisibles consists, for example, of foreign workers in Britain transferring money back to their dependants. A large item for the United Kingdom is government transfers by way of economic aid to developing countries and also in contributions to the European Community budget. Total transfers were in deficit of over £2bn in 1986.

The invisibles as a whole showed a surplus of £7.5bn. Deducting this from the £8.5bn visible trade deficit resulted in a total **current account deficit** of £1bn. The current account balance is commonly referred to as the **balance of payments deficit or surplus** even though it excludes all the items in the capital account. The point though is that the current balance shows the relationship between the country's total foreign income and expenditure. Excessive spending overseas will show itself in a current account deficit. The deficit in turn has to be **financed** by running down the country's overseas assets or by borrowing. In other words, a current account deficit must be financed by a capital account surplus. Similarly, a current surplus when foreign income exceeds spending is necessarily financed by a capital account deficit as the country uses the surplus to invest overseas or to reduce its foreign debts.

CAPITAL ACCOUNT

As we noted, this is now referred to in the United Kingdom's accounts as 'transactions in United Kingdom external assets and liabilities', but for brevity we continue to use the traditional term. Distinction is made between long-term and short-term capital flows. For instance, the acquisition by a British pension fund of foreign securities—equities and bonds—normally counts as **long-term investment**. Securities are added to the investment portfolio in order to earn income and increase its value in the longer term. Such investment is called **indirect** or **portfolio investment**. The other kind of long-term investment is **direct investment**. This is almost invariably undertaken by large companies—**multinational enterprises**—to expand their operations overseas. Typically, the multinational sets up new subsidiary companies overseas or it takes over existing foreign companies. The vital characteristic of direct as against portfolio investment is the ownership and control of overseas enterprises.

In 1986 there was a large outflow of long-term capital from Britain of £34bn, divided between £11bn of direct investment and £23bn of portfolio investment. Note that this outward investment is a debit item in the accounts since there is an actual or implicit demand for foreign exchange to pay for the foreign assets. There was also an inflow of long-term investment amounting in 1986 to nearly £14bn so that long-term capital showed a deficit of almost £21bn.

The rest of the capital account consists of inflows and outflows of **short-term funds** or what are sometimes called **monetary movements**. Thus, British companies and institutions invest in short-term, liquid assets such as foreign currency bank deposits, Treasury bills issued by overseas governments and commercial bills and other short-term instruments sold by foreign borrowers. Conversely, there will be inflows of funds as foreigners place funds in sterling bank deposits and other short-term instruments issued by British residents. A feature of these funds is their extreme **volatility**; monetary flows into and out of the UK may amount to billions of pounds in a day and they can quickly alter direction in response, for instance, to a change in interest rates or to revised expectations about sterling's exchange rate with other currencies. Other things being equal, a rise in interest rates in London will almost instantly attract possibly large fund inflows; or sudden fears of a fall in the value of the pound may equally quickly bring a flight out of sterling. As a result, short-term funds are often described as **'hot money'**.

The volatility and sheer size of short-term capital movements make it impossible to identify and measure them accurately. The table shows a figure of the balance of identified flows—a surplus or net inflow of £13bn in 1986. When that is added to the long-term investment balance the capital account as a whole shows a deficit of £7.4bn, meaning that there was a net **identified** capital outflow of that amount.

Next, notice the separate figures on **official financing**. In 1986 the government (through its agent, the Bank of England) added to the demand for foreign exchange. First, the Bank bought up £2.9bn of foreign exchange which it used to increase the official reserves. Second, the government reduced its foreign currency borrowing by £0.4bn. These official financing operations thus added £3.3bn to the net demand for foreign exchange, but, to give an accounting balance of zero this official financing deficit of £3.3bn must be matched by a **surplus** of the same amount in the rest of the accounts. Yet the items identified in the current and capital accounts add up to a **deficit** of £8.4bn. There is therefore a huge discrepancy—a credit item of £11.7bn shown in the accounts as the **balancing item**. This is explained partly by inaccuracies in recording items. Many of these have to be estimated rather than measured directly and there are inevitable errors. But the bulk of the balancing item almost certainly comes from failure to identify and record some items at all, particularly flows of short-term funds. Whatever the explanation, the true **overall balance for official financing** was a **surplus** of £3.3bn which was offset by the negative balance of official financing. We might note that the balancing item has become very large in recent years and is probably associated with the rapid growth of London's position as an international banking centre.

PAYMENTS DEFICITS AND SURPLUSES

From this discussion of the payments accounts it can be seen that there is scope for considerable confusion about the meaning of a balance of payments deficit (or surplus). What is meant depends simply on where the line is drawn in measuring a balance. We have at least three different concepts of the payments balance:

1   **The current account balance** As noted above, this is probably the most commonly used measure of a country's payments deficit or surplus. Since it excludes all capital transactions we obviously need to treat the figure with caution. Many developing countries, for instance, regularly run substantial current deficits but this may be offset by regular inflows of investment and, in some cases, of economic aid from industrial countries and from international development agencies like the World Bank. Similarly, an industrial country with net outflows of investment needs to finance them with a corresponding current account surplus. However, if this is borne in mind, the trends in a country's current account may be a good guide to changes in a country's competitive position. A large deterioration in the current account may indicate the need for corrective action of the kind dealt with in 19.4.

Note that the current account balance is often wrongly identified with the **balance of trade**. This usually refers only to visible trade and we've seen that, while in most countries trade in goods is certainly the most important part of the current account, we may get a quite misleading impression of the state of a country's foreign payments from considering its visible trade balance alone. The United Kingdom traditionally runs a trade deficit which tends to be covered in the longer run by the normal surplus on invisibles. By contrast, a developing country like Brazil needs to achieve a large visible trade surplus if it is to finance its deficit on invisibles, particularly from the heavy interest payments it has to make on its huge foreign debts (see Chapter 20).

2   **The basic payments balance** Some economists argue that the payments balance should be measured by the sum of the current account and **long-term investment balances**. This is called the **basic balance**. Thus, in our example, the United Kingdom had a basic payments deficit of £21.7bn made up of the £1bn current deficit and the £20.7bn net outflow of long-

term investment. This measure has the advantage of excluding the volatile short-term capital flows but the notion of the basic balance doesn't command widespread acceptance.

3   **The overall balance** or **balance for official financing** This measures the total net flows of funds passing through the foreign exchanges but excluding official financing flows. We shall see in the next section that the overall balance for official financing is relevant when a country's central bank is fixing or manipulating the exchange rate. If so, the bank will have to buy or sell foreign exchange to support or to hold down the exchange rate and the changes in the exchange reserves or in official borrowing indicate the extent of such intervention. In the example, the Bank of England effectively sold £3.3bn of sterling in 1986 in exchange for foreign currency which was added to the reserves or used to reduce foreign debt. Over the year, therefore, it could be said to have been holding down the external value of sterling below its free-market level. The overall balance is thus useful in measuring the upward or downward market pressures on a fixed or stabilised exchange rate.

19.3   THE EXCHANGE RATE

In the next section we shall look at the alternative policies a country may pursue to adjust its balance of payments but, first, we need to look at the exchange rate which plays a vital role in determining a country's payments balance and in measures to influence the balance. The exchange rate is simply the price of one currency in terms of another—US dollar per pound, francs per US dollar, and so on. As such, the determination of the exchange rate can be analysed with conventional supply-and-demand analysis. Thus, foreign currencies are traded against the domestic currency and against each other in the **foreign exchange market**. In London, for example, the market is made up largely of banks and other exchange dealers who buy and sell currencies partly on their own account but mainly for their customers. Trading in currency banknotes, largely for individuals, is tiny compared with the billions of pounds of business conducted every day in buying and selling bank deposits. Most of this is in **spot exchange**, where delivery is taken immediately, but a large proportion of transactions are in forward exchange where customers anticipate their requirements by entering into contracts to buy or sell exchange at some date in the future.

However, let's focus on the exchange rate for spot exchange. We shall see presently that countries often try to fix the exchange rate for their own currencies but suppose we start with a free market in which the exchange rate is allowed to find its own level according to supply and demand forces—the exchange rate is said to be **freely floating**. Thus, in Figure 19.1 we show the supply and demand curves for pounds against dollars. These are drawn in the usual way—the quantity of pounds demanded increases and the quantity supplied declines as the price (the exchange rate in dollars per pound) falls. We should see why this is likely to be the case. First, note that both supply of and demand for a currency derive from the underlying trade and investment transactions detailed in the balance of payments accounts. Also, since buying pounds means selling dollars, the demand for pounds automatically corresponds to a supply of dollars and vice versa.

Take the demand curve for sterling. Holders of dollars will need to exchange them for pounds in order to make payments in sterling. To simplify, we can say that sterling is demanded either to pay for British exports or to make investments in assets, such as bank deposits, bonds and equities, denominated in sterling. The demand for pounds is therefore derived from the demand by foreigners for British exports of goods and services and for sterling assets. Suppose the initial exchange rate is $2.00 = £1 ($R_1$), at which rate foreigners (Americans) are willing to buy L_1 pounds each day. If the pound **depreciates** by 25 per cent to $1.50 ($R_2$), then at given sterling prices the dollar prices of British goods and assets will fall in proportion. For example, if a British exporter of, say, teacups prices them at £1 each the dollar price clearly falls from $2 to $1.50. Americans therefore will import more cups and buy more sterling to pay for them. Similarly, at constant sterling values, British equities, bonds and other assets are now cheaper in dollar terms so that we can expect, other things equal, increased investment by Americans in sterling assets. For both reasons there is an increased quantity of pounds demanded shown by a movement down the demand curve.

Exchange rate changes will have the reverse effect on the quantity supplied of sterling. British residents need to sell sterling in exchange for dollars to buy American exports (British imports) and invest in dollar assets. As the exchange rate falls the sterling prices of British imports and of dollar assets rise. The quantity of dollars demanded therefore falls and, provided British demand for imports and dollar assets is not inelastic, the quantity of pounds sold will also fall. In other words, if the British

FIGURE 19.1 **Determination of the US dollar/pound Exchange Rate**

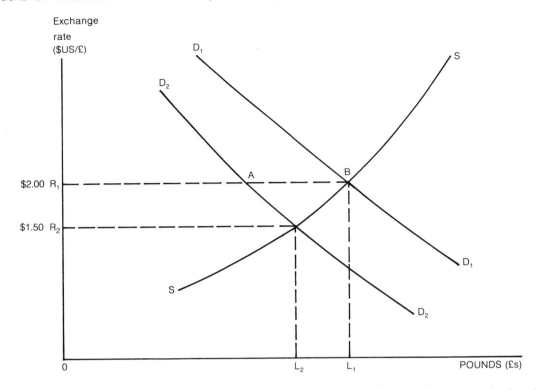

demand for American goods and assets is elastic, the supply curve of pounds is upward-sloping. We can note that inelastic demand for imports may produce a positively sloped or backward-sloping supply curve but we ignore that possibility for the moment.

Thus, with a free market for foreign exchange the exchange rate will move to the equilibrium market-clearing level at R_1. Any shifts in supply or demand for sterling will push the exchange to a new equilibrium. Suppose, for example, the British government reduces interest rates and makes British interest-bearing assets like bonds less attractive. There is less demand from overseas for British bonds and the demand curve shifts as a result to D_2 to produce a fall in the pound to R_2. Similarly, a deflation of aggregate demand in Britain will reduce the demand for imports. The sterling supply curve shifts to the left (not shown) and leads this time to an **appreciation** of the pound. Students should work out the effects on the exchange rate of other changes—increased protectionism in America, a rise in British inflation—which shift the demand or supply curves for sterling.

In a freely floating exchange rate system currencies are left to find their own market-determined levels. But in the real world governments rarely allow their currencies to float completely freely. Between the major currencies—the US dollar, UK pound, Japanese yen and the German mark (Deutschmark)—exchange rates have been nominally floating since the early 1970s, but in fact governments through their central banks have continually acted to stabilise rates or to manipulate them in desired directions. Such a system is known as **managed (or 'dirty') floating**. Moreover, in the post war years up to 1972/73 the currencies of most countries were linked fairly rigidly to the US dollar in the **Bretton Woods** monetary system (named after the place in the United States where the agreement was signed in 1944 to establish the International Monetary Fund).

19.3.1 Exchange intervention

Under the Bretton Woods system countries were obliged to maintain the dollar value of their currencies within one per cent of a declared rate or **par value**—the pound's par value was $2.80 from 1949 to 1967. The principal stabilisation method was **exchange intervention** by the country's central bank. Thus, suppose the Bank of England wants to peg the pound at R_1 ($2.00) in the diagram. There is no problem with the original supply and demand curves which give equilibrium at the desired rate. But after the leftward shift of the demand curve the equilibrium rate drops to R_2 ($1.50). At $2.00 there is now excess supply of sterling (equal to AB) which the Bank of England must absorb if it is to prevent a depreciation. The Bank must therefore intervene in the exchange market to buy up sterling in the amount AB which measures the excess supply. In doing so it sells dollars from the exchange reserves. Propping up a currency above its equilibrium level in this way therefore involves running down the country's foreign exchange reserves or borrowing currency resources from other central banks or from bodies like the International Monetary Fund (IMF). We can also note that it will appear in the balance of payments accounts as official financing of an overall deficit though a reduction in the reserves. A currency supported by intervention is said to be 'weak' or 'overvalued'.

Conversely, if the fixed rate is below the equilibrium rate (not shown in the diagram) there will be excess demand for sterling and the rate will have to be held down by selling pounds and buying up foreign exchange into the reserves. When this happens the currency is 'strong' or 'undervalued'. The major currencies today have no par values but, as we have noted, central banks, individually and sometimes together, frequently intervene to manage rates. For example, for about a year from early 1987 the Bank of England held the pound's Deutschemark value very close to DM3 = £1. This was achieved largely through intervention selling of pounds to prevent the rate rising.

Pegging a persistently undervalued or overvalued currency eventually creates problems. When the currency is undervalued the reserves continually rise and put inflationary upward pressure on the domestic money supply. It was this which finally caused the Bank of England to allow the pound to rise through DM3 in March 1988. If the currency is overvalued the reserves must ultimately run out and either the central bank has to allow the currency to float downwards to its free market level or it **devalues** the currency to a lower fixed rate or peg. Other alternatives are to raise interest rates to shift the demand curve to the right or to suppress the demand for foreign exchange with exchange and import controls.

19.3.2 Exchange rate determination

Experience of floating rates since the 1970's has shown that rates can be highly volatile and this has led economists to reassess the theory of exchange rate determination. The widely accepted theory in the 1950s and 1960s was based on the notion of a long-term equilibrium exchange rate—the rate which would maintain an equilibrium in the current account of the balance of payments (after taking into account any regular inflows or outflows of long-term capital).

This equilibrium exchange rate tended to be identified with the **purchasing power parity (PPP)** value of a currency. For example, if a representative 'basket' of goods and services costs $200 in the United States and £100 in Britain the PPP exchange rate is $2.00 = £1. It was argued that if the actual exchange rate diverged from the PPP rate, market forces would automatically push it back to equality. Thus, if the rate were $1.50, the pound would be undervalued (the dollar overvalued) and British goods would be highly competitive resulting in a trade or current account surplus against the USA. The excess demand for pounds would drive the exchange rate back to the PPP level of £2.00 = £1.

The PPP theory implies that floating rates will automatically change to reflect differences in inflation between countries. If the British inflation rate is 5 per cent higher than the American then the pound will depreciate by 5 per cent to maintain the competitiveness of British goods. Otherwise, floating rates will be relatively stable since speculators can make profits by buying undervalued currencies and selling overvalued currencies; in doing so they will drive exchange rates to their expected PPP levels. In practice, though, currencies often diverge from PPP values for long periods. The US dollar, for instance, went on rising against the Deutschmark from 1983 to 1985 to a peak of DM3.45 = $1 while the American current account went into bigger and bigger deficit—the dollar was patently overvalued relative to its PPP value. By December 1987 the dollar had slumped to as low as DM1.57, almost certainly below the PPP rate.

In order to explain this **under-** and **overshooting** of currencies in relation to PPP rates modern theorists concentrate on the capital account. They argue that the enormous increase in **international capital mobility** since the early 1970s means that exchange rates are determined for long periods, not by current account fundamentals, but by investors' **expectations** of the returns on assets, like bank deposits and bonds, denominated in different currencies. The dollar went sky-high in 1983–85 despite the worsening current account because of tight monetary policy which forced up US interest rates to attractive levels for international investors. Once the policy was loosened after the autumn of 1985 the dollar dropped as transactors switched into higher yielding currencies like sterling or into currencies like the mark and the yen which were now expected to appreciate against the dollar in the future.

International capital mobility coupled with continually changing expectations about future interest and exchange rates is a major explanation of the actual short-term and medium-term instability of currencies. Exchange rates no doubt have to reflect their PPP levels in the long run. But actual rates may under- or overshoot their PPP rates for periods of months or even years.

19.3.3   Fixed versus floating rates

Ever since the Bretton Woods system of fixed exchange rates broke down in the early 1970s there has been a debate among economists about the pros and cons of a return to a world-wide structure of stable if not absolutely fixed exchange rates. Many smaller countries in fact have retained fixed rates for their own currencies, (usually against the US dollar) while most countries in the European Community (a notable exception is the UK) keep their currencies more or less fixed against each other by participating in the so-called Exchange Rate Mechanism of the European Monetary System (EMS). The debate therefore is really about a return to fixed rates by the major currency countries. Note though that even the restoration of the Bretton Woods system would not mean absolutely fixed rates for, under that arrangement, countries were meant to devalue or upvalue their currencies to new pegs to correct severe over- or undervaluation. In fact, one of the problems of the system was that countries often resisted changes in par values for political reasons. British governments, for instance, held out against a patently needed devaluation of the pound until the Labour government was virtually forced to do so by near exhaustion of the reserves in November 1967.

The arguments put forward in favour of a return to fixed rates are largely on the following lines:

FIXED RATES PROMOTE TRADE AND INVESTMENT

Fixed or stable rates, it is argued, remove a major uncertainty of adverse exchange rate changes for traders and investors. Thus, floating rates have in practice been very unstable with large fluctuations of the $US and the pound against each other and against the yen and the mark. A British exporter who will not be paid in, say, marks for three months is exposed to the risk of a fall in the mark which will reduce the sterling proceeds and perhaps wipe out profit margins. The currency risk may therefore deter foreign trade and investment. However, even under the Bretton Woods system there was a risk of sudden and sometimes large devaluations or revaluations or of exchange and import controls imposed by countries with weak currencies to avoid devaluation.

Supporters of floating also point out that both traders and investors can **hedge** the currency risks in the **forward exchange market** and by other means. The British exporter, for example, can eliminate the risk by selling the mark proceeds forward at an exchange rate agreed now. In fact, even the wide fluctuations in rates seen in the 1980s appear to have had very little adverse effects on either trade or investment.

FIXED RATES ARE ANTI-INFLATIONARY

The claim here is that a commitment to fixed rates will impose monetary discipline on weak-currency countries with emergent payments deficits. For example, suppose France in the European Monetary System has a higher rate of inflation than Germany. The rise in prices of French goods relative to Germany's will make French industry less competitive, French exports will decline and imports rise so that the balance of payments deteriorates into deficit with Germany. With floating rates France can simply validate inflation by allowing the franc to depreciate against the mark. There is no pressure to control the money supply to check inflation. But with a fixed franc/mark exchange rate the payments deficit will cause a fall in French exchange reserves. That on its own will tend to curb the money supply but the French central bank will also be forced to put up interest rates and tighten its control on monetary growth in order to protect the reserves. In turn there will be a drop in French inflation to converge with the German rate.

Experience in the EMS suggests a good deal of truth in this. Inflation rates have fallen generally among EMS countries in the 1980s and some people give the main credit for this to the relative stability among EMS currencies, but the argument ignores the fact that inflation has fallen in nearly all countries irrespective of whether their currencies are fixed or floating. Also, it can equally well be argued that fixed rates force smaller countries to adopt undesirable deflationary policies to curb payments deficits. Critics of fixed rates point to the slow growth and high unemployment in countries like France, the direct result it is said of the constant need to pursue contractionary monetary and fiscal policies in line with those followed by the dominant EMS country, West Germany. The point is that a fixed exchange rate removes a degree of freedom in a country's economic policies and forces smaller countries to conform with those in the major economies. Also, after the failure of monetary targeting, some countries such as the UK have switched to flexible exchange rate targeting as a monetary instrument.

FLOATING RATES ENCOURAGE SPECULATION

This argument for fixing rates is related to the first one that floating rates are unstable. One cause of the instability is said to be the activities of speculators who make profits from selling weak currencies and buying strong ones. The argument, however, is naive since the very uncertainty about future exchange rates when they are floating tends to reduce speculation not increase it. By contrast, under fixed rate systems speculation is often encouraged when it is clear that a country has a badly over- or undervalued currency. In the EMS, the structure of fixed rates tends to be realigned every two or three years or so. Once it is known that another realignment is imminent speculators can make certain profits by selling the currencies which are due for devaluation and buying those to be upvalued. In fact, speculation has sometimes forced realignments as the selling of weak currencies depletes the reserves of the central banks.

Finally, however convincing the arguments in favour of fixed exchange rates, it has to be questioned how far they are practicable in today's conditions of internationally mobile private capital. The foreign exchange reserves of even the major countries are now quite inadequate to defend a currency against the tens of billions of dollars of private funds which can be shifted within minutes from one currency into another. Attempts made in the 1980s to stabilise rates among major currencies by coordinated central bank intervention have failed time and again because the markets have decided that rates should change—that the US dollar should fall or that the yen should rise. Once a general view emerges, central banks are powerless to stop rates moving to where the markets dictate. Floating rates among the big currencies look here to stay.

19.4 BALANCE OF PAYMENTS POLICIES

Countries with fundamental payments disequilibria eventually have to take measures to deal with them. The pressure is particularly great on deficit countries which are running out of reserves in the effort to support their currencies by exchange intervention. As this becomes evident speculation builds up in the expectation of a devaluation or downward float and we get what is described as an exchange or payments crisis when the central bank's resources are finally exhausted. This may be followed by emergency measures to stem the flight of capital, usually in the form of exchange and trade controls. These merely suppress, not cure the problem and the country has to adopt policies eventually to bring a durable payments adjustment. The problem lies nearly always in a deterioration in the current account and the long-term solution therefore is to reduce spending on imports relative to export earnings. This has led economists to conclude that there are logically only two broad types of policies which can be followed to restore payments equilibrium—**expenditure reducing policies** and **expenditure switching policies**.

19.4.1 Expenditure reducing policies

The principle here is simple enough. A current account deficit may be caused by excessive aggregate demand in relation to the economy's output and real income at full employment. In a closed economy this would show itself in inflation but in an open economy the excess demand can simply spill over on to imports and create a payments deficit. The deficit can be sustained only so long as there are reserves to finance it. Once these run out and assuming the country is unwilling to alter the exchange rate, the deficit can be removed only by policies to reduce demand or expenditure. Deflationary policies, as we know, may be fiscal or monetary but whichever is used the aim is to reduce aggregate demand and in turn to curb spending on imports. For a given reduction of demand

and income the effect on imports depends on the **marginal propensity to import**, the proportion of a change in income which is spent on imports (M):

$$\text{Marginal propensity to import} = \frac{\Delta(M)}{\Delta Y}$$

The larger is the marginal propensity the greater is the reduction in imports, but even in a relatively open economy like the United Kingdom's the reduction in income needed may be several times as great as the required fall in imports. In the UK the propensity to import is around one third so that a £1bn reduction in import spending needs a £3bn fall in income. Reliance on deflation of spending alone to adjust the balance of payments therefore may require an unacceptable fall in output, income and employment.

Moreover, deflation may be very slow in bringing long-term adjustment through a reduction in the country's price and money income levels to restore its international competitiveness. Even if deflation reduces inflationary pressures price and wage stickiness may deny a needed reduction in the absolute price level. If so, the country may be condemned to a long period of self-imposed recession or slow growth as Britain was both in the late 1920s and again in the 1960s. In both periods the pound was overvalued but with the maintenance of a fixed exchange rate the only means of checking the emergent payments deficit was continual deflation of spending and income.

19.4.2 Expenditure switching policies

The aim here is to reduce the payments deficit by switching spending away from foreign produced goods on to home produced goods. The two main policies are **import controls** and **devaluation** (or depreciation) of the currency.

IMPORT CONTROLS

Remember that the aim is to reduce foreign exchange expenditure. Other things equal, certain types of import restriction will have the desired result. Tariffs, for example, will reduce the volume of imports and, since the price paid to overseas suppliers remains the same or falls, there is a certain reduction in foreign exchange outlays on imports. But other things of course do not stay equal. We saw in Chapter 18 that tariffs and other restrictions may bring retaliation and a fall in the country's export earnings which could even exceed the savings on imports. In turn, the whole point of the policy is to divert spending on to home-produced goods which compete with imports. The reduction of the import leakage from the circular flow means more spending on domestic output. If there is involuntary unemployment there will be a multiplier expansion of income and employment but part of the extra income will be spent on imports despite their higher prices from tariffs. Again, it is possible that this income effect on imports outweighs the original reduction in overseas spending from the rise in price. Some economists in the United Kingdom, for example, argue that import controls (and devaluation) bring no significant improvement in the British balance of trade precisely because of these income effects. Import controls are advocated not to improve the balance of payments but as a means of achieving a Keynesian boost to demand and employment.

In any case, some kinds of **non-tariff barrier (NTB)** which might have to be used against imports are unlikely to produce foreign exchange savings and might even increase spending on imports. **Voluntary export restraints (VERs)**, for example, may lead, as we saw in the previous chapter, to cartels among foreign suppliers. If so, they may raise price directly to the scarcity level and the country may end up spending more on a reduced volume of imports! A final point is that the rise in consumer prices which nearly always results from all kinds of import controls may add to any general inflationary pressure in the economy. A rise in inflation will then reduce the country's overall trade competitiveness. In all, import controls appear to have little to commend them as a means of achieving long-term payments adjustment.

DEVALUATION

Devaluation of a country's currency has an immediate effect in lowering the foreign currency prices of the country's exports and raising the domestic currency prices of imports. The volume of exports can therefore be expected to rise and import volume to fall. Superficially, we might thus expect the balance of trade to improve. But remember that we are concerned not with the volume or quantity of exports and imports but with expenditure on them. Consider a 10 per cent devaluation (or depreciation under floating) of the British pound. If sterling export prices remain the same US dollar prices will fall by 10 per cent and foreigners (Americans) will increase the quantity demanded according to the price elasticity of their demand for British exports. Let's label this E_x. If E_x, for instance, equals 2, every 1 per cent drop in the US dollar price produces a 2 per cent rise in the quantity demanded. The more elastic is demand for exports the greater is the increase in the volume demanded and the bigger the increase in Britain's export revenue. Measured in sterling, export earnings must rise.

The same considerations apply to imports. If E_M is the British elasticity of demand for imports, the greater is E_M the bigger is the fall in import volume. But suppose demand for imports is inelastic—E_M, say, equals 0.5. The 10 per cent rise in sterling import prices will reduce the quantity demanded by only 5 per cent so that expenditure on imports, measured in pounds, will actually rise by about 5 per cent. (In Figure 19.1 the supply curve of sterling would be downward sloping.) It is possible that the higher import spending offsets the increase in export earnings so that the balance of trade does not improve or even gets worse after a devaluation.

These considerations lead to a formal condition for devaluation to improve the balance of trade—the **elasticities condition**. This is simply that the sum of the demand elasticities for imports and exports should be greater than one:

$$(E_x + E_M) > 1$$

Note the condition does not say that either elasticity should exceed one; only their sum should. This means that we could have, say, perfectly inelastic demand for imports ($E_M = 0$) but the balance of trade will still improve so long as export demand is elastic ($E_x > 1$). In the longer term the condition is likely to be met for virtually all countries but it could cause problems in the short term. This is because short-run elasticities tend to be low so that immediately after a devaluation the balance of trade gets worse rather than better. This is called the **J-curve effect**. If the balance of trade is measured against time as in Figure 19.2, the balance first declines on the downstroke of the 'J' but then turns upwards along the upstroke as the larger long-run elasticities take over.

FIGURE 19.2   **The J-Curve following a devaluation**

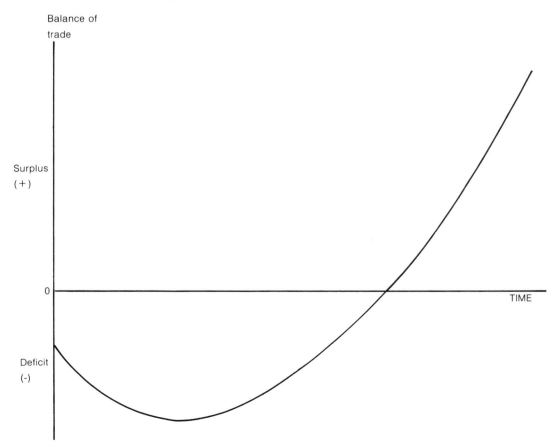

However, devaluation is unlikely to bring significant trade improvement without complementary changes in domestic financial policies. First, the expansion of exports and diversion of demand from imports both have a multiplier effect in raising demand for home output. As with import controls, the extra demand may be accommodated if there is existing involuntary unemployment but the rise in real income will feed back into higher imports. These income effects could again cancel out the substitution effects on the trade balance. Secondly, if there is already full employment the increase in demand will be inflationary or simply spill over on to imports. Either way, the trade balance may not improve. The government therefore may have to complement a devaluation with deflationary policies to make room for the increased demand for exports and import-competing products.

As many countries have found from bitter experience, devaluation is thus rarely a simple solution to a balance of payments deficit. On its own, it may only succeed in exacerbating an existing inflationary situation which was responsible for the payments problems in the first place. If so, the country cannot avoid the necessary delationary measures to curb inflation and improve the balance of payments.

SUMMARY

The balance of payments accounts record all a country's international transactions which give rise to inflows and outflows of foreign exchange. There are alternative definitions of a payments deficit or surplus but an imbalance of either kind will eventually put pressure on a country to adopt policies for payments adjustment. The exchange rate has a central influence on the balance of payments and countries can allow it to float at one extreme or try to peg the rate by exchange intervention at the other. Policies to remedy a payments deficit can be either expenditure-reducing or expenditure-switching but neither is likely to be successful on its own.

SELF-TEST QUESTIONS

1   Which one of the following is not a credit item in the current account of the British balance of payments?

(a)   A receipt of dividends on foreign shares by a British resident.

(b)   Payment of commission by a French bank for a foreign exchange transaction performed by a British bank in London.

(c)   Payment of a hotel bill in London by an American tourist.

(d)   Receipt of interest by the Bank of England on its holdings of US Treasury bills.

(e)   The purchase of equity in a British company by a Japanese corporation.

2   Which one of the following is wrong?

(a)   The current account may be in surplus even when a country has a large trade deficit.

(b)   The capital account is in surplus when investment outflows exceed investment inflows.

(c)   An increase in official foreign exchange reserves is a debit item in the balance of payments.

(d)   A reduction in foreign debt by a British company is a debit item in the British balance of payments.

(e)   An overall deficit in the balance of payments may be financed by an increase in borrowing overseas by the country's central bank.

3   In a free foreign exchange market which one of the following, other things being equal, would produce an appreciation of the pound?

(a)   An increase in the British propensity to import.

(b)   An increase in foreign investment by British companies.

(c)   A rise in foreign interest rates relative to those in Britain.

(d)   Imposition of exchange controls by the Bank of England to restrict spending abroad by British tourists.

(e)   None of the above.

4   Which one of the following statements is correct?

(a)   To prevent the pound from falling the Bank of England must sell sterling on the foreign exchange market.

(b)   In the Bretton Woods system there was no scope for profitable currency speculation on exchange rate changes.

(c)   A fixed exchange rate allows small countries to pursue independent monetary policies.

(d)   A country with an undervalued currency is likely to find its foreign exchange reserves declining.

(e)   None of the above.

5   Which one of the following statements is correct?

(a)   Deflationary policies are appropriate to correct a payments deficit when excess demand is spilling over on to imports.

(b)   Quota restrictions on imports will always produce a reduction in foreign exchange expenditure.

(c)   Devaluation cannot improve the balance of trade if the demand for imports is perfectly inelastic.

(d)   Devaluation will work on its own provided there is no involuntary unemployment in the domestic economy.

(e)   None of the above.

EXERCISE

Should the governments of countries with major currencies restore a system of fixed exchange rates like that prevailing before 1971?

Answers on page 271.

Current macroeconomic issues

In this chapter we apply economic principles—mainly but not exclusively from macroeconomic theory—to two important contemporary issues in the world economy. The first is the problem of the mountain of foreign debt owed by a number of developing countries. Difficulties in repaying debt emerged in the 1980s with some countries threatening to renege on their commitments with the danger of provoking a world banking crisis. We look here at the origins of the debt problem and the possible solutions. The second issue we consider is that of unemployment—the causes of its growth to postwar heights in many industrial countries in the 1980s and the alternative policies to secure a long-term reduction in unemployment.

20.1   THE LDC DEBT PROBLEM

20.1.1   Origins

What we know as the debt problem of less developed countries (LDCs) first surfaced in August 1982 when Mexico announced that it was no longer able to service its foreign debt (**debt servicing** means making the agreed repayments of loans together with the interest on the outstanding loans). It is not unknown of course for debtors to default but what made the Mexican case so serious was the sheer size of the potential debt failure. Mexico had outstanding debts estimated at around $90bn owed mainly to the international banks operating in the Euro-currency markets in which banks accept and on-lend deposits in currencies outside the countries in which the deposits were first created. Euro-dollar deposits, for instance, are deposits denominated in dollars in banks located outside the United States, most commonly in London which is the centre of the Euro-currency market. The Euro-banks in turn are nearly all offshoots of domestic commercial banks in the industrial countries, especially in the United States. The danger therefore was that a large-scale debt failure would spark off a loss of confidence not just in the Euro-banks but in the whole banking system of the industrial economies.

The LDC debt problem has its origins in the oil price shock of 1973/74 when the oil producers' cartel, OPEC, dramatically forced up the price of crude oil by four or five times in the space of a few months. The increased price meant a big rise in the import bills and a deterioration in the balance of trade of countries with little or no domestic oil production. LDCs were particularly badly hit not only by the oil price rise but also by the following decline in their exports of primary commodities as the industrial countries went into recession. Foreign exchange earnings suffered from both the fall in export volume and the worsening of the terms of trade—a drop in export prices relative to import prices. In short, there was a massive widening of their current account deficits.

Up to that time it was more common for developing countries to obtain external finance through aid from governments of industrial countries and from private direct investment. Since aid typically takes the form of cheap loans and grants while direct investment is repaid by the profits of the investing corporations, LDC debt servicing had not been a severe problem. Moreover in the 1960s the exports of most LDCs were increasing rapidly and this allowed them to step up their economic growth rate without jeopardising their balance of payments. While borrowing from commercial banks played a relatively small part in financing development the banks themselves began to see many LDCs as potentially profitable markets in which to expand their lending. For their part, governments in LDCs found positive attractions in borrowing from the banks, in particular, the comparative freedom to use the borrowed funds however they wanted. By contrast, economic aid is often tied to financing particular projects while the government has little control over private direct investment spending. The increased willingness both to lend and to borrow was reflected between 1967 and 1973 in an annual 30 per cent growth in long-term commercial lending to the leading LDC borrowers.

The oil shock greatly accelerated this process. Many LDCs were anxious to maintain their growth rates which were now endangered by a need to deflate their economies to curb their widening payments deficits. To avoid this they stepped up their demand for loans and found the banks only too willing to grant them, for the banks were now replete with funds deposited by the more thinly populated OPEC countries, such as Saudi Arabia, which were unable to spend the tens of billions of dollars by which their revenues had expanded. Recession in the industrial countries reduced the loans market there while the banks were positively encouraged by governments and central banks to 'recycle' the funds to deficit countries to help avoid an even deeper world recession. Banks were also attracted to lend to countries like Mexico, Venezuela, Indonesia and Nigeria to finance the expansion of existing oil production and the development of new sources.

As a result, bank lending to LDCs soared. It rose from less than $200bn in 1973 to $330bn in 1978 and then, with the second oil shock of 1979/80, to $670bn by the end of 1983. Borrowing from the banks accounted for 30 per cent of total external finance of LDCs in 1973; by 1979 it was around 60 per cent and by 1983 70 per cent. By far the biggest borrowers then were Mexico ($95bn) and Brazil ($90bn). These were followed by Argentina with $44bn of outstanding debt, South Korea with $40bn and Venezuela owing $34bn. However, the debt crisis which burst in the 1980s was the result not so much of the absolute weight of debt but of the steep increase in the cost of debt servicing relative to the borrowing countries' foreign exchange earnings from exports of goods and services and from current transfers. This **debt service ratio** (a common measure of the burden of debt) was still manageable by 1979—it had grown by then to 18 per cent from 15 per cent in 1973.

However, after 1980 the debt service ratio grew rapidly to a peak of 32 per cent in 1982—that means, remember, that nearly a third of the countries' current account earnings had to go on interest and loan repayments. There were two main causes. The first was the oil price shock of 1979/80. That benefited the oil producing debtors like Mexico and Venezuela but for the others the ensuing recession in the industrial countries meant another tumble in both volume and price of their primary product exports. The second factor was the steep rise in interest rates as the industrialised countries reacted to the inflationary effects of the second oil price shock by tightening their monetary policy. In 1981 short-term interest rates in the United States climbed to nearly 15 per cent from under 10 per cent in 1979 and around 5 per cent in 1976. The point is that a high proportion of bank loans to LDCs were at variable interest rates linked usually to rates in the money markets in New York or London. In addition, the $US exchange rate was pulled up by higher interest rates from 1981 with a corresponding increase in the domestic currency value of the outstanding debt. Finally, the drop in oil prices in 1982 slashed the export revenues of the oil producers leading to Mexico's announcement of inability to service its debt.

20.1.2 Responses to the debt crisis

The response of the banks and governments to the debt crisis was to treat it as a temporary liquidity problem. Once interest rates fell back and exports recovered Mexico and others, it was thought, would be able to resume normal debt servicing. In the meantime, they were offered new finance to enable them to go on making debt service payments if they agreed to changes in their economic policies which were intended to improve their longer-term credit-worthiness. Because the debt problem was seen as a balance of payments problem it was natural for the **International Monetary Fund** (IMF) to play a leading role. The IMF, based in Washington, was formed at the end of World War II specifically to assist its members with temporary payments (liquidity) problems. But the bridging loans given by the IMF are normally conditional on the borrower accepting an **economic adjustment programme** laid down and monitored by the Fund with the aim of improving the country's balance of payments. Once a conditional loan had been negotiated with the IMF the banks were prepared in turn to come to a **rescheduling agreement** with the debtor.

Rescheduling of debt has several ingredients. As the term implies, it usually means extending the period of repayment of loans. But in most agreements—about 70 in all since 1979—there is usually a deferral of or **moratorium** on all or part of debt servicing for a period. On top of that, most agreements have provided new finance, partly from the banks themselves and, of course, the IMF but also from the governments and central banks of the industrial countries. The debtor countries have thus been lent more money to enable them to service their existing debt! The total outstanding debt of the top 15 borrowers actually continued to rise from $260bn at the end of 1980 to $430bn at the end of 1986. For all countries the figure has soared to over $1,200bn in 1988.

Although this looks like throwing good money after bad, the lending banks and their governments really had little option in providing more finance. The alternative would have been default by a major debtor with the consequences we have already noted for the banking and monetary systems of the industrialised countries themselves. For their part, the debtor countries are reluctant to default for fear of being cut off indefinitely from the international capital markets. Peru, for example, came close to defaulting by rejecting an IMF adjustment programme and placing an upper limit on its debt-service payments in 1985 and announcing that it would pursue a policy of economic growth. The result has been no new funds from the banks and, while GDP growth was risen to 8 per cent in 1987, it was achieved by an expansion of the government's budget deficit and a consumer spending boom accompanied by a rise in inflation to over 100 per cent. The current account deficit drained the foreign exchange reserves. With no credit available, much foreign trade has to be conducted by barter while many foreign firms have withdrawn their investment. Default on loans is clearly not a solution to a country's debt problems.

As a result, many debtor countries have reluctantly accepted IMF adjustment programmes which typically lay down tight fiscal and monetary policies aimed at curbing inflationary demand pressures which the Fund tends to see as the root cause of the countries' payments deficits. The Fund often insists too on 'realistic' interest and exchange rate policies. The financial markets are often distorted by interest rates fixed below inflation rates; the resulting negative real rates of interest discourage saving and lending. Fixed exchange rates in some countries similarly may not have been adjusted to compensate for inflation so that the currency is severely overvalued making exports and import-competing goods uncompetitive. The Fund generally favours 'supply-side' policies with the elimination of these and other market distortions such as wage and price controls, subsidies, exchange and import restrictions.

TABLE 20.1   **Bank Debt and Debt/Export Ratios of biggest LDC Debtors**

	Outstanding bank debt end-1986 ($USbn)	Ratio of debt to exports (%)	
		1982	1987
Brazil	77.9	339	471
Mexico	77.3	299	366
Argentina	33.0	405	554
Venezuela	29.3	84	278
Philippines	15.4	269	309
Chile	13.9	333	370
Nigeria	11.0	84	310
Total (15 LDCs)	301.2	264	385

Implementation of this sort of policy has had some success in improving the trade balances of a number of countries. The biggest debtor countries together in fact ran a trade **surplus** from 1983 to 1986 despite another fall in their export earnings. The reason was an even steeper fall in imports from deflation of spending and devaluations which pushed up import prices. Yet, as shown in Table 20.1, the continued rise in debt and the fall of exports has forced up the ratio of outstanding debt to exports. In 1982 the ratio of debt to export earnings was 264 per cent; by 1987 it was 385 per cent. The trade surplus means that LDCs have been transferring real resources back to the industrialised countries. In some ways, therefore, the debt problem has got worse rather than better. This is because of persistent recession in many industrial economies, especially in Europe, which has held down demand for the LDCs' exports and then the great slump in the price of oil in 1986 which yet again plunged payments of the oil-producing debtors into deficit. In 1987, for example, the banks were forced to negotiate another agreement with Mexico involving rescheduling more than half of the debt of over $100bn, another $14bn in new funds and concessions on interest rates. One innovation was to make new lending contingent on the price of oil—Mexico's main export—and on the country's economic growth.

20.1.3 Solutions to the debt crisis

The approach of debt rescheduling combined with the imposition of adjustment programmes on debtor countries has not achieved a solution to the debt crisis. In 1988 the problem still rumbles on with continual threats of default from countries like Brazil and Argentina. The only long-term solution, failing a write-off of the debts by the banks, is the restoration of economic and especially export growth in the debtor countries. That in turn is dependent on an upturn of growth in the industrialised countries which are the principal markets for LDC exports.

But there is no shortage of other ideas for dealing with the debt crisis. One suggestion is **interest capping**—placing a ceiling on the interest rates on outstanding loans. If world interest rates went above the ceiling the excess would be capitalised as new loans. In 1985 US Treasury Secretary James Baker argued for a shift of emphasis from austerity to growth in the debtor countries which should be allowed to expand their debt still further to finance investment and export expansion. The **Baker Plan**, however, relied on certain assumptions, such as a revival of economic growth in the advanced countries, which have not been realised.

Another approach is to find forms of finance other than bank loans for debtor countries' investment. In particular, some banks and debtor countries have been arranging **debt-equity swaps**. Here, a corporation wishing to make an investment, say, in Mexico first buys debt at a price discounted from its face value—it pays, for example $10 million for $20 million of debt. The debt is swapped at Mexico's central bank into the local currency, pesos, and is then used to purchase a direct investment of equity. The great advantage of these debt-equity swaps is that banks are relieved of a part of their low-value loans and the debtor country of some of its debt-servicing burden. There are difficulties, though, especially the limited supply in debtor countries of projects in which foreign investors are willing to take a stake.

A final extreme solution is **forgiveness**, involving the effective writing-off of debt and compensation to the banks for their losses from their governments. The main objection is that costs would have to be borne by taxpayers in the industrialised countries. It is unlikely that any government would risk the electoral backlash from a policy which in effect bails out the banks. The banks in any case are already writing-off their loans to developing countries by putting aside a part of their profits each year into provision for bad debts. This looks sensible since realistically it is doubtful whether more than a small percentage of the LDC debts will ever be repaid. The debt problem looks like remaining as a threat to the international economy for some years to come.

20.2 UNEMPLOYMENT

Much of the second half of this book has been concerned, directly or indirectly, with the question of unemployment. In this section we pull together some of the threads of our earlier discussion to focus on the situation of the late 1980s, when (despite some recent improvement), unemployment remains very high by the standard of the twenty-five years following World War II. We discuss possible explanations of the level of unemployment, and some policies for reducing it.

20.2.1 Trends

As has been hinted before, measuring unemployment is a rather tricky business. Different countries do it in different ways: some, like the United Kingdom, by counting those who register as unemployed for the purpose of claiming welfare benefits; others, like the United States, by surveying a sample of the population to see who is seeking work. Within a country, there are changes over time in the definitions used. Since 1979, for example, the official UK definitions have been altered around twenty times, almost exclusively with the effect of reducing the official figure.

Therefore in order to make even reasonably accurate comparisons between countries and over time, it is necessary to adjust official figures and to use standardised definitions. This is done on a regular basis by the Organisation for Economic Cooperation and Development (OECD), and their estimates are used in Table 20.2. From these figures we can make a number of observations which are relevant to a discussion of current unemployment.

First, each of the seven leading Western economic powers had a higher unemployment rate in 1987 than in 1974, despite the fact that in any particular year they show considerable differences in the extent of unemployment.

Secondly, although we have a rising trend over the whole period (and in the case of France an increase in every year shown), there are two periods when unemployment has grown particularly rapidly in most countries; after the first and second big oil price increases in 1974 and 1979 respectively.

TABLE 20.2 **Standardised Unemployment Rates in seven major Economies, 1974–87 Per cent of total labour force**

Year	USA	Japan	W Germany	France	UK	Italy	Canada
1974	5.5	1.4	1.6	2.8	2.9	5.3	5.3
1975	8.3	1.9	3.6	4.0	4.3	5.8	6.9
1976	7.6	2.0	3.7	4.4	5.6	6.6	7.1
1977	6.9	2.0	3.6	4.9	6.1	7.0	8.0
1978	6.0	2.2	3.5	5.2	5.9	7.1	8.3
1979	5.8	2.1	3.2	5.9	5.0	7.6	7.4
1980	7.0	2.0	3.0	6.3	6.4	7.5	7.4
1981	7.5	2.2	4.4	7.4	9.8	8.3	7.5
1982	9.5	2.4	6.1	8.1	11.3	9.0	10.9
1983	9.5	2.6	8.0	9.3	12.5	9.8	11.8
1984	7.4	2.7	7.0	9.7	11.7	10.2	11.2
1985	7.1	2.6	7.2	10.2	11.2	10.5	10.4
1986	6.9	2.8	7.0	10.4	11.1	n.a.	9.5
1987	5.9*	2.8*	7.0*	10.8*	9.8*	n.a.	8.8*

n.a. = not available

* = 3rd quarter of year

Source: OECD

Thirdly, we can observe some significant changes in the 'ranking' of different countries over time. In the United Kingdom there has been a tendency, not surprisingly, to emphasise the particularly poor performance of the British economy, where unemployment reached the highest level amongst the leading nations in the early 1980s (although its position has improved both absolutely and relatively since then). But there have been other, perhaps more startling deteriorations in performance, notably that of West Germany. At the beginning of the period West Germany, still enjoying its postwar 'economic miracle', had an unemployment rate approximately the same as Japan, but whereas Japan has consistently maintained the lowest unemployment rate of the seven, West Germany's position has significantly deteriorated.

A final point of interest is the recent behaviour of the United States unemployment rate. From having the highest unemployment rate of the group in 1974, the United States now has the second lowest. What is particularly interesting is that in 1982–83, when unemployment everywhere else was rising, the United States was able to buck the trend. Over the next few years American unemployment was to fall very rapidly while it was still rising in other countries.

20.2.2 Demand factors

Twenty years ago, the question of unemployment was largely discussed in the context of the Keynesian model, where insufficient aggregate demand was seen as the major problem. Nowadays, as we have seen, this view is out of fashion. Certainly, given the high rates of inflation we saw in many countries in the 1970s and early 1980s, it seems difficult to argue that insufficient spending was a problem. Nevertheless, we should not totally dismiss the role of aggregate demand.

The figures we have just looked at suggest that demand does play a part. We observed that unemployment rose steeply in most countries after the OPEC-inspired oil price increases. Partly this is explicable in supply-side terms, for higher costs affect the willingness of firms to supply output, but it also has an aggregate demand dimension. The oil price rises resulted (as we saw in 20.1) in a massive diversion of spending power from the oil-using countries to the oil producers, who were unable to 'recycle' it sufficiently rapidly (ie, increase their spending sufficiently to compensate for the fall in spending by oil users) to maintain aggregate demand on the world scale.

Furthermore, we can point to specific instances when macroeconomic policy, acting on aggregate demand, almost certainly had a big impact. In the United Kingdom in 1980–81, the government operated a tight fiscal policy, cutting the budget deficit, and attempted a tight monetary policy. Furthermore, the advent of North Sea Oil, together with higher interest rates, led to a high exchange rate, with the result that United Kingdom exports fell away and imports rose. The net result of all this was a fall in effective demand and a huge leap in unemployment.

The British government believed that there was 'no alternative' to its policy, which was designed to squeeze inflation out of the system. According to monetarists and New Classicals, such a policy should only cause short-term unemployment (if that, in the New Classical case) while inflationary expectations fall. However, unemployment in the UK was rather more long-lasting than anticipated.

This suggests that a more gentle programme of disinflation, coupled with an exchange rate policy which tried to moderate the rise in the value of the pound, could have avoided the much higher rates of unemployment experienced in the United Kingdom than elsewhere. The management of demand does appear to have an effect.

This does not necessarily mean, of course, that reversing policy would immediately restore the status quo. Unfortunately, if the economy is operating at unemployment rates higher than the NAIRU (one interpretation of the United Kingdom's experience in the 1980s) for very long, the NAIRU itself will start to rise. This is because when workers are unemployed for very long their skills and morale deteriorate, making them less attractive to potential employers; moreover factories are closed and machinery is scrapped. All this means that less output is likely to be supplied, and less labour demanded, in equilibrium.

Critics of the management of the United Kingdom economy in the 1980s have pointed to the experience of the American economy as an example of what could have occurred if a different policy had been followed. They observe that under President Reagan the United States government ran an enormous budget deficit in the face of a recession—surely a Keynesian measure, even though put forward by an administration nominally dedicated (as we saw in Chapter 17) to 'supply-side' measures! However, the much greater size and importance of the United States in the world economy means it can get away with policies which would plunge the United Kingdom into a balance of payments crisis. (Although even the United States can only do so for a time; the Stock Market crash of Autumn 1987 is widely understood to have been triggered by investors' apprehension about the conduct of American macroeconomic policy.)

20.2.3   The supply side: labour market rigidity

We have seen in Chapter 17 how monetarist and New Classical economists see the problem of unemployment as largely a 'supply-side' question. Their focus is on factors affecting the microeconomic demand for and supply of labour. Here we elaborate further on some of the themes we have touched on earlier in the book.

To begin with, we ought to say something about **technological unemployment**. Many non-economists feel that the rapid pace of technological advance, with computer-controlled machinery increasingly doing work which was previously performed by people, is the ultimate cause of unemployment. This accounts for the often-expressed view that in the future there will not be enough work to go round, and we must of necessity get used to lifestyles where there is a much larger component of enforced 'leisure' and many fewer full-time jobs.

In company with most economists, we reject this view. Firstly, because similar forecasts have been made in the past, for example when technological change in agriculture in the first half of the nineteenth century made millions of British farmworkers' jobs disappear. In the long run, technological change increases output, incomes and the demand for new types of goods and services; new areas of employment are generated. We see no reason to believe that this process has come to a halt. As we saw in Chapter 1, the demand for better standards of living and the goods and services to support them is far from satiated. The experience of the United States in the last few years supports this view; millions of new jobs have been created and unemployment has fallen back to the level of the early 1970s.

Secondly, the jobs lost in countries like the United Kingdom in the 1980s cannot reasonably be put down to technological change, but rather to a mixture of factors such as loss of price competitiveness because of inappropriate exchange rates, increasing competition from newly-industrialising countries, cuts in public spending and so on. One United Kingdom study of the recession of the early 1980s suggested that only about 5 per cent of job losses could be put down to technological factors. Finally, it is instructive to see from Table 20.2 that the country which most observers consider to have been most technologically dynamic in the 1970s and 1980s—Japan—has also been the economy which continues to have the lowest unemployment rate.

Technological change does present a challenge to an economy, of course. Together with changes in raw material prices, labour availabilities and shifts in patterns of demand for final output it creates a requirement for structural adjustment, for the movement of resources (including, most importantly in this context, labour) out of declining industries and geographical locations into those which are expanding.

Much discussion about the causes of unemployment has concentrated on **labour market rigidity**. In this view, technological and other changes require a flexible labour market. Elements of flexibility include variability of pay, both in absolute terms and in relativities between groups and between areas, willingness of workers to move between locations and jobs, willingness to retrain by workers and the availability of facilities for them to do so.

Taking **pay** first. It has been claimed that the United Kingdom's exceptional vulnerability to unemployment in the 1980s is related to the way in which pay increases continued to outstrip price increases in the recession, thus increasing unit labour costs. Moreover, wage relativities between regions remained roughly constant despite different parts of the country facing very different levels of demand for labour. By contrast, United States wages seem to have been more flexible, with groups of workers taking substantial pay cuts during the recession where jobs were threatened, rather than existing relativities being maintained. In Japan, the existence of an element of profit-linked pay through bonus systems played a rather similar role in reducing the rigidity of labour's remuneration. It is possible to exaggerate the significance of wage rigidity in the United Kingdom, for there are other systems—for example, the variability of the proportion of overtime worked—which introduce some element of responsiveness to market conditions. Nevertheless it is important to give some attention to this.

Another aspect of rigidity is the difficulty of **redeploying labour** from job to job. In Japan, the system of 'lifetime' employment by which male workers stay with (and are very loyal to) one employer for most of their working lives, carries with it the willingness by workers to switch from job to job within companies. A system of trade unionism based on the firm rather than the craft or the industry (as is often the case in the United Kingdom) assists this process. In the United Kingdom and other European countries, unions have not been so cooperative, although this has been changing recently. Critics of the trade union movement, such as New Classical Professor Patrick Minford (see unions) as we have noted before, as a major source of rigidities in the labour market. They point to the way in which the United States, with a unionisation rate half that of the United Kingdom, has been much more successful in redeploying labour in the 1980s.

Another area where there are differences between countries is in the **welfare benefits system**. As we have seen, benefits are considered by 'supply-siders' to have a significant impact on the NAIRU by affecting the willingness of people to work and the effort they put into search in the labour market. This is an important potential source of rigidity. The level of benefits relative to the earnings which people can earn in work is relevant here; so is the rigour with which rules on eligibility are applied. Critics of the United Kingdom system have pointed to the rise in benefits relative to after-tax earnings which occurred in the late 1970s, and to the fact that the rules concerning eligibility were more liberally interpreted in this period; this, they claim encouraged workers to remain unemployed longer. There is probably some truth in this. The average spell of unemployment is much longer in the United Kingdom and West Germany, where benefits are extended to the unemployed indefinitely, than in the United States where a childless man who has been out of work for more than six months receives no benefit. However this cannot explain everything about unemployment. Welfare benefits in the UK have been getting steadily less attractive relative to after-tax earnings in the 1980s without unemployment falling back to its mid-1970s level.

The ability of people to switch from job to job is increased by providing adequate retraining facilities, and there has been a considerable expansion of these in most countries in the 1980s. Perhaps more fundamentally, though, the **basic education and training** received by people before they enter the labour market may determine their attitudes and aptitudes over many years. Recently much attention has concentrated on this in the United Kingdom. It has been pointed out that over half British school leavers have no significant educational qualification, that the school curriculum pays insufficient attention to vocational training, and that the United Kingdom has a smaller proportion of the relevant age group entering higher education than any leading developed country. Unfavourable contrasts can be drawn with Japan, where education is afforded much higher priority than in the United Kingdom. On the other hand, it is difficult to argue that education and training are panaceas. The United States spends about the same proportion of its national income on education as the United Kingdom and has educational problems which are perceived in the United States as being at least as great as those of the British (including a high level of illiteracy and a substantial proportion of the population for whom English is a second language); yet, as we have seen, unemployment appears to be less of a problem.

Some see the whole issue as being essentially one of attitudes. As we have seen earlier, it has been argued that what the United Kingdom and some other European countries require is a much greater awareness of the '**enterprise culture**', the willingness to think commercially, to take risks and have a spirit of independence and responsibility for yourself and your family. There are currently attempts being made to introduce such ideas in schools and colleges in the UK. If successful, another aspect of labour market rigidity will presumably be reduced.

20.2.4   Policy

We have seen, then, that unemployment is a major economic problem for most developed countries. The causes of the high level of unemployment in the 1980s are complex. Although there are common factors in many countries, it is clear that the experience of different countries has been sufficiently variable for it to be possible to learn from the experience of the more successful economies.

A policy for unemployment in the late 1980s and 1990s must be one which is appropriate to the country involved and the times in which we live. For a variety of reasons, we have seen in this book that there cannot be a return to a simple-minded Keynesian policy of pumping extra spending power into the economy. However, we cannot afford to neglect aggregate demand and assume that it is irrelevant to the determination of employment. Rather, we need to ensure that there is sufficient aggregate demand available (even if this implies some inflation) to smooth the transition back to higher levels of employment. Attempts to disinflate economies too rapidly, as in the UK in the early 1980s, can have a disastrous effect on unemployment.

In saying this, we are implying that some selective expansion of demand may be appropriate, particularly when combined with relevant measures to improve the supply-side responses of the economy. Thus a certain amount of public expenditure on repairing and improving the infrastructure of roads, schools, hospitals and sewers, particularly in regions of high unemployment, using technologies with a low import content and using a relatively large amount of labour may make sense, doubly so if simultaneously measures are being undertaken to reform the tax and benefit systems to make work an attractive option. What we do not want to go back to is blanket reflation of the economy through large pay increases for public sector workers or wasteful government expenditure on costly 'high-tech' projects like Concorde, which do little for overall employment and tie up workers and other resources who could be used elsewhere.

The precise mixture of supply-side measures to be used need not be spelt out here; we have suggested in this chapter and in Chapter 17 the range of possibilities from which governments of different political complexions will choose in the coming years.

SELF-TEST QUESTIONS

1   Which of the following was not a reason why LDCs expanded their borrowing from banks in the 1970s?

(a) There was a fall in export earnings from most primary commodities as industrial countries went into recession.

(b) Banks offered cheap, subsidised loans.

(c) Oil producers needed an outlet for their investment funds.

(d) LDC governments did not want to borrow from other governments.

(e) The rise in oil prices raised the cost of imports to most LDCs.

2   Which of the following would probably not relieve the debt problems faced by LDCs?

(a) A rise in world interest rates.

(b) An upturn in the export earnings of LDCs.

(c) A fall in world interest rates.

(d) An expansion of debt-equity swaps.

(e) An improvement in the terms of trade of LDCs.

3   Which of the following statements is correct?

(a) A further rise in oil prices would not benefit any LDCs.

(b) The biggest debtor countries had a trade deficit from 1983 to 1986.

(c) In 1987, Mexico had the largest ratio of debts to exports among LDCs.

(d) The Baker Plan proposed that in no circumstances should LDCs be allowed to expand their borrowing.

(e)   International Monetary Fund adjustment programmes tend to impose tight monetary controls.

4   Which of the following statements is not correct?

(a)   France's unemployment rate grew faster than that of Japan from 1974–87.

(b)   The USA had a higher unemployment rate than West Germany from 1974–85.

(c)   The UK had a higher unemployment rate than Italy throughout the period 1974–85.

(d)   France's unemployment rate rose every year throughout the period 1974–87.

(e)   Throughout the period 1974–87, Canada had a higher unemployment rate than West Germany.

5   With which of the following statements would you expect most economists to agree?

(a)   Technological change is the main cause of the recent rise in unemployment.

(b)   There is a very strong case for a general reflation of aggregate demand on Keynesian lines.

(c)   If an economy remains above its NAIRU for a long time, the NAIRU will fall.

(d)   The tax and benefit system in the UK encourages unemployed workers to seek jobs much more quickly than their American counterparts.

(e)   There is no single policy to reduce unemployment which will be equally effective in all countries.

EXERCISE

Why has unemployment in the 1980s been so much higher than in the 1960s?

Answers on page 273.

Solutions to questions

Solutions to Chapter 1 questions

ANSWERS TO SELF-TEST QUESTIONS

1 (b)   **4** (e)
2 (c)   **5** (c)
3 (a)

MODEL ANSWER TO EXERCISE

The notion of consumer sovereignty arises in a competitive market economy in which it is argued that consumers or households are able to use their purchasing power to determine the allocation of resources to the production of different goods and services. Thus, in a pure market economy in which all goods and services are bought and sold in free and competitive markets, consumers allocate their spending among the many products available in order to maximise their satisfaction from consumption. A primary consideration is the relative prices of different goods.

Suppose we have an initial position of general equilibrium with the quantity supplied of every good just equal to the quantity demanded by consumers. Then imagine there is a change in consumer preferences, for example, households reduce consumption of butter because of newly discovered health risks. At the present price, producers' output is excessive relative to the lower quantity demanded. In a competitive market the excess supply will lead to a fall in price and reduced profits for butter producers. Some may reduce output and others will give up butter production completely. In either case, resources will be shifted out of butter into more profitable products such as margarine. In a competitive market system, therefore, the price mechanism will ensure that the pattern of production continually adapts to changing consumer preferences. Moreover, competition between producers will lead to goods being produced with maximum efficiency and at prices which reflect the lowest costs of production to the benefit of consumers.

In reality this ideal outcome from consumer sovereignty is upset by various market imperfections. Particularly important is the existence of large corporations operating as monopolies or in oligopolistic markets. These firms, it is said, may abuse their market power to the detriment of consumer sovereignty in several ways:

(a)   They may use their power to raise prices above competitive levels. Consumers will lose the benefit of lowest-cost prices and part of their income is effectively transferred to the corporation which earns excessive profits and returns on capital.

(b)   Without competitive pressures, the firm may operate inefficiently with over-staffing and with poor standards of quality control and customer service. The firm may neglect product development and innovation and restrict product choice.

(c)   As American economist, J K Galbraith, argues, large corporations, often operating on a global scale as multi-national enterprises, may attempt to manipulate and distort consumer preferences by advertising and other sales promotion. Because of the heavy cost and risk involved in developing, producing and marketing products on a large scale the corporation will want to guarantee the largest possible sales as far ahead as it can. The corporation thus has an incentive to exploit consumers' ignorance about competing products by using advertising to increase demand and even to create wants which did not previously exist. In the extreme, therefore, we may have 'producer sovereignty' in which large firms first decide what they will produce and then shape the pattern of consumer preferences by advertising to match the predetermined pattern of production.

However, it is easy to take these claims to excess. It is doubtful how far consumers can be persuaded to go on buying products which patently do not satisfy genuine wants. In practice, many large firms with apparent market power encounter effective competition from potential entry if they make excessive profits and from substitute products satisfying similar consumer wants. Also, consumer associations in many countries are effective in disseminating information about competing products and in countering dubious or even false advertising claims.

Solutions to Chapter 2 questions

ANSWERS TO SELF-TEST QUESTIONS

1 (e)   **4** (b)
2 (e)   **5** (c)
3 (c)

MODEL ANSWER TO EXERCISE

The effects of rent controls can be examined with the aid of a supply-and-demand diagram such as the one below. This simplifies by assuming that rented accommodation is homogeneous while it shows both a short-run supply curve, along which the quantity of housing is relatively price-inelastic, and a more elastic long-run supply curve. In a free market, the equilibrium rent is P_1, and the amount of housing demanded and supplied is M_1. Suppose the government now imposes a maximum rent at P_2, below the market-clearing price.

Clearly, existing tenants will benefit from the reduction in rent but this will induce an increase in the quantity demanded down and along the demand curve to M_3. Similarly, at the lower rent landlords now obtain a smaller return on capital so that, as tenancies expire, they will withdraw property from the privately-let housing market. In the short run, quantity supplied therefore falls to M_2. The result is excess demand for rented housing equal to M_2M_3.

Rented housing—supply and demand

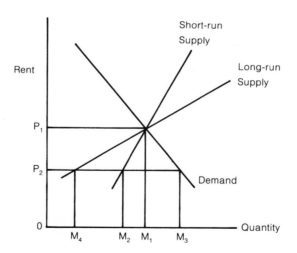

Rent control thus creates a market shortage of rented housing and the need for some system of rationing out the reduced quantity available. In the absence of official rationing and allocation of housing by the government, landlords themselves will have to operate an informal rationing system, allocating vacant tenancies, for example, by such means as 'first-come-first-served' or by discriminating against certain kinds of prospective tenants, like those with children. Also, depending on how strictly the controls are enforced and the severity of penalties for evading them, we can expect a 'black market' to emerge in which landlords collude with tenants to charge rents effectively higher than the legal maximum by such devices as 'key money' and exorbitant prices for furniture and fittings.

In the longer term the excess demand is likely to increase as landlords take more and more property out of the rented housing market—the long-run supply curve will be more elastic. The quantity supplied falls away to M_4 and excess demand expands to M_4M_3. Some houses will be sold for owner-occupation and others for commercial and industrial redevelopment. Landlords who are unable to get rid of controlled property are unlikely to maintain it properly as it depreciates. Rent controls are usually imposed together with legislation to give security of tenure to tenants. But this may not be enough to prevent some landlords from harassing or bribing their tenants to induce them to give up their controlled tenancies so that the property can be transferred to more profitable uses.

Solutions to Chapter 3 questions

ANSWERS TO SELF-TEST QUESTIONS

1 (a)   **4** (d)
2 (e)   **5** (d)
3 (b)

MODEL ANSWER TO EXERCISE

1 Primary commodities are agricultural and mineral products many of which are traded, sometimes internationally, in highly competitive markets. That in itself is a major factor in the unstable prices of many commodities. Since prices are determined in relatively free and competitive markets they tend to change swiftly in response to shifts in supply and demand. By contrast, manufactured goods are often produced in much less competitive industries where individual firms have a greater degree of control over the prices of their products. They may therefore hold prices stable even after substantial changes in costs or demand, particularly when they believe the changes to be only temporary.

    However, even in competitive markets the degree of price instability is influenced by the price elasticity of demand and supply. Price will change after shifts in demand or supply but the extent of the price change depends on the size of the relevant price elasticity. Take first a shift in demand—suppose there is an increase in demand shown by a shift to the right of the demand curve from D_1 to D_2:

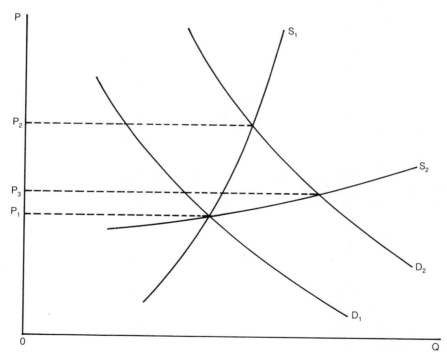

    There are two possible situations. If supply is inelastic, as along S_1, the industry cannot easily respond to the rise in demand and there is a relatively large increase in price from P_1 to P_2. This is typical in many primary producing industries, especially in the short run. With agricultural products an immediate rise in output is usually ruled out by the 'gestation period'

J

in growing crops and raising livestock. In mining, new investment may be necessary to raise production significantly.

The other possibility is that supply is relatively elastic, as along S_2. The industry can comparatively easily expand output and there is only a comparatively small rise in price to P_3. This situation may be more characteristic of manufacturing industries, particularly if they were already operating with spare capacity. Output can then be increased quickly by the existing labour force working overtime, taking on extra workers and buying in more materials.

There are similar possibilities when supply shifts. Suppose there is an increase in supply shown by the shift to the right of the supply curve:

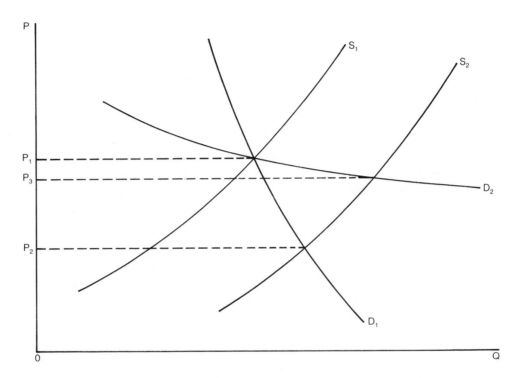

If demand is inelastic as on D_1, the rise in supply will only be absorbed with a relatively large fall in price from P_1 to P_2. If demand is elastic along D_2, however, consumers need only a relatively small fall in price to P_3 to induce them to take up the extra supply. Thus, after a given shift in supply the price change is greater the less elastic is demand. Inelastic demand may well be a contributory factor to the widely fluctuating prices for some commodities. Demand may be inelastic, particularly in the short term, for some raw materials with no close substitutes or for staple foods which take up a large proportion of consumers' incomes. Also, the supply of agricultural products tends to be inherently unstable because of uncertain weather conditions, crop diseases and so on which are outside the control of producers. The resulting price change will be magnified when demand is inelastic.

Solutions to Chapter 4 questions

ANSWERS TO SELF-TEST QUESTIONS

1 (b)
2 (c)
3 (e)

4 (a)
5 (c)

MODEL ANSWER TO EXERCISE

The notion of consumer surplus is derived from the principle of diminishing marginal utility which states that the greater the quantity consumed of a good the less is the additional satisfaction (utility) derived from consuming one more unit of the good. This implies that a consumer will attach a higher value to the first unit of a good consumed than to subsequent units and is therefore willing to pay more for the first units than for later units. In short, the marginal willingness to pay (MWP) (the amount the consumer is prepared to pay for one more unit) declines as the quantity consumed increases. This is shown in the diagram which assumes that consumption of, say, orange juice can be varied in very small amounts at a time so that a smooth MWP curve can be drawn.

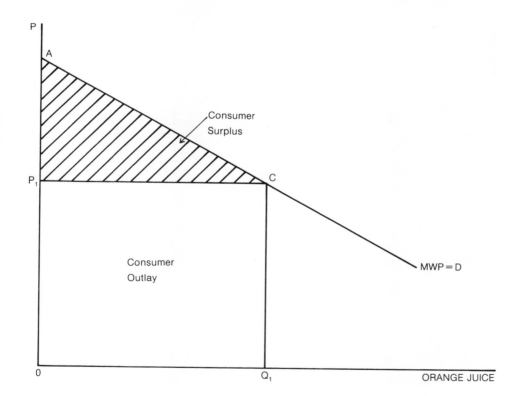

Suppose the price of orange juice is P_1. This is the cost of acquiring one more unit—the marginal cost to the consumer. In turn, the consumer will gain net satisfaction from each unit consumed so long as the MWP is greater than price or marginal cost. Thus, net satisfaction increases as consumption is expanded from zero to Q_1. Any units purchased after that will lead to a decline in net utility because the price is greater than MWP. The MWP curve is therefore equivalent to the consumer's demand curve showing the quantity demanded at each price. At P_1 the consumer buys Q_1 at a total cost of $P_1 \times Q_1 = $ rectangle OP_1CQ_1.

The total amount the consumer would be prepared to pay for Q_1—the total willingness to pay (TWP)—is found by adding up the MWP for all units consumed up to Q_1. TWP is thus measured by the area beneath the MWP curve up to $Q_1(OACQ_1)$. TWP represents the consumer's valuation of Q_1. If we deduct the rectangle measuring the total cost of that amount we are left with a surplus of utility which is not paid for—the triangular area P_1AC. When a uniform price is charged, therefore, consumers gain surplus satisfaction over and above the cost of acquiring any given quantity.

Producers can sometimes exploit this consumer surplus by price discrimination (charging different prices to different consumers or to the same consumer for different quantities). Price discrimination is only possible when producers can prevent resale of their product bought at lower prices to consumers who are being charged higher prices. If this is possible, the orange juice supplier could in principle appropriate the whole of the consumer surplus by charging up to OA for the first unit and then gradually reducing price down to P_1 for the last unit at Q_1.

In reality, price discrimination cannot be operated so precisely but producers do gain part at least of consumer surplus by such practices as quantity discounts—£2 for the first unit, £1.80 each for two, £1.60 for three, and so on. An entry fee into a golf club or the fixed charge for gas and electricity reflects the high marginal valuation placed on the first units consumed of most goods. Also, price discrimination between consumers allows producers to exploit the different MWP or demand curves of different consumers. A theatre may offer cheap seats to pensioners and students because typically their MWP is smaller for any given quantity and their demand curves are more elastic. When price discrimination is possible therefore producers increase their revenue by charging a higher price to groups with less elastic demand (for a given quantity their MWP is higher) than to groups whose demand is more elastic.

Solutions to Chapter 5 questions

ANSWERS TO SELF-TEST QUESTIONS

1   (e)
2   (c)
3   (c)

4   (b)
5   (c)

MODEL ANSWER TO EXERCISE

The distinction between fixed and variable costs arises only in the short run period defined as that in which at least one factor of production is in fixed supply to the firm. Productive capacity is therefore constrained by the fixed factor and the costs associated with it are the firm's fixed costs. Typically, the fixed factor is the firm's physical capital or assets—its premises, machinery, plant and equipment. Fixed costs thus tend to consist of rental payments or, where the assets are owned, the cost is measured as the opportunity cost of the assets—the rental value of the assets in alternative uses. Fixed costs must be met in the short run whether the firm stays in business or not.

Variable costs are those associated with variable inputs of factors such as labour and materials. These costs will increase as the firm expands its output and they can be avoided completely, even in the short run, by closing down. The diagram is a generalised illustration of a firm's short run costs.

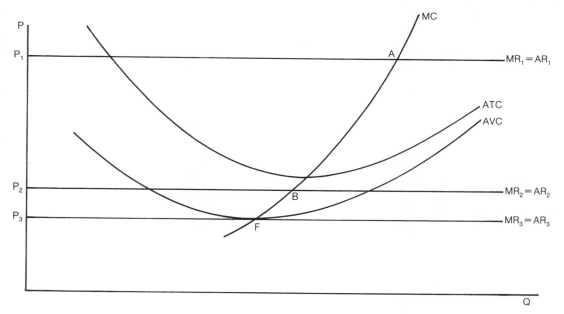

Average variable cost (AVC) is the cost of the variable inputs per unit of output. The AVC curve is U-shaped because AVC will increase at some output (F in the diagram) as a result of diminishing marginal productivity of the variable factors. This is reflected in the rising marginal cost (MC) curve which cuts AVC at its minimum point, F. The average total cost (ATC) is found for any output by adding average fixed cost (AFC) to AVC. Since total fixed cost is constant it is spread over more and more units of output as output expands. AFC therefore gets smaller as output rises as shown by the narrowing vertical distance between AVC and ATC. The MC curve cuts the AVC and the ATC curves at their minimum points.

If the firm is in a competitive industry it must take the market price as given. The price is the firm's average revenue (AR) and also its marginal revenue (MR)—the extra revenue from one more unit of output. If price is above minimum ATC, for example, at P_1, the firm can clearly more than cover its total costs. It maximises profit when $MC = MR$ at point A. Since the firm is making super-normal profits there is no question of closing down.

Suppose price falls to P_2, below minimum ATC but above minimum AVC. The firm can no longer cover its total costs but minimise losses by equating MR with MC at point B. Here, AR is greater than AVC so that revenue still more than covers variable costs. This surplus over variable costs will contribute to the fixed costs which must be met in the short run. It thus pays the firm to stay in business because by doing so it minimises its losses. It will close down in the long run when it is able to rid itself of the fixed costs, for instance, when leases expire or it can sell its assets.

But, if the price drops below P_3, equal to minimum AVC, the firm should close down in the short run. AR is now less than AVC at all outputs so that revenue cannot cover even the variable costs. These can be avoided by closing down and losses will then be restricted to the fixed costs. Generally, fixed costs are irrelevant in short-run close-down decisions. The only consideration in the short run is whether revenue is sufficient to cover the avoidable variable costs.

Solutions to Chapter 6 questions

ANSWERS TO SELF-TEST QUESTIONS

1   (a)
2   (d)
3   (b)

4   (b)
5   (d)

MODEL ANSWER TO EXERCISE

Product differentiation is a form of non-price competition in which a firm attempts to establish in the minds of consumers that its own brand of a product is superior to its competitors' products. If successful, the firm will be able to charge a higher price than its rivals and gain market power, reflected in a downward-sloping demand curve for its product. This contrasts with the perfectly elastic demand curve faced by each firm in perfect competition where firms produce a homogeneous product. Each firm is then a price taker. The firm with a differentiated product has some control over its price and, like a monopolist, can set price to maximise profits. This can be seen in the model of monopolistic competition where there are large numbers of firms producing differentiated products. But the model also assumes free entry so that any super-normal profits attract new firms to drive long-run profits to the normal level:

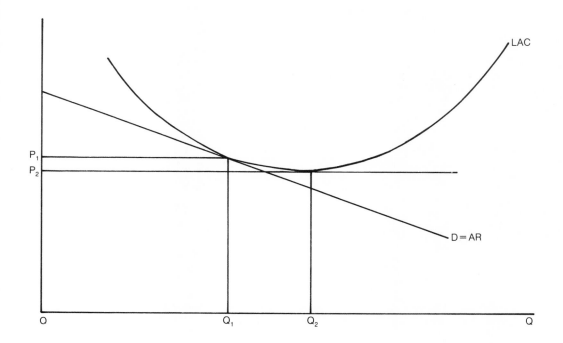

In the long run the representative firm's demand or average revenue (AR) curve is shifted down and to the left until it is tangent to its long-run average cost (LAC) curve. The firm produces Q_1 which it sells at the price P_1. This leads to the notion of 'excess capacity' in monopolistic competition. Under perfect competition with no product differentiation the long-run equilibrium output would be Q_2 with price P_2 equal to minimum LAC. The implication is that product differentiation results in an inefficient allocation of resources with a lower output and a higher price than under perfect competition. Consumers therefore lose from the higher price paid because of product differentiation.

However, the analysis fails to capture the possible benefits of product differentiation to consumers. Two kinds of differentiation can be distinguished:

1   **Contrived or artificial differentiation** Here, the firm's product is essentially the same as its competitors' but it differentiates its own brand by means of advertising, packaging and other forms of sales promotion. An example is a firm selling branded aspirins with an identical composition to unbranded generic aspirins sold much more cheaply. If product differentiation is purely contrived, the advertising and other marketing costs can reasonably be regarded as a waste of resources and the conclusions from the model of monopolistic competition apply.

2   **Real differentiation** Differentiation, however, is rarely wholly artificial. If it were, consumers would eventually discover that they have needlessly been paying higher prices and give up the branded product. Successful product differentiation invariably relies on at least some degree of real differences between firms' products, for example, in style, design, colour and even in packaging which might be more convenient to the consumer. Firms find real product differentiation profitable because consumer preferences differ. Preferences for, say, TV sets may well be clustered around a particular screen size but there may be large minority groups of consumers who prefer bigger or smaller screens. Some firms can profit by catering for these minority tastes while they may differentiate their products in other ways such as improved sound quality and sophisticated remote controls.

These real product differences increase product choice for consumers who would mostly be worse off if there was only one standard product available. Moreover, consumers benefit over time from non-price competition because it leads to product improvement and innovation. On the whole, therefore, consumers are likely to benefit from product differentiation except in the probably less frequent cases of contrived differentiation.

Solutions to Chapter 7 questions

ANSWERS TO SELF-TEST QUESTIONS

1 (c)   **4** (e)
2 (c)   **5** (c)
3 (a)

MODEL ANSWER TO EXERCISE

The conclusion that monopoly results in inefficient resource allocation is usually based on a comparison between the long-run equilibrium position of a profit-maximising monopoly and that of a perfectly competitive industry.

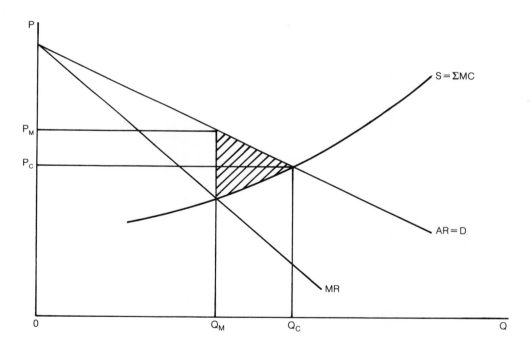

Under perfect competition, the industry's supply curve is the sum of the long-run marginal cost (MC) curves of the individual firms. Every firm accepts the market price, P_C, determined at the intersection of the supply and demand curves. The equilibrium price-output combination is therefore P_C and Q_C. This is said to be socially optimal because MC is equated to price which in turn is equal to consumers' marginal valuation of the good. Any deviation from Q_C would lead to a loss of welfare.

Under monopoly, the market demand curve is now the single firm's average revenue (AR) curve and marginal revenue is now less than AR. Profits are maximised where $MR = MC$ at the output Q_M for which the monopoly charges a price P_M. This price, equal to consumers' marginal valuation, is now greater than MC so that consumers will gain an increase in net welfare from an increase in output up to Q_C. The shaded area shows the deadweight burden—the social cost from inefficient resource allocation—of monopolising the industry.

The analysis suggests that social welfare would be increased by breaking up the monopoly into a large number of competing firms. In practice, however, the analysis is subject to severe qualifications:

1   It is unlikely to be practicable to break up one firm into large numbers of small firms. More likely, the result would be an oligopoly with no necessary improvement in social welfare.

2   The monopoly may have lower costs because of economies of scale. If so, the monopoly's MC curve would lie below that for the competitive industry and, conceivably, to such an extent that the monopoly price is lower and the output higher than under competition. There would be particular problems with breaking up a natural monopoly where the scale economies are so large that the market will support only one firm.

3   The monopoly may not be a profit-maximiser. It may face potential entry which forces it to hold price and output close to the competitive level. The same threat of entry may also lead to a high level of research and development and product improvement and differentiation as a deterrent to new entrants. This may be to the benefit of consumers.

Of course, other qualifications may strengthen the case against monopoly. Its costs may be higher, not lower, than competitive firms, particularly when it is protected by legal barriers to entry, such as patents, or if it is a nationalised industry. With the threat of competition removed, the monopoly is likely to suffer from 'X-inefficiency' where managers fail to produce with minimum cost. They may opt for a quiet life by allowing over-staffing and poor quality and poor customer service. Whatever the case, though, it is clear that the standard comparison of monopoly and perfect competition is too simplistic; policy towards real-world monopolies must be decided on a case-by-case approach.

Solutions to Chapter 8 questions

ANSWERS TO SELF-TEST QUESTIONS

1 (e)
2 (c)
3 (b)

4 (e)
5 (e)

MODEL ANSWER TO EXERCISE

Consider first the effect of forming a union in a competitive industry with a previously competitive labour market.

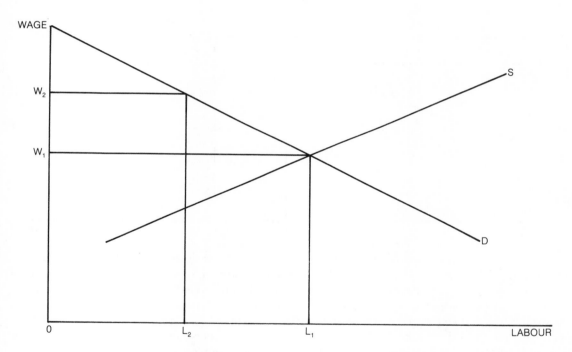

Before unionisation the competitive wage is W_1 and employment is at L_1. Assume that the union is then formed with complete 'monopoly' control over the supply of labour. The main constraint on the union's ability to raise the wage is the demand curve for labour. This is assumed to be downward-sloping so that a rise in the wage to, say, W_2 results in a fall in employment. The union must trade off higher wages against lower employment. Which wage the union chooses will depend partly on the union's goals. If its aim is to maximise union membership it may not push up the wage at all. If it wants to maximise the total income of its employed members the wage should be fixed where the elasticity of demand for labour is equal to unity.

Given the union's trade-off between wages and employment, the fall in employment for any wage rise will be less, the less elastic is the demand for labour. This will be so:

1 the less elastic is the demand for the industry's product. In industries subject to competition from substitute products therefore the union's ability to raise wages may be limited.
2 the more difficult it is to substitute other factors such as machines for labour. This may be so in industries which are already highly capital intensive.

3   the smaller the contribution of wages of unionised workers to the total costs of the industry. If the union, for example, represents a small group of skilled workers it may be able to push up wages more than a union representing the main body of workers in the industry.

However, unions may be difficult to organise in competitive industries with large numbers of small employers, possibly using a high ratio of casual workers, such as in agriculture and catering. Unionisation may be easier in monopolistic or oligopolistic industries, but there is then more likely to be collective bargaining of wages between the union on the one hand and an employers' association or the monopsony employer of labour on the other. A single buyer (monopsony) of labour faces an upward sloping supply curve and the marginal labour cost (MLC) (the cost of employing one more worker) is greater than the wage.

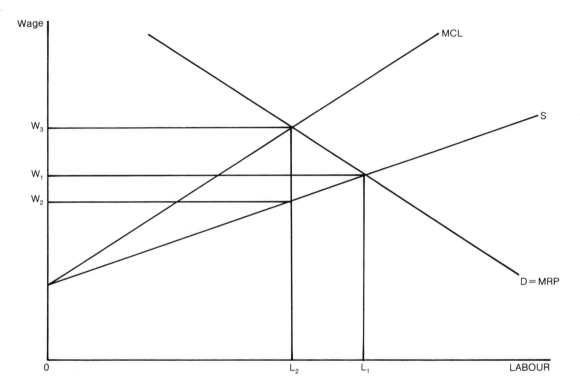

With no union, the monopsony firm maximises profits by equating MLC with MRP of labour at employment L_2 and paying the wage W_2. This is less than the competitive wage W_1 and employment L_1. A new union may now be able to raise both wages and employment or it can push the wage to W_3 with no reduction in employment. How much further it is prepared to go depends on its trade-off between wages and employment and on the elasticity of demand for labour. If the employer also has monopoly power in the market for its product and is making super-normal profits the union may be able to force the firm off its demand curve for labour, for example, forcing the wage up above W_3 while holding employment at L_2.

Unions may have significant bargaining power in both the private and public sector providing essential services such as electricity, while their general ability to control labour supply will be affected by legislation such as that on closed shops. Finally, unions may raise wages indirectly by negotiating productivity deals, better working conditions and training facilities, all of which may shift the demand curve for labour up and to the right. The wage will then rise the more the more tightly the union can restrict entry of new workers into the industry.

Solutions to Chapter 9 questions

ANSWERS TO SELF-TEST QUESTIONS

1   (c)   **4**   (d)
2   (a)   **5**   (d)
3   (e)

MODEL ANSWER TO EXERCISE

Externalities are the positive (external **benefits**) or negative (external **costs**) effects which production or consumption may confer on third parties. An example of the former is the advantage to the population as a whole of basic education which makes it easier to commmunicate and to train the workforce for specific tasks. An example of the latter is the costly effect of environmental pollution which some production processes impose on people who are not necessarily either producers or consumers of the good in question.

Normally, in the absence of externalities, we argue that a market is producing efficiently where the marginal private cost of production (measured by the competitive market's supply curve) is just equal to the marginal private benefit (measured by the demand curve). But if there are external benefits, as in the diagram, the marginal **social** benefits exceed the marginal **private** benefits. The price-output combination generated by the free market is inappropriate. The equilibrium price P_{me} and the equilibrium output Q_{me} are too low. If the social benefits were fully reflected in the demand curve, equilibrium price would be P* and equilibrium output Q*.

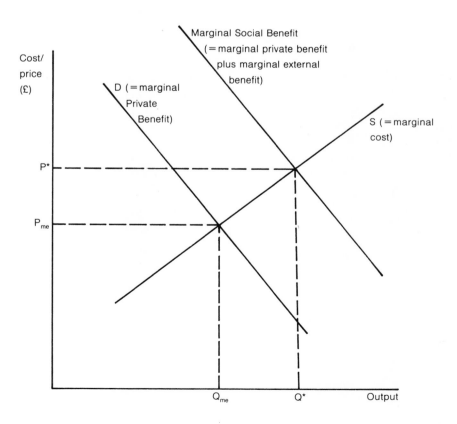

A similar diagram could be drawn to show the effects of external costs; here the conclusion would be that the free market equilibrium would involve a price that was too low and an output that was too high.

The existence of externalities has been held to justify a wide range of government policies intended to 'correct' the deficiencies of the free market. These include:

1   attempts to **persuade** people and firms to alter their behaviour, through advertising and publicity campaigns.

2   **nationalisation** of industries.

3   **regulation** of markets: laying down rules and controls on the behaviour of private sector firms and individuals.

4   **taxes** on activities which impose substantial external costs.

5   **subsidies** to activities which bring substantial external benefits.

6   the **assignment of property rights** in such a way that external costs fall on clearly defined groups which can then claim damages against those imposing these costs.

In deciding whether or not such measures are justified, economists will bear in mind that all these measures themselves impose costs on the economy. Regulation of industries, for example, uses scarce resources of highly trained professionals and back-up staff, buildings and equipment to determine, implement and monitor rules. Advertising campaigns can also be very costly. We have to be sure that measures to deal with externalities produce returns which justify their costs.

One problem is that policies towards externalities bring benefits to various groups, who will then have a vested interest in promoting such policies even if circumstances have changed. Experts and lawyers will find regulation of an industry a rich source of earnings possibilities. Trade unionists will prefer an industry to be nationalised (public enterprises are more highly unionised, and jobs often more secure) rather than in the private sector. Governments may come to depend on revenues from taxing particular activities, while those working in subsidised areas come to expect support even when they could do without them.

It is therefore sometimes difficult to separate economic logic from special pleading when discussing externalities. Although external costs and benefits need to be taken seriously, we cannot always assume that specific forms of government intervention can be justified.

Solutions to Chapter 10 questions

ANSWERS TO SELF-TEST QUESTIONS

1 (d)   **4** (b)
2 (d)   **5** (c)
3 (e)

MODEL ANSWER TO EXERCISE

'Privatisation' means the reduction of the role of the public sector and an expansion of the private sector by a variety of means. These include abandoning the provision of services previously offered to the public free or at subsidised prices; reducing the losses of nationalised industries; selling off public housing, land and other resources to private buyers; and contracting-out of services previously produced directly by public employees. However, the most obvious aspect of privatisation has been the selling-off of nationalised enterprises to private shareholders via the flotation of new companies.

It is hoped that privatisation will increase the efficiency of the economy and widen consumer choice by exposing enterprises to new competition. Of course, not all privatisations will necessarily increase competition in the market for goods and services. In some cases, privatised firms will already have been facing significant competition, for by no means all nationalised enterprises are monopolies. However, privatisation may offer scope for moving into other fields, not possible when enterprises had their market tightly defined by the government. So competition may be increased in this way.

In some cases, parts of the British privatisation programme has been criticised because the firms sold were so large that they have a dominant position in their markets and there is little effective competition. British Gas and British Telecom are the obvious examples here. Notice that in order for new competition to be stimulated, it needs also to be accompanied by deregulation measures, releasing existing firms from unnecessary restrictions on competitive behaviour and offering opportunities for new firms to enter the market.

Even where product market competition is relatively limited, privatisation may still stimulate efficiency through instituting a 'market for corporate control'. When a firm's shares are sold on the stock market, its management is under pressure to ensure that the firm performs satisfactorily. Otherwise its share price falls and there is the possibility of a takeover by outsiders who will dismiss the inefficient managers. Such a spur to efficiency is greater, however, in smaller firms; management is more difficult to replace in giant firms like British Telecom.

Privatisation receipts provide a source of government revenue. This helps to reduce the Public Sector Borrowing Requirement. As the PSBR is claimed by some people to have an influence on the rate of growth of the money supply, this may have a favourable impact on anti-inflation policy, or it may keep interest rates lower than they would have been. Alternatively, the lower tax rates privatisation proceeds made possible may have a beneficial effect on incentives.

However, the importance of these benefits should not be exaggerated. For one thing, a sale of shares to the public may have rather similar effects on interest rates as government borrowing (a share issue is, of course, in a sense a form of borrowing). For another, if the enterprise sold off was profitable (eg, British Gas), government revenue is increased today at the expense of lower government revenue in the future.

Finally, privatisation of this kind is argued to promote wider shareholding. This is claimed to be good in itself, as well as helping to promote a positive attitude to risk-taking, to business and to the 'enterprise culture'.

As for the other forms of privatisation, reducing public expenditure generally is held to free resources which can be used more efficiently elsewhere in the economy. In the case of contracting-out, if services are subject to competitive tender either a new firm will come in and do the job more cheaply than existing public employees, or else the stimulus of competition will force existing managers and workers to increase productivity and cut costs in order to keep their jobs. Ideally, too, it is hoped to increase the responsiveness of the public sector to consumer choice. If firms wish to keep contracts, they must keep customers—the general public as well as local or central government—happy.

Briefly, then, privatisation is seen as a means of increasing efficiency and widening consumer choice. But whether it succeeds in these goals is an empirical question which needs further examination.

Solutions to Chapter 11 questions

ANSWERS TO SELF-TEST QUESTIONS

1   (b)   **4**   (e)
2   (d)   **5**   (d)
3   (a)

MODEL ANSWER TO EXERCISE

The national income or product is a measure of the value of a country's total income from domestic output and from overseas. Estimates are made in three ways—measurement of income, of output and of expenditure on output. If the total income is divided by the population we have a figure of average income per head. After conversion at the appropriate exchange rates, these figures are often used to compare living standards between countries. However, the data so obtained can at best give only a very crude comparison and there are many problems which need to be taken into account when using data internationally:

1   **Income distribution** Income per head is an average and there can be wide differences in the distribution of income around the average. In many developing countries, income is highly concentrated and to that extent may exaggerate incomes for the mass of the population.

2   **Non-consumption output** Much output does not satisfy consumer needs and wants. A proportion goes on investment in capital goods which may raise income in the future but actually reduces current living standards if investment resources come from reducing consumption. Government spending, for example, on defence or building prestige office blocks again may reduce current household incomes without raising future income. The figures of national income therefore need to be adjusted to show the income available for household spending. The proportion of national product in the form of non-consumption output varies widely between countries.

3   **Non-marketed output** Substantial non-marketed output is not counted in the official income accounts. Production of goods and services in the household—housework, do-it-yourself activities, growing fruit and vegetables—is not usually recorded but may account for a substantial percentage of output. In poor agricultural economies much of a peasant's real income is from food and other goods for direct consumption in the household and recorded income per head may thus be artificially low. There is a similar problem with government services, such as education and health, provided free at the point of consumption. Output is measured by the cost of provision, which is likely to underestimate the market value.

4   **Exchange rates** These often fail to reflect the relative purchasing power of different currencies in the domestic economy. Official fixed exchange rates are frequently badly under- or over-valued and floating rates are distorted by capital flows. Corrections can be made by calculating 'purchasing power' exchange rates though there are still problems, for instance, which country's relative prices should be used to value output?

5   **Inflation** Over a period of time national income figures in money terms must be corrected for inflation to show the trends in real terms. Adjustments are necessarily very crude in countries with high rates of inflation.

6   **Errors and unrecorded income** Much of the income, output and expenditure has to be estimated. The inevitable inaccuracies may be magnified in developing countries with a large proportion of non-marketed income and poor data collection. Also, there is the problem of the 'black economy' consisting of unrecorded, usually illegal, transactions such as working for cash to avoid paying tax. This is thought to be very large in some countries whose national income may therefore be badly understated.

Clearly, there is a need for extreme caution in using national income data to make comparisons of living standards. In any case, they can indicate only material living standards and take no account of factors such as the environment and climate which affect the 'quality of life'. Many statisticians prefer therefore to supplement national income data with other indicators such as the level of ownership of cars and telephones, population density, housing space per head, and so on.

Solutions to Chapter 12 questions

ANSWERS TO SELF-TEST QUESTIONS

1	(d)		**4**	(a)
2	(e)		**5**	(c)
3	(d)			

MODEL ANSWER TO EXERCISE

The multiplier plays a crucial role in the 'Keynesian' analysis of the workings of the economy as a whole. If an economy is in equilibrium (with injections matching leakages) at a less-than-full-employment level of output, increases in injections will lead to a larger increase in aggregate demand and thus national income. The ratio of the total change in national income (ΔY) to the initial change in injections (ΔJ) is the multiplier, k.

$$k = \Delta Y / \Delta J$$

The concept is best explained by taking a simple example. Suppose that we have a closed economy (ie, one with no trade) with no government, so that investment is the only form of injection. Consumption depends on income, and the marginal propensity to consume (mpc, the change in consumption as a fraction of an increase in income, $\Delta C / \Delta Y$) is 0.6. If there is an increase in investment of £100m per week, this creates extra incomes of the same amount. Part is saved, but 0.6 of the increase—£60m—is spent on consumption. This spending in turn generates extra income of £60m, of which £36m is spent, and so on. The total extra spending and income generated is the sum of this series:

$$100 + (0.6)100 + (0.6)^2 100 + (0.6)^3 100 + ... =$$
$$100 + 60 + 36 + 21.6 + ... = 250$$

The multiplier is equal to $\Delta Y / \Delta J = 250/100 = 2.5$. In this case, the multiplier is equal to (1/1-mpc) because there is only one leakage (savings) from the circular flow of income. Additional leakages (imports and taxation) would cause the value of the multiplier to fall, as less spending would go back round the circular flow on each round of expenditure).

The idea of the multiplier suggests to policy-makers that, if there is unemployment, an increase in government spending will set off a multiplied increase in national income, perhaps to such an extent that it will pay for itself in increased tax revenue from the higher national income. This is the basis for Keynesian policies of demand management which became very influential after World War II.

We need to emphasise a number of limitations to this approach. First, the multiplier is only relevant to situations where there is **demand-deficient** unemployment. If unemployment is largely **voluntary**, however, increased spending will simply generate inflation rather than extra employment and output. Second, there may be long **time-lags** involved before the effects of increased injections work their way through the economy; by then circumstances may have changed, making extra spending inappropriate. Third, there may be an **unstable marginal propensity to consume**, making the multiplier effect unreliable in practice. Fourth, in many countries **high marginal tax rates** and **high import propensities** may combine to reduce the value of the multiplier to a low level. Increased government spending may have a greater effect in worsening the balance of payments than it has in increasing domestic output.

It is therefore important to qualify any discussion of the multiplier by an awareness of its limitations. Nowadays the appeal of the simple Keynesian multiplier analysis has greatly declined as economists and politicians have realised that the economy works in a rather more complicated way.

Solutions to Chapter 13 questions

ANSWERS TO SELF-TEST QUESTIONS

1 (e)   **4** (a)
2 (b)   **5** (a)
3 (b)

MODEL ANSWER TO EXERCISE

Investment is that part of expenditure which maintains (replacement investment) or adds to (net investment) a country's capital stock. It is a part of aggregate demand which varies very considerably from year to year and over the business cycle.

Rational individuals will choose to invest if a project's net present value is positive, or if its **internal rate of return** (that discount rate at which net present value is zero) is greater than the interest rate, which measures the opportunity cost of capital. In any period there will be a range of available projects (given the state of knowledge, demand and supply conditions, expectations about the future and what Keynes called 'animal spirits' (pessimism or optimism) of entrepreneurs. These will have different estimated internal rates of return. If these are arranged in order of their rate of return, we have a downward-sloping line which Keynes called the **marginal efficiency of capital schedule** (the marginal efficiency of capital is the rate of return on each extra unit of investment).

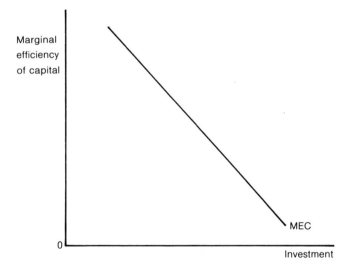

The MEC schedule in the diagram should be modified to reflect the fact that increases in investment drive up the price of capital goods and reduce the return on investment, but if we ignore this complication we can treat the schedule as the demand curve for investment. Investment will be carried up to the point where the MEC is equal to the opportunity cost of investment funds, the interest rate. Variations in the **interest rate** will therefore be one cause of variations in the level of investment.

However, Keynes thought that variations in investment as a result of interest rates would be relatively insignificant by comparison with variations resulting from changes in optimism or pessimism on the part of business. Shifts in the MEC schedule would be more important than movements up or down a given schedule.

Later writers have not been satisfied with Keynes's view. Some have asserted that interest rates **are** important and have claimed to find a significant interest-elasticity of investment demand in empirical studies. Others, however, have accepted that shifts in the MEC schedule are of more importance, but have tried to pin these shifts down by relating them to observable economic variables.

The argument is that businesses will be more optimistic, and therefore invest more, if indicators suggest that future business prospects are favourable. In each period, when contemplating investment, firms will have some information about what has been happening to key economic indicators. One will be the **level of profits**. Another will be the level of national income.

It is on the latter variable that most attention was concentrated in the 1940s and 1950s. Models were built on the **capital-stock adjustment principle**, that firms wish to maintain a desired ratio between the capital stock and the level of output. When the expected level output increases, the desired capital stock rises.

Suppose the desired capital-output ratio is v. Suppose, too that output increased in the previous period and the new higher output level is expected to continue. Then I_n, desired new investment, will be:

$$I_n = v\Delta Y$$

where ΔY is the change in national income in the previous period. If all the desired investment can be carried out in the current period, v is the **accelerator coefficient** (it will be smaller than v if some of the investment cannot be completed until later periods). This coefficient shows the ratio of actual new investment to output changes. More elaborate versions of this basic sort of model have frequently been used in forecasting models.

Solutions to Chapter 14 questions

ANSWERS TO SELF-TEST QUESTIONS

1   (d)   **4**   (c)
2   (e)   **5**   (e)
3   (a)

MODEL ANSWER TO EXERCISE

In the United Kingdom, the Public Sector Borrowing Requirement (PSBR) is the difference between what the public sector spends and what the government raises in taxes, charges, nationalised industry surpluses and asset sales. For most of the postwar period the government has been a net borrower, although in the 1988 budget statement Chancellor of the Exchequer Nigel Lawson announced that the PSBR would fall to zero in 1989–90.

In the 1970s, monetarist economists placed great emphasis on the relationship between the PSBR and the increase in the money supply. It was believed that the public sector borrowing requirement led to an increase in bank lending and thus increased 'broad' measures of the money supply (such as M3), which in turn generated inflation. Thus a reduction in the PSBR was seen as essential in controlling inflation.

It is perfectly true that **other things being equal**, the PSBR has an impact on the money supply, but in fact the connection between them is fairly complicated. The PSBR can be funded through borrowing direct from the non-bank sector, through the issue of government bonds, national savings certificates etc. The limits on this policy arise because increased borrowing from the public tends to drive up interest rates. This has the effect of 'crowding out' some private sector spending (especially investment) which would otherwise have taken place, and this is undesirable. It also attracts an inflow of foreign funds, which are deposited in UK banks and tend to lead to an expansion in the domestic money supply as a consequence.

An increase in M3 can be split into a number of 'counterparts' as shown:

ΔM3 = PSBR − sales of government debt to general public
                  + increase in bank lending to United Kingdom private sector
                  + increase in bank lending to overseas sector
                  + change in non-deposit liabilities

(We should note that 'non-deposit liabilities' are mainly sales by the banks of their own shares.) From this it can be seen that the PSBR only generates an equivalent increase in the money supply if all the other counterparts sum to zero. Such an event can occur, but it is unlikely.

For example, in 1980, the change in £M3 (**sterling** M3, the measure then used) was £10,595m, close to the PSBR (£11,813m). This occurred because the effects of the other counterparts nearly cancelled each other out. However in 1986 the increase in £M3 was £23,250m, even though the PSBR was only £2,502m! Low sales of debt to the private sector (£4,052m) were offset by negative figures on bank lending overseas and non-deposit liabilities. The real cause of the expansion of the money supply was a huge expansion in bank lending to the United Kingdom private sector of £29,367m, in contrast to the low PSBR figure and in defiance of the medium-term financial strategy, which had set a much lower target for £M3.

One problem with this approach is that the definition of the PSBR misleads. The proceeds of sales of shares in privatised companies are included in government revenue, and the PSBR is calculated net of privatisation proceeds (about £4.7m in 1986), but sales of shares compete with government bonds for private sector funds, and arguably should be counted as borrowing themselves. In that case, the 'real' PSBR was significantly larger than the figures suggested.

Another problem is that the relationship between £M3 and inflation altered over this period. Increasing competition between the commercial banks and other financial institutions meant that £M3 as a proportion of all private sector liquidity changed. So did the ratio between the monetary base (MO) and £M3.

So the relationship between the PSBR and the money supply, and between the money supply and inflation is a complicated one. As we noted earlier, an increase in the PSBR, other things being equal, will tend to generate increased inflation; but there are so many intervening factors that it would be mistaken to draw the simple relationship between them which was confidently stated a few years ago.

Solutions to Chapter 15 questions

ANSWERS TO SELF-TEST QUESTIONS

1	(d)	**4**	(e)
2	(b)	**5**	(c)
3	(b)		

MODEL ANSWER TO EXERCISE

(a)   Money is anything generally acceptable in payment of debts arising from economic transactions; its exact form will depend on both legal and social conventions.

It is traditional to distinguish four functions which money fulfils in the economy. These are:

1   **a medium of exchange.** This is implied in the definition. Money simplifies and promotes transactions by obviating the need for barter, with its requirement for the 'double coincidence of wants'.

2   **a unit of account.** In this function, money makes rational calculation and decision-making easier. Money makes it easier to keep accounts, to calculate costs and profits or losses.

3   **a standard of deferred payment.** Having a common monetary unit facilitates trade and production which involve future commitments rather than immediate exchange. It is possible, with a reasonably stable monetary unit, for contracts to be formed for payments and obligations specified in common terms.

4   **a store of wealth.** Money is also an asset, a way of storing purchasing power. As such, it competes with other assets, but is has the advantages of perfect liquidity and certain nominal value. These may be important characteristics in a world of uncertainty.

(b)   Monetarism is essentially an updated version of the old Quantity Theory of money. It amounts to the claim that the income velocity of circulation of money (V) is constant. If this is so, and if the economy is fully employed (in the sense that there is no 'involuntary' unemployment), then it must follow that an increase in the money supply (M) will lead to an increase in the average price level (P) in the same proportion.

In terms of the Fisher equation:

$$MV = PY$$

with a constant V, and output Y at its full employment level, $\Delta M/M$ must equal $\Delta P/P$. Modern monetarists argue that Y is best represented by *permanent income* (that is, the average income individuals expect to maintain over time), and that V should only be understood to be stable over a business cycle, but their position is essentially the same. Inflation necessarily follows from attempts to increase the money supply faster than the underlying (trend) rate of growth of the economy.

By contrast, Keynes and later writers sympathetic to his approach would stress that output can fall below its full employment level, which means that an increase in the money supply which led to increased spending might raise output as well as prices. Moreover the velocity of circulation is not constant; rather, its value will depend on (amongst other things) the interest rate. The demand for money is *interest-elastic,* and part of any increase in the money supply may be held as idle balances rather than spent, if the interest rate is low. Thus, there is not the simple connection between the rate of growth of money supply and inflation which monetarism suggests.

Although it is clear that there must be some relationship between money supply changes and inflation (a doubling of the money stock would surely stimulate inflation!), it does not seem likely that the relationship can be predicted with any accuracy. Even monetarists admit that the velocity of circulation varies over the business cycle, and such cycles are themselves of varying length.

Moreover, the monetarist analysis assumes that we can identify the relevant measure of the money supply. In practice this is difficult; different measures (eg, M0, M1, M3) have grown at different rates during the same period.

Certainly, the experience of the 1980s, when many countries tried to control particular measures of the money supply as a prerequisite to controlling inflation, showed that the process of inflation was very complex and that there were no simple answers.

Solutions to Chapter 16 questions

ANSWERS TO SELF-TEST QUESTIONS

1 (d)
2 (b)
3 (e)

4 (d)
5 (a)

MODEL ANSWER TO EXERCISE

In the 1960s, many economists and politicians thought it likely that there was a 'trade-off' between unemployment and inflation. The Phillips Curve was thought to show a stable relationship between the rate of increase of prices (or money wages, in the original version) and the rate of unemployment. As shown in Figure 1, governments were not obliged to choose point A, where inflation was zero, but could opt for another point such as B, where increased government spending produced a higher level of employment and a higher inflation rate.

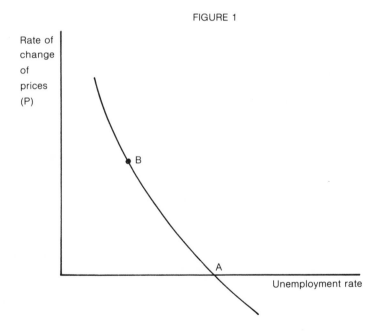

FIGURE 1

    Nowadays, however, fewer people take this position. A common view, following the argument of Professor Milton Friedman, argues that the trade-off is only a temporary one, which depends on people's expected rate of inflation lagging behind the actual rate of inflation. As a result of this, increases in **money** wages, for example, are misinterpreted to mean changes in **real** terms. Workers who would have rejected job offers and remained unemployed now accept them. Employment rises.

    However this effect only persists until expected inflation catches up with reality; then workers revert to their previous behaviour and unemployment returns to its initial level. One way to think about this is to argue that the Phillips Curve shifts as expectations about inflation alter. In Figure 2 we show how **short-run** Phillips Curves can be drawn for each rate of expected inflation. However the **long-run** Phillips Curve is vertical at the **natural or non-accelerating inflation rate of unemployment** (NAIRU).

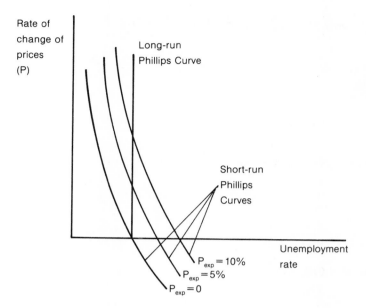

Some economists, notably the **New Classical economists**, go further than Friedman and argue that there is no trade-off between unemployment and inflation even in the short-run. This is because people form **rational expectations**, based on information about government policy and other matters which is widely available. If they see the government is pumping extra spending power into the economy, and that is likely to cause higher inflation, they will take this into account in their decision-making. The government will not be able to 'fool' the people.

Against these arguments, Keynesians may make a number of points. For one thing, it should be said that many economists find it implausible that ordinary people form expectations on the sophisticated basis that the New Classical writers suggest. More fundamentally, it can be observed that both Friedman and the New Classicals believe that, in the absence of expansionary government policy, the economy would be at its NAIRU, where all those willing to take jobs can obtain them and there is no involuntary unemployment. If this is the case, only 'supply-side' measures can permanently reduce unemployment.

Keynesians would dispute this, arguing that the level of aggregate demand **does** have an effect, and that labour and product markets can exist for considerable periods of time in a state of disequilibrium. They appear to have some evidence on their side: it is difficult to see how the big increase in unemployment in the United Kingdom in the early 1980s can be explained solely by supply-side factors.

So, despite the big change in intellectual fashion which has made earlier ideas about the unemployment-inflation trade-off unpopular, there may still be something in it. Policies to reduce unemployment should not ignore the need to maintain the level of aggregate demand, even if they place much more emphasis than before on microeconomic measures to reduce the NAIRU by altering the incentives facing those currently out of work.

Solutions to Chapter 17 questions

ANSWERS TO SELF-TEST QUESTIONS

1	(a)		**4**	(c)
2	(e)		**5**	(d)
3	(d)			

MODEL ANSWER TO EXERCISE

Supply-siders argue that an economy tends to settle at its natural rate of unemployment (or NAIRU, non-accelerating inflation rate of unemployment). This is the rate of unemployment at which the labour market is in equilibrium in the sense that, at going wage rates, the supply of labour **actually willing to accept jobs** is just equal to the demand for labour. There is consequently no tendency for the rate of inflation to change. Increases in aggregate demand eventually lead, it is argued, to a proportionate rise in all prices, costs and incomes, leaving the underlying pattern of incentives the same. So long-run aggregate output remains the same.

The only ways in which increases in aggregate demand can increase output and reduce unemployment are:

1 If people are temporarily fooled into believing that changes in the price level (or money wages) represent changes in relative prices (or real wages). However supply-siders believe people are not fooled for very long (and New Classicals argue that they cannot be systematically fooled at all).

2 If the prices of different goods and/or the wages of different groups adjust at different speeds. This may occur if some workers are on long-term contracts, or if some prices are administered by governments or cartels and only change infrequently. What happens then is that patterns of relative prices and wages are altered, leading to a change in the incentive to supply output. However, most supply-siders assume that individual markets adjust rapidly to new equilibria, and therefore any such effects are slight.

Despite their lack of belief in the effectiveness of demand management, most supply-siders are not content to ignore the unemployment rate. The NAIRU can be above the optimum level if there are some forms of significant **market failures**. For example, if firms possess considerable monopoly power and restrict output, or if there are major externalities which lead to underproduction of certain goods and services (including training and education). In such cases, government intervention—at the microeconomic level—may be justified. Left-wing 'supply-siders' might argue for considerable government intervention on these grounds. The argument for government investment in research, for example, might be put in terms of the view that fundamental research is a public good which will be undersupplied by the free market.

More commonly, however, supply-siders have stressed various forms of **government failures** which need to be remedied in order to reduce unemployment. The tax system may be argued to act as a disincentive to work effort; so may the benefit system. Public enterprises may be seen as inefficient, and government controls on the private sector may be thought to discourage innovation and efficiency; thus privatisation and deregulation are advocated. In the labour market, minimum wage and employment protection legislation, and privileges granted to trade unionism are criticised.

Thus an acceptance of the supply-side argument that demand expansion is incapable of reducing unemployment does not mean that we should passively accept that the actual rate of unemployment must remain at the current NAIRU indefinitely. The exact mix of policies proposed to deal with unemployment will vary, but they will be microeconomic in orientation.

Solutions to Chapter 18 questions

ANSWERS TO SELF-TEST QUESTIONS

1	(d)		**4**	(e)
2	(a)		**5**	(e)
3	(a)			

MODEL ANSWER TO EXERCISE

The principle of comparative advantage is that countries can benefit from trade based on differences in their comparative or opportunity costs. This can be seen with an example of two countries, A and B, producing two goods, wheat (W) and cloth (C). Assuming full employment and constant opportunity costs suppose productivity in the two industries is:

	Output per unit of resources	
	A	B
Wheat (units)	300	600
Cloth (units)	60	300
Opportunity cost	5W:1C	2W:1C
ratios	1W:0.2C	1W:0.5C

Though Country B is absolutely superior in producing both goods it has a comparative advantage in cloth—the opportunity cost of one unit of cloth is only 2W compared with 5W in country A. Country A similarly has a comparative advantage in wheat which it produces with a lower opportunity cost than B. If trade opens up at an intermediate terms of trade, say, 1C:4W, both countries can gain from importing the good in which it has a comparative disadvantage at a lower opportunity cost than it can produce it at home. Country A can now obtain a unit of cloth by exporting 4W; domestic production of cloth requires a sacrifice of 5W. Country B can import wheat at a unit cost of 0.25C compared with the domestic cost of 0.5C.

If prices reflect opportunity costs, free trade will automatically lead to each country specialising in and exporting the good which it produces with a lower opportunity cost and importing more cheaply in return the good it produces with a higher opportunity cost. The result is a more efficient division of labour between countries and greater real income.

Widespread protectionism, particularly by restriction of imports, may partly be explained by failure of the full employment assumption to hold in practice. When an economy is in recession with heavy unemployment governments may attempt to stimulate demand for domestic output by import controls to divert spending away from foreign output. This may be followed by a multiplier expansion of demand, production and employment. However, if one or more major countries attempt to boost employment in this way it may lead to an escalation of tariffs and other trade barriers as others retaliate in kind. This happened in the 1930s and there has been another surge of protectionism in the recessions of the 1970s and 1980s.

Governments in any case are under continual pressure to grant protection to specific industries suffering from foreign competition. Employers and workers may deploy a wide range of arguments to achieve protection. The employment argument is probably most frequently used and is more effective when the complaining industry is a major employer. Other arguments used on their own or in combination include the following:

1 **Dumping** The industry may claim that foreign suppliers are unfairly selling goods below cost. Dumping is technically difficult to prove and complaints are often related more to the next set of arguments.

2 **Low wages/cheap labour** This argument is used by industries in rich countries for protection against imports from less developed countries (LDCs). As a general argument it is invalid since low wages in LDCs are the result of low absolute productivity. It is not unfair if they export goods in which they have a comparative advantage.

3 **Revenue** Some countries justify tarrifs as a means of raising revenue but this is only a good argument when the country has a narrow domestic tax base.

4 **Infant industries and economic development** LDCs often claim that their new industries need protection to meet the excess costs involved when they are first established. At best, this is an argument for temporary protection. Similarly, many LDCs protect domestic manufacturing industries to diversify out of primary production. But the evidence is mixed on whether protection promotes or hinders economic development.

5 **Terms of trade** Large industrial economies like the USA may exploit their market power to drive down import prices by means of import restrictions although any gains may be nullified by retaliation.

6 **The balance of payments** Imports may be restricted in order to reduce a payments deficit but the argument falls down once again if there is widespread retaliation.

These arguments do not explain protection; rather they provide justification for protection, the real reasons for which are political—governments may concede protection when they see a political or electoral advantage. Even if protection raises prices and lowers consumers' welfare, governments will often see political benefit in granting protection to producer interests which are usually more powerful than diffused consumer interests.

Solutions to Chapter 19 questions

ANSWERS TO SELF-TEST QUESTIONS

1 (e)   **4** (e)
2 (b)   **5** (a)
3 (d)

MODEL ANSWER TO EXERCISE

In the Bretton Woods system after World War II and prevailing up to 1971 member countries of the International Monetary Fund (set up at Bretton Woods in the United States) declared 'par values' for their currencies against the $US and were obliged to hold their actual exchange rates within 1 per cent of the par value. However, exchange rates were not absolutely fixed since countries were expected to alter these par values or 'pegs' to correct persistent payments surpluses or deficits. Surplus countries were supposed to upvalue their currencies and deficit countries to devalue. The system was therefore an 'adjustable peg' system—exchange rates were fixed for indefinite periods but were altered from time to time.

Since the breakdown of the Bretton Woods system in the early 1970s exchange rates between the major currencies have been floating with currency values determined primarily by supply and demand in the foreign exchange market. Supply of, say, sterling is derived from payments for United Kingdom imports and outflows of capital. Demand comes from United Kingdom exports and inflows of investment into the United Kingdom. But fluctuations in supply and demand have caused great instability of exchange rates. The dollar/pound rate in the 1980s, for instance, has been over $2.40 and has been as low as $1.05. These large swings in exchange rates have led to demands for a return to the semi-fixed rates like those under the Bretton Woods system.

One argument is that the uncertainty and risk from unstable rates damage trade and investment. A fall in the currency in which an exporter has invoiced goods could, for example, wipe out profit margins. Though traders can hedge (insure against) adverse exchange rates it can be expensive and the costs, it is said, discourage trade and investment. However, the adjustable peg system had its own heavy costs. The central bank of a country with a fixed rate and a balance of payments deficit must support its currency by buying it on the exchange market. This means a loss of the country's exchange reserves. When they near exhaustion speculators will expect a devaluation and provoke a payments crisis by selling the currency. The country then has to impose exchange and import controls or else it is forced to devalue. In either case, it is clear that the adjustable peg system does not avoid risks and costs for traders and investors.

Perhaps more important, countries in the Bretton Woods system were compelled to pursue monetary policies dictated by the dominant country, the United States. If, say, the United Kingdom had high inflation its payments would move into deficit and, without the freedom to allow a depreciation of sterling, the only means of correcting the deficit was through domestic deflation to curb imports. The result may have been a rise in unemployment which might have been avoided if the United Kingdom could more easily have permitted a fall in the exchange rate. Conversely, if the United States pursued inflationary policies its higher inflation was exported to other countries through an American payments deficit.

With floating rates countries can in principle pursue independent monetary policies and can insulate themselves against importing unwanted inflation or recession in other countries. A payments deficit can be corrected by currency depreciation, a surplus by appreciation. However, floating rates since the 1970s have really been managed rates with central banks intervening or manipulating interest rates to push exchange rates in desired directions. Arguably, this has actually caused even greater instability once exchange rates held at unwarranted levels for long periods have eventually had to be altered. High American interest rates, for example, held the dollar up from 1983 to 1985. By 1988 the $US had lost about half its value and was still threatening to fall further to remedy the large United States trade and payments deficit.

Although there appear to be strong arguments for stable exchange rates their feasibility is doubtful so long as countries pursue divergent monetary policies in a world in which huge volumes of private funds can easily overcome any attempts by central banks to hold what the markets deem to be unrealistic exchange rates. Billions of dollars can be moved from one currency to another in the space of hours or even minutes. This new factor of mobile funds means that a restored Bretton Woods system would almost certainly be unworkable unless countries were prepared once again to allow their monetary policies to be dictated by the United States.

Solutions to Chapter 20 questions

ANSWERS TO SELF-TEST QUESTIONS

1 (b)
2 (a)
3 (e)

4 (c)
5 (e)

MODEL ANSWER TO EXAMINATION QUESTION

Throughout the developed Western world, unemployment in the 1980s has been higher than in the 1960s. Circumstances differ from country to country, but there have been some common factors.

For one thing, **political priorities** have altered. In the 1960s, governments in many countries were run by politicians whose ideas were shaped by memories of inter-war mass unemployment, and who were determined not to allow it to return, even if the cost was somewhat higher rates of inflation than would ideally be preferred (this was a period when it was believed that there was a trade-off between unemployment and inflation). By the 1980s a new generation of politicians was in charge, and they experienced a decade of rapid inflation which had altered their priorities. It was no longer acceptable to tolerate high rates of inflation, particularly as many believed that the trade-off between unemployment and inflation (if it had ever existed) had now disappeared.

So governments in the 'eighties were more concerned to conquer inflation than to keep unemployment down. This was most strongly reflected in the policies of Mrs Thatcher's government in the United Kingdom, where tight fiscal and monetary policies had the effect of increasing unemployment very sharply.

But unemployment had already started to rise in the 1970s. The two **oil price 'shocks'** of 1974 and 1979 had much to do with this. They had effects on aggregate demand; spending power was transferred away from oil-using countries, and total spending did not rise sufficiently to bridge the gap: thus unemployment rose.

There were also effects on the supply side of the economy. Relative costs of production were affected, making fuel-intensive technologies inefficient and raising the 'natural' rate of unemployment or NAIRU. In addition, the increased inflation helped to stimulate **trade union militancy** in a number of countries, and this has been argued by some economists and politicians to have been a further cause of higher unemployment. In Britain, trade union power may have increased as a result of greater privileges accorded to trade unions by the Labour government of 1974–79.

In addition there was in the United Kingdom, most European countries and the United States a variety of new **legislation which regulated the labour market**. Laws against racial and sexual discrimination, equal pay provisions and employment protection legislation have all been argued to have reduced employers' willingness to employ labour. Although they helped those already in jobs, such measures may have made it more difficult for new entrants to the labour market to obtain work in various ways.

Mention of new labour market entrants draws attention to the fact that in the early 1980s in many countries there was a big **increase in the number of young workers** coming on the labour market, the children of the baby boom of the early to middle 1960s. Young people always tend to find it difficult to obtain suitable jobs as they have little experience or skills to offer and they tend to display higher 'search' and 'frictional' unemployment. This generation, however, found it particularly difficult. For one thing, youth wages had risen as a proportion of adult wages in the 1970s, making them relatively less attractive to employers. For another, in several countries they faced competition for low-paid jobs from large numbers of married women, who were re-entering the labour market in unprecedented numbers.

Another factor tending to increase the NAIRU was the changes in the **tax and benefit**

K

systems which had occurred since the 1960s. There is evidence that benefits had become somewhat more generous for those out of work in a number of countries, and in the United Kingdom at least it seems to have been the case that rules about eligibility were less stringently applied from the mid-1970s onwards. In virtually all countries taxation bore more heavily on workers' incomes by the early 1980s than they had twenty years before. Thus the 'replacement ratio' (the ratio of income received when out of work to earnings when in work) had risen, making it less imperative to get a job immediately. Thus the average duration of unemployment rose. Even if there were only the same number of people becoming unemployed each month, this would imply a rising average number of people unemployed at any time.

So the rise in unemployment from the 1960s to the 1980s had many causes. It seems likely that some of the factors which led to higher unemployment are becoming less significant; for instance trade union power may have been reduced, tax rates are falling and the number of young people entering the labour market is dropping. It seems unlikely, however, that there will be a rapid return to the rates of unemployment prevailing in the 1960s.

Additional questions

Students are encouraged to attempt these questions. However, the answers are provided only in the manual issued to lecturers. Lecturers may obtain a free copy of the manual by writing to: Sales and Marketing Department, Longman Group UK Ltd., 21–27 Lamb's Conduit Street, London WC1N 3NJ.

1 (a) Explain with examples the concept of 'market failure'

   (b) Do market failures justify central planning of the economy?

2 (a) Distinguish between the price elasticity of demand and the income elasticity of demand

   (b) What relevance do these concepts have to the pricing and investment decisions of a business with a large share of the markets for its products?

3 (a) Explain what is meant by 'price discrimination'

   (b) In what conditions is price discrimination profitable? Can consumers ever benefit from price discrimination?

4 In many countries governments protect farmers by supporting the prices of agricultural products. Examine the effects of price support and the costs and benefits of such policies.

5 'Competition is preferable to monopoly'. Explain why this is usually thought to be the case. Are there any exceptions to this rule?

6 (a) Explain the concepts of 'the multiplier' and 'the accelerator'

   (b) How can these concepts help us in understanding cycles in economic activity in industrial countries?

7 What factors determine the pattern of wage differentials which we observe?

8 'Unemployment can only be reduced by measures which affect the incentives to supply goods and services'. Discuss

9 What costs are imposed on an economy by (i) inflation and (ii) unemployment?

10 Should Western economies revert to a system of fixed exchange rates?

11 If countries benefit from free trade why is protection so widespread?

12 Examine the difficulties faced by a government which wishes to control the money supply

The Chartered Association of Certified Accountants

June 1988

Level 1—Preliminary Examination

Paper 1.3

Economics

Time allowed—3 hours
Number of questions on paper—8
The paper is divided into 2 sections
FIVE questions ONLY to be answered, choosing at least TWO from each section
All questions carry equal marks. (Credit will be given for diagrams where appropriate)

FIVE questions ONLY to be answered

Candidates are required to answer as follows:
EITHER—
THREE questions from Section A, AND TWO questions from Section B
OR—
TWO questions from Section A, AND THREE questions from Section B

Section A

1   **Explain the following**:
    (a) Why the demand curve for a good or service is normally downward sloping.
                                                                                    (10 marks)

    (b) The notion of consumer surplus.   (5 marks)

    (c) What you understand by the concept, 'consumer equilibrium'   (5 marks)
                                                                                    (20 marks)

2   A local entrepreneur has built up a successful business which is still growing. He is aware that the
     increasing scale of operations has a number of cost advantages but is finding the administration
     of the organisation increasingly difficult. He asks you as a student of economics to explain the
     relative merits of expanding the size of his business still further.
     Write him a brief report on this subject.   **(20 marks)**

3   **To what extent can the marginal productivity theory account for actual earnings?**
                                                                                    (20 marks)

4   Faced with increasing costs, the world's five big car manufacturing companies are considering
     raising the prices of their cars.
     **What factors, would they, as individual firms, take into account in deciding whether
     or not to raise prices?**   **(20 marks)**

Section B

5   (a) How, under a system of 'dirty' floating exchange rates is the rate of a particular currency determined?   (10 marks)

    (b) What are the likely effects of an appreciation in the value of the Japanese yen on:

        (i) the Japanese economy?
        (ii) the economies of Japan's trading partners?   (10 marks)
                                                                                (20 marks)

6   How far, if at all, is government action necessary in order to secure full employment equilibrium in a market economy?   **(20 marks)**

7   (a) List the main functions of the central bank of a country.   (5 marks)

    (b) Describe the means which are available to the central bank for regulating the demand for, and the supply of, money and credit.   (15 marks)
                                                                                (20 marks)

8   (a) To what extent is the precise measurement of economic growth possible?
                                                                                (10 marks)

    (b) What factors are responsible for economic growth?   (10 marks)
                                                                                (20 marks)

End of Question Paper

Reproduced with permission of The Chartered Association of Certified Accountants

Author's model answers to this examination paper are on page 279.

Authors' model answers to June 1988 ACCA Economics paper

1 (a) A downward sloping demand curve for a good or service means that consumers will be willing to consume more of it after a fall in its price. This can be explained in terms of diminishing marginal utility—the greater the consumption of a good the less is its marginal utility to the consumer, that is, the less the additional satisfaction derived from consuming one more unit of the good. This is an empirical 'law' based on the observation that particular human wants are satiable so that increasing consumption of goods which satisfy those wants must ultimately yield no additional utility.

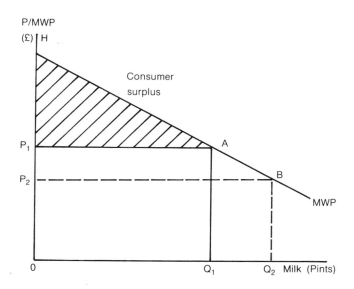

Since utility is subjective it is only measurable indirectly by the consumer's 'willingness to pay' for different quantities of a good. Thus, suppose the good in question is milk. The diagram shows a curve of the consumer's marginal willingness to pay (MWP) for different amounts of milk per week. MWP is the additional sum the consumer is prepared to pay to acquire one more unit of the good, in this case, an extra pint of milk. It can therefore be interpreted as the consumer's valuation of the marginal utility of milk. Assuming diminishing marginal utility the MWP curve will be downward sloping.

The MWP curve is also the consumer's demand curve for milk showing, other things equal, the quantity demanded at each price. For example, if the price is P_1 this measures the marginal cost of milk to the consumer—the cost of obtaining one more pint. If the consumer is 'rational' he or she will seek to maximise satisfaction from milk consumption and this is achieved by consuming up to the point where the marginal cost (the price P_1) equals the MWP at quantity Q_1. Up to Q_1 the MWP exceeds the price so that an extra pint yields additional net satisfaction. Beyond Q_1 MWP is less than price so that extra consumption reduces net satisfaction. This is therefore maximised by consuming Q_1 at the price P_1. If the price falls to P_2 net satisfaction is maximised by equating MWP with the lower price and increasing consumption to Q_2. Since the MWP curve relates price to quantity demanded it is the consumer's demand curve. On the assumption of diminishing marginal utility it is downward sloping.

(b) Consumer suplus is the excess of total utility or total willingness to pay (TWP) for a given quantity of a good over and above the consumer's actual outlay on the good. In the diagram TWP for Q_1, is measured by the area beneath the MWP curve up the point A, ie the area $OHAQ_1$. However, at the price P_1 the total cost to the consumer is P_1. Q_1, the rectangular area OP_1AQ_1. The excess of TWP over the consumer's outlay—the consumer surplus—is therefore measured by the shaded triangular area P_1HA. If the price falls to P_2 consumer surplus, which measures the consumer's net satisfaction or utility, expands to P_2HB.

(c) Consumer equilibrium refers to the position achieved by a consumer when he or she has allocated income between goods in such a way that the total utility from consumption of all goods is maximised. Assuming diminishing marginal utility (MU) the consumer will logically achieve equilibrium when the MU of expenditure (the utility gained by spending one more pound) is the same for all goods.

For example, assume only two goods X and Y. The MU of expenditure is given by the MU of each good divided by its price—MU_x/P_x and MU_y/P_y. for equilibrium it is necessary that:

$$MU_x/P_x = MU_y/P_y$$

If the condition is not satisfied the consumer can increase total utility by reallocating expenditure between the two goods. Thus, start with an initial equilibrium but then assume a fall in the price of X. We now have:

$$MU_x/P_x > MU_y/P_y$$

The consumer can now make a net gain by switching expenditure from Y to X. As he or she does so, MU_x will decline and MU_y will increase. The equality will therefore be restored at some point and the consumer is then at a new equilibrium. We can note that this gives an alternative explanation of a negatively sloped demand curve since normally, to restore equilibrium, the consumer increases consumption of the good whose price has fallen.

2   You are quite correct in thinking that there are usually cost advantages from increasing the scale of business operations. Your firm is currently operating in what economists call a short run situation in which production capacity in limited by the fixed supply of one or more of your productive inputs (factors of production). In particular, your output is constrained by the size of your premises and fixed assets such as plant and machinery—the fixed factors in the short run. If you try to expand your output you will inevitably at some point encounter 'diminishing returns' as you take on more variable factors such as labour and have to use your fixed inputs more and more intensively. The result will be falling marginal productivity (the extra output from employing one more worker) with corresponding increases in marginal cost (the addition to costs from producing one more unit of output).

In the long run all factors, including your physical assets, are variable. That means that you can increase your scale of output by investment in bigger premises and installing more plant, machinery and equipment, thus raising your productive capacity. Since your sales are growing you should obviously consider such an expansion which will almost certainly result in economies of **scale**. Thus, most firms find that an increase in the size of their operations gives rise to increasing returns, that is, increased productivity of their labour and capital and therefore reductions in the average cost per unit of output. These economies of scale have various sources:

1   **Specialisation** Factors of production can become more specialised with a beneficial effect on productivity. A larger scale allows a greater **division of labour** with workers and managers becoming more specialised to particular tasks and operations. They can concentrate on the kind of work they are best at doing and increase their skill and expertise in doing so. Experience shows that the resulting increase in productivity can be quite startling. The larger scale may also permit a reorganisation of production with the introduction flow or assembly lines. Workers along the line may be specialised in minor

operations but output rises and materials and components are hardly ever at rest. The same principle applies to other factors. Specialised machines, for example, can be introduced to replace less productive general purpose equipment.

2   **Substitution** A bigger scale makes it possible to employ, say, expensive equipment, which would be underutilised at a lower scale, to substitute for less costly but also less productive factors. Computers may replace book-keepers; specialist accountants can be directly employed to substitute for services previously bought in.

Depending on the nature of the business there may be scope for a wide range of other scale economies. Some of these are:

1   **Set-up costs** Where products are turned out in batches or 'runs' (in engineering and printing, for example) there are fixed costs in setting up plant and equipment for each run. The longer the run, clearly the lower the set-up per unit of output.

2   **Administrative and overhead costs** These are often quasi-fixed costs—they do not rise in proportion to the scale of the business. Again, an increase in scale means that these costs can be spread more thinly over the greater output.

3   **Technical or dimensional economies** The cost of building storage and factory space and processing equipment normally doesn't rise in proportion to the increase in capacity. A factory with twice as much floor area almost certainly costs less than twice as much to build and maintain.

4   **Stocks or inventories** Firms can usually economise on stockholding of materials, spares and finished goods since the optimum level of stocks rises proportionately less than the level of output.

5   Finally, bigger firms can often exploit their increased market power to purchase inputs at lower prices. They may be able to negotiate bulk discounts, cheaper loans and better credit terms.

However, before you decide to undertake an expansion of the business you should also consider the possibility of **diseconomies of scale**. You are already finding administration difficult and as the firm expands you may find these managerial diseconomies more evident as your own decision-making capacity is stretched and as you have to delegate to possibly less efficient managers who do not have the same level of commitment to the business. Communications in the firm will also deteriorate and you will find it harder to obtain and analyse the information needed for efficient decision-making. Finally, you should consider the possible adverse effects on labour productivity from overspecialisation of workers who may feel increasingly remote from the final product and lose any identification with the goals of the firm. Labour relations may suffer and the effects of industrial action are potentially more damaging to a larger firm.

In short, your business and profits are likely to benefit from an increase in scale but before you go ahead with your expansion plans you should carefully consider and anticipate the potentially adverse impact on your ability to manage and on industrial relations in the firm.

3   Marginal productivity theory provides an explanation of the demand curve for labour. In the simplest case, where a firm is operating in perfect competition and its price is therefore equal to its marginal revenue, we can define the marginal revenue product of labour as its marginal physical product multiplied by its price:

$$\text{MRP of Labour} = \text{MPP} \times \text{P}$$

In the first diagram the MRP curve cuts the average revenue product ($= \text{APP} \times \text{P}$) curve at its maximum; the shape of these curves results from the action of the Law of Diminishing Returns. If the wage, the marginal cost of employing labour, is indicated on the diagram, we can see that at a wage rate W_1 it will be profitable to employ labour up to the level Q_1. If less labour is employed, the MRP exceeds the marginal cost of labour and employment should be increased; at a higher level of employment the wage exceeds MRP and profits would be increased by reducing employment. The MRP curve therefore traces out the demand for labour by a profit-maximising firm, though it should be noted that only the section of the MRP curve lying below the ARP is economically relevant (this section is shown by the thicker line). At a wage rate of

Diagram 1

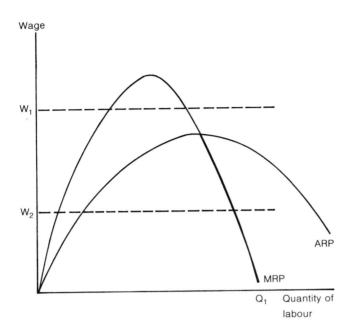

W₂, for instance, the wage (the average, as well as the marginal), cost of employing labour exceeds the ARP and the firm will be failing to cover its variable costs and will therefore close down.

The marginal revenue product curve gives us the demand curve for labour, but the equilibrium wage or earnings can only be determined through the interaction of the demand curve with the supply curve. Clearly, different supply conditions will mean a different equilibrium wage and employment level. To clarify this, see the second diagram. On both the right and left hand sides we show the same demand curve for labour, but the different supply curves lead to different equilibrium wage rates and consequent earnings:

Diagram 2

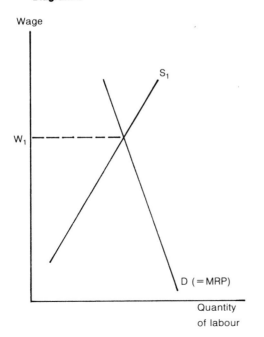

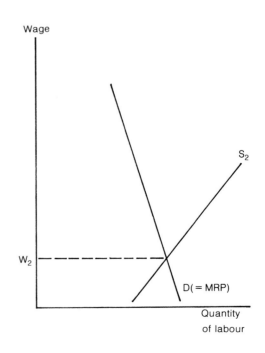

The quantity of labour supplied at a particular wage rate in different types of job will depend on such factors as the inherent attractiveness of jobs (people usually prefer office jobs to working down sewers), the riskiness of the occupation, the amount of education and training required and so on. Economists argue that it is the *net advantages* of the job (the wages and these other factors taken together) which determine how many people will want to accept employment at a given wage. Sometimes, however, their choices may be constrained—for example where trade unions or other groups are able artificially to restrict entry to a field.

So, the interaction of demand and supply in the dermination of wages is crucial to an understanding of the marginal productivity approach. Its critics, however, point to a number of circumstances where it may not be an adequate explanation of wage and earnings determination.

For example, it assumes firms are narrow profit maximisers. Particularly where firms are in protected markets, this may not be the case; they may not maximise the effectiveness with which resources are used, and may be prepared to tolerate inefficiency, perhaps giving workers higher wages (paid for out of the supernormal profits resulting from market power) than the model suggests. However, it seems unlikely that firms can persist in this type of behaviour forever; there are examples—such as the UK printing industry—where such behaviour, once prevalent, has now largely disappeared as a result of new competititon.

Another possibility is that firms may discriminate against racial and ethnic groups, or against women, on 'non-economic' grounds. Such behaviour, however, may again be threatened by competition. An employer who pays his or her workers what they are worth in marginal productivity terms gains a competitive edge over one which does not.

Then there are many examples of enterprises which are not intended to make profits—cooperative enterprises, charities and government departments. Here the notion of wages closely reflecting marginal productivity may not be very helpful. Nevertheless, it is still likely that the demand curve for labour is downward-sloping. For example, government departments facing 'cash limits' have a fixed employment budget available; higher wages mean less can be employed. So it may be that the government behaves 'as if' the marginal productivity model holds.

4   The market we are concerned with is an *oligopoly* market, one where only a few sellers dominate. Each firm is a 'price-setter' rather than a 'pricetaker' of the sort found in perfectly competitive markets. However, unlike a monopolist, the oligopolist acting alone has to take into account the reaction of competitors. Much will depend, of course, on whether the car firm sees the cost increase as being permanent or temporary. But assuming that the increase is permanent, then, other things being equal, a rise in costs will tend to reduce profits at the existing price-output combination, and should lead the firm to alter its price. However, in oligopoly there is a great deal of uncertainty about the outcome of such a change. The firm will be aware that its rivals have the choice to copy its behaviour and alter their prices in a similar direction, or to keep their prices the same (or, for that matter, to alter them in the opposite direction). The result of the original firm's price change will depend on which policy its rivals choose.

This interdependence between firms, and the associated uncertainty, means that economic models of oligopoly behaviour are less clear-cut and determinate in their predictions than those of simpler markets such as perfect competition and monopoly. A model which tries to capture some aspects of oligopoly behaviour is that of the 'kinked' demand curve, originally put forward nearly fifty years ago.

This model does not attempt to explain how a particular price-output combination is chosen by a firm, but rather suggests reasons why a price, once set, may be 'sticky' (ie, not changed very frequently) in oligopoly conditions. Suppose, in our example, that a car producer is originally at the price-output combination A in the diagram (page 284). It is considering whether to increase or decrease its price. If the firm raises its price, the result of its action on sales will depend on what its rivals do. A pessimistic view is that the other firms won't alter their prices. As a result, the firm will lose a lot of sales to its competitors. For price increases, the demand curve is relatively elastic. What happens if the firm instead *reduces* its price? Here a pessimistic view is that the other firms will make price cuts as well, in which case the firm's price change will only lead to a small increase in sales; the demand curve is much less elastic and may become inelastic. This is illustrated in the diagram; the 'kink' at point A occurs because the demand curve is less steep to the left of A than to the right, on these pessimistic assumptions.

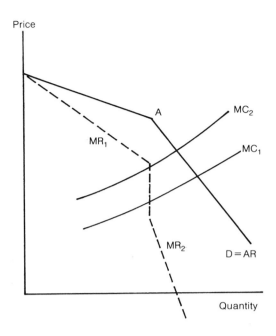

An implication of this kink in the demand (or average revenue) curve facing the car producer is that there is a discontinuity in the marginal revenue curve, MR_1 is the marginal revenue curve corresponding to the elastic section of the demand curve, while the steeper MR_2 corresponds to the less elastic section.

There is a gap between the two MR curves. Shifts of the marginal cost curve (eg, from MC_1 to MC_2) may therefore lead to no change in the level of output at which $MC = MR$. The 'prediction' of the model is therefore that in oligopoly markets, changes in costs are less likely to be reflected in changes in price and output than would be the case either in monopoly or perfect competition.

In fact, this prediction is by no means always supported by the evidence. It depends on the assumption that firms take a particular, pessimistic view of the outcome of their behaviour; arguably, firms taking such a view consistently are likely to be less successful than more optimistic, risktaking firms. However, the model remains interesting as one attempt to consider the impact of uncertainty on firms' behaviour.

It also points to the incentives which car firms and others have to reduce uncertainty. One obvious way to do this is for firms to *collude*; to agree to act together in relation to price changes. It is illegal in many countries for firms to act as formal cartels; a possibility is a tacit, unwritten agreement for one firm to act as 'price leader'. When costs rise for all producers, one of them puts up its price and is immediately followed by all others.

5   (a)   A 'dirty' or managed floating exchange rate for a currency means that, while the currency has no official fixed or 'par value' against other currencies, the central bank of the country intervenes in the foreign exchange market to stabilise the exchange rate or to manipulate it in a desired direction. How this works can be seen in the diagram on page 285.

The supply curve for pounds derives from sales of sterling in exchange for foreign currency (dollars) in order for British residents to buy US exports and to invest in the USA. The demand curve is similarly derived from foreign (US) purchases of sterling to buy British exports and to make investments in Britain. With a freely floating exchange rate the equilibrium rate is $1.80 = £1 which equates the quantity of sterling demanded with the quantity supplied.

However, the British government may wish to push up the rate to, say, $2.00 (to bring down inflation, for example). But at $2.00 there is excess supply of sterling on the exchange market equal to AB. The central bank (Bank of England) must therefore **intervene** on the market to buy up the surplus sterling in exchange for dollars sold from

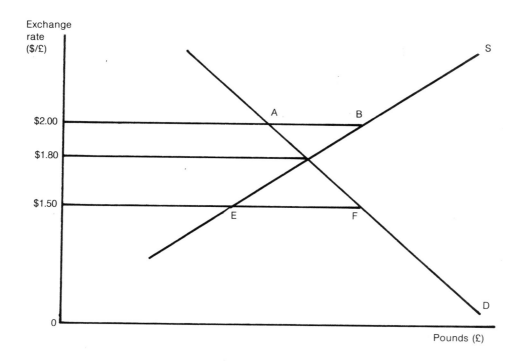

the exchange reserves. Alternatively, the bank might increase the demand for sterling by pushing up interest rates to attract foreign funds. If so, it may force the demand curve for sterling to the right (not shown) to cut the supply curve at B.

Conversely, to engineer a depreciation of sterling to, say, $1.50 (perhaps to improve export competitiveness) the bank must absorb the excess demand for sterling (equal to EF) by selling pounds on the market and buying dollars in return which are added to the reserves. Again, it has the option this time of lowering interest rates to shift the demand curve for sterling to the left to pass through the supply curve at E.

The 'dirty' floating has been practised periodically by the governments of most major countries since the abandonment of fixed rates in the early 1970s. But it is not always successful. Keeping an overvalued currency risks an eventual exhaustion of reserves or indefinite maintenance of high interest rates. Holding down the currency may set up domestic inflation through excessive accumulation of exchange reserves or keeping interest rates too low. Either way, experience shows that governments cannot counter market forces for more than short periods. Eventually, they are forced to allow currencies to return to their market-clearing levels.

(b)　(i)　An appreciation of the yen will have the primary effect of raising the foreign currency (dollar) price of Japanese exports and lowering the yen price of Japanese imports. The immediate effect therefore is to improve the Japanese terms of trade—the country's residents can now buy imported goods and services more cheaply.

However, the loss of competitivenes is likely to reduce the volume of exports and boost the volume of imports. If the price elasticities of demand for exports and imports add up to more than one (which is likely, certainly in the long run) there will be, other things being equal, a deterioration in the Japanese balance of trade. This, of course, will not be a problem if (as has been the case in practice) Japan was already running a large trade surplus.

The effects on the domestic economy are potentially more serious. The loss of export volume and displacement of domestic output by imports will have a deflationary effect on Japanese output and employment. Profit margins of exporters and firms producing import-competing goods will be squeezed and this could cause a fall in business investment followed by a multiplier contraction of output. However, in practice the deflationary effects of the rise of the yen since 1985 have been offset by a fiscal expansion by the Japanese government to maintain aggregate demand. This compensating expansionary policy was possible because of the enormous trade surplus while any inflationary effects have been offset by the improved terms of trade. Also, Japanese exports have hardly suffered as Japanese corporations have made efforts to increase labour productivity and labour costs have been cut through the frequent linking of a proportion of pay to profits.

(b) (ii) In principle, the effects of the yen's rise on Japan's trading partners are simply the opposite of those on Japan. Thus, in the USA (Japan's most important export market) imports from Japan are less competitive and the yen's appreciation has greatly stimulated import-competing production in the USA not least because Japanese firms themselves have been switching production from Japan to the USA. The fall in the dollar has also boosted American exports (to other countries as well as Japan) and the multiplier expansionary effects have sustained rapid growth and produced a fall in unemployment back to the levels of the 1970s.

However, the rise in US import prices together with rapid output growth has so far (1988) swelled the import bill and maintained the huge trade deficit. But there are now signs that the J-curve effect of currency depreciation (where the trade deficit gets worse in the short run but eventually narrows as demand elasticities increase) is working its way through to reduce the American trade gap. However, inflationary pressures are also emerging from the worsening of the terms of trade and from the domestic demand expansion. These pressures may have to be removed by a tightening of monetary policy (higher interest rates) and eventually by a curbing of the massive US government budget deficit.

The effects on Japan's other major trading partners (eg, Western Europe) have been less pronounced because for the most part their currencies have risen against the dollar along with the yen.

6 Those who believe strongly in the free market stress its advantages in encouraging efficiency, consumer choice and innovation. They believe it responds optimally to changes in the economic environment, altering the pattern of employment and output rapidly and smoothly as technology, consumer tastes and the availability of raw materials, natural resources and labour alter.

In this context, unemployment is seen as a transitional phenomenon. If people are unemployed, it is because they and firms have not fully adjusted to economic change. For example, if the demand for steel falls, steelworkers are made unemployed. They do not move immediately to new jobs because workers are not completely informed about their changed job prospects. They may hold out for similar types of job at the same rate of pay as before. Similarly, firms may not yet have realised that the equilibrium rate of pay has altered, and continue to offer the same wages even though faced with a queue of applicants. Eventually, in the 'long run', wages (like the 'price' of other goods and services) will adjust to clear the market. In equilibrium, all those willing to accept jobs for which they are qualified are able to find them at the going rate. Any unemployment remaining is *voluntary*, the result of the preference of some workers for leisure rather than wages at the margin.

This is a highly idealised picture, which leaves no room for government intervention in the economy to reduce unemployment. Economists in the Keynesian tradition argue that the economy does not function so smoothly. Wages do not adjust rapidly to clear markets. Workers may have incomplete information about labour market conditions, and persist for long periods in seeking their old wages. Those who remain in work will react against wage cuts by working less effectively; managers know this, and are therefore unwilling to cut wages in order to make jobs available to the currently unemployed. Keynes argues that this wage 'stickiness' meant that considerable *involuntary* unemployment could persist for long periods. In such a case, it was necessary for goverments to intervene to boost aggregate demand, thus making it profitable to hire more labour at existing wage rates. If necessary, this could be financed by running a budget deficit.

Keynesian policies of this sort were popular in the UK and other countries for many years after World War II. Although Keynes himself had seen the role of government as essentially one of 'pump-priming', providing an initial boost to demand (by, for example, building roads and other public works) which would be increased through the 'multiplier' process, his arguments were often used to justify more and more interference with the free market. By the late 1970s it was widely argued that such policies had contributed to inflation and were not in practice very successful in keeping unemployment down. Monetarists and New Classical economists argued against the use of demand management policies in favour of *supply-side* measures.

Supply-siders argued that unemployment had risen in the 1970s and early 1980s because of various rigidities which had undermined the smooth operation of the labour market. This led to the persistence of unemployment when the labour market was forced to adjust to changes resulting from oil price rises, exchange rate fluctuations and technological change. Some of these rigidities were blamed on trade unions; others were blamed on governments themselves. For instance, it was argued that unemployment and social security benefits made it worthwhile for some workers to remain unemployed ('voluntarily') rather than take low-paid jobs. In either case, it was argued to be necessary for governments actively to seek ways of making the labour market work more efficiently by dismantling barriers to the free workings of the market—reducing trade union power and cutting benefits to make life on social security less attractive. So there was a role here for governments too, albeit one very different from that envisaged by Keynesians.

Supply-side policies tend to have been associated with the political Right, and with opposition to the idea of the government having a major role in the economy. However, it is possible to argue for rather different approaches while still retaining a 'supply-side' orientation. For instance, both Left and Right may agree on the need for governments to provide expanded education and training facilities, to make it easier for individuals to qualify for more highly-skilled jobs of the sort which the market increasingly requires; they both implicitly recognise an area of 'market failure' which the government needs to rectify. Moreover, others on the Left, while rejecting 'Keynesian' demand management, may argue for an industrial strategy involving substantial government funding for new technologies, research and development: it is argued that this is another area where the free market alone may be inadequate.

So, it appears that few people are prepared to say that, in modern conditions, unemployment is a phenomenon with which the government need not concern itself at all. Policies advocated may be very different, but it seems likely that there will continue to be a major role for government in this area. The dispute is over what that role should be.

7   (a)   The precise functions have evolved historically and differ, therefore, from country to country. However, all central banks have a primary function of **regulating the supply of currency and credit** in the country. In this, the central bank's goal, unlike that of commercial banks, is not to make profits but to regulate the financial system in the national interest. The detailed functions of central banks tend to follow from this primary one:

1   **Control over the supply of notes and coins** Most central banks have a monopoly of note issue; if not, they can regulate the issue by other banks.

2   **Regulation of the volume of credit** created by commercial banks in their lending operations.

3   **Supervision of the banks** (for example, in relation to prudential reserve holding) and often of other financial intermediaries in order to regulate general liquidity.

4   **Acting as 'lender of last resort'** to the banks in order to maintain confidence and to avoid a 'run on the banks' by their depositors.

5   **Banker to the banks** The central bank normally requires that commercial banks holds deposits with it; the banks in any case voluntarily keep accounts in the central bank which they use to settle inter-bank indebtedness.

6   **Banker to the government** The central bank maintains the government's bank account and manages the National Debt on behalf of the government.

7   **Implementation of monetary policy** In some countries (eg, West Germany) the central bank both determines and implements monetary policy. In others (UK) the government lays down policy goals in cooperation with the central bank and the bank is responsible primarily for implementation.

8 **External financial relations and exchange management**. Central banks hold the official foreign exchange reserves and execute rate policy through intervention and exchange controls. They liaise with other central banks and conduct or advise on negotiations, for example, with the International Monetary Fund.

(b) Central banks have a number of instruments available to regulate the supply of and demand for money and credit:

1 **Open market operations (OMOs)** The bank intervenes to buy and sell various financial securities. Thus, to curb the supply of money and credit the bank may sell securities (usually government bonds and bills) on the open market. These are paid for by cheques drawn on commercial banks whose balances are thus reduced at the central bank. Since these are equivalent to holdings of cash the banks may be forced into a multiple contraction of their lending in order to restore their cash reserve ratios.

In Britain the Bank of England now largely restricts OMOs to the money market by buying bills (short-term debt) from the banking system to maintain liquidity or selling bills to mop up surplus liquidity. The aim is to stabilise the money market and to influence short-term interest rates.

2 **Reserve ratios** Central banks can insist that commercial banks hold minimum reserves of cash and other liquid assets relative to their deposit liabilities. Raising the minimum ratio may force the banks to curb lending. In Britain, though, use of reserve ratios has largely been abandoned in favour of OMOs in the money market.

3 **Special deposits** The central bank may demand additional deposits from the commercial banks. This is equivalent to an increase in reserve ratios and again has largely fallen into disuse in Britain.

4 **Direct controls** The central bank may impose direct quantitative limits on bank lending and other credit expansion. These ceilings may be general or selective, eg, applied to consumer credit, and may be extended to non-bank credit such as hire purchase finance and mortgage lending. The Bank of England has rarely used direct controls since the 1970s.

5 **'Moral suasion'** The Bank of England has a tradition of informal regulation and used to rely on goodwill of the banks to conform with requests to restrict lending. Reliance on OMOs has made moral suasion largely irrelevant.

6 **Influencing interest rates** OMOs and other central bank controls can significantly influence interest rates which in turn affect the demand for credit. In the past, the Bank of England relied on a combination of OMOs and an announced official discount rate (a penal rate for supplying liquidity to the banks) to influence interest rates. Bank Rate (subsequently to become the Minimum Lending Rate) has again formally been abandoned but the Bank now has an unpublished flexible discount rate. The Bank can push this up by its OMOs in the money market and in turn force the commercial banks to increase their own borrowing and lending rates (with a benchmark known as Base Rate). The aim is to restrain the demand for credit by raising the cost of borrowing.

The Bank of England has gone further than most central banks in abandoning direct controls in favour of indirect market intervention as its main method of regulating the money supply. However, other central banks are increasingly following suit as part of the general trend towards deregulation of financial markets.

8 (a) By economic growth we mean the rate of increase of national income. It is convenient to be able to put a definite figure on this, so that we can compare, say, the UK's average growth over the 1980s with that over the 1970s. However, there are considerable difficulties in doing this.

National income in any year can only be estimated with a considerable margin of error. In principle, the income, output and expenditure methods of calculation should all give the same result: in practice they do not. They are collected in different ways, and this gives rise to different types of error. Income data, for example, are derived from Inland Revenue (tax) figures, and people may often under-report incomes for tax purposes—particularly those who are active in the 'black' economy. Expenditure data, on the other hand, are based on (voluntary) surveys of households' expenditure, and may not be completely representative.

Ideally, we are aiming for national income data net of depreciation, but the unreliable nature of our information forces us to use *gross* domestic or national product figures. Moreover, 'open' economies like the UK trade large proportions of output, and there are massive capital flows in and out of the country. Data on these only become available after a considerable time and are less accurate than data for domestic production and consumption. Some types of income (eg, the return on capital invested in the provision of publicly-owned schools and hospitals) are imputed: they do not correspond to any actual monetary payment and are thus of doubtful accuracy. Work carried out by households in their own homes (home decorating, housework, child care etc,) is not included in national income, although it would be if the equivalent services were purchased in the market. These factors make even accurate income data a dubious measure of a country's welfare.

The difficulties of estimating national income are compounded when we measure its rate of change over time. For one thing, prices will have changed; we need to take account of inflation to get at the change in *real* income. This means using an index of prices, and there is no perfect index available. For another, changes over time in the accuracy of recording national income may produce a spurious effect: for instance, if the Inland Revenue is more effective in reducing tax evasion, measured national income is likely to rise. Then there is the difficulty of reflecting changes in the quality of goods and services used over time as new products are invented and old ones fall into disuse. Finally, social changes which lead to more married women working outside the home increase measured national income, although there may be some offsetting reduction in production in the home, so the net welfare of society has not increased by as much as measured income.

We should, therefore, be sceptical of the accuracy of data on economic growth rates, both in terms of the magnitudes they claim to measure and (even more so) as a measure of social welfare. Nevertheless, such data are better than nothing and are increasingly treated as the main indicator of a government's success in running the economy.

(b)   There is no magic formula for promoting economic growth, despite the claims of politicians. One approach is to look at the quantity and quality of the factors of production available to a country, and to seek ways of augmenting these.

For example, the availability and fertility of *land* for both farming and non-agricultural purposes is obviously important. Endowments of *natural resources* are also relevant: in the 1970s, for example, countries possessing abundant supplies of oil were able to grow very rapidly.

Obviously, too, the size and quality of the *capital stock*, consisting of buildings and equipment used to produce output directly plus the infrasture of roads, communications, etc, is of great importance. At any moment, the capital stock is the result of past investment decisions, but over time the capital stock is augmented as a result of the investment decisions of firms and governments and the savings decisions of firms and households. Generally speaking, countries with a higher rate of investment tend to grow faster, though it is important to stress that the quality of investment is crucial. There are many examples of large scale investments (often undertaken by governments for reasons of prestige) which have turned out disastrously.

The *labour force* is also of major importance. It is possible for countries to be either under-populated (so that communications are poor, transport costs are high and it is impossible to achieve economies of scale); it is also possible for a country to be over-populated in relation to its resources of land and capital, as a result of a high dependency ratio (the ratio of the non-working to the working population). Some economists speak of an 'optimum population' which will maximise economic growth, but this is a very difficult concept to define.

Apart from the absolute size of the workforce, there is also the question of its standard of education and training—the quantity of *human capital* embodied in the population. Many studies indicate that, other things being equal, higher growth rates are associated with higher average levels of such indicators as the proportion of the population which has completed high school or the equivalent (though it is fair to point out that some people have disputed the direction of causation here). In any case, there is no doubt that governments are increasingly stressing the role of education and training in any policy to promote economic growth.

Another important factor has to be the nature of *institutions* such as laws and regulations, tax rates, political parties and systems of government, the nature and strength of trade unionism and so on, all of which can be seen to have an effect on economic performance.

Perhaps more fundamentally, attitudes towards business are likely to be of importance. Many years ago sociologist Max Weber distinguished the 'Protestant ethic', a particular value system which he argued to have been crucial in the rise of capitalism in Europe. Nowadays, people point to Japan and the United States, where (in different ways, admittedly) dominant cultural values clearly favour business to a greater extent than elsewhere. In the UK, Mrs Thatcher's government has placed great stress on the need to generate an 'enterprise culture' as the key to economic success.

Glossary

Accelerator coefficient. The ratio between the change in total planned new investment in a period and the change in national income in the previous period.

Aggregate demand. The sum of all planned expenditure in an economy in a given period.

Aggregate demand curve. Curve showing the relationship between the average price level and aggregate demand for output in an economy (drawn for a given level of the nominal money supply).

Aggregate supply curve. Curve showing the relationship between the average price level and total supply of output in an economy.

Balance of payments. The accounting record of all a country's international financial transactions over a given period.

Bank credit multiplier. The ratio of the change in total deposits to the change in cash deposits which sets off a process of credit expansion.

Business cycle. The regular pattern of fluctuation of related economic indicators of activity (such as output, employment and the average price level) over time.

Capital. As a factor of production, refers to the stock of physical assets accumulated from past investment and used to produce other goods and services.

Cartel. A group of suppliers of a commodity who combine to fix prices or other supply conditions.

Central bank. Regulates banking and finance and carries out monetary policies of the government.

Central planning. A system where all major economic decisions are made by a government ministry or planning organisation.

Commercial banks. Also known as deposit banks, they are institutions which are licensed to make loans and accept deposits, including those against which cheques can be written.

Comparative advantage. A country possesses a comparative advantage in the production of a good which it can produce at a relatively low opportunity cost.

Complementary goods. Goods which are consumed together (eg, fish and chips, motor cars and petrol).

Conglomerate integration. Occurs when firms producing completely different goods or services merge.

Consumer surplus. The excess of the consumer's valuation of a commodity over the amount which he or she has paid for it.

Consumption function. The relationship (expressed in mathematical or diagrammatic form) between planned consumption and other independent variables, particularly income.

Contestable market. A market where sunk costs are very low, so that supernormal profits cannot be maintained because they will rapidly lead to new firms entering the market and competing them away.

Cross-elasticity of demand. Measures the responsiveness of quantity demanded of one commodity to changes in the price of another; percentage change in quantity demanded of one commodity divided by percentage change in price of another.

Debt service. The agreed repayment of loans together with the interest on outstanding loans.

Depreciation of currency. Fall in the value of a currency relative to other currencies.

Deregulation. Relaxation or abandonment of rules imposed on business to restrict the free play of market forces.

Devaluation. Reduction in the pegged exchange rate of one currency relative to other currencies.

Dirty floating. Central bank manipulation of a floating exchange rate.

Division of labour. The division of a productive process into separate tasks performed by different individuals.

Economic rent. Surplus obtained for the services of a factor of production above its transfer earnings or opportunity cost.

Economies of scale. These raise factor productivity reducing the average cost of output as the productive capacity of a firm increases.

Entrepreneur. Person who organises, and risks his or her money, in economic activity.

Equilibrium price. The price at which the quantity of a good buyers wish to purchase is just equal to the quantity suppliers wish to offer.

Equilibrium income. That level of national income at which total planned spending equals income.

Exchange controls. Controls on the amount of foreign currency which can be bought to purchase goods or services from abroad.

Exchange rate. The value of a unit of a country's currency in terms of that of another country.

Externality. The positive or negative effect which the activities of production and consumption has on third parties (ie, neither producers nor consumers of the product).

Eurodollars. Deposits denominated in $US in banks located outside the USA (especially London).

Factors of production. Productive resources, conventionally classified into land, labour and capital.

Fisher equation. See *Quantity Theory of Money*.

Fixed costs. Those costs which do not vary with the level of output at which a firm produces.

Floating exchange rate. An exchange rate which is free to fluctuate in value in relation to other currencies depending on supply and demand conditions in foreign exchange markets.

Giffen good. Good for which demand increases after a rise in its price, as a result of the (positive) income effect outweighing the (negative) substitution effect.

Horizontal integration. Occurs when firms producing similar products merge.

Human capital. Stock of skills resulting from investment in education, training and other ways of enhancing labour productivity.

Imperfect competition. See *Monopolistic Competition*.

Income effect. Effect on the consumption of a commodity of a change in real income resulting from a change in its price.

Income-elasticity of demand. Measures the responsiveness of quantity demanded of a commodity to changes in income; percentage change in quantity demanded of the commodity divided by percentage change in income.

Indirect taxes. Taxes imposed on the sale of goods and services.

Inferior goods. Goods for which demand falls as consumers' incomes increase.

Inflation. Increase in the average level of prices.

Interest rate. Payment, normally expressed as a percentage of the sum lent which is paid over a year, for the loan of money.

Internal balance. Combination of full employment and zero inflation.

Invisible trade. Exports and imports of services (including services of factors of production).

J-curve. Curve showing how the balance of payments first worsens as a result of a devaluation and then improves.

Labour. As a factor of production, refers to all types of physical and mental power of human beings which can usefully be employed in the production of goods and services.

Laffer curve. Curve showing the relationship between tax revenue and average tax rate.

Land. As a factor of production, embraces land and other natural resources which contribute to the production process.

'Law' of diminishing returns (or law of variable proportions). When the quantity of a variable factor of production is increased while another factor is held constant, the marginal physical product of the variable factor will eventually decline.

Liquidity preference. Keynes's term for the desire to hold cash balances.

Liquidity trap. Extreme (theoretical) case of interest-elastic demand for money; when the demand curve for money becomes perfectly elastic, increases in the money supply have no effect on the equilibrium interest rate.

Long run. Period in which all factors of production are variable.

Macroeconomics. Study of the economy as a whole.

Marginal cost. Addition to total cost as a result of increasing output by an extra unit.

Marginal efficiency of capital. Rate of return on each additional unit of investment.

Marginal physical product of a factor of production. Addition to total output as a result of employing one extra unit of a factor of production.

Marginal propensity to consume. Proportion of an extra unit of income received which is consumed.

Marginal revenue. Addition to a firm's total revenue as a result of selling one extra unit of output.

Marginal revenue product of a factor of production. Addition to total revenue as a result of employing one additional unit of the factor.

Marginal utility. Change in total utility derived from a commodity as a result of consuming one extra unit of the commodity.

Market economy. A system where economic decisions are decentralised and made by consumers, producers and owners of factors of production.

Market for corporate control. Market for shares in companies; enables firms to be taken over by outside financial interests.

Market failure. Situation where the free market economy produces an inefficient (sub-optimal) outcome.

Microeconomics. Study of economic behaviour at the level of the individual, the firm and the market.

Mixed economy. Economy which makes use of both public and private enterprise.

Monetarism. The modern version of the old idea of the Quantity Theory of Money; monetarists recognise that in principle the velocity of circulation can vary as a result of interest rate changes, but claim that the evidence points to its stability.

Money. A generally acceptable means of settling a debt resulting from an economic transaction.

Monopolistic competition or imperfect competition. Market structure characterised by a large number of competing firms each selling a differentiated product.

Monopoly. Market where there is only one supplier of the commodity.

Monopsony. Market where there is only one purchaser of the commodity.

Multiplier. Ratio of the change in national income resulting from a change in injections to the change in injections which caused it.

National income. The sum of all incomes derived from production of goods and services generated by a country's economy in a given period (usually a year).

NAIRU. See *Natural Rate of Unemployment*.

Nationalised industries. Government-owned industries producing goods or services for sale to the public.

Natural level of output. Equilibrium level of output at which aggregate demand is equal to aggregate supply. The output level corresponding to the natural rate of unemployment.

Natural rate of unemployment (NAIRU). Rate of unemployment at which the demand for labour and the supply of those willing to accept work is equal; there is no Keynesian, involuntary unemployment. At this rate of unemployment, compatible with any expected rate of inflation, there is no tendency for inflation to increase or decrease. Thus it is also known as the non-accelerating inflation rate of unemployment or NAIRU.

Negative income tax. A system of income redistribution, administered through the income tax system, which would give income supplements (negative income tax) to those whose incomes fell below a cut-off level.

New Classical economics. The belief that an economy is always close to its natural level of output, from which it can only be disturbed by genuinely unexpected supply or demand 'shocks'. An extreme version of monetarism.

Non-accelerating inflation rate of unemployment (NAIRU). See *Natural Rate of Unemployment*.

Normal goods. Goods for which demand increases as consumers' incomes increase.

Normal profits. Minimum return required to attract capital into a business; it is the opportunity cost of risk capital.

Normative economics. That part of economics which is concerned with how people ought to behave in order to achieve certain economic objectives.

Oligopoly. Market where there are only a few suppliers of the commodity.

Opportunity cost. Cost of a good, service or activity in terms of the best alternative use to which productive resources could be put.

Pareto-optimality. Efficient allocation of resources, such that any reallocation can only benefit one individual or group at the expense of another.

Participation rate. Percentage of the potential working population who are willing to become members of the active labour force.

Perfect competition. Market structure characterised by a large number of competing firms selling a homogeneous product.

Permanent income. Income which individuals expect to maintain in the long run.

Phillips curve. Curve, first drawn by A W Phillips, showing combinations of the rate of unemployment and price or wage inflation.

Positive economics. That part of economics which attempts to explain or predict economic behaviour, based on models which can in principle be tested against the evidence.

Price discrimination. Charging different prices for the same product to different consumers, or for different units of the product to the same consumer.

Price-elasticity of demand. Measures the responsiveness of quantity demanded of a good to a change in its price; percentage change in quantity demanded divided by percentage change in price.

Price-elasticity of supply. Measures the responsiveness of quantity supplied of a good to a change in its price; percentage change in quantity supplied divided by percentage change in price.

Privatisation. Policy to increase the scope for private sector in the economy through a number of means, including stock market flotation of nationalised industries, sale of public housing and contracting-out of publicly-funded services.

Production frontier or production possibilities curve. Curve showing possible combinations of outputs of two goods or services which can be produced with a given set of resources.

Production possibilities curve. See *Production Frontier*.

Profit. Return to owners of a business for organising the enterprise and bearing the risk involved.

Public good. Good which provides benefits which are not confined to one individual or household. A 'pure' public good possesses the characteristics of non-rivalness and non-excludability.

Quantity theory of money. Belief that changes in the money supply are the main cause of changes in the price level. Summed up in the Fisher equation, $MV = PT$ (or PY).

Quasi-rent. Surplus over transfer earnings obtained for the services of a factor of production which is temporarily in short supply.

Rational expectations. Expectations about economic variables formed on the basis of all relevant available information; although not perfectly accurate, will not be consistently wrong in one direction or another.

Rent. Payment for the use of the services of land, buildings or machinery. See also *Economic Rent*.

Short run. Period in which a firm's productive capacity is constrained by a fixed supply of at least one factor of production.

Speculative demand for money. Desire to hold cash in the expectation that bond prices will shortly fall.

Substitution effect. The effect on the consumption of a commodity of a change in its price relative to other commodities for which it is a substitute.

Sunk costs. Costs which cannot be recovered on leaving a market.

Super-normal profit. Profit in excess of the opportunity cost of risk capital.

Supply-side economics. Belief that increases in aggregate demand are ineffective in raising output in the long run; thus policy must be directed towards increasing incentives for firms and individuals to supply goods and services.

Tariff. Tax or duty on imports.

Terms of trade. Ratio of export prices to import prices.

Transactions demand for money. Desire to hold cash in order to make planned transactions.

Transfer earnings. Minimum payment necessary to attract and retain the services of a factor of production; essentially its opportunity cost.

Transfer payments. Payments, made by governments to individuals, which are not based on the performance of a productive task, eg, welfare benefits and old-age pensions.

Utility. Capacity of a commodity to satisfy consumers' wants.

Value added. Value of output minus the value of the raw materials and/or intermediate goods used in its production.

Variable costs. Costs which vary with the level of output at which a firm produces.

Velocity of circulation. Average frequency with which money changes hands.

Vertical integration. Occurs when a firm moves either into earlier (backward integration) or later (forward integration) stages of the production of the good it produces.

Visible trade. Exports and imports of physical goods.

X-inefficiency. Failure to maximise technical efficiency, associated with protected markets where firms face little competition.

Index

Free

ACCA
LATEST ACCA EXAMINATION PAPER
QUESTIONS AND ANSWERS

YES Please send me the latest ACCA examination Questions
and Suggested Answers... **Free of charge**

SUBJECT OF EXAM PAPER_____

DATE OF EXAM PAPER REQUIRED_____

NAME_____

ADDRESS_____

_____

_____

POSTCODE_____ TEL_____

Do you study... ☐ Full time
☐ Part Time
☐ Corresp/ Dist Learning

Did you purchase this book...
☐ Direct from Longman
☐ Direct from College
☐ From a Bookshop

At which level... Level 1 / 2 / 3

Institution Name _____ Name of Bookshop _____

Longman 🚢

Free

ACCA
LATEST ACCA EXAMINATION PAPER
QUESTIONS AND ANSWERS

YES Please send me the latest ACCA examination Questions
and Suggested Answers... **Free of charge**

SUBJECT OF EXAM PAPER_____

DATE OF EXAM PAPER REQUIRED_____

NAME_____

ADDRESS_____

_____

_____

POSTCODE_____ TEL_____

Do you study... ☐ Full time
☐ Part Time
☐ Corresp/ Dist Learning

Did you purchase this book...
☐ Direct from Longman
☐ Direct from College
☐ From a Bookshop

At which level... Level 1 / 2 / 3

Institution Name _____ Name of Bookshop _____

Longman 🚢

1

BUSINESS REPLY CARD
Licence No. KE6356

**LONGMAN ACCA SERIES
LONGMAN GROUP UK LTD
21-27 LAMB'S CONDUIT ST
LONDON WC1N 3NJ**

FOR OVERSEAS PLEASE AFFIX STAMP

Stamp

**LONGMAN ACCA SERIES
LONGMAN GROUP UK LTD
21-27 LAMB'S CONDUIT ST
LONDON WC1N 3NJ**